Restorative Justice in Context

Restorative Justice in Context
International Practice and Directions

Edited by Elmar G. M. Weitekamp
and Hans-Jürgen Kerner

WILLAN
PUBLISHING

Published by

Willan Publishing
Culmcott House
Mill Street, Uffculme
Cullompton, Devon
EX15 3AT, UK
Tel: +44(0)1884 840337
Fax: +44(0)1884 840251
e-mail: info@willanpublishing.co.uk
website: www.willanpublishing.co.uk

Published simultaneously in the USA and Canada by

Willan Publishing
c/o ISBS, 5824 N.E. Hassalo St,
Portland, Oregon 97213-3644, USA
Tel: +001(0)503 287 3093
Fax: +001(0)503 280 8832
e-mail: info@isbs.com
website: www.isbs.com

First published 2003

ISBN 1-903240-73-5 (cased)
ISBN 1-903240-84-0 (paper)

British Library Cataloguing-in-Publication Data
A catalogue record for this book is available from the British Library

Printed by T.J. International, Padstow, Cornwall
Project management by Deer Park Productions
Typeset by GCS, Leighton Buzzard, Beds.

Errata

The Publishers regret that some errors were made in Chapter 2, 'Making variation a virtue: evaluating the potential and limits of restorative justice', during the production process of this book. Please accept our apologies for the inconvenience caused by this. These are the corrections which need to be made:

p. 30: please see the reverse of this sheet where p. 30 is reprinted as it should appear.

p. 33: Table 2.3c (YP and offence victim demographics): the signs for three coefficients are incorrectly shown. For race-ethnicity of primary YP, it is .17 *not* −.17; for sex of primary offence victim, it is .24, *not* −.24; and for race-ethnicity of offence victim, it is .13, *not* −.13.

p. 41: Table 2.4e (Indicators of re-offending): the sign for the coefficient for n=89 primary YPs is incorrectly shown. It should be −.15, *not* .15.

p. 45: Table 2.5a (Indicators of attitudes toward the YP in 1998): the sign for the coefficient for 'feel angry toward the YP before the conference' is incorrectly shown. It should be −.03, *not* .03.

p. 46: Table 2.5d (Indicators of conference impact on victim recovery): the sign for the coefficient for 'How victim feels about the incident in 1999' is incorrectly shown. It should be −.12, *not* .12.

p. 47: Footnote 1 at the bottom of the page: the superscript d should say 'sig at .01 level', *not* .10 level.

Table 2.2. Limits on the restorative ideal

a YP interviews in 1998 (n = 93 YPs)		
Before the conference, was it important to you?		
no		31
Before the conference, did you think about what you wanted to do or to say to the victim?		
no, not at all		53
After listening to the victim or rep's story, did it have an effect on you?		
no, not at all or not much (n = 73 YPs for whom a victim was present)		49
At the conference, was it more important to you to make the victim feel better or to get what you wanted?		
make victim feel better		58
make sure I got what I wanted		16
both equally		17
neither		9
Looking back at the conference, was it more important that you be treated fairly or that you were able to do something for the victim?		
be treated fairly		40
do something for the victim		39
both equally		20
neither		1
As a result of the conference, you have a better understanding of how your behaviour affected the victim		
agree		87
The conference was largely a waste of time		
agree		15
Before the conference and now: how sorry did/do you feel for the victim		
not at all or less sorry		42
still not sorry at all	19	
feel less sorry for victim after the conference	23	
a bit or more sorry		58
still a bit, somewhat, or very sorry	45	
more sorry for victim after the conference	13	
b Victim interviews in 1998 (n = 61 conference victims)		
Before the conference, did you think about what you wanted to say to YP?		
no, not at all		34
In listening to the YP's account of the offence, how much impact did it have on you?		
none or not much		62

Contents

List of figures and tables

I. Figures:

II. Tables:

Notes on contributors

Britta Bannenberg is currently Professor of Criminology and Criminal Law at the University of Bielefeld, Germany. She studied jurisprudence at the University of Göttingen and took her First State Examination in 1989. She worked then as research associate at the Institute of Criminal Law and Criminology, University of Göttingen (with Professor Schöch and Professor Rössner). After her dissertation on 'Restitution in Practice of Criminal Law' (Dr. jur. 1993, Göttingen) she lectured at the University of Leipzig in the summer 1993 (Lecture on Rights in Prison Law). Her Second State Examination took place in 1994 in Kassel/Hesse. Between 1995 and 2001 she was Assistant Professor at the University of Halle/Saale and the University of Marburg (with Prof. Rössner), where she gave lectures and exercises in criminology, juvenile criminal law and prison law. In 2001 she served as short-term expert for the EU-Phare Projekt 'Anti-Corruption' in Riga/Lettland. In her Habilitation in 2001 she presented an empirical study on corruption (published under the title: *Korruption in Deutschland und ihre strafrechtliche Kontrolle, eine kriminologisch-strafrechtliche Analyse*, Luchterhand 2002). Dr. Bannenberg's main focus of research is victim–offender mediation, violence, corruption and crime prevention. She is a member of several associations, e.g. 'Forschungsgruppe Täter-Opfer-Ausgleich', 'Neue Kriminologische Gesellschaft', and 'Arbeitskreis deutscher, schweizerischer und österreichischer Strafrechtslehrer (AE-Kreis)'. She is collaborating with the further education programme

'Mediation' of the 'Fernuniversität Hagen'. She is manager of 'Prevent – Institut für Prävention' in Köln.

William Bradshaw is an Associate Professor and Senior Research Associate at the Center for Restorative Justice and Peacemaking at the University of Minnesota, School of Social Work. Dr. Bradshaw is a former probation officer and specializes in work related to restorative justice interventions in crimes of severe violence.

John Braithwaite is a member of the Centre for Restorative Justice at the Research School of Social Sciences, Australian National University. His most recent books are *Restorative Justice and Responsive Regulation* (2002), *Shame Management Through Reintegration* (with Eliza Ahmed, Nathan Harris and Valerie Braithwaite, 2001), *Restorative Justice and Civil Society* (edited with Heather Strang, 2001) and *Restorative Justice and Family Violence* (edited with Heather Strang, 2002).

Robert Coates is a Senior Research Associate at the Center for Restorative Justice and Peacemaking at the University of Minnesota, School of Social Work. Dr. Coates is a former faculty member at the University of Utah, University of Chicago, and the Harvard Criminal Justice Center. He has been a co-principal investigator in several studies of the Center related to peacemaking circles, victim–offender mediation, work with victims of severe violence, and systemic change toward restorative justice policies.

Irwin M. Cohen is a post-doctorate fellow at the School of Criminology at Simon Fraser University, Burnaby, BC, Canada. Dr. Irwin's areas of interest focus on young offenders, juvenile justice, political crime, mental health and Aboriginal victimization. He has co-authored several manuscripts on torture, terrorism, juvenile justice, young offenders, restorative justice and mentally disordered offenders. Irwin has also acted as the project director and a co-principal investigator on several research projects focusing on serious and violent young offenders, and Aboriginal victimization. Irwin is a member of the Institute of Mental Health, Law and Policy at Simon Fraser University.

Raymond R. Corrado is a Full Professor in the School of Criminology and the Department of Psychology at Simon Fraser University, Burnaby, BC, Canada. He also is a Visiting Fellow at Clare Hall College and the Institute of Criminology, University of Cambridge and a founder member of the Mental Health, Law, and Policy Institute at Simon Fraser University. Dr. Corrado has co-authored three edited books, *Issues in Juvenile Justice,*

Evaluation and Criminal Justice Policy and *Juvenile Justice in Canada*, as well as having published various articles and book chapters on juvenile justice, young offenders, terrorism, mental health and victimization. Currently, Dr. Corrado is completing a variety of projects involving comparative juvenile justice, state terrorism, mentally disordered offenders and Aboriginal victimization.

Kathleen Daly is an Associate Professor in Criminology and Criminal Justice at Griffith University, Brisbane, Australia. Her book *Gender, Crime, and Punishment* (1994) received the Michael Hindelang Award from the American Society of Criminology. During 1998–99, she directed a major research project on restorative justice in South Australia. In 2001–3, she is directing a second project on the race and gender politics of new justice practices in Australia, New Zealand, the United States, and Canada.

Dieter Dölling, Dr. jur., is Director of the Institute of Criminology, University of Heidelberg, Germany and Full Professor at the Faculty of Law, with special responsibility for the fields of criminology, juvenile (penal) law and corrections (including prison law). He is a member of the Research Group on Victim–Offender Reconciliation, Heidelberg, Germany.

Els Dumortier is Scientific Researcher at the Free University of Brussels (VUB). She graduated in Law (1995) and Criminology (1997). She has published in the fields of juvenile justice and juvenile criminology. She is preparing a PhD dissertation on the topic of 'Juvenile Judges and Legal Rights for Juvenile Delinquents in the 20th Century'.

Arthur Hartmann is currently Deputy Director of the Institute of Criminology, University of Tuebingen, Germany. He received his Dr. jur. and a diploma in sociology at the University of Munich. The topic of the thesis was 'Schlichten oder Richten?' (a study on victim–offender mediation and the legal system in Germany). From 1995 to 2001 he worked as research associate at the Institute of Criminology, University of Heidelberg, Germany. His habilitation thesis (2001) dealt with the 'Theory of Organised Crime'. During the summer and winter terms 2001 he lectured at the Humboldt University of Berlin on penal law and criminology. He has done research in victim–offender mediation since the first projects started in Germany in the 1980s. He is co-founder of the German Research Group in Victim–Offender Mediation and is responsible for the VOM Statistics.

Hans-Jürgen Kerner is currently Director of the Institute of Criminology, University of Tübingen, Germany. He is Full Professor at the Faculty of Law, with special responsibility for the fields of criminology, juvenile (penal) law, corrections (including prison law), and penal procedure. He serves as co-ordinator of the post graduate LL.M. Programme of the Faculty of Law for foreign law graduates. He is also co-ordinator of the Tübingen Criminology and Criminal Justice Theory–Practice Programme, i.e. a series of continuous workshops in further education for practitioners and academics alike. He is Honorary President of the International Society for Criminology, Paris, France; President of the German Foundation for Crime Prevention and the Reintegration of Offenders, Bonn; Chair of the German Association for Court Aid, Probation and Parole Assistance, and Care and Resettlement of Offenders, Berlin; member, Research Group on Victim–offender Reconciliation, Heidelberg, Germany; life member, American Society of Criminology, and Academy of Criminal Justice Sciences, USA.

Peter Lindström received his PhD in sociology from Stockholm University in 1993. He is currently Head of the Division for Reform Evaluation at the National Council for Crime Prevention, Sweden. His research interest focuses on juvenile justice systems including victim–offender mediation, police research, drug research and finally domestic violence.

Marianne Löschnig-Gspandl is currently Assistant Professor at the Institute for Criminal Law, Criminal Procedure and Criminology of the University of Graz, Austria. She did her thesis, which was published in 1996, on 'Die Wiedergutmachung im österreichischen Strafrecht. Auf dem Weg zu einem neuen Kriminalrecht?' She has published several articles in national and international journals in the fields of substantive criminal law, criminal procedure and victimology. Together with Prof. Dr. Schick has published a casebook in substantive criminal law (*Löschnig-Gspandl/Schick, Casebook Strafrecht*, 2. Aufl., Wien 2001) At the moment she is preparing her 'Habilitationsschrift' on 'Strafrechtliche Verantwortlichkeit juristischer Personen' at the Max-Planck-Institute for Foreign and International Criminal Law in Freiburg, Germany; to be able to do this she got a Humboldt Scholarship for one year. She is also very much engaged in victim assistance, victim support and crime prevention in Austria in practice.

Ulrike Meier is currently Rechtsassessorin in Dresden, Germany. She was Research Assistant at the Institute of Criminology, University of Tübingen, specializing in juvenile delinquency and community policing.

Susanne Nothhafft lives and works in Munich, Germany, as a lawyer and mediator at the 'Fachstelle für Täter-Opfer-Ausgleich und Konfliktschlichtung' running a program of victim–offender reconciliation. Her main focus lies on the development of a specific methodology refering to domestic violence cases. She is, therefore, engaged in the Munich campaign 'Aktiv gegen Männergewalt' and takes part as representative of the Deutscher Juristinnenbund in the legislation procedure concerning the now-passed 'Gewaltschutzgesetz' which gives – among other protection orders – to the victims of domestic violence the right to stay home while the perpetrator has to leave.

She had a research assignment by the Bavarian Ministry of Eduction and the Arts concerning the evaluation of a pilot programme on conflict resolution and peer mediation in Munich secondary schools. First findings were presented at the Conference on Restorative Justice in October 2000 in Tübingen. In addition, she teaches criminology at the Munich University of Applied Sciences and works as a trainer for mediation and the prevention of domestic violence.

Candice Odgers is a PhD student in the Department of Psychology at the University of Virginia. Her MA research at the School of Criminology at Simon Fraser University was focused on serious and violent young female offenders. She has co-authored a number of articles and book chapters focusing on restorative justice, youth justice processing of young female offenders, serious and violent young female offending, and youth violence. She has worked as a project co-ordinator on a number of projects, including a North Atlantic Treaty Organization Advanced Research Workshop focusing on the risk and needs factors associated with serious and violent juvenile offending.

Tony Peters is Professor Emeritus at the Katholieke Universtiteit Leuven, Faculty of Law, Department of Criminology, Leuven, Belgium. He teaches Criminology, Victimology and Penology. His research focuses on punishment, victimization, mediation and restorative justice. He is President of the Scientific Committee of the International Society of Criminology, Director of the MA Programme in European Criminology at the Catholic University of Leuven.

Luc Robert, criminologist, works as researcher in Punishment and Restorative Justice at the Katholieke Universiteit Leuven, Faculty of Law, Department of Criminology, Leuven, Belgium.

Dieter Rössner is currently Professor of Criminal Law and Criminology and Director of the Institute of Criminal Science at the Philipps-University Marburg. He was President of the German Society of Criminology (NKG). Before his university career he was a judge and a prosecutor. He initiated several first models of victim–offender reconcialiation in Germany and has done extensive research and teaching in this field. Other topics of research and teaching are comparative studies on criminality, crimes of violence, hate crimes, theory of criminal law, and sentencing.

Lawrence W. Sherman is currently the Director of the Jerry Lee Center of Criminology, Chair of the Graduate Group in Criminology and the Albert M. Greenfield Professor of Human Relations in the Department of Sociology at the University of Pennsylvania, Philadelphia, PA. He is also President of the American Society of Criminology, and President of the International Society for Criminology, Paris, France. Since beginning his career as a civilian research analyst in the New York City Police Department as an Alfred P. Sloan Urban Fellow in 1971, he has collaborated with over 30 police agencies around the world. The author or co-author of four books and hundreds of articles, he has received awards for distinguished scholarship from the American Society of Criminology, the American Sociological Association, and the Academy of Criminal Justice Sciences. His publications include the 1997 Congressionally-mandated report to Attorney General Janet Reno, *Preventing Crime: What Works, What Doesn't, What's Promising*, which he co-authored with a team of distinguished University of Maryland criminologists. With support of the National Institute of Justice, he is also author of *Policing Domestic Violence: Experiments and Dilemmas*, as well as articles identifying the 'hot spots of crime' phenomenon and effectiveness of concentrating police patrols in small street corner zones where crime is heavily concentrated.

Heather Strang, PhD, criminologist, is currently Director of the Centre for Restorative Justice in the Research School of Social Sciences at the Australian National University. Over the past five years she has directed the Reintegrative Shaming Experiments (RISE), investigating the effectiveness of restorative conferencing as an alternative to normal criminal justice processing of offenders. She has a special interest in victims of crime, which is focus of her own research contribution to RISE. She is currently in the United Kingdom managing a further series of experiments to test the impact of restorative conferencing on violence and property crime at various points in the criminal justice system.

Barb Toews holds a Masters degree in Conflict Transformation from Eastern Mennonite University. She is currently the Restorative Justice Program Manager for the Pennsylvania Prison Society. Working with incarcerated men and women, she is exploring the application of restorative justice in prison and facilitating programmes that provide restorative opportunities for inmates. She has worked in the restorative justice field since 1992 when she began working in Fresno, CA at the Victim–Offender Reconciliation Program of the Central Valley. Following this experience, she was the founding director of the Lancaster Area Victim–Offender Reconciliation Program in Lancaster, PA. She facilitates educational forums and skills training in restorative justice and victim–offender mediation in Pennsylvania and around the U.S. She has experience as an Adjunct Professor at Eastern Mennonite University (Harrisonburg, VA), teaching classes in restorative justice and criminal justice as peacebuilding. She is a member of the Victim–Offender Mediation Association and has published articles in the area of restorative justice. She holds a masters degree in Conflict Transformation from Eastern Mennonite University.

Thomas Trenczek is currently Professor of Law at the School of Social Work of the University of Applied Sciences in Jena, Germany, where he teaches Criminal and Juvenile Law as well as Mediation and Dispute/Conflict Resolution. He holds both German Law degrees, and a PhD (Dr. iur.) as well as a MA in Social Sciences of the University in Tübingen. In 1987/88 he spent a year of research at the University of Minnesota in Minneapolis, USA and in 2001 was a Visiting Scholar at the Corrs Westgarth Dispute Management Center and the T. C. Beirne School of Law of the University of Queensland, Brisbane, Australia. Prof. Trenczek has worked as a law clerk and in the state attorney's office, in a law firm as well as in governmental bodies. From 1988–1991 he was Secretary General of the German Association of Juvenile Courts and Court Services. In addition, he is an accredited mediator, a cofounder and on the board of the WAAGE conflict resolution centre in Hanover, the largest VOMP in Germany.

Mark S. Umbreit is currently Professor and Founding Director of the Center for Restorative Justice and Peacemaking at the University of Minnesota, School of Social Work in St. Paul. Dr. Umbreit is an internationally recognized speaker, author and trainer in restorative-justice practices. His most recent book is *The Handbook of Victim Offender Mediation: An Essential Guide to Practice and Research* (Jossey-Bass Publishers). He initiated the first cross-national study of victim–offender mediation in Canada, England and the United States, and has recently completed the first multi-site empirical study on the impact on victims of severe violence who request a meeting with the offender in prison.

Elmar G. M. Weitekamp is Professor of Criminology, Victimology and Restorative Justice at the Katholieke Universiteit Leuven, Belgium, and Distinguished Adjunct Professor of Sociology at the Central China Normal University in Wuhan, People's Republic of China. He is a member of the Executive Board of the World Society of Criminology and Co-Director of the Postgraduate Courses in Victimology, Victim Assistance and Criminal Justice in Dubrovnik, Croatia. His primary research and writing interests are restorative justice, longitudinal research, comparative criminology and victimology and youth violence.

Toshio Yoshida studied law at Hokkaido University and at the University of Hamburg as DAAD-student (German scholarship). In 1987, he obtained Dr. jur. degree (Japan). He has visited various universities in Germany and the Max-Planck-Institut for Foreign and International Criminal Law in Freiburg, Germany. He teaches criminal law, criminal justice and criminology as Professor at Hokkaigakuen University (Sapporo). His research interests include criminal responsibility, sentencing policy, corrections and restorative justice. He regularly publishes articles in German and English.

Howard Zehr joined the graduate 'Conflict Transformation Program' at Eastern Mennonite University, Harrionsonburg, Virginia, in 1996 as Professor of Sociology and Restorative Justice, and is currently serving as Interim Director of that programme. Prior to that he served for 19 years as Director of the Mennonite Central Committee U.S. Office on Crime and Justice. Zehr's book *Changing Lenses: A New Focus for Crime and Justice*, has been a foundational work in the growing restorative justice movement. In their recent book *Restoring Justice*, Dan Van Ness and Karen Heederks Strong cite him as the 'grandfather of restorative justice.' As a result, he lectures and consults internationally on restorative justice and the victim– offender conferencing programmes, which he helped pioneer. Other publications include *Crime and the Development of Modern Society* (1976), *Doing Life: Reflections of Men and Women Serving Life Sentences* (1996) and, most recently, *Transcending: Reflections of Crime Victims* (2001). He has also worked professionally as a photographer and photojournalist, both in the North America and internationally. His primary interest currently is in the use of photography and interviews for documentary work. Zehr received his BA from Morehouse College (Atlanta, GA), his MA from the Univeristy of Chicago and his PhD from Rutgers University. From 1971–78 he taught humanities and history at Talladega College in Alabama.

Preface

This book brings together a number of the leading authorities on restorative justice to explore this burgeoning field, and to provide a comprehensive review of international practice and directions, and the context in which the practice is developing. The book moves beyond a focus on restorative justice for juveniles to a broader concern with the application of restorative justice in such areas as corporate crime, family violence, and cases of severe crimes like murder. The contexts examined are drawn from Europe, North America, Australia and Japan. The chapters in this book have been developed from papers and discussions at the Fourth International Conference on Restorative Justice for Juveniles, which was held in Tübingen, Germany, on October 1–4, 2000 to address 'Restorative Justice as a Challenge for the New Millennium'. This event was part of a series of conferences arranged by the members of the International Network for Restorative Justice for Juveniles. Their purpose is to bring together academics, policy makers and practitioners to discuss specific topical issues relating to restorative justice, and to develop ideas about its further expansion in as many juvenile justice and criminal justice systems in the world as possible.

Raymond Corrado, *Irwin M. Cohen* and *Candice Odgers* start with the notion that since the general introduction of restorative justice in the 1970s, there has been a growing debate concerning the role of restorative justice in addressing, deterring and responding to young offenders. A crucial issue is the ability of the restorative justice paradigm to transform, or even replace, existing retributive justice systems. Quite often practical programmes consider only first-time offenders, or those who commit minor offences, as 'good candidates' for restorative interventions. The lack of theoretical attention to, or practical experimentation with restorative justice principles with serious and violent young offenders is deplored. In their chapter the authors illustrate some of the challenges facing the implementation of restorative justice interventions for those offenders. The results presented are based on research into a sample of some 400 incarcerated serious and/or violent young offenders from the Vancouver Young Offenders Study.

Kathleen Daly argues in her chapter that a good measure of the vitality of a new justice idea is the ratio between the claims made by advocates and the evidence to support those claims. The argument goes: the less evidence that exists, the greater the excitement and debate about the new idea. Her intention is to add sound and thorough evidence to the debate. She presents findings from the South Australia Juvenile Justice research on conferencing projects. From observational measures gathered on some 90 youth justice conferences she constructs a measure that differentiates those conferences that have higher levels of 'restorativeness', procedural justice, and coordinator management skill from other, less ideal conferences.

Britta Bannenberg and *Dieter Rössner* then turn our attention to the special issue of violence in families or in partnerships. They present empirical results about such violence, especially in Germany, based on various sources, and they critically analyse the usual reactions of the police and the judiciary. The chapter ends with explorations of new forms of legal response in order to settle violent conflicts in partnerships, including suggestions to implement effective victim–offender mediation schemes.

Susanne Nothhafft presents first results of a pilot programme in secondary schools in the city of Munich, which was started in the 1990s and aims at resolving in-school conflicts with three 'target groups' , namely pupils, teachers and parents. The objective of the programme is to open to these target groups new kinds of peer mediation and dispute resolution that are constructive, peaceful and oriented towards win–win solutions.

Luc Robert and *Tony Peters* dedicate their chapter to a very challenging endeavour: introducing ideas of restorative justice into prison practice on a national scale. Their example is Belgium where a pilot project, in operation in six prisons since the beginning of 1998, developed into a large movement when policy makers saw that this first attempt at 'restorative detention' had quickly taken root in the global Belgian penal establishment. The authors describe the contextual framework of the project whose name seems to be at first sight a 'contradiction in terms'. They go on to analyse the experience of implementing the programme, with respect to the prison system as such, its personnel, the prisoners, and the restorative justice consultants who are working in close cooperation with research teams from universities. Special attention is given to the 'real threat' that traditional prison praxis might 'hijack' restorative initiatives.

Mark S. Umbreit, William Bradshaw and *Robert B. Coates* deal with a perhaps even more challenging issue: whether and how far it might be possible to bring victims of severe violence, including cases of murder, into dialogue with the offender. By referring to the extensive experience with programmes that have been offered in the United States through victim-services units of departments of corrections in several states, they describe differing approaches of 'victim-sensitive offender dialogue' and develop a relevant typology. Five programmes are analysed in more detail. Preliminary research data indicates exceptionally high levels of client satisfaction with the process and outcome of victim–offender mediation and dialogue in crimes of extreme violence that were handled by specially qualified mediators.

Marianne Löschnig-Gspandl analyses the question of how restorative justice could deal with corporate crimes as well as with corporations as crime victims. As far as corporations-as-offenders are concerned, corporate liability is considered to be a necessity from a criminal policy point of view. Possible restorative sanctions are then explored. With corporations as victims the concept of 'evaporating' victims is discussed. The author then presents an interesting practical case of victim–offender mediation that shows the potential for further developments in that field.

John Braithwaite puts the problem of restorative justice in the corporate world in a different perspective. He starts with the notion of 'justice that empowers the most powerless', referring to some of the most moving and effective restorative justice conferences he has seen: namely business regulatory conferences, especially following nursing-home inspections in the US and Australia. He holds that deliberative empowerment is one of the core values of restorative justice, and it is nowhere more profoundly realized than in nursing-home regulation at its best. He then goes on to describe the work of his research group on those inspections and regulations. Other examples then dealt with are the field of safety regulation and its relation to re-integrative shaming and empowerment, and the field of whole-school anti-bullying programmes. Seen from that perspective, giving the least powerful people in our societies a voice is an important restorative justice value. Regulatory conversations are seen to be capable of building micro-communities in contexts where they are sorely needed. They create models of 'active responsibility' which means taking responsibility for solving existing problems. In contrast, punitive criminal justice, like the accountability mechanisms of the contemporary state more generally, are considered to follow a 'passive model' of responsibility, holding someone responsible for what they have done in the past, which is not consistent with ideas of citizenship.

Toshio Yoshida asks in his chapter whether Japan is actually a model of restorative justice, as could be inferred from reports of foreign observers that the Japanese criminal justice system emphasizes compensation and apology to the victim, and the restoration of community peace. His answer to the question posed is based on two comprehensive surveys administered by the Japanese 'Working Group for Investigating the Present Situation of Crime' and by the 'Research and Training Institute of the Ministry of Justice'. They draw a very different picture. The attitudes of criminal justice practitioners are on the whole punitively oriented. The currently pre-dominant 'relative theory of retribution' in criminal justice administration leaves little room for socially constructive crime-resolution schemes like victim–offender mediation. Apologies are less frequent in criminal justice settings than they are in everyday Japanese life. Settlements out of court aim rather exclusively at paying compensation instead of trying to reach non-material restoration. However, the survey results show that there seems to be a basis for further restorative justice developments in the Japanese criminal justice system.

Els Dumortier analyses the state of development of legal rules and safeguards within Belgian mediation practices for juveniles, concentrating on how basic procedural safeguards are organized within the Brussels mediation practices and, more specifically, in a very active mediation centre with the name BAS! (Counselling Service for Community Service). This organization started, in 1996, an experiment on victim–offender mediation at the level of the public prosecutor. The chapter deals in depth with the tensions between the 'discourse' of mediation (stressing voluntary co-operation, and diversion) and the everyday 'mediation practices' in the field (where it may be hard to pretend that a minor actually has a free choice to join or not to join the programme, when his unwillingness to co-operate can eventually be sanctioned by prosecution before the juvenile court). This leads to the urgent need for some legal assistance in practice, and for special additional qualification for those appointed to provide young people with legal advice.

Dieter Dölling and *Arthur Hartmann* report the results of a German research project on re-offending after victim–offender mediation in juvenile court proceedings. The comparative analysis of some 130 mediation cases and some 140 control cases reveals the favourable influence of Victim–offender mediation on re-offending, but its extent with regard to other characteristics that differentiated the two samples could not be measured very precisely. However, the hypothesis put forward by opponents of

Victim–offender mediation, namely that it will reduce the preventive effect of criminal law, was definitely not supported by the data.

Lawrence W. Sherman, Heather Strang and *Daniel Woods* report in their chapter an analysis of the varying effects of some restorative justice models when led by different individuals, with different levels of experience, and different systems of caseload management. They refer to some 500 restorative justice conferences conducted during the RISE (Reintegrative Shaming Experiments) programme by individual conference leaders. It can be shown that there are indeed substantial differences between those leaders in the effect they appear to cause in offenders, including repeat offending and offender perceptions of the legitimacy of law, as measured by post-conference respect for police. The effects are controlled for both drink/drivers and for three different kinds of juvenile offences. The biggest differences in outcomes were associated with individual facilitators, regardless of their level of experience.

Barb Toews and *Howard Zehr* explore in their chapter some of the similarities in the values and practices of the dominant approaches to research and to justice, and contrast them with those of restorative justice and transformative research. Among the important issues are 'respect for the people affected by the criminal event', and the 'recognition that the meaning of the crime event is subjective, constructed and inter-relational and, as a result, is complex and limits the nature of the justice response' . The chapter suggests a whole set of 'transformative guidelines' for research that are more consistent with the values of restorative justice.

Thomas Trenczek questions in his chapter the conceptual orientation and enforcement of TOA (the German version of victim–offender reconciliation) in the juvenile justice and criminal justice systems. His argument is that the real nature and character of conflict mediation is hidden, and that the dominant approach prevents elements of restorative justice from asserting themselves. The multiple search for niches of acceptance is considered conspicuous, as is the adaptation to inappropriate ideas taken from traditional juvenile welfare and criminal law.

Peter Lindström looks, in his chapter on Sweden, for possible hidden links between zero-tolerance criminal policy and restorative justice. He reports that in recent years, discussions in the area of crime policy have on the one hand focused on a reduced level of tolerance in relation to offenders, and on the other hand on increased possibilities of winding up a case at an earlier stage of its progress through the justice system. It seems impossible to integrate both concepts in a coherent way. The chapter elaborates the problems with the example of the offence of shoplifting, and then goes on to examine trends in the way the system reacts to the crimes of young offenders. The goals of reducing crime and increasing security are considered so general that most people can easily agree on them. This may even generate populist slogans in crime policy. In countering those developments, putting more emphasis in the future on redressing the injury that has been done is considered highly necessary.

Finally, *Elmar G. M. Weitekamp, Hans-Jürgen Kerner* and *Ulrike Meier* develop some basic elements of a concept of community policing and problem-oriented policing in the context of restorative justice. Drawing on the international literature on the guiding principles of these two modern ways of policing as compared to traditional styles, they argue that they offer sound possibilities for integration into a restorative problem-solving police prevention programme that takes into account the perceptions, wishes and needs of the victims, the offenders, the community and the police alike.

As conference organizers and editors we were lucky and happy to have with us two people who were highly dedicated to the task of making our endeavours a success. We would like to mention particularly Beatrice Lunkenbein and Maria Pessiu. Carsten Brombach and Ulrike Höschle deserve special thanks for helping to refine the final text of the chapters.

Elmar G. M. Weitekamp
Hans-Jürgen Kerner

Chapter 1

Multi-problem violent youth: a challenge for the restorative justice paradigm

Raymond R. Corrado, Irwin M. Cohen
and Candice Odgers

Restorative justice first gained popularity with academics, researchers and criminal justice policy-makers, in part due to a general feeling that traditional, retributive systems of justice were failing victims, offenders and the community. Supporters and proponents of the restorative justice paradigm argued that interventions based on the principles of restorative justice could achieve the necessary criminal justice goals of offender accountability, community safety and victim restoration, and could attain these objectives in ways that were meaningful and impacted the lives of those responsible and affected by crime. Since its general introduction in the 1970s, there has been a growing debate concerning the role of restorative justice in addressing, deterring and responding to young offenders. Crucial issues debated in the literature concern the theoretical and practical roles for restorative justice within existing criminal justice systems for youth, and the ability of the restorative justice paradigm to transform, or even replace, existing retributive justice systems. Other significant issues in the literature include a focus on the actual implementation of restorative justice initiatives and programmes for young offenders, and evaluations of the effectiveness of these restorative justice programmes.

Regardless of whether one considers restorative justice from a theoretical perspective or from a policy standpoint, it is frequently only first-time offenders, or those who commit minor offences, who are considered 'good candidates' for most restorative justice interventions. As a result, while there have been a myriad of different approaches and initiatives proposed or undertaken by researchers, academics and policy-makers that aim to achieve the fundamental goals of restorative justice, these attempts frequently share the shortcoming of only accepting novice and low-risk offenders, or those who engage in relatively minor offences.

For instance, Canada has used formal restorative justice programmes for decades. The primary target population for the overwhelming majority of victim–offender reconciliation programmes for young offenders, which is the most common form of restorative-justice programming in Canada, are youth, who have no previous criminal record, have no previously recorded referrals to an alternative measures programme, and have not committed a violent offence or exhibited antisocial behaviour patterns (Pate 1990; Griffiths and Corrado 1999).

Moreover, there are a wide range of serious offences, and types of offenders, for which restorative justice programmes are not even an option (Archibald 1999). As Bazemore and Umbreit conclude, '… all acknowledge that some proportion of the youthful offender population will need to be removed from the community and confined in secure facilities for public safety reasons' (Bazemore and Umbreit 1995: 306–7). While this may be self-evident, there are, nonetheless, no compelling reasons why serious and violent young offenders should not be considered, or cannot participate, in restorative justice initiatives during or following their incarceration.

The lack of theoretical attention, or practical experimentation, of restorative justice principles with serious and violent young offenders has led to several informal schools of thought to address the amenability of this paradigm to this unique group of young offenders. Some scholars, such as Roach (2000) contend that it is unlikely for restorative justice to completely replace traditional retributive youth-justice systems in cases of serious and violent young offenders. This conclusion is due in part to the apparent lack of severe sanctions, such as long-term imprisonment, for the most serious and violent offenders under the restorative justice paradigm. Other scholars, such as Umbreit (1995) and Walgrave (1995), suggest that restorative justice can be effective with all offenders, but concede that it will be difficult to work, in a practical sense, with high-risk, violent offenders using the restorative justice paradigm. They contend that this difficulty is primarily due to the public's need to feel safe from youth who engage in serious, habitual offending or violence. To many in the public, restorative justice is synonymous with soft justice. As such, there is little public support for the use of restorative justice with serious, violent or habitual criminals at the expense of traditional, retributive methods of justice. Finally, there are those restorative justice scholars, such as Bazemore (1994), who maintain that it is still possible to restructure the entire juvenile justice system to reflect restorative-justice principles for all offenders, including serious and violent young offenders.

Therefore, the aim of this chapter is to illustrate some of the challenges facing the implementation of restorative justice interventions for serious and violent offenders. To do so, we will review the restorative justice paradigm and the most common forms of restorative justice interventions. Moreover, we will provide an overview of a sample of 402 incarcerated serious and/or violent young offenders from the Vancouver Young Offender Study (VYOS). The purpose of including a basic review of this sample is to demonstrate the significant problem profiles of serious and violent young offenders and the unique challenges that these kind of offenders pose for restorative justice interventions. Finally, we will analyse the potential benefits of the Transforming Conflict perspective, as discussed by Moore and McDonald (2000), and the Victim Offender Mediation Project in British Columbia, Canada (1995), in dealing with serious and violent young offenders within the restorative-justice paradigm.

Restorative justice is most commonly used to describe informal and non-adjudicative methods of solving disputes or conflicts that give victims, offenders and the community a central role in decision making (Braithwaite 1990; Roach 2000). A fundamental tenet of the restorative-justice paradigm is a shift in accountability from the young offender owing a debt to society for their criminal behaviours to the offender's responsibility to their victim(s). As Umbreit (1995) explains, in the restorative-justice paradigm, the primary victim of a criminal offence is not the state, as is the case in retributive, adversarial criminal justice systems. Instead, the person who is victimized is viewed and treated as the primary victim in this paradigm (Niemeyer and Shichor 1996). Moreover, the restorative-justice paradigm is based on the notion that the offender 'incurs an obligation' to the victim (Umbreit 1994). This obligation can take many forms, such as financial restitution, community service, victim–offender mediation, or personal services to the victim.

Regardless of the specific form the offender's obligation takes, the general purposes of the intervention remain the same in the restorative-justice paradigm. All interventions must focus on problem solving, on restoring or reconciling both parties, and on repairing any social injury (Umbreit 1995). Some of the other fundamental principles of the restorative-justice paradigm include ensuring community protection, promoting offender responsibility, removal of the stigma of crime through restorative action, and the direct involvement of all effected persons, including representatives for the offender, the victim and the community (Umbreit 1995).

3

Typically, restorative justice programmes aim to bring together the victim and the offender for the purposes of allowing both sides to understand the context of the offence, the impact of the offence on both parties, and, in some cases, to establish some form of agreed-upon reparation to the victim by the offender (Bazemore and Umbreit 1995; Walgrave 1995; Niemeyer and Shichor 1996; Braithwaite 1990). While there are several general elements held in common by most restorative justice initiatives in order for these interventions to be considered successful, such as a fundamental change in how the offender, the victim and the community think, feel and respond to crime, there are a number of different structures to interventions that are consistent with the restorative-justice paradigm.

Perhaps the intervention most readily identified with the restorative-justice paradigm is victim–offender mediation. The focus of this form of intervention is to hold offenders accountable by making them aware of the impact their offending has had on their victims. This is achieved by having the offender meet and discuss the offence with their victim(s) in the presence of a trained mediator (Umbreit 1995). Importantly, this approach does not allow the offender to be passively punished. Instead, the offender plays an active role in restoring themselves, the victim, and the community. While there is an abundance of research demonstrating that both offenders and victims feel that this form of intervention is beneficial to them, it must be kept in mind that the overwhelming number of evaluations of victim–offender mediation programmes focus almost exclusively on minor offences or novice offenders (Trimboli 2000; Walgrave 1995; Levrant et al. 1999; Niemeyer and Shichor 1996; Braithwaite 1990).

Research that does investigate the success of offender–victim mediation with serious or violent offenders suffer from two basic limitations. First, these studies have very small sample sizes. Second, the mediations with serious or violent offenders are always held after the offender has served a significant period of time incarcerated (Flaten 1996). While this second limitation does not put into dispute the validity of the findings, or the ability of restorative justice to assist violent offenders and their victims, it does indicate that there still exist obstacles for those who wish to see restorative justice replace existing criminal justice methods for dealing with serious and violent offenders.

Financial restitution is another common form of restorative justice programming. Restitution allows victims to receive financial compensation from the offender for the losses they have incurred due to their victimization (Umbreit 1995). Restitution exhibits several of the key elements of the restorative-justice paradigm, such as making the offender directly accountable to their victim(s); in addition, financial restitution serves to restore victims by compensating them, to some degree, for their losses. The use of financial restitution as a form of intervention continues to grow internationally (Galaway and Hudson 1990); however, it is still overwhelmingly used with property or minor offenders. With respect to serious and violent offenders, it is difficult to see how offenders might financially compensate victims for personal offences, such as murder or sexual assault, as part of a restoring process. While financial restitution can help replace stolen or damaged property, it is more difficult to link this form of intervention to personal offences other than as a symbolic demonstration of responsibility.

Another intervention that is increasing in popularity is community work service. In these programmes, offenders must work for a specific number of hours at tasks aimed at benefiting the general community. The principle underlying community work service is that the community is also a victim in any offence, and, as such, the offender has an obligation to restore, and is accountable to, the community. Umbreit (1995) correctly points out, however, that unless the primary victim is involved in decisions concerning this intervention, such as by selecting the site for the community work service, this intervention may simply serve as retribution or punishment, and not achieve the goals of the restorative justice approach. Moreover, even with victim input, this form of intervention may not assist the victim in feeling restored. One possible method of alleviating this possible problem is through personal service to the victim.

Some victims would rather have the offender perform some type of unpaid service to them directly, rather than have their offender(s) perform duties for the general community. Personal service to the victim make the offender directly and personally accountable to them. These interventions only work with certain victims because, for some, personal service increases their fear of being victimized again (Umbreit 1995). Other victims do not wish to have any contact with their victimizers once they have completed their initial participation in mediation. These considerations are particularly salient in view of the nature of serious and violent offences and offenders.

Once again, regardless of the specific form that the intervention takes, all restorative justice initiatives stress the participation of the offender, the victim and the community (Simms 1997). All decisions must be based on the principles of fairness and reconciliation. Moreover, the needs of the offender and the victim, and the safety of the community, must be paramount. All interventions must ensure that the offender accepts responsibility, and is accountable to themselves, their victims and the community. Interventions must offer the opportunity for offenders to make amends to their victims and the community for their criminal offences.

Finally, victims of property offences must be provided with the opportunity for restitution, while victims of violent offences must be provided with the opportunity to achieve some degree of closure (Umbreit 1995).

As mentioned above, while there exist many studies demonstrating that those who do participate in restorative justice programmes tend to view the process as positive, even with violent offences, there are several clear limitations to achieving even the most basic of restorative justice goals. For instance, the participation of victims in mediation is often affected by the type of offence committed against them. It is evident that offenders and victims are most likely to agree to mediation when the offence is either a property offence or a minor personal offence (Levrant *et al.* 1999). Moreover, victims who avail themselves of financial restitution interventions may not receive full monetary restoration, or may feel that the offender continues to feel or act hostile toward them (Levrant *et al.* 1999).

With respect to offenders, some may not feel that they have been forgiven, even after completing their intervention, by either the victim or the community. Perhaps most important to the public is the ability of restorative justice to protect society by reducing recidivism. Meta-analyses of restorative justice programmes conclude that restitution and mediation programmes have, at best, a modest impact on recidivism (Lipsey and Wilson 1999). As Levrant *et al.* suggest, 'given research findings that suggest that intensive services are required to reduce recidivism among high-risk offenders, it is unlikely that, for example, a one-hour victim–offender mediation session will lessen criminal propensities among these offenders. Thus, the restorative approach runs the risk of becoming the progressives' equivalent of conservative Scared Straight programmes ... It is also highly unlikely that restorative justice programmes will, as currently implemented, produce lasting changes in an offenders' criminogenic needs ... restorative justice programmes are currently implemented in a piecemeal fashion and are focused primarily on victim restoration' (1999: 20).

Given even this cursory review of some of the more common limitations of restorative justice programmes, there are clear challenges when considering applying the restorative justice paradigm to serious and violent offenders. As mentioned above, the seriousness of the offence and the criminal history of the offender are frequently the most crucial factors in deciding who is a suitable candidate for restorative justice. However, Walgrave (1995) contends that the seriousness of the offence need not be a determining factor. Walgrave suggests that while simple victim–offender mediation may not be adequate to address all serious offences and offenders, he does not believe that serious offenders cannot benefit, or be positively affected, by interventions such as community service. Still, we contend that serious and violent offenders are sufficiently different from minor offenders that they require special consideration with respect to restorative justice programmes.

Serious and violent young offenders differ from minor offenders in several distinct ways. However, it can be argued that the simplest way to understand these differences is to recognize that there are certain variables that have consistently demonstrated some degree of predictive value with respect to youthful offending. In general, certain personal factors and characteristics (gender, ethnicity, IQ, medical/physical condition), social factors (social ties, antisocial peers), family characteristics (antisocial parents, abusive parents, broken home), and anti-social behaviours (aggression, problem behaviour, substance use) are all correlated with serious and violent offending (Anderson 1994; Huizinga and Jokob-Chien 1999; Tolan and Gorman-Smith 1999; Lipsey and Derzon 1999; Hawkins *et al*. 1999; LeBlanc 1999). While young offenders who commit minor offences will have some of these predictors, serious and violent offenders will have more of these predictors, and have them to a significantly greater degree. As such, serious and violent young offenders pose unique, but not insurmountable, challenges to the successful implementation of the restorative-justice paradigm. In order to identify these challenges, it is important to understand the multi-problem profile of serious and violent young offenders.

Between 1998 and 2000, a sample of 402 young offenders from a major urban centre in British Columbia, Canada were interviewed as part of the Vancouver Young Offenders Survey (VYOS).[1] In order to be included in this study, a youth (aged 12–18) had to be sentenced to a custodial disposition under the Young Offenders Act (YOA). The sample was drawn from four separate youth custody institutions: two secure custody institutions and two open custody institutions. The primary differences between a secure and an open custody facility in Canada are the level of security and the programming options available to residents. Moreover, the ability to access and participate in community-based programmes and initiatives is increasingly restricted for those sentenced to secure custody. Youth serving their sentences in open custody settings also experience greater freedom of movement within the institution and are afforded a greater number of privileges, such as increased visitation rights and the ability to retain a wider variety of personal belongings in the institution.

Typically, younger, less serious and/or first time offenders are sentenced to open custody, while the chronic, serious and violent offenders are more likely to be sentenced to a secure custody facility. As a result, the ability to sample from both secure custody and open custody institutions provides a diverse sample of youth and offending patterns, ranging from relatively minor offenders to the most serious and violent incarcerated youth. This provides an excellent sample with which to discuss the amenability of restorative justice principles.

The Vancouver Young Offender Study (VYOS) employed a multi-method approach in order to develop a holistic picture of incarcerated serious and violent youth and the myriad of social, educational, family, peer, mental health and abuse variables that characterize their lives and offending patterns. A combination of extensive file reviews and in-depth interviews were used to gather information on a wide range of key variables, as well as allowing the researcher to contextualize the lives and experiences of this group of offenders. Due to this multi-method approach, the resulting data set includes both rich qualitative information, provided by both the youth via self-report questionnaires and through the official case files, as well as in-depth quantitative responses that are tied to key youth justice models, such as deterrence, special needs, procedural rights, fairness, due process and restorative justice.

As mentioned above, in order to obtain as complete a picture as possible of each youth, an extensive file review was conducted on each youth prior to their interview. The typical profile of documents reviewed for each youth included: (1) a pre-disposition report that details the youth's social, educational, family, peer, substance use and correctional history; (2) psychological reports that include the mental health history of the youth, along with any psychological testing information; (3) institutional Reports that describe the youth's behaviour within the institution as assessed by staff members; (4) provincial case files that outline the youth's charge, court and disposition history; and (5) extraneous documents, such as specific programming reports, staff alerts and medical information.

During the interview, participants were asked questions relating to their experiences with the youth justice system and its agents, past and present offending behaviour, peer and sexual relationships, family dynamics, school and work history, substance use, attitudes towards their offending and victims, experiences of physical and sexual abuse, identity, deterrence, social bonding, past interventions, institutional experiences, and their attitudes toward restorative justice principles. In addition, the youth were rated by trained interviewers on the youth version of the Psychopathy Checklist (Hart *et al*. 1995), a series of family, work, and school bonding measures, and an aggressive incident coding instrument. Each interview lasted approximately 2–3 hours.

The mean age of the participants was 16 years. The sample consisted of 323 males (80.3 per cent) and 79 females (19.7 per cent). As indicated in previous research (Roberts and Doob 1997; Boe 2000; Griffiths and Verdun-Jones 1994), the ethnic composition of the sample was not representative of the larger youth population. Caucasian youth comprised 64 per cent of the participants, while 25 per cent of the youth were Aboriginal, 3 per cent were Afro-Canadian, 5 per cent Asian, and the remaining 3 per cent were classified as other. The discordance with the larger youth population was even more pronounced when one considers just the female sample. In this sample, 42 per cent of the incarcerated females identify themselves as Aboriginal. It is interesting to note that there has been virtually no research focusing on serious and violent female youth in Canada, and more specifically there is no research to date that focuses on female youth and restorative justice models. Given the unique needs that have been found with female youth in terms of overall criminal justice processing (Corrado, *et al.* 2000), the application of restorative justice principles to this population warrants a substantial amount of research and policy attention.

Offence information was gathered from both the youth's file and through self-report measures within the questionnaire. Official charge(s) disposition(s) and court information was collected on each youth in order to examine sentencing patterns and profile the offence history of the sample. Self-report measures were also included in order to tap into the dark figure of offending, with a special emphasis on gathering information relating to the youth's involvement in serious and violent offending. In addition, the self-report crime and delinquency measures included attitudinal measures regarding their offending, the official and unofficial reactions to their criminal behaviour, and, perhaps most importantly, their perceptions of the anticipated consequences of their behaviour. This last measure is extremely important for an analysis of the applicability of restorative justice principles for serious and violent offenders because this indicator addresses the issue of how both official youth justice consequences and unofficial consequences, such as stigmatization and labeling, affect future behavior and future decisions to participate in crime.

Table 1.1 presents the general offending profiles of the youth in the sample. While the majority of the youth were serving time for relatively minor offences, such as minor property offences (36.6 per cent) or breaches[2] (20.1 per cent), the previous offence history indicates the serious nature of the sample's offending profiles. On average, these youth have spent just under one year in a custodial institution (356 days) and have a mean of four previous sentencing dispositions. In addition, 62.4 per cent of the youth have been sentenced for a violent offence, and 72 per cent of the sample are classified as chronic offenders. Using Synder's definition (1999), a chronic young offender is one who has been sentenced four or more separate times for separate criminal incidents.[3] With respect to the frequency of violence, our sample does demonstrate a high level of official and unofficial violence. For instance, approximately 26 per cent of the youth report getting into fights at least once a week. Within this group, there are 17

Table 1.1 Offence characteristics

	Percentage	Mean
Current offence		
Murder	2.5%	
Sex offences	1.8%	
Robbery	16.5%	
Assaults	16.0%	
Property offences	36.6%	
Drug offences	3.0%	
Breaches	20.1%	
Other	3.6%	
Prior offence		
Number of prior offences		4.0
Average days spent in custody		356.3
Age at first contact with the criminal justice system		14.6
Serious and violent offending		
Violent offender	62.4%	
Chronic offender (4 or more dispositions)	72.0%	
How often do you get into physical fights?		
Never	7.7%	
Daily	4.2%	
Few times a week	12.6%	
Once a week	7.3%	
Few times a month	11.5%	
Once a month	9.4%	
Rarely	47.2%	

of the youth reporting that they fight daily and 51 of the youth reporting that they are involved in fights a couple of times a week.

As can be expected with a sample of serious offenders, there is a high level of family dysfunction. This dysfunction is characterized by extremely high levels of physical and sexual abuse, family separation, and chronic linear family problems (see Table 1.2). In particular, the percentage of youth who report that they have left home of their own choice (78.6 per cent) and/ or have been kicked out of their homes (48.6 per cent) indicates the lack of strong family bonds. Moreover, on average, these youth have lived in seven places other than their primary home.[4] Of those youth who were living with their immediate family, a substantial portion were residing with single-

Table 1.2 Family variables

	Percentage	Mean
Linear family history		
Alcohol abuse	73.0%	
Drug abuse	60.4%	
Criminality	70.5%	
Mental illness	22.0%	
Foster care	38.9%	
Living at time of offence		
Immediate family	47.1%	
Extended family	7.5%	
Independent	22.8%	
Ward of the state	22.5%	
Kicked out of home	48.6%	
Earliest age		12.5
No. of times		10.5
Left home	78.6%	
Earliest age		13.5
No. of times		4.9
No. of places lived other than home		7.0

parent families (72.2 per cent), with the mother being the more frequent primary caregiver in these instances. In addition, at the time that the youth in this sample committed the offence(s) for which they were currently serving a custody sentence, over 45 per cent of the youth were either living on their own (on the street or with a friend), or were classified as a ward of the state and were living in foster-care placements.

The problem is not limited, however, to simply where the youth was living. A large portion of the youth in our sample have immediate family members or close relatives with significant social, mental, substance-abuse and criminal problems. For instance, 73 per cent of the youth in our sample report a close family member as having an alcohol-abuse problem. Moreover, 60 per cent report that a close family member has a drug-abuse problem. Of interest to those who advocate the use of family members as essential players in any restorative justice initiative, in addition to the large number of youth who have little or no contact with their immediate family, 70 per cent of the youth in our sample report an immediate family member as having a criminal record.

Self-report and file indicators of abuse indicate that a substantial number of the youth in our sample are victims of physical and sexual abuse. While 55 per cent of the youth report that they have been victims of physical abuse at some point in their lives, 19.2 per cent of the youth indicate that they had experienced sexual abuse. As can be expected, a significant gender difference exists on the measures of abuse. 39.3 per cent of the male youths in our sample report being a victim of physical abuse, while 66.7 per cent of our females report being abused physically. An even greater difference exists with respect to sexual abuse. Of the female youth in our sample, 52.6 per cent report being a victim of sexual abuse, while 11.3 per cent of the male youth report being a victim of sexual abuse.

Another important variable in understanding the profiles of serious and violent youth is their school and education histories. Overall, the school histories of this group of serious and violent offenders display a consistent pattern of low commitment to school, poor performance in school, and high levels of conflict with fellow students, teachers and staff (see Table 1.3). A key indicator of one's commitment to school is truancy, or the number of times one is absent from school without a legitimate reason. In our sample, 91.4 per cent of the youth report skipping school an average of a few times a week. In addition, they report beginning to skip school, on average, at the age of 13 years. The high level of truancy, the high rate of truancy, and the early onset of truancy clearly reflects the low levels of commitment to education among this sample of youth.

With respect to poor school performance, while the majority of the youth in our sample feel that it is important or very important to get good grades (59.4 per cent), the modal average final grade for the sample was C–. Moreover, the average grade completed for the sample was grade 8. It must be kept in mind that the mean age for our sample was 16. As such, the average grade of completion is 3–5 grades below what it typical for a youth aged 16 years old.

Our sample of serious and violent young offenders is also characterized by a high level of school conflict. 95.4 per cent of our sample report getting into trouble at school, beginning at the age of 10. It should be noted that the vast majority of the reasons that these youth provided for 'getting into trouble' at school were serious conduct problems, such as fighting, selling drugs, violence towards teachers, and intimidation. In other words, the behaviours that these youth engage in at school are not minor transgressions, but behaviours that, once discovered by school officials, typically result in either suspension or expulsion, or the involvement of the criminal justice system.

The seriousness of these school problems, and the frequency with which they occur, often result in the youth having to change schools. On average,

Table 1.3. School variables

	Percentage	Mean
Enrolled in school at time of offence	53.5%	
Last grade competed		8.6
How important is it for you to get good grades?		
Very important	26.7%	
Important	32.7%	
Neutral	9.7%	
Not very important	21.8%	
Totally unimportant	9.1%	
How often did you have trouble with teachers?		
Never	8.5%	
Rarely	24.8%	
Sometimes	25.6%	
Often	20.2%	
Always	20.9%	
Skip school	91.4%	Few times a week
Age started skipping		12.8
Trouble at school	95.4%	
Age first started getting into trouble		10.2
Times changed schools		5.6

our sample report having to change schools 5.6 times.[5] Although a portion of these changes were due to residential moves, the majority of transfers were the result of chronic disruptive behaviour and discipline problems. In addition, approximately 41 per cent of the youth report having trouble with teachers 'often' or 'always', indicating a high frequency of classroom disruption.

As indicated above, a central feature of many restorative justice initiatives is compensation for the victim through work performed by the offender. As such, it is useful to examine the work history of offenders and their commitment to employment.

While a portion of our sample was employed at the time of the offence, a similar portion report getting into trouble at work (Table 1.4). The typical behaviours that these youth are getting into trouble for at work include lateness, arriving at work drunk or stoned, verbal and physical conflicts with co-workers, and verbal and physical conflicts with employers. As a result, the conclusion drawn from an analysis of the youth in our sample is

Table 1.4. Employment variables

	Percentage
Employed at the time of the offence	32.1%
Ever in trouble at work	30.1%

that most of these youth have little to no work experience. Those who do have some work experience tend to have experience in service or physical labour jobs. And, of those who have been employed, nearly a third have had problems that have resulted in either their dismissal or that could result in dismissal. Our sample's bonds to work and employment are sufficiently low to suggest that there is little current commitment among these youth to employment.

As expected in a sample of serious and violent youth, the levels of substance use among this sample are extremely high. Virtually all of the youth (92.9 per cent) report using drugs (see Table 1.5). Although the most frequently reported drug used was marijuana, the levels of serious or hard drug use were also relatively high. 56.5 per cent of the youth report using cocaine, while 44.2 per cent of the youth report using crack cocaine an average of a 'few times a week'. In addition, a large portion of our sample report a high rate of heroin use. For instance, 35.1 per cent of the sample indicate that they use heroin an average of 'once a week'. Interestingly, the levels of drug use among the female youth were significantly higher that their male counterparts. For example, 64.5 per cent of females report crack use, 59.0 per cent report heroin use, and 72.7 per cent indicate that they use cocaine. By comparison, 38.9 per cent of the males report using crack, 28.6 per cent report heroin use, and 52.3 per cent indicate that they use cocaine. The frequency of hard drug use was also significantly higher among the females.

On average, the onset of both drug and alcohol use began at the age of 12 years. Similar to the rates of drug use reported above, 91.2 per cent of the sample report using alcohol, with 70.5 per cent of the youth reporting that they consume alcohol at least once a week or more. These rates serve to highlight that there is a major drug and alcohol problem associated with our serious and violent young offenders. As such, any initiative designed to restore a youth to being a healthy, law-abiding member of the community must consider drug and alcohol treatment as a central element in any offender–victim agreement.

Another feature that distinguishes serious and violent young offenders from other offenders are their rates of mental disorders, specifically conduct disorders (see Table 1.6). While not all serious and violent offenders suffer from a mental disorder, there are several mental disorders

Table 1.5. Substance use variables

	Percentage	Mean
Ever used drugs	92.9%	
Earliest age started using drugs		11.9
Type of Drug		
Marijuana	91.6%	Daily
Crack	44.2%	Few times a week
Heroin	35.1%	Once a week
Cocaine	56.5%	Few times a month
Ever used alcohol	91.2%	
Age started using alcohol		12.0
Frequency of drinking		
Daily	20.1%	
Few times a week	33.4%	
Once a week	17.0%	
Few times a month	11.1%	
Once a month	5.3%	
Rarely	12.3%	

and/or conditions that present unique challenges to the restorative-justice paradigm. For instance, the youth in our sample have a high rate of psychopathy, as measured by the Youth Version of the Psychopathy Checklist (Hart et al. 1995). In fact, 22.3 per cent of our sample scored high enough on this scale to be defined as psychopaths. Due to the fact that youth who score high on psychopathy typically present themselves as superficial, lack empathy, lie compulsively, and tend to deflect responsibility, this population may simply be inappropriate for restorative justice initiatives.

In addition, attention-deficit hyperactivity disorder (ADHD) is also somewhat common in our sample. In our sample, 40.6 per cent of the youth have been told they have ADHD by either a clinician or a non-clinician. Interestingly, only 23.5 per cent of our sample believe that they have ADHD. However, in terms of an official diagnosis of ADHD appearing in their official records, only 11.2 per cent have an official diagnosis of ADHD. Finally, there are also high rates of aggression, anger management problems, and anti-social personality disorder found in our sample. Each of these mental disorders present specific and unique challenges for any restorative justice programme.

Based on this review of the profiles of a sample of serious and violent

Table 1.6. Mental health variables

	Percentage	Mean
PCL – Youth Version score		22.3
ADHD		
Has been told by other people that they have ADHD	40.6%	
Youth thinks that he/she has ADHD	23.5%	
Official diagnosis of ADHD	11.2%	
Previous psychiatric contact	59.8%	
Self-report: Have a bad temper	72.7%	

young offenders, it is clear that this group of offenders requires an integrated model of intervention that can address the myriad of problems facing these youths. Two innovative approaches to addressing the needs of serious and violent offenders are the Victim Offender Mediation Project (VOMP) in British Columbia, Canada, and the Transforming Conflict initiative discussed by Moore and McDonald (2000). While holding certain restorative justice principles in common, these two processes differ in specific ways. For instance, VOMP deals exclusively with violent offences, while conferencing under the Transforming Conflict model is typically used for relatively minor offences or first-time offenders. Moreover, it is important to recognize that neither programme specifically targets young offenders. Still, each approach does provide viable alternatives to existing methods for dealing with serious and violent young offenders.

The primary goal of VOMP is to promote the healing and well-being of all parties affected by an offence. This programme's target is serious and violent offenders either during or following a significant period of incarceration. It must be kept in mind that this programme is not designed exclusively for young offenders, and the sample presented in this programme's evaluation includes only adults. Nonetheless, we believe that the central themes and methodology of this programme are transferable to serious and violent young offenders.

VOMP is unique for a couple of reasons. First, this programme does not require face-to-face meetings, written agreements, or restitution between the offender and the victim as part of the process. This is due to the fact that VOMP focuses on healing and on rebuilding well-being rather than reconciliation as a goal (VOMP 1995: 21). Second, prior to VOMP, there were no systematic attempts to use victim–offender mediation with incarcerated serious and violent offenders.

An evaluation of VOMP included 39 cases of victim–offender mediation. These cases were all violent offences. Specifically, 18 of the cases were of sexual assault, seven were cases of murder, and nine were cases of armed robbery. Of the 39 cases evaluated, 22 of the cases were initiated by the victims, and in 22 cases there was a prior relationship between the victim and the offender. The average time between an offender being sentenced and their participation with VOMP was 3.7 years (VOMP 1995: iv).

Possible inclusion in this programme is assessed in several ways. Without significant modifications, the protocols for acceptance in VOMP could be used with serious and violent young offender's. With respect to determining whether an offender would be a suitable candidate for participation, a review of the offender's file examines whether the offender would be willing and/or able to respond to the types of questions that a victim might ask. Other relevant information gained from a review of the offender's file includes the types of programmes that the offender has been involved in, the degree of responsibility that the offender accepts for their behaviour, and their mental and emotional stability (VOMP 1995: 31). Offenders are interviewed prior to their inclusion in the programme to assess their level of remorse, respect for the victim(s), their willingness to accept responsibility for their offence(s), and their willingness to make 'symbolic and/or practical amends that might be possible under the circumstances' (VOMP 1995: 33).

Victims are also assessed in order to determine their suitability for a victim–offender mediation. Similar procedures to that of the offenders are used to assess victims. An interesting addition to the assessment of victims is an interview with a third party in order to avoid any possible re-victimization of the participant. This contact typically focuses on determining whether it is appropriate for VOMP to contact the victim, and to gauge the victim's willingness to participate in this type of programme.

As mentioned above, face-to-face meetings are only one possible outcome of the VOMP. Other options include written correspondence or videos made by the victim or the offender. Again, these options may achieve the same goals as a face-to-face meeting without some of the possible difficulties associated with direct contact between a violent offender and their victim(s). Regardless of the method selected, there are several common themes that all victim offender mediations have in VOMP. The most frequent issues raised by victims and offenders include (1) the rehabilitation of the offender or changes in the offender; (2) the impact, pain and consequences of the offence for the victim; (3) descriptions and explanations of the circumstances and events related to the offence; and (4) forgiveness and apologies (VOMP 1995: 62-65).

Of the 39 cases examined during the 1995 evaluation of VOMP, there was unanimous support for the programme from both victims and offenders (VOMP 1995: 76). Specifically, support was given to the reality of the experience and the flexibility of the programme in terms of making the participants feel that they were in control of the experience. In terms of the goals of the restorative justice paradigm, victims who participated in VOMP claimed that this programme provided closure for them. For instance, victims stated that the experience was positive because they had finally been heard, the offender no longer exercised control over them, they felt less fear, and they felt that they were no longer preoccupied with the offender (VOMP 1995: 104). Offenders stated that participation in this programme increased their feelings of empathy, increased their awareness of the impact of their behaviour, and helped them achieve peace of mind in knowing that they had might have helped, in a small way, a former victim (1995: 105).

While the statements made by victims, offenders and mediators involved in VOMP all suggest that this programme is not only beneficial to offenders and victims, but can also achieve many of the goals of restorative justice, there are key questions that remain unanswered. Specifically, this evaluation does not provide any information about the impact of participation in this programme on the recidivism of its participants. Furthermore, while all victims stated that participation provided them with a sense of closure, it is impossible to discern the long-term effects of this experience on victims. For instance, many victims stated that they maintained essentially negative views of their offenders, and their views of the criminal justice system were not necessarily made more positive by their VOMP experience (VOMP 1995: 107). As such, it is unclear whether or not victims will maintain a positive view of VOMP in the future.

A final interesting question is whether a programme like VOMP could be used either at the pre-sentence stage or earlier in an offender's sentence. It is important to keep in mind that a common thread through all of the studies reviewed for this chapter which examine restorative justice initiatives with serious and violent offenders is that they use these interventions after a significant period of incarceration or after an offender has completed their incarceration. In addition to needing to provide victims and their families with an opportunity to heal, and needing to provide offenders with time to consider the impact of their actions, there are no guidelines with respect to when victim–offender mediations are most appropriate, other than the common suggestion that enough time must be provided for both offenders and victims to reflect on the offence and to have enough time to prepare for mediation.

Another interesting initiative that might have some potential for addressing serious and violent young offenders is conferencing, according to the transforming conflict perspective. Transforming conflict is a model of conferencing that has been used with minor offences or novice offenders. Its theoretical foundations are very similar to other restorative justice initiatives. For instance, conferencing aims to bring together those directly affected by the offending behaviour, increase participant satisfaction with the process of dealing with an offence, and reduce recidivism rates. Still, conferencing differs in several ways from other victim–offender mediation programmes or alternative dispute resolution programmes. In keeping with the principles of transforming conflict, the process of conferencing allows for participants to freely express their feelings about the event and the people affected by the event. During the process of conferencing, the intention is to transform the negative feelings associated with the conflict into positive feelings focused on reintegration and rehabilitation (Moore and McDonald 2000).

Conferencing under the transforming conflict paradigm, in other words, does not focus on labelling the offender as the root of the problem. In addition, conferencing aims to break down the barriers, and the preconceived notions, that allow the victim and the offender to remain entrenched in their roles of victim and victimizer. Instead, the process of conferencing seeks to determine what, not who, caused the conflict, who has been affected by the conflict, and what can be done to repair the harm caused and reduce the potential for future harm (Moore and McDonald 2000: 111).

Both of the aforementioned approaches, transforming conflict and VOMP, suggest avenues for pursuing restorative justice initiatives with serious and violent young offenders. While neither study specifically discusses serious and violent young offenders, the theories, protocols and methodologies of these programmes could effectively be implemented with this unique population. While there is little evidence to suggest whether or not restorative justice initiatives are fulfilling and/or useful for serious and violent young offenders, there do seem to be several compelling arguments for introducing these programmes as an option in conjunction with a young offender's incarceration.

In considering exclusively the needs of a serious and violent young offender, the range of possible benefits to participating in a restorative justice programme include being made aware of the harm they have caused to another human being, understanding the nature and impact of their offending, providing insight into the basis for their offending behaviour, and assisting in their reintegration into the community. In conjunction with a period of incarceration, restorative justice programmes for serious and violent offenders might also serve to enhance the public's concerns over safety, rehabilitation, deterrence and reintegration. While clearly not a panacea, there seem to be few compelling arguments for excluding serious and violent young offenders from the potential benefits of the restorative-justice paradigm, especially when the programme occurs during or after a period of incarceration.

Notes

1. This research was supported by a grant from the Social Science and Humanities Research Council of Canada (R-410-98-1246) to Raymond Corrado.
2. The term breach refers to section 26 of the Young Offenders Act, offences against the administration of youth justice, where a youth is charged with a new offence for violating probation conditions set by a judge on, or as part of, a previous sentence.
3. The number of prior sentencing dates does not correspond with the number of previous charges. Typically, a youth is sentenced for two or more charges on the same date.
4. In most cases, the places that these youths have lived other than home are in a foster or ministry placement, and to a lesser extent with a relative.
5. The number of times that a youth changed schools refers to changes due to reasons other than normal grade progressions or graduations. In other words, having to change schools because of one's advancement from junior high to high school would not be considered a change in school.

References

Anderson, M. (1994) 'The High Juvenile Crime Rate: A Look at Mentoring as a Preventive Strategy', *Criminal Law Bulletin*, 30(1); 54–75.

Archibald, B. (1999) 'A Comprehensive Canadian Approach to Restorative Justice: The Prospects for Structuring Fair Alternative Measures to Crime' in D. Stuart, R. Delisle, and A. Manson (eds.), *Towards a Clear and Just Criminal Law*. Toronto: Carswell.

Bazemore, G. (1994) 'Developing a Victim Orientation for Community Corrections: A Restorative Justice Paradigm and a Balanced Approach,' *Perspectives*, Special Issue, American Probation and Parole Association.

Bazemore, G. and Umbreit, M. (1995) 'Rethinking the Sanctioning Function in Juvenile Court: Retributive or Restorative Responses to Youth Crime', *Crime and Delinquency*, 41(3); 296–316.

Boe, E. R. (2000) 'Aboriginal Inmates: Demographic Trends and Projections', *Forum on Corrections Research*, 210(1); 7–9.

Braithwaite, J. (1990) *Crime, Shame, and Reintegration*. Cambridge: Cambridge University Press.

Corrado, R., Odgers, C. and Cohen, I. (2000) 'The Incarceration of Female Young Offenders: Protection for Whom?' *Canadian Journal of Criminology*, 42(2); 187–207.

Flaten, C. (1996) 'Victim–Offender Mediation: Application with Serious Offences Committed by Juveniles' in B. Galaway and J. Hudson (eds) *Restorative Justice: International Perspectives*. Monsey, New York: Criminal Justice Press.

Galaway, B. and Hudson, J. (1990) *Criminal Justice, Restitution, and Reconciliation*. Monsey, New York: Criminal Justice Press.

Griffiths, C. and Corrado, R. (1999) 'Implementing Restorative Youth Justice: A Case Study in Community Justice and the Dynamics of Reform' in G. Bazemore and L. Walgrave (eds) *Restorative Juvenile Justice: Repairing the Harm of Youth Crime*. New York: Willow Tree Press, Inc.

Griffiths, C. T. and Verdun-Jones, S. N (1994) *Canadian Criminal Justice*, (2nd edn.). Toronto: Harcourt Brace and Co.

Hart, S. D., Cox, D. N. and Hare, R. D. (1995) *Manual for the Psychopathy Checklist: Screening Version (PCL:SV)*. Toronto: Multi-Health Systems.

Hawkins, J., Herrenkohl, T., Farrington, D., Brewer, D., Catalano, R. and Harachi, T. (1999) 'A Review of Predictors of Youth Violence' in R. Loeber and D. Farrington (eds) *Serious and Violent Juvenile Offenders: Risk Factors and Successful Interventions*. London: Sage.

Huizinga, D. and Jakob-Chien, C. (1999) 'The Contemporaneous Co-Occurrence of Serious and Violent Juvenile Offending and Other Problem Behaviors' in R. Loeber and D. Farrington (eds) *Serious and Violent Juvenile Offenders: Risk Factors and Successful Interventions*. London: Sage.

LeBlanc, M. (1999) 'Screening of Serious and Violent Juvenile Offenders: Identification, Classification, and Prediction' in R. Loeber and D. Farrington (eds) *Serious and Violent Juvenile Offenders: Risk Factors and Successful Interventions*. London: Sage.

Levrant, S., Cullen, F., Fulton, B. and Wozniak, J. (1999) 'Reconsidering Restorative Justice: The Corruption of Benevolence Revisited?' *Crime and Delinquency*, 45(1); 3–27.

Lipsey, M. and Derzon, J. (1999) 'Predictors of Violent or Serious Delinquency in Adolescence and Early Adulthood: A Synthesis of Longitudinal Research' in R. Loeber and D. Farrington (eds) *Serious and Violent Juvenile Offenders: Risk Factors and Successful Interventions*. London: Sage.

Lipsey, M. W. and Wilson, D. B. (1999) 'Effective Intervention for Serious Juvenile Offenders: A Synthesis of Research' in Loeber, R. and Farrington, D. P. (eds) *Serious and Violent Juvenile Offenders: Risk Factors and Successful Interventions*. London: Sage.

Moore, D. and McDonald, J. (2000) *Transforming Conflict*. Maryborough, Australia: Australian Print Company.

Niemeyer, M. and Shichor, D. (1996) 'Preliminary Study of a Large Victim/ Offender Reconciliation Programme', *Federal Probation*, 60(3); 30–4.

Pate, K. (1990) 'Victim–Young Offender Reconciliation as Alternative Measures' in B. Galaway and J. Hudson (eds) *Criminal Justice, Restitution, and Reconciliation*. Monsey, New York: Criminal Justice Press.

Roach, K. (2000) 'Changing Punishment at the Turn of the Century: Restorative Justice on the Rise', *Canadian Journal of Criminology*, 42(3); 249–80.

Roberts, T. (1995) *Evaluation of the Victim Offender Mediation Project*. Prepared for Solicitor General Canada.

Roberts J. V. and Doob, A. N. (1997) 'Race, Ethnicity, and Criminal Justice in Canada' in Tonry, M. (ed.) *Ethnicity, Crime, and Immigration: Comparative and Cross National Perspectives*. Chicago: University of Chicago Press.

Simms, S. (1997) 'Restorative Juvenile Justice' *Corrections Today*, 59(7), 68–114.

Synder, H. N. (1999) 'Appendix: Serious, Violent, and Chronic Juvenile Offenders: An Assessment of the Extent of and Trends in Officially Recognized Serious Criminal Behavior in a Delinquent Population' in Loeber, R. and Farrington, D. P. (eds) *Serious and Violent Juvenile Offenders: Risk Factors and Successful Interventions*. London: Sage.

Tolan, P. and Gorman-Smith, D. (1999) 'Development of Serious and Violent Offending Careers' in R. Loeber and D. Farrington (eds) *Serious and Violent Juvenile Offenders: Risk Factors and Successful Interventions*. London: Sage.

Trimboli, L. (2000) *An Evaluation of the NSW Youth Justice Conferencing Scheme*. Sydney, Australia: New South Wales Bureau of Crime Statistics and Research.

Umbreit, M. (1994) *Victim Meets Offender: The Impact of Restorative Justice and Mediation*. Monsey, New York: Criminal Justice Press.

Umbreit, M. (1995) 'Holding Juvenile Offenders Accountable: A Restorative Justice Perspective', *Juvenile and Family Court Journal*, 46(2); 31–42.

Walgrave, L. (1995) 'Restorative Justice for Juveniles: Just a Technique or a Fully Fledged Alternative?', *The Howard Journal*, 34(3), 228–49.

Chapter 2

Making variation a virtue: evaluating the potential and limits of restorative justice

Kathleen Daly

Introduction[1]

A good measure of the vitality of a new justice idea is the ratio between the claims made by advocates and the evidence to support those claims. The less evidence exists, the greater the excitement and debate about the new idea. When evidence arrives, we may begin to lose interest. The results may be equivocal, or worse, we may despair that the new idea does not 'measure up' in the expected ways. Matthews (1988: 1–2) captured this problem well in 1988, when he reflected on what happened in Britain and the United States in the 1970s and 80s with the introduction of the new idea of informal justice.

> In the beginning there was optimism. The introduction of more informal forms of dispute processing would, it was claimed, provide a greater level of participation and access to justice ... After a period of experimentation, ... the initial enthusiasm subsided and many observers became sceptical about the possibility of informal justice realising its promises. Less than a decade after the emergence of the first wave of optimism, [there was] an equally forceful wave of pessimism ... The verdict was that informalism was a distraction, an error, an experiment which had failed. Despite these critiques, support for informal justice continued, and we are now entering a

new phase, which involves moving beyond the poles of optimism and pessimism, and evaluat[ing] the movement towards informal justice in different theoretical and practical terms. [In doing so] ... We are push[ed] in two ... directions. On one hand, we [must] examine the specific details of informal dispute processing; and on the other hand, we [must consider] the wider political and social frameworks within which they operate. In this way, we might avoid the twin pitfalls of idealism and impossibilism which [have] informed much of the debate so far.

All of us conducting research on restorative justice should heed Matthews' advice. Today, we are in an optimistic phase. There are raised expectations, which will be impossible to meet. Apparent negative or contrary results will produce a mood of impossibilism, and this will set in motion a sterile debate in which advocates and critics argue past each other. A more constructive approach is to analyse how the ideal works in practice, while assuming there are limits on achieving the ideal. Rather than despair that restorative justice practices and outcomes vary, I propose we turn variation into a virtue.

In this paper, I present findings from the South Australia Juvenile Justice (SAJJ) research on conferencing project. From observational measures gathered on 89 youth justice conferences, I constructed a measure that differentiates those conferences that were judged by SAJJ observers to have higher levels of 'restorativeness', procedural justice, and coordinator management skill from other, less ideal conferences. This measure is an explicit recognition that some conferences succeed better than others and have more engaged participants who are prepared to think and act in restorative ways. A key question for research is whether it matters if the ideal is reached. For example, do those conferences classified as 'high' on restorativeness, procedural justice and coordinator skill produce more favourable outcomes for victims and offenders? If we find no association between a measure of conference variability and outcomes for victims and offenders, then the theory of restorative justice is in doubt. However, if we do find that better conferences yield greater positive benefits to victims and offenders, then the theory of restorative justice has merit.

SAJJ methodology

The SAJJ project had two waves of data collection in 1998 and 1999 (see Daly *et al.* 1998; Daly 2001).[2] In 1998, we observed 89 conferences that were held during a 12-week period in the metropolitan Adelaide area and in two country towns. The conferences were selected on the basis of the offence category. SAJJ-eligible offences were personal crimes of violence and property offences that involved personal victims or community victims such as schools, churches and housing trusts. Excluded were shoplifts, drug cases and public order offences. Some features of the conference sample were:

- forty-four per cent of conferences dealt with personal crimes of violence; the rest dealt with property offences (break and enter, illegal use of a motor vehicle, property damage);

- in two-thirds of conferences, the victim was a personal victim of crime; the rest were an organizational or occupational victim;

- in nearly 30 per cent the victim was injured, and in 70 percent the victim sustained economic losses;

- in 74 per cent of conferences, the victim was present at the conference;

- half the conferences involved people who were completely unknown to each other;

- in 15 per cent of conferences, there was more than one offender in the conference.

For each conference, the police officer and coordinator completed a self-administered survey, and a SAJJ researcher completed a detailed observational instrument. SAJJ researchers aimed to interview all the young people/offenders (YPs, $n = 107$) and the primary victim associated with each offence ($n = 89$) in 1998 and a year later, in 1999. Of a total of 196 offenders and victims, we interviewed 88 per cent in year 1; of that group, we interviewed 94 per cent in year 2. Therefore, the overall response rate (that is, completed interviews for victims and offenders in years 1 and 2) is 82 percent.

The interview schedules had open- and close-ended items. All the interviews were conducted face to face, except those with victims who did not attend the conference, which were conducted by phone. For the offenders, the length of the interview was 35 to 40 minutes; for the conference victims, the length was 45 to 60 minutes. The interviews were tape-recorded and the open-ended questions were transcribed.

In year 1 the focus of the interviews was on the offenders' and victims' judgements of whether elements of procedural justice and restorativeness were present in the conference. In year 2, we were interested in how the passage of time affected offenders' and victims' judgements of the process and promises made; their attitudes towards each other; whether the conference had an impact on 'staying out of trouble' (for offenders) or on 'getting the offence behind them' (for victims); and for victims, how their experience in the conference process affected (or not) their views of young people and the politics of crime control. In addition to the observational and interview data, the project analyzed official police data on the offending histories, pre- and post-conference for the 107 YPs. The findings presented here rely on the quantitative items. I see the project's strength, however, in the blend of quantitative and qualitative data on the conference process and its impact on participants.

Procedural justice and restorativeness

Like other studies of conferencing in Australia (e.g., Palk *et al.* 1998; Strang *et al.* 1999), the SAJJ project finds very high levels of procedural justice at conferences. Table 2.1a gives a small sampling of procedural justice variables; these tap the degree to which conference participants were treated with respect, the conference process was fair, the coordinator acted neutrally, and participants had a say in the outcome. SAJJ observers found that procedural justice was evident in 80 to nearly 100 per cent of conferences, depending on the variable. From the interviews with the offenders and victims in 1998 (data not shown here), the SAJJ observations were confirmed: to procedural justice items such as the police treated you fairly, you were treated with respect, you had a say, among others, 80 to 95 per cent of both groups said they were treated fairly and had a say.[3]

Compared to these very high levels of procedural justice, there is relatively less evidence of restorativeness. Table 2.1b lists a variety of restorativeness indicators in the observational protocol. Some items such as 'the YP accepted responsibility for the offence', 'the YP was actively involved in the conference', and 'the victim was effective in describing the offence and its impact' are indicators of potential restorativeness. Others are more direct measures of whether restorative actions or words of some kind occurred. They include the 'degree of positive movement or mutual understanding between the victim and YP', 'degree of positive movement or mutual understanding between the YP's supporter(s) and the victim or the victim's supporters', 'the YP understands the impact of the crime on the victim', and 'the victim understands the YP's situation'. These direct and relational measures tap the degree to which offenders and victims recognized and were affected by each other; they indicate whether there was positive movement between the offender, victim and their supporters during the conference. Whereas procedural justice was present in 80 to 95 per cent of conferences and potential restorativeness was present in 60 to 80 per cent, actual restorative actions or words occurred in about 30 to 50 per cent of conferences, and perhaps most solidly in about one-third. These

Table 2.1. Indicators of procedural justice and restorativeness (SAJJ observers' judgements for n = 89 conferences)

a Indicators of procedural justice, in percentages

Process of deciding the outcome was fair agree/strongly agree	89
Police officer talked to or treated YP in a respectful manner agree/strongly agree	99
Coordinator permitted everyone to have their say agree/strongly agree	97
Coordinator seemed impartial, not aligned with any one person agree/strongly agree	93
YP was respectful to the police officer present agree/strongly agree	94

b Indicators of restorativeness

YP gave a clear story for what happened yes, mostly/fully	71
YP accepted responsibility for the offence yes, mostly/fully	62
YP was actively involved in the conference yes, mostly/fully	78
YP was remorseful for his/her actions yes, mostly/fully	49
YP was defiant (cocky, bold, brashly confident) indicator of non-restorative behaviour) (somewhat, mostly or fully)	30

(for conferences where the victim or rep was present (n = 71))

YP made spontaneous apology to victim or rep yes, mostly/fully	41
Victim was effective in describing the offence and its impact yes, mostly/highly	72
YP assured victim the behaviour wouldn't happen again yes, mostly/highly	58
YP understood the impact of the crime on victim yes, mostly/fully	51
Victim understood YP's situation yes, mostly/fully	34
Positive movement or mutual understanding between the victim and YP, expressed in words yes, mostly/fully	31
Positive movement or mutual understanding between YP supporters and victim (or victim supporters) (yes, mostly/fully)	37

ggest that although it is possible to have a fair process, it can be
for victims and offenders to resolve their conflict completely or to find
ommon ground, at least during the conference itself.

Limits on the restorative ideal

It is essential to explore the finding that restorativeness is more difficult to
accomplish than is procedural justice in the conference process. It is often
remarked that if conferences do not go well (or do not measure up to the
ideal), this may be overcome by better practice and more resources (see
discussion in Maxwell and Morris 1996: 108). I am not so sure. Instead,
from the SAJJ data, there appear to be limits on offenders' interests to
repair harms and on victims' capacities to see offenders in a positive light.
Indicative of these limits is a sampling of responses to interview items by
the YPs and the victims who attended conferences (Table 2.2 a–d).

From the 1998 YP interviews, about 30 per cent said that the conference
was not important to them, half had not thought about what they would
do or say to the victim at the conference, and half said that the victim's (or
victim representative's) story had an effect on them (Table 2.2a). While
very high proportions of the YPs said they had a better understanding of
how their behaviour affected the victim (87 per cent), a slim majority (58
per cent) said they felt sorry for the victim. Some 58 per cent said it was
more important to make the victim feel better than to get what they
wanted, while in another item, about 40 per cent said it was more
important to do something for the victim than to be treated fairly. These
latter items suggest that the YPs are split between those who are other-
regarding (make victim feel better, do something for the victim) and self-
regarding (get what I wanted, be treated fairly). Therefore, while some
offenders are prepared to act in ways that can produce the restorative
ideal, others are less willing.

The 1998 victim interviews also show a mixed bag of restorative
interests and capacities: most victims (over 60 per cent) said that the YP's
account of the offence had little impact on them, and about half said they
have a better understanding of why the YP committed the offence (Table
2.2b). Like the YPs, the victims were split in their other- and self-regarding
interests: a slim majority (56 per cent) said it was more important to
connect at a personal level with the YP than to get what they wanted, and
43 per cent said it was more important to find common ground with the
offender than to be treated fairly. While relatively small percentages of
victims and YPs (15 to 16 per cent) thought the conference was a waste of
time, their restorative and 'other-regarding' orientations were more mixed
and equivocal.

Selected items from the 1999 YP and victim interviews ; constraints on the restorative ideal (Tables 2.2c and d). Many not believe that the YPs were really sorry for what they did per cent of victims thought the YP was really sorry, a substantially ing share of the YPs (68 per cent) said that they were. (In analysing the smaller subset of YP and victim pairs, the percentages are similar.) One feature of a restorative justice process is that 'bad acts' should be distinguished from 'good actors' (Braithwaite 1989). Most victims (68 per cent) saw young people as good actors and most YPs (68 per cent) believed that victims saw them in this positive light. However, about one-third of the victims believed that the YP was a 'bad person' with a similar percentage of YPs believing that victims saw them in this negative light. Conference victims in 1999 were split between those who thought it was more important that the YP make up by paying money or doing work (44 per cent) and those who thought it was more important that the YP make a genuine apology (40 per cent).

How often do conferences succeed in optimal ways?

The foregoing results show that conferences display varying degrees of restorativeness, along with varied interests and capacities of victims and offenders to see each other in positive or other-regarding ways. To capture this variability compactly, I devised a measure that combined the SAJJ observer's judgement of the degree to which a conference 'ended on a high, a positive note of repair and good will' with one that rated the conference on a five-point scale ranging from poor to exceptional. While the first measure taps the degree of movement of victims and offenders (or their supporters) toward each other, the second taps elements of procedural justice and coordinator skill in managing the conference. The conference measure initially had four levels: ended on a high and rated very highly (10 per cent), ended on a high and rated good (40 per cent), did not end on a high and a fair/good rating (20 per cent), and did not end on a high and a fair/poor rating (30 per cent). I collapsed the four levels into two, with a measure that distinguished between 'high/good' and 'low/ mixed' conference classifications. These groups are nearly identical in size (n = 45 for high/good and n = 44 for low/mixed).

I then analysed the relationship of the high/low conference measure to several clusters of variables, including the type of offence, conference attendance and numbers, offender and victim demographics, in addition to measures of procedural justice, restorativeness and coordinator skill. To have construct validity, the high/low measure should be able to distinguish

Table 2.2. Limits on the restorative ideal

a YP interviews in 1998 (n = 93 YPs)

Before the conference, was it important to you?	
no	31
Before the conference, did you think about what you wanted to do or to say to the victim?	
no, not at all	53

After listening to the victim or rep's story, did it have an effect on you?		
no, not at all or not much (n = 73 YPs for whom a victim was present)		49
At the conference, was it more important to you to make the victim feel better or to get what you wanted?		
make victim feel better		58
make sure I got what I wanted		16
both equally		17
neither		9
Looking back at the conference, was it more important that you be treated fairly or that you were able to do something for the victim?		
be treated fairly		40
do something for the victim		39
both equally		20
neither		1
As a result of the conference, you have a better understanding of how your behaviour affected the victim (agree)		87
The conference was largely a waste of time		
agree		15
Before the conference and now: how sorry did/do you feel for the victim		
not at all or less sorry		42
still not sorry at all	19	
feel less sorry for victim after the conference	23	
Before the conference and now: how sorry did/do you feel for the victim		
a bit or more sorry		58
still a bit, somewhat, or very sorry	45	
more sorry for victim after the conference	13	

b Victim interviews in 1998 (n = 61 conference victims)

Before the conference, did you think about what you wanted to say to YP?	
no, not at all	34
In listening to the YP's account of the offence, how much impact did it have on you?	
none or not much	62

At the conference, was it more important to you to connect at a
personal level with YP or to get what you wanted?

connect at personal level	56
get what I wanted	33
both equally	1
neither	10

Looking back at the conference, was it more important that you be treated
fairly or that you find common ground with the offender?

be treated fairly	49
find common ground	43
both equally	5
neither	3

As a result of the conference, you have a better understanding of why YP
committed the offending behaviour

agree	53

The conference was largely a waste of time

agree	16

---

c YP interviews in 1999 (only YPs with conference victims present)

What was the main reason you apologized to the victim at the conference?
(n = 60 YPs with known apologies)

Didn't feel sorry, but thought you'd get off easier	10
Felt pushed into saying sorry	15
Thought it would make your family feel better	7
You wanted the victim to know you really were sorry	68

What do you think the victim would say about you? (n = 62 YPs)

You did a bad thing because of who you are	26
You're not bad, but what you did was bad	68
YP says do not know	6

---

d Victim interviews in 1999 (n = 57 conference victims)

What was the main reason YP apologized at the conference?
(n = 54 conference victims with known apologies)

YP wasn't sorry, but thought s/he would get off easier	31
YP was pushed into saying sorry	26
YP thought it would make family feel better	15
YP was really sorry	28

How would you describe the offender?

YP did a bad thing because of who they are	32
YP is OK, but what s/he did was bad	68

What was more important to you?

YP make genuine apology	40
YP pay money or do work	44
both equally	11
neither	5

---

between conferences that have more and less restorativeness, procedural justice and skilful work by coordinators. In addition, I was interested to determine if other conference elements were associated with the high/low measure. Table 2.3 presents a series of 2 × 2 tables, using the Phi statistic as the measure of association, to determine which variables are associated with the high/low measure. (The table also shows the frequency of each independent variable; for example, in Table 2.3c, 76 per cent of primary offenders are male, 80 per cent are white Australian, and 51 per cent of primary victims are male.)

Table 2.3. Relationship between the conferences of the high-low classification and observed features of the conference process. Frequencies for each variable are given for the level of the independent variable coded '1'.

Of the 89 conferences, $n = 45$ were classified high/good (coded 1), and $n = 44$ were classified low/mixed (coded 0). Row percentages are shown for each level of the independent variable.

a Features of the offence

	Conference classified		Phi and stat. sig.
	High	Low	
Victim–offender relations			
1 = known to each other, including by sight			
(52%)	52	48	.03 (ns)
0 = strangers, had never seen before	49	51	
Type of offence			
1 = violence (assault, sexual assault, robbery)			
(44%)	46	54	−.08 (ns)
0 = rest (break and enter, prop damage, illegal			
use or theft of car, embezzlement)	54	46	
Type of victim			
1 = personal, including personal-organizational			
and personal-occupational (80%)	49	51	−.05 (ns)
0 = organisation only	56	44	
Number of offenders in the whole offence			
1 = two or more (55%)	53	47	.05 (ns)
0 = one	48	52	

b Conference attendance, numbers and indicator of emotion

	Conference classified		Phi and stat. sig.
	High	Low	
Number of YPs at the conference			
1 = two or more (15%)	64	36	.10 (ns)
0 = one	49	51	
Victim was present at conference			
1 = yes (74%)	50	50	−.02 (ns)
0 = no	52	48	
Victim or victim rep was present at conference			
1 = yes (80%)	49	51	−.05 (ns)
0 = no	56	44	
Number of conference participants(excluding police officer and coordinator)			
1 = 6 or more (Higher than average) (30%)	58	42	.09 (ns)
0 = 5 or less	48	52	
Participants were crying during the conference			
1 = yes (25%)	50	50	−.01 (ns)
0 = no	51	49	

c YP and offence victim[1] demographics

	Conference classified		Phi and stat. sig.
	High	Low	
Sex of primary YP			
1 = male (76%)	52	48	.03 (ns)
0 = female	48	52	
Race–ethnicity of primary YP			
1 = white Australian (80%)	55	45	−.17[b]
0 = Aboriginal or other ethnic group	33	67	
Sex of primary offence victim			
1 = male (51%)	62	38	−.24[c]
0 = female	39	61	
Race–ethnicity of offence victim			
1 = white Australian (84%)	53	47	−.13 (ns)
0 = Aboriginal or other ethnic group	36	64	
Age of offence victim			
1 = adult, 18 years or older (72%)	42	58	−.27[d]
0 = child or adolescent	72	28	

d Indicators of procedural justice and conference outcome

	Conference classified		Phi and stat. sig.
	High	Low	
Process of deciding the outcome was fair			
1 = agree (89%)	56	44	.29[d]
0 = disagree	10	90	
Police officer talked to or treated YP in a respectful manner			
1 = agree (99%)		see note	
Coordinator permitted everyone to have their say			
1 = agree (98%)		see note	
Coordinator seemed impartial, not aligned with any one person			
1 = agree (93%)	53	47	.18[b]
0 = disagree	17	83	
YP understands relationship between the offence and outcome			
1 = agree (80%)	62	38	.45[d]
0 = disagree	6	94	
Outcome was decided by genuine consensus			
1 = yes (65%)	69	31	.50[d]
0 = YP accepted w/modification by police officer or w/reluctance	16	84	

e Indicators of restorativeness

	Conference classified		Phi and stat. sig.
	High	Low	
YP gave a clear story of what happened			
1 = mostly or fully (71%)	56	44	.16[a]
0 = somewhat or not at all	39	61	
YP accepted responsibility for the offence			
1 = mostly or fully (62%)	53	47	.06 (ns)
0 = somewhat or not at all	47	53	
YP was actively involved in the conference			
1 = mostly or fully (78%)	59	41	.33[d]
0 = somewhat or not at all	20	80	

YP was remorseful for his/her actions			
1 = mostly or fully (49%)	66	34	.30[d]
0 = somewhat or not at all	36	64	
YP was defiant (indicator of non-restorative behaviour)			
1 = somewhat, mostly, or fully (30%)	44	56	−.08 (ns)
0 = not at all	53	47	
YP made a spontaneous apology to victim or rep[2]			
1 = mostly or fully (41%)	66	34	.25[b]
0 = had to be drawn out or not at all	38	62	
YP made any apology to victim or rep[2]			
1 = yes, including had to be drawn out (73%)	56	44	.21[b]
0 = not at all	32	68	
Victim was effective in describing the offence and its impact[2]			
1 = mostly or fully (72%)	59	41	.30[d]
0 = somewhat or not at all	25	75	
YP assured victim the behaviour wouldn't happen again[2]			
1 = mostly or fully (58%)	59	41	.22[b]
0 = somewhat or not at all	37	63	
YP understands the impact of the crime on the victim[2]			
1 = mostly or fully (52%)	62	38	.27[c]
0 = somewhat or not at all	35	65	
Victim understands the YP's situation[2]			
1 = mostly or fully (34%)	79	21	.43[d]
0 = somewhat or not at all	34	66	
Positive movement or mutual understanding between the victim and YP, expressed in words[2]			
1 = mostly or fully (31%)	82	18	.44[d]
0 = somewhat or not at all	35	65	
Positive movement or mutual understanding between YP supporters and victim (or victim supporters), expressed in words[2]			
1 = mostly or fully (37%)	73	27	.36[d]
0 = somewhat or not at all	36	64	

f Coordinator skill

	Conference classified		Phi and stat. sig.
	High	Low	
Coordinator managed movement through conference stages well			
1 = agree (91%)	56	44	.32[d]
0 = disagree	0	100	
Coordinator negotiated the outcome well			
1 = agree (89%)	56	44	.29[d]
0 = disagree	10	90	

[1]Characteristics of *offence* victims can differ from those for *conference* victims in that the latter group may be speaking on behalf of a direct victim at the conference. Of the 89 conferences, 71 were attended by victims or victim representatives, of whom 5 were from the Victim Support Services and 2 were parents speaking on behalf of their children.
[2]Per cents shown are of $n = 71$ conferences for which victims or victim reps were present. Of these, 35 were classified high/good and 36, low/mixed.
(ns) not significant
[a]significant at .15 level
[b]significant at .10 level
[c]significant at .05 level
[d]significant at .01 level

Note:
Observed levels of procedural justice are so high for some variables (e.g., greater than 95 per cent) that it is inappropriate to test for differences between the high/low groups.

Table 2.3 reveals some fascinating patterns. First, there is no association between high/low conferences and characteristics of the offence, including victim–offender relationship, type of offence, type of victim, and number of offenders in the whole offence (Table 2.3a). Second, there is no association between high/low conferences and the number of people at the conference, whether the victim was present at the conference, the number of YPs at the conference, or the degree of emotionality present (such as participants crying) (Table 2.3b). These results challenge the conventional wisdom that conferences are more likely to be successful when victims are present and the number of participants is higher than average. Third, some demographic features of victims and offenders are related to the conference measure. Of the conferences with white Australian offenders, 55 per cent are classified high, whereas of those with Aboriginal or other ethnic group offenders, 33 per cent are so classified. In addition to the race–ethnicity of the offender, conferences with male victims or with child/adolescent victims are more likely classified high (Table 2.3c). I did not expect these findings and do not yet have a satisfying explanation for them.

Almost all of the measures of procedural justice, restorativeness and coordinator skill are associated with the high/low classification in the expected direction (Tables 2.3d–f). High conferences are associated with the SAJJ observer's judgement that the process of deciding the outcome was fair, the coordinator seemed impartial, the young person understood the relationship between the offence and the outcome, and the outcome was decided by genuine consensus (Table 2.3d). With very high observed levels of procedural justice (95 per cent or higher), some procedural justice variables cannot be used to distinguish high/low conferences. For the restorativeness indicators, high conferences are associated with offenders giving a clear story of what happened, being actively involved in the conference, being remorseful, apologizing to the victim or victim representative (both spontaneously or having to be drawn out), assuring the victim the behaviour wouldn't happen again, and understanding the impact of the crime on the victim. High conferences are associated with victims' effectiveness in describing the offence and its impact, victims' understanding of the YP's situation, positive movement or mutual understanding between the victim and YP or between the victim (or victim supporters) and the YP or YP's supporters, and coordinator skill in managing movement through the conference stages and negotiating the outcome well. There are only two variables that show no association with the high/low measure: whether the YP accepted responsibility for the offence or was defiant.

These results tell us three things. First, each of the five SAJJ observers was consistent in their global conference ratings (measures of 'ended on high' and 'overall conference rating') and the many items tapping procedural justice, restorativeness and coordinator skill. Second, and of significant theoretical interest, it is possible to identify a set of activities and behaviours that are related to better conferences, or to enhanced levels of actions and behaviours anticipated by restorative justice theory. Finally, the high/low measure has construct validity as a compact measure of procedural justice, restorativeness and coordinator skill. It should be emphasized that because procedural justice and coordinator skill are evident in a high share of conferences (80 to 95 per cent), whereas restorativeness is more varied and relatively less evident (30 to 80 per cent), 'high' conferences are those that have a greater degree of restorativeness, along with very high levels of procedural justice and coordinator skill.

High or low conference: does it matter?

A major untested assumption in the literature is that when conferences succeed in optimal ways, there are positive effects for participants. For example, it is thought that if offenders learn from a restorative justice encounter to develop more empathetic feelings about the impact of crime on victims, they may be deterred from future offending. It is also believed that the conference process may assist in victims' recovery from crime. One way to test the theory of restorative justice is to determine whether conference variation, as measured by the high/low variable, is associated with variation in victims' and offenders' post-conference behaviour and attitudes.

I carried out analyses of the high/low measure with items from the offender and victim interviews and with measures of the YP's post conference re-offending. Tables 2.4 and 2.5 present a series of 2 × 2 and 2 × 3 tables, with the appropriate Phi and Chi-square statistical tests of association. In general, the results show that the high/low measure is predictive of offender attitudes toward the victim and toward the law, of victim attitudes toward offenders, and of both victims' and offenders' global judgements of the conference experience – all in the expected direction. The 1998 interviews were conducted one week to two months after the conference (the median time was 25 to 33 days for the YPs and victims, respectively). Therefore, the temporal ordering of the conference followed by participants' reflections on their experience (or official data on re-offending 8 to 12 months post conference) could invite a claim of causal effects of the conference. However, as we will see for some variables, the high/low measure resulted, in part, from orientations and capacities that offenders and victims brought with them to the conference.

Before turning to a discussion of the results, a word on statistical significance is in order. When the Phi coefficient is .12 to .14 in magnitude, it nears statistical significance for the YP analyses, but is just above the .15 error level. Because statistical significance is based partly on sample size (that is, there needs to be an even greater percentage point difference as the sample size grows smaller because of sampling error), we need to be mindful that some variables, while not statistically significant, are of substantial magnitude and related in the predicted direction. This is particularly important in characterizing the results for the victims, for whom the Phi coefficient needs to be even larger to reach statistical significance compared to the YPs. This is because the number of YPs in the analysis (about 90) is larger than the number of victims (about 60).

From the YP interview results (Table 2.4), we can see the difficulty of making causal claims about conference effects. While high conferences

Table 2.4. High/low conference: Does it matter to offenders?
Of the $n = 93$ YPs interviewed in 1998,
$n = 47$ were in conferences classified high/good (coded 1) and
$n = 46$ were in conferences classified low/mixed (coded 0)

For re-offending using police data, three n-sized groups are shown ($n = 107$ all
YPs, $n = 89$ primary YPs, and $n = 93$ YPs interviewed in 1998)

a Indicators of attitudes toward the victim

	Conference classified		Phi and stat. sig.
	High	Low	
From the conference, you have a better understanding of how your behaviour affected the victim			
1 = agree (87%)	52	48	.07 (ns)
0 = disagree	42	58	
Feel angry about the victim before the conference			
1 = not at all (75%)	54	46	.13 (ns)
0 = yes, a little, somewhat, or a lot	39	61	
Feel angry about the victim now, after the conference			
1 = not at all (83%)	56	44	.23[c]
0 = yes, a little, somewhat, or a lot	25	75	
Feel sorry for the victim before the conference			
1 = yes, a little, somewhat, or a lot (74%)	55	45	.15[a]
0 = not at all	38	62	
Feel sorry for the victim now, after the conference			
1 = yes, a little, some or a lot (75%)	59	41	.28[d]
0 = not at all	26	74	
At conference, what was more important, 1 = make victim feel better and mixed response (75%)	56	44	.18[b]
0 = get what you wanted and neither	35	65	
Looking back, what was more important 1 = do something for the victim and mixed response (59%)	56	44	.14 (ns)
0 = be treated fairly and neither	42	58	

b Participation in agreement discussion

	Conference classified		Phi and stat. sig.
	High	Low	
YP said that s/he was involved in the agreement discussion			
1 = yes (76%)	54	46	.11 (ns)
0 = no	41	59	

c Global judgements of conference experience

	Conference classified		Phi and stat. sig.
	High	Low	
Conference was largely a waste of time			
1 = agree (15%)	29	71	−.19[c]
0 = disagree	54	46	
Would you go to a conference again?			
1 = yes (86%)	55	45	.22[c]
0 = no or not sure	23	77	
Would you recommend conferencing to friends who get into trouble?			
1 = yes (90%)	54	46	.19[b]
0 = no or not sure	22	78	
Would you recommend the government keep conferencing?			
1 = yes (93%)	52	48	.13 (ns)
0 = no	29	71	
Were you satisfied with how your case was handled?			
1 = yes (90%)	52	48	.11 (ns)
0 = no	33	67	

d Indicators of attitudes toward law and staying out of trouble

	Conference classified		Phi and stat. sig.
	High	Low	
As a result of the conference, respect for legal system			
has gone down (12%)	27	73	Chi sq.
has stayed the same (49%)	59	41	3.8[a]
has gone up (39%)	47	53	

As a result of the conference, respect for the police

has gone down (13%)	25	75	Chi sq.
has stayed the same (58%)	54	46	3.7 (ns)
has gone up (29%)	56	44	

As a result of conference, respect for the law

has gone down (4%)	50	50	Chi sq.
has stayed the same (46%)	58	42	1.9 (ns)
has gone up (50%)	50	50	

What happened in the conference will encourage
you to obey the law

1 = agree (75%)	56	44	.18[b]
0 = disagree	35	65	

e Indicators of re–offending (official police data)

	Conference classified		Phi and
	High	Low	stat. sig.
Offended one or more times 8 to 12 months after the conference (measure of prevalence) All $n = 107$ YPs			
1 = yes (38%)	42	58	−.14[a]
0 = no	56	44	
$n = 93$ YPs interviewed in 1998			
1 = yes (37%)	38	62	−.19[b]
0 = no	58	42	
$n = 89$ primary YPs			
1 = yes (40%)	42	58	.15 (ns)
0 = no	57	43	

f Relationship between officially detected re-offending and conference impact on changing attitudes toward law and re-offending

Of the $n = 93$ YPs interviewed in 1998,
$n = 34$ re-offended 8 to 12 months after the conference (coded 1) and
$n = 59$ did not re-offend (coded 0)

	re–offended 8–12 mos after conference		
	no	yes	
As a result of the conference, respect for legal system			
has gone down (12%)	36	64	Chi sq.
has stayed the same (49%)	61	39	5.7[b]
has gone up (39%)	75	25	

As a result of the conference, respect for the police

has gone down (13%)	50	50	Chi sq.
has stayed the same (58%)	57	43	5.6[b]
has gone up (29%)	82	18	

As a result of conference, respect for the law

has gone down (4%)	25	75	Chi sq.
has stayed the same (46%)	56	44	5.8[b]
has gone up (50%)	74	26	

What happened in the conference will encourage
you to obey the law

1 = agree (75%)	69	31	–.19[b]
0 = disagree	48	52	

YP said that they were involved in the agreement discussion

1 = yes (76%)	65	35	–.05 (ns)
0 = no	59	41	

(ns) not significant
[a]   significant at .15 level
[b]   significant at .10 level
[c]   significant at .05 level
[d]   significant at .01 level

may have enhanced positive effects on offenders compared to low conferences, what young people bring to a conference can also matter. The items asking the YPs about the degree of anger they felt toward the victim before and after the conference suggest there was a conference effect of reducing YP anger: while there is no statistically significant association between pre-conference anger and high/low conferences, there is a definite post-conference difference. A different pattern is evident for the items asking if the YP felt sorry for the victim before and after the conference. High conferences are associated with YPs who said they felt sorry for the victim both before and after the conference. High conferences are also related to YPs who are 'other-regarding',[4] although this measure (like the 'sorry' items) may be tapping what the YPs bring to the conference as well as what they take from it.

For the YP's global judgement of the conference experience, high conferences are inversely related to those who said the conference was a waste of time, and positively related to those who said that they would go to a conference again and would recommend conferencing to friends who get into trouble. Three other measures, the YP's recommendation that the government keep conferencing, satisfaction with how his/her case was handled, and being involved in the agreement discussion, are in the predicted direction, but not statistically significant.

For the impact of the conference on changing the YP's attitude toward the legal system and the police, and toward more law-abiding behaviour, the results suggest that better conferences achieve these results (Table 2.4d). For items asking whether their respect for the legal system and police went up, down or remained the same, for those YPs who said their respect went down (about 12 per cent), few were in high conferences. The Chi-square statistic was significant for 'respect for legal system' and just neared significance for 'respect for police'. High conferences are also linked with those who said that what happened in the conference would encourage them to obey the law.

For re-offending, 38 to 40 per cent of the YPs (depending on which group is analysed) re-offended one or more times 8 to 12 months after the conference. Details on the data and methods for this analysis are available in Hayes and Daly (2001); re-offending was defined as officially detected illegalities, which were dealt with by formal caution, conference or court.

For all the YPs ($n = 107$) and those interviewed in 1998 ($n = 93$), there is a statistically significant inverse relationship between the YP participating in a high conferences and re-offending. (For the $n = 89$ primary offenders, the Phi coefficient neared statistical significance.) These are important and striking results. They show that when conferences have higher levels of restorativeness and very high levels of procedural justice and coordinator skill, young people are less likely to re-offend.

Table 2.4f explores the relationship between the YP's re-offending and items in the 1998 YP interview. Re-offending is more likely when the YPs say that as a result of the conference, their respect for the legal system and for the law went down. Re-offending is less likely when the YPs say that as a result of the conference, their respect for the police went up, and that what happened at the conference would encourage them to obey the law. There is no relationship between the YP's participation in the agreement discussion and re-offending.

From the 1998 conference victim interviews, we see that like the YPs, the attitudes that victims bring to a conference contribute to the high/low classification; at the same time, high conferences can be said to produce positive outcomes (Table 2.5a). Victims in high conferences are significantly less likely to say they felt frightened of the offender after the conference, and less likely to say they felt angry toward the offender after the conference (neared statistical significance); both results suggest an enhanced effect of reductions in victim's fear and anger in high conferences. However, high conferences are associated with victims who felt positive or neutral toward the YP both before and after the conference. This means that the victims' attitudes toward the YP before the conference likely affected how the conference went.

Like the YPs, there is no relationship between a victim's own sense of being involved in the agreement discussion and a high/low conference (Table 2.5b). Also in line with the YPs, there is an association between global judgements of the conference experience and high/low conferences. In 1998, low conferences are related to victims' judgements of the conference being a waste of time, and high conferences, with being satisfied by how their case was handled (Table 2.5c).

A puzzling set of findings emerges for victim recovery (Table 2.5d). In 1998, high conferences are related to victims saying that the conference was helpful in overcoming emotional or psychological effects of crime. However, when asked in 1999 whether they had fully recovered from the incident or only partly recovered from it, high conferences are not related to victim recovery. In fact, the sign of the coefficient shows that high conferences are associated with partial recovery (although not statistically significant). A third variable, which asked if the conference process aided the victim in recovering from the offence, shows no relationship to the high/low measure. These results suggest that while the conference process may have an immediate positive effect on victims, over time other things may make more of a difference.

Victims' attitudes toward offenders in 1999 suggest that high conferences continue to be associated with reductions in victims' fear toward offenders (Table 2.5e). A new attitude measure in the 1999 interview – the victim's judgement of the YP as a 'good' or 'bad' person – shows that high conferences are associated with victims who see the YP as a good person. In other analyses not shown here, this measure also proves to be strongly related to victims' recovery: of those victims who said they had fully recovered from the offence, 81 per cent said the YP was a good person; whereas of those who had partly recovered from the offence, 48 per cent saw the YP as a good person. The good/bad person measure is also strongly related to victims' attitudes toward the offender before and after the conference (from the 1998 interview) and with the victims' attitudes toward the offender in the 1999 interviews. Thus, while high conferences are associated with changes in victim attitudes toward offenders, for one-third of victims their attitudes toward YPs are fixed and generally unmoved by the conference experience.

Global judgements of the conference by victims in 1999 show that high conferences are related to victims saying that the conference was worthwhile and being satisfied with how their case was handled. While high conferences are related to victims who were pleased their case went to conference rather than court, the result was not statistically significant.

Table 2.5. High/low conference: does it matter to conference victims? 1998,
Of the $n = 61$ victims who attended the conference
$n = 32$ conferences were classified high/good (coded 1) and
$n = 29$ were classified low/mixed (coded 0). 1999,
Of the $n = 57$ victims who attended the conference
$n = 31$ conferences were classified high/good (coded 1) and
$n = 26$ were classified low/mixed (coded 0)

a Indicators of attitudes toward the YP in 1998

	Conference classified		Phi and stat. sig.
	High	Low	
As a result of the conference, you have a better understanding of why YP committed the offending behaviour			
1 = agree (53%)	56	44	.08 (ns)
0 = disagree	48	52	
Feel angry toward YP before conference			
1 = no, not at all (23%)	50	50	.03 (ns)
0 = a little, somewhat, or a lot	53	47	
Feel angry toward YP now, after the conference			
1 = no, not at all (56%)	59	41	.14 (ns)
0 = a little, somewhat, or a lot	44	56	
Feel frightened of YP before conference			
1 = no, not at all (62%)	55	45	.07 (ns)
0 = a little, somewhat, or a lot	48	52	
Feel frightened of YP now, after the conference			
1 = no, not at all (75%)	59	41	.22[b]
0 = a little, somewhat, or a lot	33	67	
At conference, what was more important,			
1 = connect with YP and mixed response (57%)	57	43	.11 (ns)
0 = get what you wanted and neither	46	54	
Looking back, what was more important,			
1 = find common ground and mixed response (48%)	59	41	.12 (ns)
0 = be treated fairly and neither	47	53	
Before conference, feelings toward the YP			
positive and neutral (39%)	67	33	.23[b]
negative	43	57	
After conference, feelings toward the YP			
positive and neutral (67%)	59	41	.17 (ns)
negative	40	60	

b Participation in agreement discussion in 1998

	Conference classified		Phi and
	High	Low	stat. sig.
Vic said that s/he was involved in the agreement discussion			
1 = yes (79%)	54	46	.07 (ns)
0 = no	46	54	

c Global judgements of conference experience in 1998

	Conference classified		Phi and
	High	Low	stat. sig.
Conference was largely a waste of time			
1 = agree (16%)	30	70	−.20[b]
0 = disagree	57	43	
Would you go to a conference again			
1 = yes (84%)	55	45	.11 (ns)
0 = no or unsure	40	60	
Recommend conferencing to other victims of crime			
1 = yes (87%)	55	45	.12 (ns)
0 = no or unsure	38	62	
Satisfied with how your case was handled?			
1 = yes (82%)	58	42	.24[b]
0 = no	27	73	

d Indicators of conference impact on victim recovery in 1998 and 1999

	Conference classified		Phi and
	High	Low	stat. sig.
Conference was helpful in overcoming emotional or psychological effects of crime (1998)			
1 = yes, helpful (20%)	78	22	.25[b]
0 = no	46	54	
How victim feels about the incident in 1999			
1 = all behind me, have fully recovered (63%)	50	50	.12 (ns)
0 = partly behind me, not recovered	62	38	

What was more important to get offence behind you, participation in justice process or only things you could do for yourself?

1 = participation in the justice process and both (60%)	59	41	.11 (ns)
0 = only things I could do for myself or neither	48	52	

e Indicators of attitudes toward the YP in 1999

	Conference classified		Phi and stat. sig.
	High	Low	
Feel angry toward YP in 99			
1 = not at all (61 %)	57	43	.07 (ns)
0 = a little, somewhat, or a lot	50	50	
Feel frightened of YP in 99			
1 = not at all (83%)	60	40	−.23[b]
0 = a little, somewhat, or a lot	30	70	
Attitude toward YP in 99			
positive and neutral (60%)	62	38	.18 (ns)
negative	44	56	
Thinks that the YP is OK, but what s/he did was bad			
1 = yes (68%)	62	38	.21[a]
0 = no (YP seen as bad person)	39	61	

f Global judgements of conference experience and conferencing as a response to crime in 1999

	Conference classified		Phi and stat. sig.
	High	Low	
Was the conference worthwhile?			
1 = yes (79%)	62	38	.31[c]
0 = no or unsure	25	75	
Were you satisfied with how your case handled?			
1 = yes (75%)	61	39	.21[b]
0 = no	36	64	
Pleased your case went to conference or wish it had been dealt with in court?			
1 = conference ok (83%)	57	43	.13 (ns)
0 = wish it had gone to court	40	60	

[1]In the 1998 victim interview, for the item asking if the conference was helpful in overcoming non-material harms, this was asked only of the 46 victims who said they had these problems (22 were in the low/mixed, and 24 were in the high/good categories).
[a]sig at .15 level [b]sig at .10 level [c]sig at .05 level [d]sig at .10 level

Making variation a virtue

From the SAJJ project, we see high levels of procedural justice: observational and interview data show that the conference process is viewed as fair and conference participants are treated fairly, with respect, and have a say. At the same time, it is relatively harder for victims and offenders to find common ground with each other and to recognize 'the other'. For these and other measures of restorativeness, there appear to be limits on victims' capacities to see offenders in a positive light and on offenders' capacities to feel sorry for what they did and to be affected by victims' accounts of the incident.

Contrary to the moving stories of repair and goodwill between victims, offenders, and their supporters that populate the literature (e.g., Braithwaite 1996: 9; Umbreit 1994: 1, 197–202), the high/low measure devised from the SAJJ conferences suggests that half can be characterized as high/good with a smaller share (10 per cent) as especially high. It is important to keep in mind that South Australia is a high-volume conference jurisdiction, where conferences are used routinely, not selectively, and for more serious kinds of offences (see Daly and Hayes 2001 for a review of jurisdictional variation). Thus, when conferences are applied to large and diverse populations, we should expect to see a good deal of variation in the degree to which they succeed, especially on indicators of restorativeness. Rather than seeing failure in conferences that do not 'measure up', I have proposed that we turn variation into a virtue. By making variation explicit and expectable, we are able to test the theory of restorative justice and its limits.

The high/low conference measure has high construct validity: all of the behaviours and movements one ideally hopes to see in conferences occurred to a significantly greater degree in the high conferences than in the low conferences. One way to test the theory of restorative justice is to determine whether it matters to victims and offenders if a conference succeeds in optimal ways. The results suggest that generally it can and does matter: high conferences are associated with a range of positive benefits. For offenders, high conferences are associated with some improvement in their attitudes toward the victim, with even stronger positive evaluations of their conference experiences, with increased respect for the legal system and the police, and with reduced levels of re-offending. For victims, high conferences are associated with reduced anger toward and fear of the offender, with even stronger positive evaluations of their conference experience, but with mixed results for victim recovery.

While high conferences are associated with increased levels of positive 'effects' for victims and offenders, in comparison to low conferences, I have cautioned against making strong causal claims about conference effects. One reason that conferences succeed or fail is that offenders and victims come to conferences with varied degrees of readiness to make the process work. Here is where we see the limits of restorative justice theory. Offenders and victims are not equally disposed to be restorative toward each other, to listen to each other, or to be willing to repair harms. Some come to conferences with negative orientations and closed minds that cannot be changed, and others come with positive orientations and open minds. The conference process may engage restorative orientations already present in offenders and victims, or it may create openings for those orientations to emerge. However, for those victims with fixed negative attitudes (e.g., those who think the offender is a 'bad person'), the conference process is unlikely to move them in a more positive or restorative direction.

Research and policy in criminal justice are not well served by the poles of idealism and impossibilism in evaluating new justice ideas. For youth justice conferences, we need to analyse the degree to which the process succeeds, assuming all the while that there are limits on individuals' capacities and interests to think and act restoratively. We should expect variation in restorative processes and outcomes; without it, we would be unable to test the theory of restorative justice. Variation occurs because there is both potential for and limits on transforming relations between victims and offenders in the aftermath of crime.

Notes

1. Acknowledgments: My thanks and appreciation to the members of the South Australian Family Conference Team, the SAJJ research group, and Michele Venables, Brigitte Bouhours and Sarah Curtis-Fawley, who assisted in preparing the data and reviewing the manuscript.
2. Conferencing practices in Australia and New Zealand are varied (see Daly and Hayes 2001). Conferencing in South Australia (as in most other jurisdictions in the region) is 'New Zealand' style, having both a police officer and co-ordinator present. The Re-Integrative Shaming Experiments (RISE) in Canberra are of 'Wagga' style conferencing, where a police officer runs the conference.
3. Space limitations preclude giving more detailed results for these items from the interviews.
4. In coding this other-regarding variable, I found that when YPs said 'both equally' (both making the victim feel better and get what you wanted), they were more likely to have been in high conferences. Thus, I constructed the variable with code 1 including this 'mixed response'.

References

Braithwaite, J. (1989) *Crime, Shame and Reintegration*. Cambridge: Cambridge University Press.

Daly, K. (2001) *South Australia Juvenile Justice (SAJJ) Research on Conferencing, Technical Report No. 2: Research Instruments in Year 2 (1999) and Background Notes*. School of Criminology and Criminal Justice, Griffith University, Brisbane, Queensland, available at www.aic.gov.au/rjustice/sajj/index.html

Daly, K. and Hayes, H. (2001) 'Restorative Justice and Conferencing in Australia', *Trends and Issues in Crime and Criminal Justice No. 186*. Canberra: Australian Institute of Criminology, available at www.aic.gov.au/publications/tandi/tandi186.html

Daly, K., Venables, M., McKenna, M, Mumford, L. and Christie-Johnston, J. (1998) *South Australia Juvenile Justice (SAJJ) Research on Conferencing, Technical Report No. 1: Project Overview and Research Instruments*, School of Criminology and Criminal Justice, Griffith University, Brisbane, Queensland, available at www.aic.gov.au/rjustice/sajj/index.html

Hayes, H. and Daly, K. (2001) 'Family Conferencing in South Australia and Re-offending: Preliminary Results from the SAJJ Project', paper presented to Australian and New Zealand Society of Criminology Conference, Melbourne, February, available at www.gu.edu.au/school/ccj/kdaly.html

Maxwell, G. and Morris, A. (1996) 'Research on Family Group Conferences with Young Offenders in New Zealand' in J. Hudson *et al.* (eds) *Family Group Conferences*. New York: Willow Trees Press, Inc.

Matthews, R. (1988) 'Reassessing Informal Justice' in R. Matthews (ed.) *Informal Justice?* Newbury Park, CA: Sage.

Palk, G., Hayes, H. and Prenzler, T. (1998) 'Restorative Justice and Community Conferencing: Summary of Findings from a Pilot Study', *Current Issues in Criminal Justice*, 10: 138–55.

Strang, H., Sherman, L. W., Barnes, G. C. and Braithwaite, J. (1999) *Experiments in Restorative Policing: A Progress Report to the National Police Research Unit on the Canberra Reintegrative Shaming Experiments (RISE)*. Canberra: Centre for Restorative Justice, Australian National University, available at www.aic.gov.au/rjustice/rise/index.html

Umbreit, M. S. (1994) *Victim Meets Offender: The Impact of Restorative Justice and Mediation*. New York: Criminal Justice Press.

Chapter 3

New developments in restorative justice to handle family violence

Britta Bannenberg and Dieter Rössner

Introduction and the nature of the problem

This chapter aims to describe and analyse empirically the situation of violence in partnerships. Based on this analysis, the authors hope to answer the politico-criminal question of the extent to which criminal law and mediation can be necessary and helpful, especially for women, the usual victims of violence in relationships.

The way in which the public and the legal authorities generally deal with violence in families and relationships still differs from the way they handle violence between strangers. The number of unrecorded cases is enormously high, and reports to the police, both by private individuals and by victims, are rare. Police and prosecution take a passive stance and often react by diverting the criminal proceedings without consequences. But over the course of time, people have become more aware of the problem of domestic violence. International studies have examined the 'hidden' violence and the victims' needs for mediation, i.e. for a settlement of the conflict, and their wish to bring the cycle of violence to an end. The latest studies show the disastrous effects which a violent atmosphere at home has on children, carrying the risk of future delinquent behaviour, inadequate resolution of conflicts and repeated victimization. Neither criminal law nor informal strategies of control have yet been able to bring the situation under control. The idea of mediation is an innovative one which might possibly contain ways of responding to violence against partners as well as against strangers. New approaches have to be tried out, such as regulating conflicts by victim–offender mediation, aiming to strengthen the weaker party in violent partnerships which, as a rule, is the woman – or confronting the offender with the offence and the victim's viewpoint without the victim necessarily having to attend the meetings. Elements of current theories such as 're-integrative shaming', which test community group conferences as well as the popularity of mediation in the present politico-criminal debate, show the way. In future responses to violence in partnerships these new ideas ought to be pursued with the objective of improving the protection of the victim and preventing the conflict from escalating, as well as preventing future violence.

The function of restorative justice in crime control

We recognize crime control as one part of the general system of social control. This recognition raises questions about the function of criminal law. We need to identify what the specific tasks of criminal law are in relation to the system of social control as a whole. We must realize that the two methods of control depend on each other. Traditional criminal theory does not take this mutual dependence into account and therefore determines the function of criminal law without respect to the reality of social control.

The specific functions of criminal law can only become clear in relation to the general system of social control. They contain the following elements, which are necessary in a modern system of crime control and have no other place in social control:

(1) isolation of the wrongful act by a reaction of a powerful criminal-justice system;

(2) assessment of responsibility for an offence;

(3) justice and protection for the victim;

(4) reinforcement of the broken law and the lost trust;

(5) reasonable, balanced and formalized procedure;

(6) constructive conflict resolution through integrative sanctions such as victim–offender reconciliation.

This is not the place to explain thoroughly these elemental principles of a new criminal law. We will limit ourselves to demonstrating how, logically, peacemaking by mediation can be incorporated into the state system of crime control.

The starting point and main focus of crime control are the offence and its treatment. This offence-oriented perspective is evidently found in the criminal sentence: it convicts the defendant of a physical injury rather than as a thug. The verdict respects the defendant and their dignity: it does not stigmatize the offender but only contradicts, marks and isolates the offence. There is an important difference between the person and their act. This subtle dogmatic distinction in criminal law opens the way for a self-responsible peacemaking on the part of the offender: by compensation, when the offender accepts that they have done wrong and show that they generally respect the rights of other people and existing norms. With voluntary compensation to the victim, offenders accept the difference between their wrongful act and their person.

Initially, it may appear to be difficult to put the new theory of re-integrative sanctioning into practice. The wrongdoing must be isolated and objected to and clearly labelled (without stigmatizing the person); at the same time, the offender must be given the opportunity for voluntary association, rule-affirmation and integration into the community.

These principles can only be realized in a justice model of restorative justice which is incorporated into the state's criminal justice system. This is the appropriate way to handle the complex problem of re-integrative sanctioning, especially the necessary protection of the victim. The victim should not suffer a second time in the process of conflict resolution.

This incorporation into the state justice system guarantees that the victim's and the offender's rights are taken into account in the process of mediation. We must recognize that criminalization implies not only oppressive and severe consequences for the offender, but also protects freedom and belief in social rules for the sake of the victim and society. Crime control by the state is an instrument of balancing power and freedom among weak and strong members of the community. To put this theoretical consideration into more concrete terms, physically strong individuals are protected by the legal ban on all violent acts from the selfish pursuit of their interests. The weaker individuals may trust that their justified interests are not overwhelmed by physical strength or fraud.

Criminal acts must be controlled by the criminal justice system. Restorative justice accepts this system, which guarantees the elimination of violence in human social life and is a keystone of civilization in modern society. So the criminal justice system presents the setting for victim-protective mediation.

Acceptance of responsibility and victim compensation by the offender fulfil the goal of punishment through norm affirmation and victim rehabilitation, so that repressive measures become superfluous in the process of sanctioning.

Peacemaking by mediation neither abolishes state control of crime nor establishes an informal 'shadow justice'. It is an alternative to retributive punishment within the penal system, which is based on the principles of human rights.

The more penal control contains autonomous elements, and the less it depends on repression, the more it repairs institutional authority in the final instance. Today's criminal law is no more committed to a law of criminal punishment than it was in the past. Non-intervention, informal sanctions, and measures of prevention all play important roles in the system. The characteristic of the criminal law system is state control, not punishment.

In conclusion, peacemaking by mediation is a central element of state-incorporated crime control. This important 'third way' – appropriately placed between intervention and punishment – harmonizes crime control and the interests of the victim. By assuming a more active and positive role in responding to crime, the victim can avoid – at least to some extent – becoming the object of further harm or being victimized again during (and by) the process.

Empirical results about violence in partnerships

Violence in couple relationships is, first and foremost, violence against women and children, including offences such as insult, threat, coercion, deprivation of liberty, assault and various sexual offences, up to attempted and accomplished homicides. But various obstacles to prosecution exist: the majority of offences do not become known to the authorities, and the number of unrecorded cases is estimated to be extremely high. If an offence becomes known, it is rarely prosecuted. Only felonies, the most serious offences, are regularly prosecuted. Many of the offences committed in relationships are so-called 'private prosecution offences' or require an application for prosecution. Even if the victim has an interest in the offence being prosecuted, this does not necessarily lead to criminal proceedings being carried out: in principle, these offences are only prosecuted if the victim makes an application, but that might not happen in cases of domestic violence. Reasons such as fear, shame, uncertainty concerning the authorities, or pressure exerted on the victim by the offender can be of importance. Nevertheless, offences which normally require an application can be prosecuted if this is 'in the public interest' (para. 230 I 1 of the German Criminal Code (StGB)). Deciding this question is at the discretion of the public prosecutor; as an exception, an affirmative answer is to be given if the offender acted in a particularly coarse and brutal way, inflicted serious injuries or has considerable previous convictions (no. 223, 86 RiStBV). It is particularly emphasized in no. 233 s.2 RiStBV that this applies to assaults in close relationships as well. But in practice the 'public interest' in cases of violence in partnerships is usually denied: in a study analysing more than 2000 cases of domestic violence, only 30 per cent of their perpetrators were charged by the police, and 84 per cent of the proceedings pursued by the prosecution were dismissed/discharged without any consequences (Steffen and Polz 1991: chart 7). The crucial question for the prosecution authorities is whether or not a demand for a penalty has been submitted. If not, or if the application has been withdrawn, the order to stay proceedings then comes from the public prosecutor, because even the victim does not show an interest in criminal action (see also Beulke 1995: 12 f.). But most of the victims cannot imagine pursuing private prosecution proceedings themselves. Each charge requires that prosecution is in the public interest (para. 376 of the German Criminal Procedure, StPO). Prosecuting authorities decide this question by taking into account no. 86 II RiStBV. A charge is usually regarded as in the public interest if the peace under the law in the victim's area of life is disturbed and society at large has an interest in prosecution for various reasons. As a result of this rule and of the view that domestic conflicts are a private matter, the public interest is frequently negated. In spite of this, an affirmative answer to the question of public interest is legally possible if a private prosecution is not reasonable for personal reasons and the victim is unable to clarify the circumstances of the punishable deed, which are the typical problems of women who are faced with violence in relationships. If a woman in this situation expects the protection of the criminal law, referring her to private prosecution means in effect refusing legal protection (AK-StPO-Rössner para. 376 no. 2 (Rössner 1996)). In addition, Beulke (1995: 9) points out that by referring victims of domestic violence to private prosecution, their situation runs the risk of getting worse. The offender, with whom the victim still lives, might possibly react in an even more aggressive way upon finding out that the report and the accusation depend exclusively on the victim's initiative and that the prosecuting authorities themselves are not interested in investigation.

On the occasion of the 33. StrÄndG of 1 July 1997, which came into force on 5 July 1997, para. 177 StGB (sexual coercion/rape) was changed. Before the restatement, marital rape could only be prosecuted as coercion (para. 240 StGB). Now marital rape is a special abstract of record. However, we have to wait and see whether this change in the law will cause a change of people's attitudes and whether effective protection of the woman can be achieved by criminalizing marital rape. But in view of the high number of unrecorded cases and the unchanged problems occurring in criminal proceedings concerning rape, this is unlikely to happen. For the most part, the prosecution authorities generally depend on offences being reported to them. Only a few offences become known by active criminal investigation on the part of the police and the prosecution. Furthermore, the number of unrecorded cases concerning crimes of domestic and social violence is estimated to be very high. Those offences become known to the prosecuting authorities almost exclusively through private reports made by the victims or other persons. The fact that this kind of offence is less visible for the public and is often committed in private places is of crucial importance in this.

The problematic nature of 'family violence' includes various combinations of victims and offenders, especially violence against children and elderly people. In this report, the viewpoint is limited to partnerships including married and unmarried couples, regardless of whether they live together or apart from one another. Even though in the majority of the cases men are the offenders and women the victims, the fact that men are victims of violence in relationships as well and that women also commit homicides by killing their spouses should not be disregarded. Studies carried out by Straus and Gelles (1980; 1988; 1990) have proved that the number of offences committed by women against men is considerable. But there is a crucial difference: women normally strike out in order to express fear, hurt and despair, and – as a result – they provoke brutal male revenge which aims to re-establish their superiority and subordination. Men use violent behaviour in order to assert their authority. If one follows the development of cases in which men or women kill their partners, there are usually many years of escalating conflicts preceding the homicide. The same holds true for women who commit an offence: the criminal act is the result of the disastrous dynamics of the relationship and the previous humiliations and acts of violence inflicted by their male spouses. Many violent offences are based on unresolved and escalating conflicts (Straus and Gelles 1980; 1988; 1990; Steck 1997: 404f.).

The figures announced by the PKS (German Police Crime Statistics) are only partly able to record the violence in partnerships. The percentage of relatives and partners committing violent crimes in 1996 amounted to 5.5 per cent (in 1995: 5.3 per cent; in 1993: 7.4 per cent; in 1989: 7.6 per cent), and the percentage of cases in which victim and offender were acquainted with one another was 17.4 per cent (in 1995: 17.1 per cent; in 1993: 21.6 per cent; in 1989: 22.8 per cent). Even though couple relationships are not recorded separately, the statistics suggest that there is an evident risk of becoming the victim of a closely related offender. This becomes particularly clear if one looks at the data by differentiating between the two criteria of 'sex of victim' on the one hand and 'kind of the offence' on the other hand. In doing this, the probability of becoming a female victim of an offence committed by a relative, the partner or an acquaintance is much higher than that of falling victim to a stranger (Schneider 1993: 117). Looking specifically at the numbers showing attempted and accomplished murder, one can see that 30 per cent (178) out of 593 victims were related to the offender (including intimates), and another 27.3 per cent were acquainted. Among the 772 cases of attempted and accomplished manslaughter, in 335 (46 per cent) of the cases the offender was a relative or the partner, and in 224 (31.6 per cent) he was part of the victim's circle of acquaintance. When death occurred as a result of an assault, 17.4 per cent (26 out of 149) of the offenders were relatives/partners and 37.6 per cent (56) were acquainted with the victim.

The same ratio appears when looking at serious and dangerous battery/assault: altogether, 25,933 cases were recorded; in 20.4 per cent (5,303) the offender was related or the partner, and in 34 per cent (8,822) the victim knew the offender personally. According to the prosecution statistics (1996, Tab. 6.1, p.74f.), in 96.7 per cent of the total cases in which the offenders were committed for trial, the reason for arrest was flight or risk of escape. When analysing the reasons for pre-trial arrest and the offences causing an order to commit the offender for trial, one can draw the cautious conclusion that it is rarely used in cases of violence in partnerships, because an order for pre-trial arrest is the exception in relation to violent offences in general, if one takes those offences that normally cause an order for pre-trial arrest as a starting point (10.3 per cent without and 19.9 per cent including robbery). It is impossible to say how many of these are cases of violence between intimates. However, it can not be assumed that flight or danger of flight can be of considerable importance in the case of relationship violence, because most of the offenders have a fixed place of residence. Any more than that, danger of collusion is unlikely to be the reason for pre-trial arrest. The only likely reason is danger of recurrence, para. 112a StPO, because obviously the offender might use force again. Apart from the legal problems, one can tell from the small number of orders (against 671 persons in 1996) that ordering pre-trial custody for this reason cannot be of practical significance in cases of violence in relationships.

There are no precise numbers available stating how frequently physical violence is used in partnerships, but the number of unrecorded cases is estimated to be considerable. One can get an idea about this by looking at the number of women who take refuge in a battered wives' refuge. According to the latest information, about 40,000 women and just as many children live in more than 320 battered wives' refuges. Those affected are mainly working-class women who are financially dependent on their husbands. A study carried out by a battered wives' refuge in Berlin showed that 21.4 per cent of the women seeking protection lived on their husband's income, 21.6 per cent obtained social welfare benefits and 58.9 per cent of the violent men were workers (Schall and Schirrmacher 1995: 11; Hagemann-White 1992). But this kind of study can only show a part of social reality, because women who come from middle-class or upper-class families usually choose other ways of leaving their husbands. As a result, we have to be aware that, in addition to the occupants of battered wives' refuges, an unknown number of women leave their violent husband in other ways. Violence is not solely a working-class problem, but those cases that become known to the police do come primarily from socially disadvantaged families.

No accurate estimate of the number of unrecorded cases exists (vague estimates range from 100,000 to 4 million women yearly). The sub-committees of the Commission for Violence also refer to the unreliability of the information available. The Subcommittee for Criminology, for example, refers to American studies (for the USA, researchers take a percentage of 50–60 per cent of marriages as a starting point and consequently conclude with an extremely high number of unrecorded cases), or to the results of the extensive study carried out by Schneider who assumed that, concerning violence inflicted by male offenders on female victims, no reliable estimates are possible (Schwind and Baumann 1990, UK Kriminologie no. 232 f.; Schneider 1987, 63f.; 1993, 117f.).

The KFN (Criminological Research Institute of Lower-Saxony 1995) conducted a full survey into violence in the private arena, especially into the spread of sexual abuse of women, by questioning victims. It emerged that approximately 14.5 per cent of the women had been victims of a rape or sexual coercion at least once in their lives. Rape in partnerships does by no means necessarily lead to a separation: only 56.7 per cent of those victims who lived together with the offender at the time when the sexual offence was committed declared that they split up with him permanently; the others did so only temporarily or not at all. Most of the violent sexual offences do not become known to the police and the prosecuting authorities. Only just under 7 per cent of the cases had been reported to the police. What matters to the women affected is not to avoid punishment of the offender. Rather, the dominating emotion is one of embarrassment, the opinion that what happened was a private matter, and the assumption that the police are not able to achieve anything anyway. Some of the women were afraid that living together with the partner/offender would become even more difficult if they gave notice of the offence to the police.

The study carried out by Beulke (1995: 6, 122) about public violence showed that a large proportion of the offences that become known to the prosecuting authorities were slight and medium assaults. In 83.1 per cent of the cases, the assault had been the only offence reported (64.2 per cent), or it had been reported in addition to other offences. Thirteen per cent of the crimes reported were insults, acts of coercion and threats, and 5.8 per cent were sexual offences. Steffen and Polz (1991: 112) also found that concerning violent offences committed in families, assaults and grievous bodily harm (with or without other offences) were the main cause for calling the police. The latest American statistics about partner violence published by the US Department of Justice (Greenfield *et al.* 1998) shows that in 1996 about 1,800 deaths were caused by partners with whom the victim lived. In nearly three out of four cases the victim was female. But the numbers are falling: in 1976, nearly 3,000 victims died as a result of violence in partnerships. In 65 per cent of these homicides a weapon was used. The number of non-fatal acts of violence dropped as well: in 1996, about 840,000 cases of rape, sexual abuse, robbery, assault and grievous bodily harm in relationships were registered, whereas in 1993 it had been 1.1 million cases. Women aged between 16 and 24 years have the highest rate of violent experiences per head. Violence inflicted upon men by their partners did not change significantly between 1992 and 1996. In 1996, approximately 150,000 offences of violence committed by spouses/partners were registered in which the victims were male. About half of the cases in which women had fallen victim to their partners had been reported to the police. Victims who did not turn to the police declared that they considered the incident to be a private matter. Furthermore, they stated that they were afraid of revenge by the offender and that the police would not be able to change anything in their case anyway. In one out of five cases, the police arrested the offender.

Slightly more than half of the female victims and about half of the male offenders who are imprisoned as a result of family violence live in a household with children who are less than 12 years old. More than half of the victims are physically injured, one out of five women went to a doctor. Reports given by emergency doctors show that 84 per cent of the women staying in hospital because of physical injuries have been harmed by their partners. More than half of those injuries were bruises, contusions and similar injuries. Furthermore, more than half of them were located on the victim's face or head. More than half of the offenders convicted as a result of force used against their spouses/girlfriends were under the influence of alcohol or drugs at the time of the offence. The numerous American studies investigating the number of unrecorded cases of domestic violence are based on official statistics, on information given by emergency doctors and hospitals, and on questioning victims and offenders about self-reported delinquency. Researchers agree that the number of unrecorded cases is very high and that the significance of domestic violence has been underestimated for decades, although it is a large part of the problem of violent criminality. Questioning victims revealed that nearly 40 per cent of all criminal acts are committed by a friend, a relative or the intimate partner of the victim (Garner and Fagan 1997: 53f.). Twenty-eight per cent of all homicides with female victims occur at the victim's home. It is assumed that no more than 20 per cent of all offences of violence committed in families become known to the police. Compared with victims of other offences, the psychological and social situation of victims of domestic violence differs considerably in nearly all of the cases.

Conventional criminal procedure is not able to react to those violent experiences in close relationships in any appropriate way. Victims often do not want penal proceedings, because this cannot guarantee actual help in a difficult personal situation. On the contrary: criminal action might even worsen the domestic situation. Those victims who really want the offender to be prosecuted have to reckon with disappointment, because most prosecutions are dismissed without consequences, or the victim is referred to private prosecution.

The following distinctive features between victims of family violence and victims of anonymous offenders can be established:

- a situation of mental pressure precedes a decision to report the incident to the police;

- in many cases, the victims are still at the mercy of the offender (if they were not brave enough to break up with him);

- the victims have to reckon with increased aggression;

- the situation is worsened by children, financial dependence and, in some cases, syndromes of 'learned helplessness';

- often, ambivalent emotions are of importance: the women do not necessarily want to leave the offender or they come back;

- the police are usually called in order to intervene in an urgent crisis, but a prosecution is often rejected because of the consequences expected;

- the victims do not pin much hope on improving their situation by criminal proceedings.

The particular dynamism of physical violence inflicted by men upon their female partners is evident in the fact that various kinds of abuse (psychological, economic, sexual and physical) do not start with the use of physical violence straight away: the different kinds of abuse merge into one another and, from the partner's point of view, the use of violence appears to be a creeping and gradual process in which the intensity of the violence used increases steadily (Schall and Schirrmacher 1995: 13f.). At the beginning, the woman is the subject of psychological and economic restrictions, for example as a result of the man being in charge of the family income, taking away material resources from the woman, forbidding her to have a job, denying that she has personal capabilities, trying to keep her under control and cut her off from the outside world. In addition, in some cases the man threatens to use violence or even to kill the woman. The first act of physical violence is often excused as an isolated case and is not regarded as a warning sign for the beginning of a violent relationship. Such a misinterpretation is supported by the fact that in many cases the man himself feels guilty, apologizes to the woman and promises that something like that will never happen again. As far as the women are concerned, at this stage they are mostly willing to believe that the act of violence will be an exceptional incident, because the relationship had once been based upon love and confidence. However, this often results in repeated use of force, which occurs more regularly and finally escalates into serious physical abuse. Consequently, on the one hand, the woman is humiliated constantly, on the other hand she is kept in the relationship.

The phenomenon of the *battered woman syndrome* (cf. Buchwald and Kilian 1997: 66f.) can be classified into three typical categories of symptoms.

1. The first, typical way in which victims of violence react (like the victims of all kinds of traumatic events) is by showing depression, confusion, lack of motivation, fear, rage, feelings of guilt, etc. This is followed by reactions which are, at first glance, difficult to comprehend, for example affection towards the aggressor and the feeling of being the one who is to blame. Since the maltreatment typically occurs repeatedly, and escalates, the women who are ill-treated are convinced that nobody understands them or that people could even hold *them* responsible for what happened. As a result, they seek protection by secluding themselves from the outside world. In addition to that, especially in the case of abused women, the main effect of being maltreated by the partner is a drastic loss of self-esteem. In the end the affected women feel worthless, powerless, helpless and humiliated.

2. The main component of the range of symptoms is the so-called 'learned helplessness' as a special kind of depression. It can be summed up as the victim learning that she is unable to bring unpleasant events under her control and, as a result, losing the motivation to change her situation. The way the woman reacts to the first acts of violence is of critical importance. Women who have been abused for only a short period of time are more likely to threaten the offender with drawing the obvious conclusions and to pursue their threats. If they are successful, they feel in control of the situation and are convinced of their ability to help themselves. However,

if the woman failed to do this, the *offender* learned that the negative reaction failed to materialize, and this has a reinforcing effect. It has been concluded from this and from other studies that aggression can be learned and that violent behaviour develops only in the course of a relationship. Therefore it is important for the women affected not to accept her partner's behaviour as being unavoidable, but to try to prevent violence from being inflicted on her by all possible means. Possibilities such as discussion with the offender, threatening to get a divorce, making him make promises and so on must be considered. But this method can only be of short-term success and might even confirm the behaviour if the woman does not act positively. Further possible informal ways are to inform relatives, friends or neighbours. Formal action that may be taken by the victim includes calling institutions such as the police, battered wives' refuges, the church or a lawyer. The main problem in this respect is that the women concerned make use of these possibilities very hesitantly and often do not see them through. Various reasons can be found, especially the conviction that it would not be much use anyway, increased threats from the offender, or fear of giving up the relationship. It is crucial for the woman to find out which of her strategies is effective and how she can fight against the maltreatment. If she does not succeed in doing this, she is going to go round in circles, because as soon as she considers herself helpless, she actually becomes so. Afterwards, the victim tries to explain the unavoidable feeling of helplessness by blaming herself and feeling solely responsible for what happened and the ability to assess a situation in an objective way is lost. As a result, if – at some time – the chance to escape from the relationship arises, the women are often no longer able to recognize this opportunity and to take advantage of it.

3. If the worst comes to the worst, the woman reacts with self-destruction in order to try to cope with the situation and the violence she has experienced. So-called co-alcoholism, repressing by playing down, idealizing the offender, medicine and drug abuse, as well as various mechanisms to suppress reality and to justify one's own behaviour have repeatedly been observed.

   The victim usually tends to deny that the offender's acts are to be called criminal. She does not blame *him* for the abuse, but external causes and unusual circumstances like unemployment and illness. Victims deny that they are victims at all. They do not take the initiative which would enable them to break free from the violent relationship such as, for example, moving to another job, or making appointments with social workers or friends. Once the victims have stayed in the relationship for a long period of time, they no longer regard a divorce or a new beginning as possible.

To summarize, two different kinds of conflict situations can be established: on the one hand, violence in relationships in which the woman – for various reasons – does not part from the offender and a spiral of violence, or at least repeated use of force, is to be expected; and on the other hand, violence and threats against women whose former partners do not want to accept the separation.

Reactions by the police and the judiciary on violence in partnerships

The police are of crucial importance in violence in close relationships. Police and emergency hospitals are the sole institutions which can be contacted seven days a week, 24 hours a day, almost everywhere. By means of the emergency-call system, the police are able to reach the scene of an offence within a very short period of time. This alone shows the significance of the police in the termination and prevention of violent situations. Not surprisingly, victims of domestic violence call the police in such situations.

Despite this, the reactions of police and prosecution are viewed critically: according to international findings, the way the police react to domestic violence differs from the way violence inflicted by strangers is handled; in fact, victims of family violence are often denied protection. Furthermore, the police treat emergency calls from battered wives as being lower on the list of priorities than emergency calls from other victims. It is assumed that the prosecution authorities play down violent offences committed at the victim's home, or underestimate them, and that they do not take the emergency calls seriously. Compared to the usual form of intervention, the action taken against violence in partnerships is more settling, mediating, non-repressive and passive. One reason held to be responsible for this conduct is the fact that the legal authorities regard the family as being a place of privacy and, as a result, the use of force as a private matter, as a matter for which the victim and the offender are jointly responsible, or as something which has even been provoked by the victim (United Nations 1993: 26, 27).

Steffen and Polz (1991) investigated the way the police intervene in domestic conflicts on behalf of the Research Group for Criminology of the Bavarian police. Steffen and Polz confirm the findings of national and international research, according to which the available data and existing attempts to explain family violence are unsatisfactory and that, especially in Germany, empirical studies are lacking. Over a period of two months, 2,074 cases of family violence were analysed and evaluated. The questionnaires were filled in by the police officers and partly reflect their assessments. Victims were not questioned.

It turned out that police interventions relating to violence in partnerships are extremely rare (less than 1 per cent of all operations). Family altercations include various kinds of disputes with different persons participating, vociferous but nevertheless relatively harmless quarrels, as well as crude fights resulting in clashes or even in homicides (Steffen and Polz 1991: 55). In 65 per cent of the cases, the police were called by the victim, in 14 per cent by family members who were not involved in the dispute, in another 14 per cent by neighbours, and in 6 per cent by other persons or anonymous callers. Most of the cases occurred between adults and mainly between Germans: only 16 per cent of the offenders and 14 per cent of the victims were foreigners. More than half of all disputes were fought out verbally, also involved serious threats being made. In 42 per cent of the cases, physical force was used – 30 victims and 5 offenders (in 2,074 cases) were seriously injured and needed treatment as in-patients, and three victims were killed (Steffen and Polz 1991: 61). Aggression against the police officers was very unusual and occurred in only 3 per cent of all cases in which the police were called. In none of the cases did the victim act in solidarity with the offender against the police. The 61 cases in which the offender attacked the police officers differed significantly from the 'peaceful' missions. They turned out to be especially problematic disputes, and the way the police reacted was more often repressive, and measures according to PAG (police operation law) and StPO as well as coercive means and reports were frequently taken (Steffen and Polz 1991: 70).

Nearly two-thirds of the police interventions involved families who had never called the police before. Seventy-nine per cent of the victims were female and 21 per cent were male. In 91 per cent of the cases, the offenders were male, in 9 per cent female. In 28 per cent of the operations it was impossible to clearly classify the persons involved as either offender or victim. However, the situation was unambiguous when force was used or when reports were made: classifying the persons affected as victims/ offenders was easy to accomplish in 90 per cent of those cases. Seventy-six per cent of the missions dealt with violence between intimates. The majority of the cases concerned maltreatment or insults of the woman by the man. Compared with other combinations of persons involved, in these cases the offender was most frequently drunk (57 per cent), approximately half of the disputes involved physical violence, and the women were injured in 31 per cent of the cases. Twenty-two per cent of all victims were prepared to press charges. Sixty-three per cent of the harmed victims were slightly injured, 10 per cent were seriously injured, and there were three homicides. Second in the order of frequency (14 per cent of all incidents) was where both victim and offender were male. Fifty-nine per cent of these cases were aggressive fights between fathers and adult sons, resulting most frequently (in 42 per cent of the cases) in criminal proceedings (see Table 1).

It was quite rare for the police officers to take the male offender away with them (Steffen and Polz 1991: 106). In 137 out of 2,074 cases they took him to the police station (to sober up, to take a blood sample, for preventive detention or provisional apprehension), in 46 cases to a hospital/mental hospital, in seven cases to other persons, and in 101 cases he was expelled from the home.

Steffen and Polz (1991: 173f) suggest pursuing criminal proceedings in cases of serious conflicts and/or if the victim desires them. For less grave cases they recommend a procedure of advice and admonition.

Like the police, the public prosecutors act reluctantly and passively when dealing with family violence (Steffen and Polz 1991: 117). The majority of the proceedings are dismissed without consequences and the victim is referred to private prosecution. The women who are seeking help are told that it is impossible to do anything by means of the criminal law against the threatening and violent men who are not willing to accept separation. What was also proved to be true by the empirical results of the study carried out by Steffen and Polz is that out of all cases of violence in partnerships which became known to the police and were subject to criminal investigation (out of 2,074 cases that became known to the Bavarian police during a two-month period in 1988, in 622 cases criminal proceedings were taken into consideration, and 568 cases were handed over to the prosecution authorities), 95 per cent were already terminated at the time the data was analysed. The breakdown here was as follows.

Table 3.1. Measures taken by the police recorded by Steffen and Polz

Measure	Number of Measures	%
Legal process	1,490	72
Settlement of dispute	1,339	65
General measures concerning victim	1,188	57
Charge	622	30
Measures according to PAG/StPO	597	29
Refer victim to other persons/institutions	315	15
Induce victim to leave flat	248	12
First aid/emergency doctor	113	5
Use of coercive means concerning offender	108	5
Taking blood sample (offender)	72	4
Taking victim to other persons	72	4
Total number of calls	2,074	100

The vast majority of the proceedings had been dismissed by the prosecution *without consequences*. Four hundred and forty-five (84 per cent) were dismissed, most of them (288) according to para. 170 II StPO (dismissal of cases because sufficient cause for accusation is lacking), 111 cases were referred to private prosecution, and 46 cases were dismissed according to para. 153, 154 StPO (dismissals without conditions and instructions, because the public interest in a charge is lacking), and ten cases were dismissed with conditions or according to other provisions. Only 16 per cent (84) of the offenders had been charged. When the study was carried out, 31 per cent (26) of the proceedings had not yet been disposed, and out of the settled proceedings, five cases were dismissed by judgment, in seven cases the offender was acquitted, 13 orders of summary punishment, 23 fines and ten prison sentences were imposed.

Concerning the way the police and the public prosecutors handle family violence proceedings, Steffen and Polz found that orders to dismiss proceedings are not influenced by how seriously the victim is injured. If the demand for prosecution is lacking, this leads to a dismissal in 90 per cent of the cases, 73 per cent out of these procedures are dismissed according to para. 170 II StPO. But even if a demand for prosecution existed, the passive way of deciding predominated: the prosecution dismissed 73 per cent of the incidents, 38 per cent of which were dismissed according to para. 170 II StPO, and 47 per cent by referring the victim to private prosecution according to para. 374, 376 StPO.

Beulke (1995: 393) observed that – even in the course of the pilot scheme imposing the condition of advice – the major part (51.5 per cent) of the proceedings was dismissed according to para. 170 II StPO, and that the public interest was denied with the consequence of referring the victim to private prosecution (18.2 per cent).

A short questionnaire carried out by criminal justice practitioners in Marburg, where cases of partner violence are handled by a special department, showed that such cases are usually referred to private prosecution. As a result of the relationship remaining in existence, the victim failed to bring a charge against the offender, because prosecution was considered to be unsuitable. The offender was only accused if the victim was physically injured in a serious, visible way (for example distorting injuries to the face, wounds that required to be stitched, or fractures). If the demand for prosecution is lacking, the proceedings are regularly dismissed without conditions.

In Austria, the Sicherheitspolizeigesetz (police operation law) came into force in 1993. In reacting to family violence, it provides the possibility of using preventive means (expelling the offender from the home), and to co-ordinate police and local institutions (female contact officers, social institutions, youth authorities and welfare services). According to the Sicherheitspolizeigesetz, the police are required to settle the fights by mediation in order to prevent the situation from escalating (Mahrer 1997: 105; Bohrn 1997: 113).

Victim–offender mediation and violence in partnerships

The idea that mediation (in variations such as restitution, victim–offender mediation, reconciliation) is one possible way of responding to criminality has become more and more important in discussion on crime and crime prevention in Germany and other countries. Victim–offender mediation is supposed to settle the conflict resulting from the offence by reconciling victim and offender, especially by means of mediation carried out by the offender. Concerning the central idea of victim–offender mediation, a number of criminological and legal studies have been carried out. As far as they integrate victim–offender mediation into the legal framework of criminal law, its function can be characterized as follows: by means of the offender voluntarily taking responsibility for and redressing the consequences of the offence, a reinforcement of the rule of law infringed by the offence and the integration of the offender into society are supposed to be achieved. In this way, the victim is supposed to be treated justly and the victim's need for a settlement of the conflict, for establishing responsibility and for restitution, can be satisfied. Integrating the victim–offender mediation into the formal rules of criminal procedure provides a rational way of solving the conflict (cf. the summary by Dölling *et al.* 1998: 487f.).

Earlier legal responses to violence in partnerships seem unsatisfactory. The idea of mediation might possibly provide an alternative. Analysing the experiences of services which carry out victim–offender mediation in practice (especially the experiences regarding adults), as far as violence between spouses is concerned, one cannot help but be disillusioned: out of all German victim–offender mediation services, only a few projects in Germany (e.g. Hannover–HAIP) specialize in reconciliation in violent partnerships. All the other projects do have experience with this kind of case, but handling them proved to be very difficult. Though most of the cases handled do result from offences of violence (on the nationwide victim–offender mediation statistics see Hartmann and Stroezel [1998] in Dölling *et al.* 1998 149f.), the projects worked on cases involving long-lasting conflict in the victim–offender relationship, which moreover differed depending on whether juveniles or adults were affected (Bannenberg 1993: 255). Thus, the results of a study comparing the different juvenile projects show that 5.7 per cent of the cases were fights between pupils and former friends. With adults, a considerable number of continuing violent disputes between spouses (and neighbours) was registered: at the project in Tübingen, in 14.2 per cent of the cases close family relationships were affected, in 4.4 per cent other relatives, in 5.5 per cent friends, and in 2.2 per cent acquaintances. The considerable tension observed, particularly in partnership relationships (resulting from divorces, disputes about maintenance, physical and psychological violence), were described by the mediators as bearing an 'explosive cause for conflict'. The problem regarding this kind of cases was – according to the mediators – that the conflict was not limited to the criminal offence; rather, the problem to work on was the complex conflict background. Moreover, it was assumed that the prosecution deliberately passed on problematic cases to the legal aid service in order to attempt mediation, because a solution by means of criminal law was not regarded as sufficient. Accordingly, one public prosecutor stated that the prosecuting authorities were, on the one hand, supposed to focus on serious offences and their prosecution, but on the other hand they had to bear in mind that the function of criminal law was to limit conflict. An employee of the legal aid service assessed this selection of cases by saying that '[t]hese cases are allocated to me, because the prosecutors don't know what to do about them and the criminal law obviously does not work.' (Rössner 1993: 117).

Looking at one of the cases (unfortunately one that had a particularly tragic ending), the conflict becomes peculiarly clear: neither the present victim–offender mediation projects nor the judiciary are able to handle partner conflicts in an appropriate way or to protect the victim.

The legal aid service in Düsseldorf was allocated a case in order to attempt reconciliation, because the prosecution felt a need to solve the conflict but had no possibility of intervening by means of the criminal law. The case concerned a 38-year-old woman who lived apart from her husband. She had reported him to the police for battery and menace. After the separation, the woman lived together with her 12-year-old son and was permanently afraid of her husband, because he lay waiting for her and constantly called her. The 12-year-old did not leave the house without being armed with a knife. The woman voluntarily received psychiatric treatment and told her contact at the legal aid service that 'her nerves cannot take any more'. The prosecution did not do anything to protect her. They handed the case over to the legal aid service in order to try victim–offender mediation. Though the acts clearly proved to be 'criminal' according to the law (assault, menace), the husband was not willing to try to settle the conflict when the mediator asked him to do so. The mediator had the impression that the husband was dangerous, mentally ill, and prepared to carry out his threats to kill his wife. With this result, the case was handed back to the public prosecutor, who felt unable to take legal measures. Mediator and prosecutor discussed having the husband admitted to a psychiatric hospital, but concrete measures were not taken. Eight months after the case had been handed back to the prosecution (the victim had since gained a divorce), the husband waylaid his ex-wife, forced her to drive to the forest, hit her with a baseball bat and killed her with a knife. Afterwards he gave himself up to the police and declared that he had not been able to bear the separation.

In 1995, Beulke carried out a pilot project concerning domestic violence. The problem of violence in close relationships was investigated with special reference to the prosecuting authorities. Linking the prosecution with advice services was held as a way to make use of the legal pressure inflicted by opening criminal proceedings, but only in order to dismiss proceedings after a voluntary participation with the advice services, and to avoid unsuitable legal sanctions. In this way, the victim was not left in the lurch by the prosecuting authorities and the accused was offered a form of sanction that he could use to set about changing his behaviour, and to help him avoid future offences of violence (Beulke 1995: 33). The conditions for receiving advice included a limit of five hours' duration and were first directed solely at the offender. Including the victim (especially the partner) was possible at any time, by means of the mediator, the victim and the offender coming to an agreement to hold joint or separate meetings with both parties. Beulke came to the conclusion that although the pilot project was not quantitatively successful (only about 11 per cent of all cases were held to be suitable by the prosecutors), qualitatively it had been successful.

Possible legal reactions in order to settle violent conflicts in partnerships

Suggestions for testing different possibilities already provided by criminal law

In the light of the fact that the police and the judiciary currently handle violence in partnerships inadequately and without taking account of the victims' need for protection, mediation and restoration seem to be alternatives that are legally as well as practically possible to implement.

It is assumed that every voluntary and non-legal attempt to solve conflicts in cases of domestic violence is the best and most promising possibility. Voluntary mediation, advice procedures and therapies are alternatives to consider. Mediation (essentially existing forms of mediation in cases of separation/divorce) is interpreted as an offer which can be arranged individually by taking into account the particular needs of both victim and offender affected, and its course is flexible and not pre-fixed. These methods deserve wider support and obviously meet a growing need in society, as one can tell from their increasing utilization in practice and the change in the attitude of the judiciary as well as other sectors of society.

But we have to be aware that violent conflicts in partnerships can only be solved by means of mediation in very rare cases. Despite the fact that drawing the victim's and the offender's attention to voluntary, non-legal mediation provides one possibility of *legally* handling conflicts in relationships, the number of conflicts that can actually be solved in this manner cannot be called considerable. This method requires absolutely voluntary participants (for this reason legal pressure cannot be applied), and it presupposes that either the offender has already realized his mistake and is now looking for help in order to avoid future violence, or that the victim herself has managed to look for non-legal help to bring the unbearable situation to an end.

Fundamentally different from the situation described above and more problematic are those cases in which female victims of couple violence are not able to end the violent situation by themselves and turn to the police or judiciary for help. Even though researchers have found that the victims do not necessarily want legal proceedings, it is clear that a report or an emergency call are cries for help in a situation the victim cannot cope with on her own. This includes many kinds of different conflict situations, some aiming at short-term intervention to end an urgent, escalating situation, but also some cases of continual threats or injuries by the (former) partner, where the risk of a homicide is high. Particularly in the most difficult situations, the judiciaries appear to be extremely insecure and helpless in using the criminal law, even though protecting the victim should be their primary task.

The duty of criminal law to protect the victims and to avoid future offences requires a differentiated intervention and a range of measures to help victims and offenders. Criminal law no longer just provides a 'penalty' in a purely repressive sense, but also offers a wide spectrum of possible responses to criminal offences. Moreover, research on the different forms of delinquent behaviour demands further specialization and development of legal responses to this. Particularly serious cases of violence require intervention by the state for reasons that include the protection of the victim, breaking the cycle of violence, and avoiding future offences. But only in exceptional cases does the response have to be a consistently and 'classically' legal one (such as accusing the offender and sentencing him to imprisonment). In the majority of cases of violence in partnerships, a legal response which focuses on victim–offender mediation and reconciliation appears to be appropriate.

Victim–offender mediation and settlement of conflicts within the context of German criminal procedure require that the parties affected participate absolutely voluntarily. As far as the offender is concerned, a limited degree of voluntary participation has to be assumed, because regular criminal proceedings take place as a result of the absence of such willingness. This legal pressure put on the offender can also be a fundamental motivation to attempt reconciliation in the first place. But on the other hand, none of the offenders has ever been forced to participate, and being unwilling to take part in the mediation procedure must not have a detrimental effect in relation to the assessment of the penalty. Therefore we have to differentiate between the offender who accepts the offer to seek reconciliation after he has used force against his wife/girlfriend, and the one who does not accept it. If he shows readiness, victim–offender mediation can be considered. If the victim is not willing, the offender can endeavour to achieve mediation, or examination of the question of violence and victimization, or symbolic acts. But if the offender does not want to attempt reconciliation, pressuring an offender (who has not come to his senses) by means of the criminal law is incompatible with the fundamental idea of victim–offender mediation and reconciliation. If the offender is not willing to face his criminal deed and has no insight into his act, and if he puts strong pressure on the victim, which has to be assumed in cases of serious, long-term conflicts or of the 'battered woman syndrome', the only possibilities that might be considered are confrontational methods supported by legal pressure, such as imposing conditions to seek advice, social training and so on, which work towards mediation without the victim's participation. The idea of 're-integrative shaming' (Braithwaite 1989; 1995; Matt 1997/4: 225f.) is of particular importance: the woman does not have to attend the negotiations directly in order to make the position of the victim clear. The offender, however, has to face his criminal offence and is forced to take responsibility. The experiences recorded by Weidner (1990, 1993: 247f.) in the course of anti-aggression training for violent criminals in prison prove that this works even in cases of the most serious offences of violence. This kind of anti-aggression training could be suited to the special needs of effectively opposing violence in partnerships. By means of confrontation, an examination of subjects linked with violence could take place. In particular, problems of violence between intimates, the situations in which violence is used, the image of women, and the problems children are faced with if they are growing up in a violent atmosphere, or if force is used to control them are topics that could be discussed. One could attempt to learn non-aggressive ways to settle conflicts in a group process.

Problematic items concerning the settlement of conflicts
in violent partnerships

Judging from experience in Germany, victim–offender mediation, although it is already carried out in cases of violence between intimates, is often quite difficult to employ. Compared with other offences of violence, the criminal act committed by the partner is just the cause for prosecution. Concealed behind it is a large number of past conflicts and injuries, making different demands on mediation.

Problematic items concerning mediation in cases of domestic violence include the following:

- critics are of the opinion that the women are exposed to the violent offender yet again – the victim just serves its own purpose in the procedure;

- victims are the weaker part of the relationship anyway and could only lose in victim–offender mediation as well, because they cannot express and enforce their rights as firmly and strongly as the offender;

- mediators could have problems with limiting their neutrality and evening out the imbalance of powers by strengthening the women (for example by drawing their attention towards institutions that offer help and advice, by taking a stand for them or by supporting them in articulating their interests);

- furthermore, difficulties might arise concerning demands for surveillance (renewed use of force by the offender).

But in cases of long-term violent relationships from which the women themselves cannot break free (for whatever reasons), intervention from outside is most difficult. Concerning attempts to mediate, one should be aware that taking just one isolated measure (just one conversation, one attempt to mediate) cannot successfully interrupt the cycle of violence in this kind of relationship. In practice, various ideas suggest themselves.

Concerning violence in partnerships, it could probably make sense to analyse these on the basis of the *nature of the conflict in a relationship:* differences might exist and, as a result, different kinds of reactions might be required. This is also indicated by experiences relating to mediation in cases of violence in partnerships in Austria. According to these, it is quite probable that not all of the women living in violent relationships are suffering from the 'battered woman syndrome'. In cases in which violence against the woman is used for the first time or only exceptionally, and the women – supported by help from the outside – are strong enough to split up with the offender, a settlement of the conflict is more promising than in relationships with a long history of violence. Those women who have already separated from their partner are also at risk of becoming victims of violence if the man is not willing to accept the separation. In cases of this kind, regulating the conflict by using the pressure of the criminal law appears to be the most promising alternative. The existence of children might intensify the conflict. Particularly problematic cases, with a long history of violence and with many social problems (which are probably connected with the social class the couple belong to), might prove unsuitable for victim–offender mediation, because victim and offender are deeply caught up in the violent pattern of behaviour, are mutually dependent on one another in spite of the violence, and willingness to try a settlement might not exist. The only possibility worth considering in this kind of case is to confront the offender or to use the criminal law combined with an offer of advice for victim and offender.

On the basis of international experience, a modification of the standard of mediation of conflicts in violent relationships seems to be necessary:

- Two mediators would probably be in a better position to cope with problematic situations.

- A specification concerning the procedure should be carried out, taking into account the following points:

  - mediation may take up a great deal of time and require some more preliminary conversations and more mediating sessions;

  - taking a stand against violence;

  - drawing attention towards the possibly weaker position of the victim during the negotiations;

  - development of methods to even out the imbalance of powers (procedural frameworks, e.g. limiting the time for speech, supporting the formulation of interests, pre-formulated comments and demands and so on);

  - making use of criminal law if the offender commits another offence of violence;

  - links with other institutions offering aid and advice, with the police and the judiciary;

- possibly success surveillance, that is, to come to an agreement with the victim to report renewed use of violence within a certain period of time (for example three months).

Concerning the question of *who* should carry out the settlement of conflicts and victim–offender mediation in cases of violence between intimates, there is an argument in favour of greater specialization within existing victim–offender mediation services. The extensive experience and understanding which the mediators have gained through dealing with parties of unequal strength, with conflicts between spouses or neighbours, and with other difficult mediations should be utilized. Thus, the demand for creating special institutions – which is difficult to enforce in any case, because of the expense – becomes superfluous. Since these settlements of conflicts become relevant within the context of criminal law, it is important to make sure that in the course of interlinking and implementing the planned (specialized) victim–offender mediation institutions, prosecutors and judges are included, and that the judiciary and the mediators are permanently in contact with one another.

It appears problematic to go further by demanding which institutions specialize exclusively in settling conflicts between intimates, because this might result in additional hindrance to the allocation of cases by the judiciary. The more complicated the choice of cases and measures, the more difficult the practical settlement, and the less likely the judiciary's willingness to co-operate. Since up to now the main reason for the rare use of reconciliation and victim–offender mediation in penal proceedings is connected with the judiciary's conduct of allocation, the creation of further specialized institutions does not appear to be worthy of recommendation.

Specialization could rather be implemented at the level of the mediating institutions themselves. Therefore, legal aid services and independent institutions which have already carried out victim–offender mediation in the past or plan its implementation in the future have to be considered. But the main problem to be expected in the course of testing a settlement of violent conflicts in partnerships lies not in an insufficient number of mediators, but in existing ways of handling the problem: police officers do not take it seriously, and even now prosecutors and judges rarely apply for compensation in criminal law and under para. 46a StGB. In addition, decisions such as discharging the proceedings without consequences (para. 170 II, para. 153 StPO) or referring to private prosecution are very time-saving, and a settlement of conflicts delays termination insofar as the period which is necessary for the attempt at mediation has to be awaited. Only by a laborious process of convincing and establishing a consciousness of the problem can a change in the prosecutors' and judges' attitude be achieved.

The way in which the pilot project in Hannover connects the institutions and authorities involved is exemplary and can be taken as a model.

Suggestions for implementing victim–offender mediation in cases of violence in partnerships in practice

It is suggested that the two following pilot schemes are put to a practical test.

Specialized victim–offender mediation concept

Existing institutions are able to carry out victim–offender mediation in cases of violence in partnerships as well as those they currently conduct. Since some experience is already available, special features do not arise in cases that do not feature long-term conflicts, and if no former offences are reported. In such cases mediation is essentially restricted to the settlement of the conflict arising from the offence under discussion.

Serious conflict situations, however, require a special procedure that takes particular difficulties into consideration. Following the Austrian experience, if both parties are in principle ready to attempt mediation, two mediators should carry out the reconciliation. They should take into account the fact that behind the visible conflict there is a great number of further, unreported offences and injuries requiring longer and more frequent discussions. Particular attention should be drawn to the – probably – weaker position of the woman, who is, as a rule, the weaker part of a violent relationship. The frequently-advocated principle of neutrality and impartiality can be restricted if the mediators do not want to become accomplices of the violent man. Attempts should be made to link the current procedure with institutions offering help and advice for victim and offender. This should be supported actively, taking into account the problematic nature of the relationship. Direct conversations with the participation of victim and offender are to be considered as well as indirect mediation, in the course of which the victim does not meet the offender. Furthermore, one should think about providing for follow-ups, for example by means of coming to an agreement with the victim in case the offender uses force once again.

Confrontation of the offender/settlement of conflicts without the victim meeting the offender

One variation is to confront the offender with the victim's point of view and with his own violent behaviour without including the victim herself in the mediation. All-male discussions as well as mediating organizations might be considered if the victim is not ready for reconciliation, or has already split up with the offender and does not want to meet him again.

Even though a legal order does in principle require voluntary participation on the part of the offender, it seems to be important that limited voluntary participation under the pressure of the criminal law is sufficient, and that the institutions who have been instructed to seek their help by the prosecution or the court are willing to advise men. Practical experiences show that most violent men do not participate in purely voluntary offers, and for this reason a proposal made by the prosecutor or the judge is a sensible compromise.

Excursus: conferences

The third model scheme chooses another possibility, which seems to be impossible to implement in Germany. The idea of family group conferences and community group conferences (Burford and Pennel 1996; Pennel and Burford 1997) comes from New Zealand, Australia and Newfoundland/Canada. It does not use the power of the criminal law, but the power of the public and the social milieu in order to ensure the protection of the victim and to avoid recidivism. Especially where the delicate subject of sexual abuse of children, the abuse of children and domestic violence/violence between spouses is concerned, the offence is made public in family or group conferences, which take place in the offender's municipality or place of residence. Without the intervention of the criminal law, but with the participation of official authorities (youth office, organizations protecting children, probation office, court social workers, victim assistance, to an extent the police), an open discussion about the deed which the offender is accused of takes place. The objectives are to bring the offence out into the open, to rehabilitate the victim, to guarantee their future protection, and to elaborate a plan in which control mechanisms are laid down that make it impossible for the offender to repeat the offence. All this is *not* about criminal conviction. Offenders attend these conferences voluntarily, because they are interested in the outcome as a matter of course. Nobody is forced to participate. This procedure carries the fascinating thought that the intimacy imposed by the offender upon the victim, which often makes it impossible for them to escape from the situation, is broken by means of solidarity and support. Especially for offences of family violence, in which the prosecuting authorities take a passive stance and the victims are disastrously dependent on the offender, a counter-power seems to be able to put protection and rehabilitation for the victims into practice. Of course, the disadvantage of such a counter-power is to be seen in the fact that a formal framework protecting constitutional rights (such as, for example, criminal proceedings founded on the constitutional rules of law) is lacking, and that this might result in excessive reactions, false accusations and self-administered justice. Furthermore, the practical implementation appears to be hard to imagine in a society as individualistic as that of Germany.

Changes

As a result, a change in the way the police, the prosecution, and the courts handle the cases is required. The legal structure is already available, especially with regard to para. 46a StGB. The legislator is asked to either abolish private prosecution completely, or to take the offence of battery/assault out of the catalogue of private prosecution offences. If prevention of violence and prosecution of offences of violence are given a high priority, this is incompatible with classifying assault as being an offence of private prosecution, the pursuit of which is not in the public interest.

Violence in partnerships is particularly problematic. Criminal law is no panacea for solving all social problems. Victims who turn to the police and the judiciary are entitled to state protection just as much as children who live in a violent family situation. Domestic violence is no private affair. Non-intervention has unfortunate negative side effects and causes new and renewed victimization. Criminal law in a modern society provides a large number of formal and informal responses. The idea of mediation deserves increased attention because it meets people's needs. The arguments that police and criminal justice practitioners are not social workers and not meant to solve private conflicts are wrong. Legal intervention has long included a wide area of discretionary decisions. The 'harsh legal sanction' of imprisonment is the exception, and a prison sentence itself is not free of socio-educational interventions, as the existence of conditions and instructions of probation proves.

The idea that families are supposed to solve their conflicts themselves fails in cases where serious offences of violence become known to the prosecution authorities, where children are subject to such events, and where victims are – for reasons already well known – unable to help themselves and thus rightly expect state support. Mediation has been part of the legal response for a long time, and since 1994, when para. 46a StGB came into force, it has become a rule of general criminal law, by means of which the legislator has made it clear that mediation is one of the tasks of criminal law and has to be taken into account on all procedural levels. Towards the end of 1999, the legislator again strengthened victim–offender mediation by a new procedural act. It is only the force of tradition and the fact that application of the rule is not *compulsory* which has so far prevented a broad – but at any time possible – application of victim–offender mediation.

Even if, in view of this difficult problem, not every case can be solved by mediation, the objective of criminal law – namely restoration of peace under the law – demands that every effort be made to achieve a settlement of conflicts which protects the victims and prevents the offenders from recidivism (for further information see Bannenberg *et al.* 1999).

References

Bannenberg, B. (1993) *Wiedergutmachung in der Strafrechtspraxis*, Bonn.

Bannenberg, B., Weitekamp, E., Rössner, D. and Kerner, H.-J. (1999) *Mediation bei Gewaltstraftaten in Paarbeziehungen*. Baden-Baden.

Beulke, W. (1995) *Gewalt im sozialen Nahraum. Forschungsbericht.* Passau.

Bohrn, F. (1997) 'Familiale Gewalt in Österreich' in Th. Feltes (ed.): *Gewalt in der Familie – ein polizeiliches Problem?*

Braithwaite, J. (1989) *Crime, Shame and Reintegration*. Cambridge.

Braithwaite, J. (1995) 'Diversion, Reintegrative Shaming and Republican Criminology' in G. Albrecht and W. Ludwig-Mayerhofer (eds): *Diversion and Informal Social Control*. Berlin.

Buchwald, B., Kilian, B. (1997) Das Battered Woman Syndrom in Th. Feltes (ed.) *Gewalt in der Familie – ein polizeiliches Problem?*

Burford, G. and Pennell, J. (1996) Family Group Decision Making: New Roles for "Old" Partners in Resolving Family Violence. Implementation Report Summary. Institute of Social and Economic Research. Memorial University of Newfoundland. St. Johns NF, Canada.

Dölling, D. *et al.* (1998) in BMJ (ed.): *Täter-Opfer-Ausgleich in Deutschland. Bestandsaufnahmen und Perspektiven.* Bonn.

Garner, J. and Fagan, J. (1997) 'Victims of Domestic Violence' in R. C. Davis, A. J. Lurigio, and W. G. Skogan (eds), *Victims of Crime* (2nd edn). Thousand Oaks, 53–85.

Greenfield, L. A. *et al.*, (1998) *Violence by Intimates: Analysis of Data on Crimes by Current or Former Spouses, Boyfriends and Girlfriends.* U.S. Department of Justice.

Hagemann-White, C. (1992) *Strategien gegen Gewalt im Geschlechterverhältnis.* Pfaffenweiler.

Hartmann, A., and Stroezel, H. (1998) 'Die Bundesweite TOA-Statistik' in D. Dölling, *et al.* (eds) BMJ *Täter-Opfer-Ausgleich in Deutschland. Bestandsaufnahmen und Perspektiven.* Bonn.

Mahrer, K. (1997) 'Polizei und Gewalt in der Familie' in Th. Feltes (ed.): *Gewalt in der Familie – ein polizeiliches Problem?*

Matt, E. (1997) 'Täter-Opfer-Ausgleich und "Reintegration Ceremony" ', *Monatsschrift für Kriminologie und Strafrechtsreform*, 1997(4): 255–267.

Pennell, J. and Burford, G. (1997) *Family Group Decision Making: After the Conference – Progress in Resolving Violence and Promoting Well-Being*. St. Johns Newfoundland, Canada.

Rössner, D. (1993) 'Wiedergutmachung als Aufgabe der Strafrechtspflege. Auswertung des Tübinger Gerichtshilfe-Projekts und kriminalpolitische Folgerungen' in R.-D. Hering and D. Rössner (eds) *Täter-Opfer-Ausgleich im allgemeinen Strafrecht*, Bonn.

Rössner, D. (1996) *AK-StPO, Kommentar zur Strafprozeßordnung*, Bd. 3, 5. Buch, paras 374–406, Beteiligung des Verletzten am Verfahren.

Schall, H., Schirrmacher, G. (1995) *Gewalt gegen Frauen und Möglichkeiten staatlicher Intervention*. Stuttgart.

Schneider, U. (1987) *Körperliche Gewaltanwendung in der Familie*. Berlin.

Schneider, U. (1993) 'Gewalt in der Familie. Grundformen, Verbreitung, Auswirkungen, Ursachen, Vorbeugung' in *Der Bürger im Staat*.

Schwind, H.-D., et al. (eds) (1990) *Ursachen, Prävention und Kontrolle von Gewalt*. Gewaltkommission, Bd. I-IV, Berlin.

Steck, P., Matthes, B., Wenger de Chávez, C. and Sauter, K. (1997) 'Tödlich endende Partnerkonflikte', *Monatsschrift für Kriminologie und Strafrechtsreform* 1997(6): 404–21.

Steffen, W., Polz, S. (1991) *Familienstreitigkeiten und Polizei*. München: Bayerisches Landeskriminalamt.

Straus, M. A. and Gelles, R. J. and Steinmetz, S. (1980) *Behind Closed Doors. Violence in American Families*. New York.

Straus, M. A. and Gelles, R. J. (1988) *Intimate Violence*. New York.

Straus, M. A. and Gelles, R. J. (1990) *Physical Violence in American Families. Risk Factors and Adoptions to Violence in 8, 145 Families*. New Brunswick.

United Nations (1993) *Strategies for Confronting Domestic Violence: A Resource Manual*. New York.

Weidner, J. (1990) *Anti-Aggressivitätstraining für Gewalttäter*. 2. Foroum Bad Godesberg. Bonn.

Weidner, J. (1993) 'Handlungskonzepte und Praxiserfahrung. Tatverarbeitung von Gewalttaten: Die Täter in E. Marks, K. Meyer, J. Schreckling and M. Wandrey, (eds) *Wiedergutmachung und Strafrechtspraxis*. Bonn.

Wetzels, P. and Pfeiffer, C. (1995) *Sexuelle Gewalt gegen Frauen im öffentlichen und privaten Raum – Ergebnisse der KFN-Opferbefragung 1992* – KFN-Forschungsberichte Nr. 37.

Chapter 4

Conflict resolution and peer mediation: a pilot programme in Munich secondary schools

Susanne Nothhafft

Evolution

Empirical experience

In the early nineties the *Fachstelle für Täter-Opfer-Ausgleich und Konfliktschlichtung of the Brücke e.V. in Munich* (which runs a programme of victim–offender reconciliation) noticed an increasing number of cases concerning criminal offences in or near schools (in school buildings, on playgrounds, on the way to school). All types of schools (primary, secondary and high school) were represented in this. The offences committed involved mainly bodily harm, sometimes sexual harassment. Legal action was usually instituted by the school teachers or the headteacher, rarely by the victims or their parents. This call for formal proceedings often expressed the wish to put an end to a situation which had got out of control. Nearly all criminal acts arose out of ongoing conflict whose escalation was not prevented at an early stage. In the end a report to the police seemed to be the only and necessary consequence. In this situation the offenders described their experience of being excluded and stigmatized as the usual reaction to any form of their rule-breaking. Some of the victims, however, reported that their complaints were not taken seriously by their teachers so that they felt rejected and left alone.

Until the end of the eighties the question of whether and how much in-school violence actually occurs was a kind of taboo in Germany.[1] Schools as well as education authorities were worried about their reputation. Even in the seventies the media had spread disturbing news about dramatically increasing violence in schools in the United States. But in 'continental' terms isolationism was the byword. In the nineties the media finally began to take up the issue, focusing on the national phenomenon of increasing violence in schools. Since then we have had a number of serious studies dating from the nineties which do not altogether corroborate the media reports. Similar to the Anglo-American discussion on schools as a microcosm of society (where the violence in society is brought into schools) *vs.* schools as 'safe havens' (from society) where very little violence occurs,[2] there is also disagreement in the national surveys over how much in-school violence actually takes place.

Overall the mediators of the *Fachstelle* got the impression that either repressive or neglectful answers were given to the issue of violence in schools. They therefore devised a sustained, prevention-oriented programme of alternative dispute resolution, especially adapted to the basic conditions in schools.

Contents of the programme

The programme is composed of different building blocks comprising several target groups; the building blocks of the programme are illustrated in Figure 4.1.

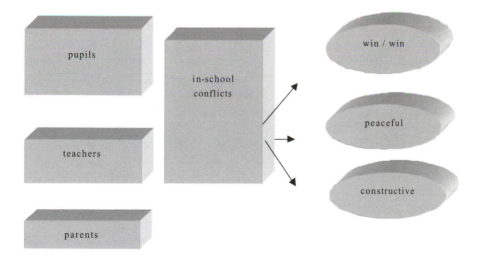

Figure 4.1   Prevention-oriented dispute-resolution programme for schools

Pupils are represented as the largest target group because the programme provides the most time for concentrated work with pupils. As regards content, the programme deals with in-school conflicts that affect the well-being of at least one side and disturb the joint structuring of (everyday) school-life (see Figure 4.2). The programme is based on the premise that, *per se*, conflicts appear wherever people interact. This is especially true for (secondary) schools. All participants are different in sex, age, origin and background and have dissimilar experiences, needs and objectives. Conflicts arise quite naturally from this mixture. This need not necessarily be regarded as disturbing, threatening or destructive. On the contrary, the occurrence of conflicts also express the existence of communication, change and evolution. Conflicts offer learning and growth potential to those who are looking for creative and constructive ways of resolving disputes. The objective of the programme, therefore, is to open to pupils, educators and parents new kinds of dispute resolution that are constructive, peaceful and oriented towards win–win solutions without anybody being perceived as being the loser.

In order to develop a constructive in-school culture of resolving disputes, the programme originally provided the following tools.

Class council/conference[3]

Class conferences offer a recurrent structure (once a week or twice a month) with which to reflect the actual atmosphere in class. Regular

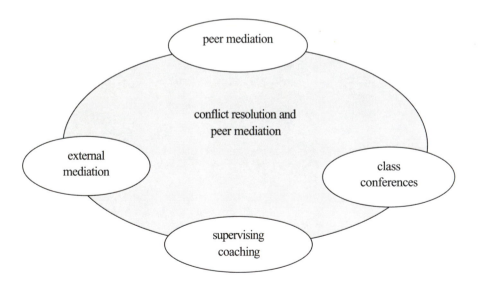

Figure 4.2 Contents of dispute-resolution programme

sessions can be a seismograph for interference. The class conference is prepared and conducted by classmates.

Supervising/coaching
This is an offer to educators – teachers and parents – to work on actual in-school conflicts within a proper structure. Individual behaviour and patterns of conflict-solving will be analysed. Action and reaction will be examined on the basis of system theory. If necessary, alternative ways of behaviour will be developed.

External mediation
External mediation opens up the opportunity to engage in alternative dispute resolution outside of the school system. This kind of offer might be helpful if in-school conflicts have seriously escalated and hardened to the point that an external (with regard to the system) mediator is required.

Peer mediation
Pupils of classes 5 to 9 will be trained as peer mediators, taking into account, among other things, the experience that juveniles are much more oriented towards their peers than towards adults/educators as far as attitudes and behaviour are concerned. Peer modelling will be used to develop social skills. The programme should only include pupils who volunteered for the training. Moreover, the training group should consider not only pupils who are regarded as rich in social skills but especially those who are often regarded as the troublemakers or who are more introverted. The peer mediation programme consists of two modules, shown in Figure 4.3.

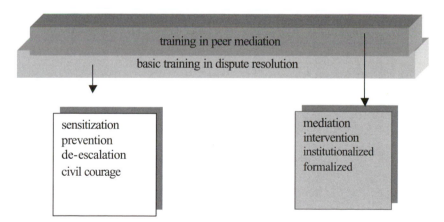

Figure 4.3   Modules of the peer mediation programme

The basic training in dispute resolution consists of several building blocks presented in two units. It provides a sensitization for (possible) conflict situations and the basis for co-operative conflict resolution. Practice, role-playing and group discussions deal with perception/awareness – experience of and conduct in conflicts – skills in conflict resolution – communication skills – (development of) empathy – (development of) tolerance – positive attitudes towards conflicts and a win–win conflict resolution (see Figure 4.4).

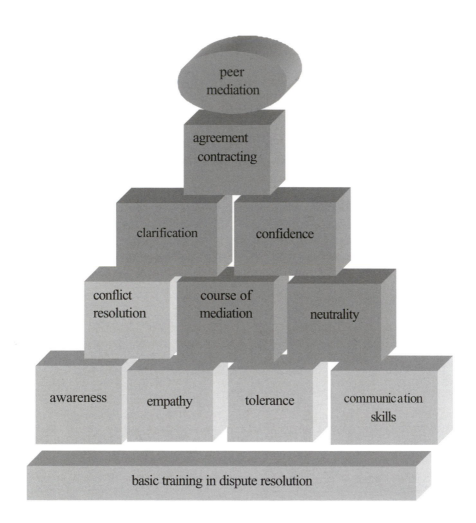

Figure 4.4   Basic training in conflict resolution

The purpose of the basic training is to develop with the pupils tools for acting constructively in conflict situations and thereby avoid escalation. The basic training has a strong preventive impetus.

The peer mediation training builds on the basic training. The main focus here lies in learning about the course of mediation procedure, the rules and the mediator's role. Peer mediation focuses on concrete mediation as an intervention. It should become part of everyday school life and therefore be an institutionalized and formalized procedure.

Implementation

The implementation of the programme proved to be rather difficult politically.

The concept of a programme on conflict resolution and peer mediation in schools (*Konfliktbehandlung an Schulen*) was presented to the Bavarian Ministry of Education and the Arts at the beginning of 1995. It took over two years of persuasion to get permission to start a pilot programme in Munich secondary schools.

The city council of Munich approved funding for one post in 1997. To guarantee the co-operative structure for the training provided in the scheme, the post was split in two halves. As a consequence, the number of schools joining the programme had to be reduced to four secondary schools (two *Hauptschulen*, two *Realschulen*).

The Bavarian Ministry of Education and the Arts had reservations concerning the work of external trainers in school and the provision of training units during lessons. Despite the active interest of many secondary schools the pilot programme therefore could not start until the beginning of 1998 – with an agreement as follows.

The basic training in conflict resolution could take place during *Projekttagen* (experience-oriented practice lessons as part of the curriculum, six to eight lessons a school day with free structuring by the school) – tolerated but not authorized by the Ministry of Education and the Arts – with the class teacher as observer (if requested by the pupils, the teacher would leave the room for a while to guarantee a confidential setting). The peer-mediation training had to be carried out after school in the afternoon.

Running of the pilot programme

The pilot programme concerning conflict resolution and peer mediation finally consisted of several modules (see Figure 4.5) that were tailor-made into an individual programme for each school.

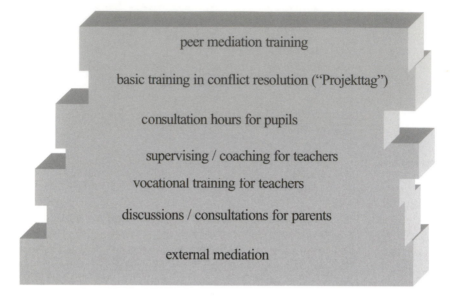

peer mediation training

basic training in conflict resolution ("Projekttag")

consultation hours for pupils

supervising / coaching for teachers

vocational training for teachers

discussions / consultations for parents

external mediation

Figure 4.5 Conflict resolution and peer mediation – pilot programme in seven schools, 15–20 training units per school

The class council/conference was to be introduced or existed already and was in the charge of the class teachers. The participation of external trainers does not seem to be necessary and is often not possible for reasons of time, because the class council should be held at least twice a month. It should be part of practising democracy in school.

In 1998 the module requested most was the basic training in conflict resolution (e.g. see Table 4.1) (two school days of at least six lessons). For each class an individual schedule was drawn up. For that reason it was necessary to begin with an analysis of the situation and the conditions in class in cooperation with the class teacher (standardized analysis sheet/ discussion). This analysis was followed by a visit to the class just to present the basic training programme in general, and for the trainers to become acquainted with the pupils of the class (one to two lessons). Recurring objectives were communication and cooperation – sense of community – conflict culture – how to fight/argue non-violently – conflicts between certain in-class groups – conflicts between boys and girls.

Whenever needed, activities, games or relaxation exercises were done. Video-taping was often used to initiate a feedback structure.

While the first unit of the basic training often focused on actual in-class conflicts and the sense of community in class, the second unit dealt with the development and the practice of alternative, non-violent conflict

Table 4.1. Example of a timetable (mediogram) for basic training – first unit (7th year)

Time	Content	Method	Objective	Materials
8.00–8.15	Arrival Welcome Contracting the rules	Nameplates Input Poster	Joint basis for work	Stickers Poster
8.15–8.30	Warming up	Game	Get active Discover common ground	
8.30–10.00	Class activity	Memory game (to be partnered) Interviews (peer to peer) Sociogram (plenary)	Perception of structures and relations in class Positioning Sensitivities	Memory cards Interview sheets 'People' 'Smiley-buttons'
10.00–10.30	Break			
10.30–11.30	In-class conflict	Small group	Clearing Empathy	Cards
11.30–13.00	Conflict resolution Contracting	Plenary Reports Discussion	Consent Agreement about further dealings	Poster

resolution, perception and communication skills (discussion groups, role-playing, interactive games, feedback, video taping – in a plenary or a small group structure).

The peer mediation training (peer mediation training: five schools with 14–15 pupils per school) was based on the basic training and put the main emphasis on the learning of the mediation proceedings, the rules and the understanding of the mediator's role (confidence, neutrality, empower-ment, autonomy of the parties). The training itself was experience-oriented with an increasingly inductive structure. Sometimes it was organized as a one-week unit, sometimes held in regularly recurring training units over a longer period; however, it never comprised less than 24 lessons. After finishing the peer mediation training, every participant received a certificate. Every group of peer mediators in the pilot programme wanted to design a visiting card identifying them as mediators. To support this team-building process and the creation of a corporate identity among the team of mediators is important; moreover, enough time should be provided for reflection about how to establish and introduce peer mediation in a specific school. Following the training, a reflecting and counselling structure has to be set up for the peer mediators in the form of, for example, monthly meetings with a teacher (and if necessary one of the trainers) as a coach.

The vocational training for teachers provides the opportunity to get to know the core concepts of system philosophy, conflict theory and conflict analysis, and to become better acquainted with their own experience in conflicts (in-school and external). The contents of the training sessions are to be suited to the needs of the teaching staff.

Supervising and coaching is a chance to exchange experiences, to discuss individual cases, and to attain an adequate level of self-reflection in an instructive setting. (Vocational training and supervisory sessions took place in eight schools.)

The discussion and consultation planned for parents had to be limited to parents' evenings to disseminate the idea of peer mediation and to inform parents about planned or current training in their school. This restriction resulted from the trainers' limited time and insufficient interest shown by the parents – even when the discussions were held in several different languages. (Parents' evenings were held in two schools.)

External mediation

In 1998 and 1999 there was an increasing demand for conflict resolution and peer mediation in Munich schools. To meet that demand the scheme was developed as a training programme for trainers (one psychologist or social worker and one teacher to form a pair of trainers per school). By 2001, each secondary school in Munich should have had a peer mediation programme set up.

Research findings – summary

Research profile

The data gathering has been finished only recently, so only preliminary findings can be presented here. The research was conceived as assessment and evaluation. The methodology consisted of observation, standardized questionnaires and group discussion.

Pupils

It was especially in so-called 'schools at risk' that the pupils were very seriously engaged in the training programme, even investing their leisure time. We had no drop-outs.

The training groups were composed of pupils of very different ethnic and social backgrounds, often with problematic biographies (civil war refugees, asylum seekers, multi-problem families). We found good social skills (such as empathy, sociability, active listening). Therefore the trainers worked more and more inductively; the phases and rules of mediation were derived from actual in-school conflicts, reprocessed in role-playing with less theoretical input and more sustained feedback structures. Pupils in secondary schools are more oriented to act than to assimilate situations cognitively. The experience-oriented attempt suited them very well. The pupils were able to evolve their own language for mediation. The rules and the interventions of mediation were all translated into their own empirical and linguistic context.

The basic training was widely accepted and found to be useful (girls appreciate it more than do boys). The pupils liked having the time to work on conflicts in a non-repressive way and expressing themselves in a setting where confidentiality was guaranteed by the external status of the trainers.

As far as the peer mediation training was concerned, a sufficient number of participants volunteered in every school. Nevertheless, when the pupils of the classes participating in the basic training were asked how they assessed the possibilities of peer mediation, some made sceptical comments: 'mediators will not be taken seriously' – 'a third party should not interfere' – 'if I go to the mediator I might show that I cannot cope with a situation' – 'problems must be solved on one's own'. Once a peer-mediation programme was set up, pupils of the 5th, 6th and 7th years used the offer more than pupils of higher classes.

Initially, the initiative for calling on peer mediation came mainly from a teacher or a mediator who noticed a conflict/fight and raised the possibility of peer mediation. Most of the mediations ended up in an agreement. We found a high rate of satisfaction with the outcomes of mediation among the parties of the conflict. In nearly all schools about a year was needed to integrate peer mediation into everyday school life. After that period, we had peer mediation running with about five mediations per week in most of the schools. A high consensus among the teachers for the support of the peer mediation programme was an important factor in its success.

Teachers

The teachers as a rule were very satisfied with the basic training in conflict resolution and the peer mediation training. They noticed an improvement in the sense of community in class. They appreciated the opportunity to hand over a part of their responsibility to pupils trained in conflict resolution. They felt relieved of the necessity to intervene in any sort of conflict. Very few experienced the delegation of competence as questioning or threatening their role. Referring especially to the coaching and counselling (and its confidential setting) they enjoyed no longer being a 'single combatant'.

Satisfaction with the conduct of the training programme

As far as the satisfaction with the running of the programme is concerned, the results of the group discussions and the answers to questionnaires were unanimous. Pupils as well as teachers were very satisfied with the programme and its modules. The fact that the work was done by external trainers was highly valued – the teachers felt relieved they did not have to tackle a topic they did not feel well prepared for, and the pupils enjoyed the confidential setting.

Effects of the training programme on moral and social skills

While in the group discussions the effects of the basic and the peer-mediation training were assessed very positively by both teachers and pupils, the results of the questionnaires (handed out to the pupils) were more mixed. For example, the use of physical force as a means of conflict resolution was only accepted by about a quarter of the pupils, before as well as after the running of the programme. Social and communicative skills were assessed positively by about three-quarters of the pupils, both before and after the programme. Throughout the questionnaires, the only actual difference to be found was between the answers of boys and girls. For example, three-quarters of the girls disapproved of physical force as a means of conflict resolution, but only about one-half of the boys. More than four-fifths of the girls valued social and communicative skills, but only two-thirds of the boys.

Training in conflict resolution and peer mediation should therefore include sex-specific units (for example sex-specific small groups and discussions) and should also work on sex-role stereotypes.

In-school structure

The more the school has already introduced elements of democracy, co-determination, self-responsibility and participation of the pupils, the more staff and trainers analyse the actual in-school situation and define the contents of co-operation

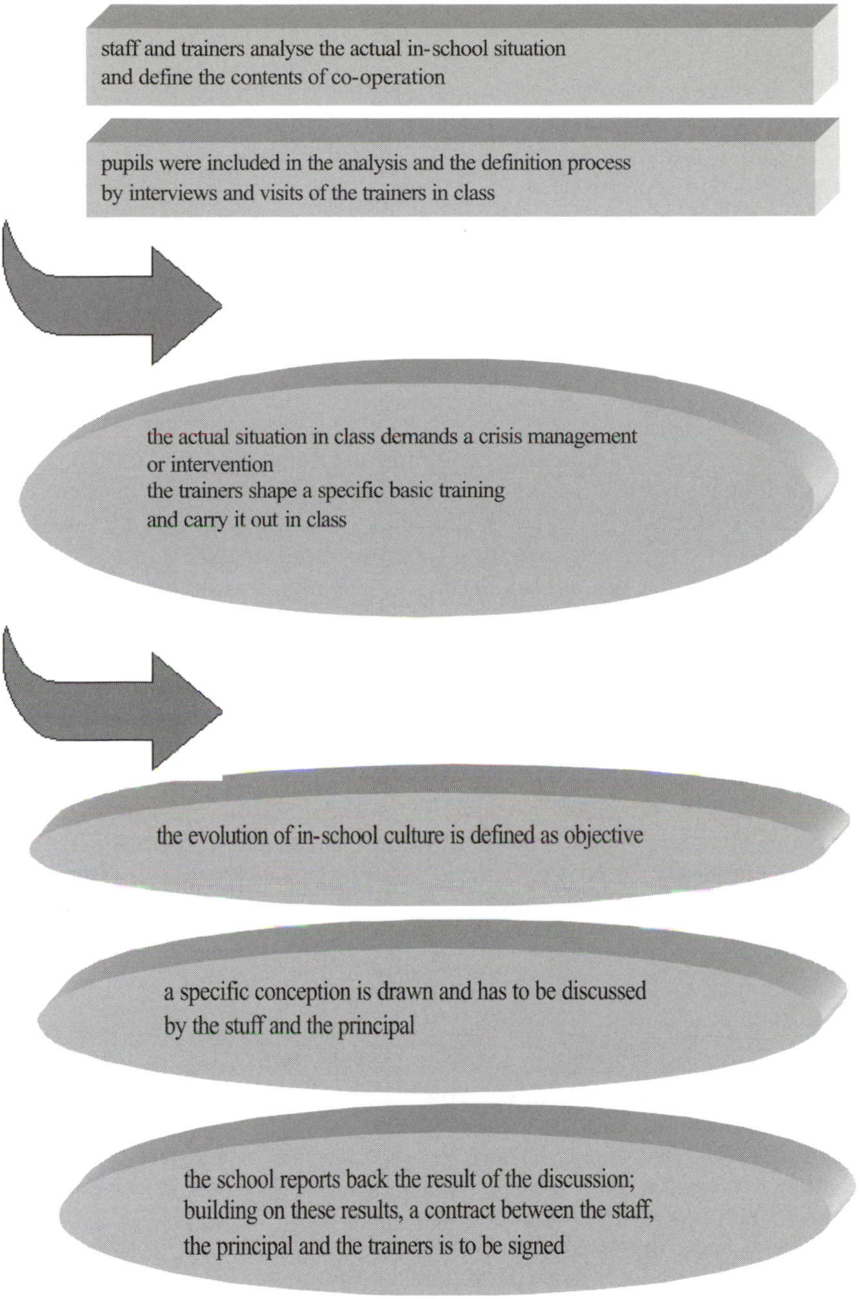

pupils were included in the analysis and the definition process by interviews and visits of the trainers in class

the actual situation in class demands a crisis management or intervention
the trainers shape a specific basic training
and carry it out in class

the evolution of in-school culture is defined as objective

a specific conception is drawn and has to be discussed by the stuff and the principal

the school reports back the result of the discussion;
building on these results, a contract between the staff,
the principal and the trainers is to be signed

Figure 4.6 Conditions for the introduction of a dispute resolution programme in schools

competent in social skills the pupils are and the more successfully a programme of alternative dispute resolution and peer mediation can be installed.

To develop a peaceful, constructive and win–win in-school culture of conflict resolution the occasional carrying out of some of the modules offered by the pilot programme is not enough. Alternative dispute resolution has to be embedded in a comprehensive concept that is supported by all participants and which tends to change in-school culture for the longer term. One result of the assessment was therefore to modify the programme to give it a strong focus on preparation for implementing an alternative dispute resolution programme and on the need for an explicit request by the school that is to be done (see Figure 4.6).

Outcome in general

Peer mediation programmes are proliferating but they are no panacea. They are not effective if they are introduced as a veneer of democracy in schools or because one wants to be *à la mode*. They have vital effects if the staff and the pupils of a school are open to letting their in-school structure and system of relations evolve. Understood in this sense, the installation of a peer mediation programme is upsetting (in the best sense) and challenging, but it is worthwhile. Pupils – especially in so-called 'schools at risk' – do manage and use peer mediation.

Despite the divergence of the subjective assessments of the effects of the pilot programme and the measurement in the questionnaires, we hold peer mediation to be an important instrument in developing moral and civil identity. We have extensive empirical literature on positive long-term effects of youth activism.[4] Participation develops a sense of responsibility and helps to identify with the community.[5] Therefore participation should be the keyword for a new millennium.

Notes

1. Schwind, H.-D., Roitsch, K., Gielen, B. (1997) 'Prävention in der Schule. Handlungskonzepte und "Tips" für die Praxis' in R. Northoff (ed.) *Handbuch der Kriminalprävention*, Baden-Baden.
2. Johnson, D., Johnson, R. (1996) 'Conflict Resolution and Peer Mediation Programs in Elementary and Secondary Schools: A Review of the Research' *Review of Education Research*, 66(4) 461 f.
3. Gordon, T. (1992) *Lehrer-Schüler-Konferenz*, München.
4. Youniss, J. *et al.* (1997) *Community Service and Social Responsibility in Youth*, Chicago: University of Chicago Press.
5. Gross, M. (1997) *Ethics and Activism*, New York: Cambridge University Press.

References

Akademie für Lehrerfortbildung (2000) *Wenn zwei sich streiten. Jugendliche vermitteln in Konflikten*, Dillingen.

Araki, C. (1990) Dispute Management in the Schools, *Mediation Quarterly*, 8(1), 51–62.

Bonafé-Schmitt, J. (1997) *La Médiation Scolaire. Etude comparative France-Etats-Unis*, Lyon.

Faller K. *et al.* (1996) *Konflikte selber lösen – ein Trainingshandbuch für Mediation und Konfliktmanagement in Schule und Jugendarbeit*, Mühlheim/Ruhr.

Fuchs, M. *et al.* (1996) *Schule und Gewalt. Realität und Wahrnehmung eines sozialen Problems*, Opladen.

Gordon, T. (1992) *Lehrer-Schüler-Konferenz*, München.

Gross, M. (1997) *Ethics and Activism*, New York: Cambridge University Press.

Hagedorn, O. (1995) *Konfliktlotsen-Unterrichtsideen*, Stuttgart.

Hale, C. et al. (1997) Achieving Neutrality and Impartiality: The Ultimate Communication Challenge for Peer Mediators, *Mediation Quarterly*, 14(4), 337–352.

Hinsch, R. *et al.* (1998) *Gewalt in der Schule*. Landau: Materialien.

Holtappels, H. *et al.* (eds) (1997) *Forschung über Gewalt an Schulen. Erscheinungen und Ursachen, Konzepte und Prävention*, Weinheim.

Institut National de Recherche Pédagogique (1998) 'La Violence à l'École: Approches Européennes' in *Revue Française de Pédagogie*, 123.

Jefferys K. *et al.* (1995) *Streiten. Vermitteln. Lösen – Das Schüler-Streit-Schlichter-Programm für die Klassen 5–10*, Lichtenau.

Johnson, D. *et al.* (1996) Conflict Resolution and Peer Mediation Programs in Elementary and Secondary Schools: A Review of the Research, *Review of Education Research*, 66(4); 459–506.

Johnson, D. *et al.* (1997) The Impact of Conflict Resolution Training on Middle School Students, *The Journal of Social Psychology*, 137(1); 11–21.

Levy, J. (1989) Conflict Resolution in Elementary and Secondary Education, *Mediation Quarterly*, 7(1); 73–87.

Lürse, D. *et al.* (1995) *Zivilcourage. Anleitung zum kreativen Umgang mit Konflikten und Gewalt*, Münster.

Maxwell, J. (1990) Mediation in Schools: Self-Regulation, Self-Esteem, Self-Discipline, *Mediation Quarterly*, 7(2); 149–155.

Pedersen, P. *et al.* (1994) *Multicultural Counselling in Schools. A Practical Handbook*, Boston.

Rademacher, H. *et al.* (1991) *Spiele und Übungen zum interkulturellen Lernen*, Berlin.

Sadalla, G. *et al.* (1990) *Conflict Resolution. An Elementary School Curriculum*, San Francisco.

Schubarth, W. *et al.* (eds) (1996) *Gewalt an Schulen. Ausmaß, Bedingungen, Prävention*. Opladen.

Schwind, H. *et al.* (1997) 'Prävention in der Schule. Handlungskonzepte und "Tips" für die Praxis' in R. Northoff (ed.): *Handbuch der Kriminalprävention*, Teil 31; Baden-Baden, 1–31.

Stevahn, L. *et al.* (1996) Effects on Highschool Students of Integrating Conflict Resolution Training and Peer Mediation Training into an Academic Unit, *Mediation Quarterly*, 14(1); 21–36.

Stevahn, L. *et al.* (1997) Effects on High School Students of Conflict Resolution Training Integrated Into English Literature, *The Journal of Social Psychology*, 137(3); 302–315.

Tennstädt, K. *et al.* (1992) *Das Konstanzer Trainingsmodell (KTM). Neue Wege im Schulalltag. Ein Selbsthilfeprogramm, vol.* 1–4, Bern.

Tillman, K. *et al.* (1999) *Schülergewalt als Schulproblem. Verursachende Bedingungen, Erscheinungsformen und pädagogische Handlungsperspektiven*, Weinheim.

Walker, J. (1993) 'Gewaltfreie Konfliktaustragung lernen – aber wie? Erfahrungen an einer Grundschule in Berlin-Kreuzberg' in M. Spreiter (ed.) *Waffenstillstand im Klassenzimmer*, Weinheim.

Walker, J. (1995) *Gewaltfreier Umgang mit Konflikten – Sekundarstufe (vol. I) – Grundschule (vol. II). Spiele und Übungen*, Frankfurt/Main.

Winter, F. *et al.* (1997) *Jugendliche schlichten. Initiierung eines Konfliktschlichtungsangebots durch jugendliche Schülerinnen und Schüler an ihrer Schule*, Mönchengladbach.

Youniss, J. *et al.* (1997) *Community Service and Social Responsibility in Youth*, Chicago: University of Chicago Press.

Chapter 5

How restorative justice is able to transcend the prison walls: a discussion of the 'restorative detention' project

Luc Robert and Tony Peters

Since the beginning of 1998, a 'restorative detention' pilot project has been active in six Belgian prisons. In 2000, more quickly than expected, the policy makers saw to it that the restorative detention project had taken root in the Belgian penal establishment as a whole. Given its all-inclusive history and due to a lack of space, here we will only briefly sketch the start-up and development of the 'restorative detention' project.[1]

The project name itself, 'Restorative Detention', seems to embrace a contradiction in terms.[2] It is also clear that the introduction to, and the underlying vision for, such a 'provocative' project require explanation. This is done in the first part of this chapter. A second part sheds light on a few aspects of the purpose of the pilot project. To provide the discussion of the project with more substance, we will then focus our attention on a range of activities at the level of the prison, and conclude with a few further considerations.

The contextual framework of the 'restorative detention'[3] project

This project did not appear out of the blue, but is situated within a research tradition and a policy on criminality. On the one hand, the project represents a 'logical' step in the development of the research activities at the Katholieke University Leuven (KU Leuven) concerning mediation and restorative justice. On the other hand, external influences play a significant role in the genesis of this research project. Continuous reciprocity between internal and external influences has given the project the form it currently has.

The internal run-up to the project

The initiative for Restorative Detention came from the penology and victimology research group.[4] This somewhat strange sounding combination of punishment-oriented and victim-oriented research is part of a tradition that spans three decades.

In the beginning the scholarly focus of the research group was on studies of the prison system and studies of punishment in general; also – a forerunner of the present attention given to restorative justice initiatives – the (too marginal) use of community sanctions was subjected to critical reflection.

With the study and analysis of violent property crimes, the need arose for victimological research. Beginning in 1986, the victim-oriented approach attracted much attention. Both qualitative and quantitative victimization studies brought into view the problematic position of the victim in the administration of criminal justice. Victims of violent property crime were the particular focus. The judicial marginality of the victim was one of the most important policy themes. One of the first Belgian victimological handbooks received the title 'the reverse side of criminality', due in part to reveal the neglect of the victim (Peters and Goethals 1993).

A shift in the approach taken in research occurred around 1990. Beginning in the 1990s, based upon the experience obtained and findings in victimological research, a more proactive approach was taken. On the one hand, a thematic development of new practices designed to meet the needs of victims was initiated. On the other hand, an examination was made of how criminal prosecution practice can be influenced and how the conventional response to criminality could be challenged.

Action research as a method implied a change in course in the approach to research. Action research is concentrated on the development and evaluation of new practices and is also focused upon the fine tuning or restructuring of existing practices. This allows the researchers to approach the criminal justice system from a more problem-solving point of view. At the same time, this method has also won approval due to its inclusive character. Action research allows several (all) parties to be actively involved in the (search for a) solution to the problem. This method was employed until the end of 2000 and also used in the Restorative Detention project. Here, use was made of previous experience with the action research method.[5]

To better involve the victim in the legal resolution of the offence, among other things an 'offender–victim mediation project' was started at the level of the courts. On 1 January 1993, a 'redress mediation' project was initiated in the legal district of Leuven with the support of the King Baudouin Foundation. After two years of operating as a project, this redress-oriented initiative won the support of the Ministry of Justice. In 1998 it became a national project which, over time, will be introduced into each legal district. Redress mediation was positioned between the public prosecutor and the courts. At the outset the choice was made to work only with relatively serious forms of criminality, and parallel to the criminal proceedings, prior to punishment.

Following the experience with mediation for redress, interest grew among the researchers for a restorative justice approach to punishment, including imprisonment.

Reflections concerning imprisonment led to the realization that while for many years prison had appeared as a last resort in government rhetoric, the actual practice revealed a completely different picture. Many Western countries, especially the USA, have been acquainted with the phenomenon of a 'prison tree' for several years now (Cayley 1998). The administration of criminal justice in Belgium is also far from immune to the excessive use of the deprivation of liberty.

The number of inmates in the Belgian prison system has increased by almost 40 per cent over the last decade. The 1980s were characterized by an average of approximately 6,000 prisoners. During the last 10 years this has increased to approximately 8,500 prisoners. The intake decreased from around 22,000 prisoners per year in the 1980s to 14,000 in the 1990s. From this it can be concluded that the average prison sentence has increased significantly. Suspects are on remand for up to 30 per cent longer, while the group with long prison sentences (more than three years) grows steadily.[6] Thus by no means can we speak of prison as a last resort. Actual practice in Belgium differs little from that in neighbouring countries.

In addition there are many disadvantages associated with imprisonment. A stay in a 'total institution'[7] represents for each detainee a high probability of personal and inter-relational harm. We have in mind the concepts that attempt to grasp these aspects of prison reality such as, for example, *prisonisation* (Clemmer 1940) and the *pains of imprisonment* (Sykes 1958). They leave little to the imagination. In addition, detention also constitutes a large social and economic loss.[8] That is why the research group has for years adhered to a reductionist point of view.[9] For that matter, the bankruptcy of the process of the administration of criminal justice has in recent decades been felt in several countries and has fed the search for alternatives. In this context, restorative justice has recently been introduced as a new and promising perspective.

Among the 'Penology and Victimology' research group, the view is prevalent 'that to deal constructively with criminality an appeal must be made to both the offender and the victim, and that the criminological and the victimological cannot be separated from each other' (Christiaensen, 2001). To that end, answers in the direction of restorative justice constitute the initial pretext for action in the response to criminality. Restorative justice is a remedy for a number of shortcomings in the 'retributive' criminal justice system, which is strongly characterised by a profound dichotomy between offender and victim. This dichotomy still receives its strongest manifestation in the prisons. The societal exclusion of both victim and offender confirms this.

The research group has thus gradually evolved into an integral restorative justice approach to criminality. For the moment, the Restorative Detention project is a final link here. When imprisonment is unavoidable, then the means must still be made available to victim, imprisoned offender, and the broader societal context in which they are located, to search for a constructive – i.e. problem-solving – approach. In other words, restorative justice should not be allowed to end with punishment or at the walls of the prison.

External motivation

The setting up of a project in which restorative justice penetrates the furthest corners of the criminal justice system can be seen as the ultimate test for the restorative justice movement. Such an enterprise only has a chance of success against the background of a policy on criminality that is favourably disposed to restorative justice. Here a short clarification of a few of the steps in restorative justice thinking in the context of Belgian criminality is appropriate.

Before the Dutroux affair took hold of Belgium, the then Minister of Justice had injected new life into the government's discourse on punishment. With his 'Orientation Memorandum on Penal and Prison Policy' of 19 June 1996, the wind suddenly changed direction. The ministerial memorandum made clear the basic objectives of imprisonment (ensuring safe and dignified punishment; preparation for reintegration and the prevention of relapse) and subsequently associated itself with the ideas of restorative justice. At the same time the problematic legal arrangement for prisoners, concerning both their substantive and their formal legal position, was broached and a proposal made to work on a penal principles act.[10]

While the first innovative point will still take some time, penal law has already been thoroughly reconsidered by Dupont. By 30 September 1997, he had already submitted his 'treatise on a preliminary draft of a prison system and execution of detention act' to the Minister of Justice. He proposed as a main objective the *limitation of harm due to detention*. In this approach of limitation of harm, the detainee is able to work on fulfilling other goals such as restoring material and non-material damages resulting from acts committed and the preparation for his or her social reintegration.[11]

These two important documents allow us to deduce that restorative justice thinking is slowly but surely seeping into government discourse. The present Minister of Justice also considers restorative justice to be of paramount importance. In the 'Federal Safety and Detention Plan' of 31 May 2000, he endorses the view that the criminal justice system, including the prison system, must have a restorative orientation across the board (Minister of Justice 2000).

At all levels of the criminal justice machine, for that matter, elements of the system are beginning to demonstrate an affinity for victims. And although the Dutroux affair was a catalyst which has quickened certain developments, many victim-friendly initiatives saw the light of day before August 1996. Thus, article 46 of the Act of 5 August 1992 on the Duties of the Police, for the first time in the history of Belgian police legislation, mentions the task of assisting the victims of criminal offences. The Act of 12 March 1998 improved the position of the victim at the level of the investigation and judicial inquiry.[12] The search for new regulations concerning parole was also begun before the Dutroux crisis, but it certainly received a boost from it. The acts of 5 and 18 March 1998 put into force a more victim-sensitive arrangement for parole.[13] Now a victim must be informed if the offender requests parole. Also the Parole Commissions may consult the victims in reaching a decision regarding the granting of parole, especially when defining the conditions.

This enumeration of shifts in policy on criminality provides the framework in which the restorative detention project saw the light of day. At the same time it demonstrates the setting of the project in a changing approach to punishment. In addition, a number of foreign restorative justice initiatives have already found their way to the 'society of captives'. Among others, the *Wiedergutmachungsprogrammema* of the Swiss penitentiary of Saxerriet (Brenzikofer 1997) and certain Victim Offender Reconciliation Programmes (VORPs) in Canada, England and the USA (Immarigeon 1996) provide examples of a restorative justice approach that transcended the prison walls.

The Restorative Detention project has developed its own character precisely due to the important link with and reciprocity between policy and research.

The purpose of the 'restorative detention' project

On 1 October 1997, a research project was initiated under the name 'Building blocks for a coherent restorative and victim-oriented criminal justice policy' (Peters 1999). Restorative Detention arose from this as sub-project and, from January 1998 on, became an independent project.

From the Ministry of Justice came the request to initiate action research in six Belgian prisons. Researchers from the University of Liège (UdL) were assigned to the prisons of Andenne, Tournai and Jamioulx, while the Penology and Victimology research group launched research activity at three Dutch-speaking prisons, namely Leuven Central, Leuven Auxiliary and the Hoogstraten Penal Educational Centre.[14] The subsequent discussion will focus primarily upon revealing aspects of the action research in the three Flemish prisons.

Before making the leap to action research, restorative justice still needs some conceptual clarification. A strong definition comes from the hand of Tony Marshall: 'Restorative Justice is a process whereby parties with a stake in a specific offence resolve collectively how to deal with the aftermath of the offence and its implications for the future' (Marshall 1998). Restorative justice can thus be understood as 'interaction between offender, victim and society, in which all parties make an effort and an investment in order to arrive at a certain level of pacification via communication' (Vandeurzen *et al.* 1999). The local community, the broader society and the societal institutions (as representative of society) may be constructively involved in this.

Central to the pilot project is the search for an answer to the question concerning how punishment in general and the prison context in particular can contribute to a juster and more balanced administration of criminal justice for offender, victim and society (Christiaensen 2001). This central issue can be reduced to the challenge to give imprisonment a more victim-focused and restorative justice orientation (Christiaensen, Vandeurzen and Verhoeven 2000).

On the Flemish side, the project took the form of action research. The point of departure was always the specific context of each penal institution. The researchers required a good view of the operation of 'their' respective institutions before proposing focused initiatives. Each of the three Dutch-speaking prisons thus functioned as an experimental site for concrete restorative justice initiatives. And that brings us to the importance of the method used.

In action research, the two dimensions of action and research are connected to each other like Siamese twins. The *action* dimension is aimed at the phased or cyclical implementation of change. The *research* dimension is focused upon both the procedure and the result. The action is regularly evaluated and fine-tuned if needed. Action research thus makes it possible to react quickly to changing situations (Aertsen and Peters 1995).

Not only does regular reflection on the action taken form an integral part of this approach to research, but the interaction between theory and practice also contributes to a process of theory formulation.[15] The research has a direct impact on the actors in the field (e.g. prisoners, victims and prison personnel). They are able to gain new (learning) experience, which then affects the pedagogic aspect of action research (Christiaensen 2001).

A double motivation lay behind the choice of the three Flemish penal institutions. First and foremost, it concerns prisons with differing tasks and thus prisons with a specific character. A second decision criterion concerns the existence of a certain level of receptivity (at least on the part of the board) for the idea of 'restorative detention'. Given that in these prisons the ideas concerning a more restorative justice oriented system of detention were able to germinate for two years, a short presentation of the three total institutions involved seems appropriate.

The *Leuven Central Prison* (1860) accommodated 227 convicts and 74 accused at the beginning of the project. Officially, the Central Prison is a 'house of punishment'. The convicted prisoners all have long prison stays. During the day, except for working hours, there is an open door regime. The institution has a level of employment of approximately 70 per cent. A broad range of offerings in the area of sport, relaxation and education seeks to ensure the meaningful use of (free) time (Brouckmans *et al.* 1998; Vandeurzen *et al.* 1999; Christiaensen 2001).

The *Auxiliary Prison of Leuven* (1869) is located only a stone's throw away from the Central Prison. Leuven Auxiliary fulfils the function of a 'house of remand custody', utilizing confinement in cells. This approach allows for little in the way of facilities for communal activities. Change is gradually occurring in this respect, and educational and cultural activities are steadily increasing. The employment possibilities limit the number of employed prisoners to between 35 and 50. The total population of Leuven Auxiliary fluctuates between 135 and 155. The turnover is high. In 1997 there were still 1,005 incoming detainees. The average length of stay is 50 days. When the project began, approximately 80 accused were in residence, as were 45 convicts, some 30 detainees and a remaining category of foreigners without the means to exist (Brouckmans *et al.* 1998; Vandeurzen *et al.* 1999; Christiaensen 2001).

The *Hoogstraten Penal Educational Centre,* the 'newest' of the three (1931), is the last of the 'penal experimental sites'. This institution houses only permanent convicts. As an open institution, the Hoogstraten Penal Educational Centre has room for 155 inmates. Prisoners must fulfil a number of conditions to be eligible for residency (Dutch-speaking, younger than 50 years of age, at least five months and no more than five years of the sentence remaining, no previous sentence of one year or more). The main accent is upon the re-socialization of the prisoners. Strong communal life and a high level of involvement with the outside world are intended to make the transition to 'free' society easier. In addition to the five-day workweek (work or vocational training) consisting of eight hours per day, prisoners can count on a range of activities. At the start of the action research, all of the 155 places were occupied. A group of 40 sex offenders were an integral part of the communal regime (Brouckmans *et al.* 1998; Vandeurzen *et al.* 1999; Christiaensen 2001).

In the autumn of 2000, the project underwent a profound metamorphosis. The Minister of justice decided to recruit a 'restorative justice consultant' for each prison, with two coordinators (one French-speaking, one Dutch-speaking) at the level of the central prison administration.[16] The action research came to an immediate end as professional public servants took over the work. With the Ministerial Circular no. 1719 of 4 October 2000, the recruitment and appointment of the restorative justice consultants followed.

Both university teams received a new function to fulfil, beginning 1 December 2000 with respect to the work of the restorative justice consultants and the two (one per language regime) coordinators. Until the present, the university research teams have fulfilled a service and support function with respect to the restorative justice consultants and the coordinator in the form of education, training, consultation, draft proposals and other opportunities for contact (Peters 2001).

This support primarily concerns the differing aspects of the action research for the three research years (1998, 1999, 2000).

Activities at the level of the prisons

In order to constructively influence the prison context, all aspects of the prison community need to be addressed. An essential characteristic here is a restorative justice prison culture, in which it is not just a few key figures who are involved, but in which restorative justice is supported by all aspects of prison life.[17] Here a restorative justice prison structure constitutes a basis for a culture of respect.[18]

Following from this is the importance of the initiatives with respect to prison personnel. This constitutes the subject matter of a first point. Prison personnel make a large contribution to the success or failure of 'restorative detention'.

A second sub-section shifts the emphasis to the prisoners. Several activities designed to stimulate responsibility appeal to the prisoners regarding their (potential) perception and processing of guilt. The accomplishment of this includes ensuring the presence of a victim dimension in the punishment.

Moreover, restorative justice may not be an isolated event. This implies a deliberate linking of the project to the periphery of the prison, the 'outside world'.

A final point of interest focuses upon a specific issue, namely the financial problems of prisoners (insolvency, impoverishment, debts, fines, legal costs, civil action settlement and the lack of possible remedies). This problem has received a considerable amount of attention.

Education of prison personnel

For restorative detention to have any chance of success, personnel from all prison departments must be personally and constructively involved. During the first years of the action-research project, much attention and energy also went into the education of personnel in the three pilot prisons. We will first examine a few general educational initiatives that are relevant to all professional groups, in order then to be more specific regarding each professional group of prison officials and the Psychosocial Service.

The first steps of the project can be reduced to an introduction of the theme 'Restorative Justice During Detention'. Providing information and sensitizing prison personnel was done in various ways. In the three pilot prisons, much importance was attached by the project workers to informal contacts with prison personnel. At the same time, somewhat formally, information days were organized and introductory texts drawn up. Information was disseminated via the existing channels as much as possible (for instance via an internal newsletter, an existing study group, etc.) (Christiaensen *et al* 2000). The project was initiated by addressing questions concerning the possible effects upon a victim – and a restorative justice approach to the prison situation. Surveys assessed the reactions to and possible need for the project (Van Win 2001).

Demand quickly surfaced for more information regarding victimization and restorative justice.[19] An educational programme on 'victims and restorative justice' was the answer to this. This course had four objectives. First and foremost, the programme was meant to provide prison personnel with knowledge and insight concerning the issue of victimization. The development of restorative detention was also explained regarding vision, objectives and methods. A third objective to this extra programme was providing a forum for discussion and reflection concerning the issue discussed. In addition, the course provided a good opportunity to explore and stimulate the interest, openness and readiness to take action among prison personnel (Van Win 2001).

The Victims and Restorative Justice educational programme consisted of three different parts.[20] Regarding methodology, the choice was made to make the theoretical explanations as lively as possible. Thus, among other things, victims came to testify. The evaluation forms that the participants filled in after the course indicated that it were precisely these testimonies that made the greatest impression (Christiaensen 2000).

Victims and Restorative Justice was able to count on an enthusiastic audience. Yet the researchers chose to change this course. The unilateral introduction of (more) victim sensitivity to prison personnel contained a possible negative effect, a more repressive attitude with respect to prisoners. Another motivation for changing the focus comes from E. Fattah. He states that 'yesterday's victims are today's offenders and today's victims are tomorrow's offenders' (Fattah 1991). Moreover, restorative justice consists precisely in bringing together both dimensions, victim and offender. 'It is important that in addition to a victim focus, there is also an offender focus and that personnel deal respectfully with prisoners' (Van Win 2001). The course was also subsequently renamed 'offenders and victims'.

The involvement of personnel does not end with the introduction to 'restorative detention'. The issue of restorative justice must thus be kept alive in a stimulating way. With this in mind, interested personnel are provided with a more systematic way to work together on the theme 'offender – victim – restorative justice'. In the Hoogstraten Penal Educational Centre and later also in the Auxiliary Prison of Leuven, such collaboration was followed up in the form of a 'personnel' study group that met regularly (Christiaensen et al. 2000).

Prison officials deserve a separate mention as they 'are the primary agents of a culture of respect in their daily contacts with prisoners' (Brouckmans et al. 1998). In the field, the researchers were regularly questioned by prison officials concerning precisely what was expected of them with respect to this project. The answers regarding the promotion of a culture of respect and respectful treatment of prisoners in turn created a need for additional education.

Thus follow-up needed to be ensured. Indeed, some prison officials had indicated that they had difficulty finishing a discussion with a prisoner in a respectful way. Two additional days of training were then also planned for the Hoogstraten Penal Educational Centre. A one-day training programme focused upon communication skills. Another one-day programme focused upon motivational discussion techniques.[21]

Another question dealt with the collegial support of guards. Several groups of prison officials had already had training on collegial victim support in situations of crisis.

The Psychosocial Service also underwent a degree of reorientation with this project. The Psychosocial Service is responsible for detention guidance and until recently has been focused exclusively on the world of the offenders. It is not easy within this offender-focused world to obtain a victim-oriented dimension in dealing with individual prisoners. For them it indeed comes down to introducing the victim dimension without harming the trust – or at least the level of cooperation with the prisoners (Vandeurzen 1999).

The staff members of the Psychosocial Services in the three 'restorative detention' experimental sites thus also had questions concerning methodological support. This has led, in the first place, to the development of an educational programme based upon the contextual therapy of Nagy. Furthermore, a training session on systems theory provided an opportunity for a response to the methodological challenge.

To provide the Psychosocial Service staff with an instrument that allows incorporating the perspective of the victim in working with the offender, an appeal was made to a fundamental attitude in contextual therapy. 'Multilateral bias' locates a person within the context and the relations in which he or she lives. This framework allows the social workers to alternate between positions of bias for their clients and bias for other parties.[22]

A contextual therapist led a three-day training programme for the Psychosocial Service staff members of each of the three prisons. In addition, a day was organized around the theme of 'Introduction to Multilateral Bias'. These programmes were also open to social workers from the judicial social work sector who assist offenders, and to social workers who assist victims (Vandeurzen *et al.* 1999).

Systematic thinking provided another framework to integrate the newly introduced victim dimension into offender-focused activity. In systems theory the person is seen as a junction of relations imprisoned within a complex of communication systems, various meaning-giving systems and social expectations. (Vandeurzen *et al.* 1999).

For three half-days, a staff member of the Interaction Academy provided commentary and answers were sought to pressing questions.[23] The members of the Psychosocial Service of Leuven Central and one Psychosocial Service staff member from each of the other two prisons attended this training programme.

Both training programmes, given in 1999, brought with them additional requirements. By improving the recognition of psychological problems among prisoners, referrals could be more focused. But here was the rub. The counsellors were not sufficiently aware of the therapy on offer. Furthermore, the need also arose for skills training to motivate the prisoners to make use of the therapy (Vandeurzen *et al.* 1999). Mindful of the arrival of the restorative justice consultants, there were no specific training programmes scheduled for the Psychosocial Services in 2000. Meeting such requirements and needs was included in the job responsibilities of the restorative justice consultants.

Currently a number of questions have surfaced concerning the general and occupationally specific training for staff. With the arrival of the restorative justice consultants, for example, one can ask whether general training on the theme of 'offenders and victims' for each professional category needs to be centrally organized, or whether 'custom' training courses should be held in each prison. Other questions are relevant to the content of the training, to whether or not attendance at such courses should be mandatory for personnel, etc. Thus there are still many questions for which an answer must be sought.

Activities for prisoners

'The essence of imprisonment lies in the fact that the basic right to move where they want and to participate in a self-selected part of society is taken away from people' (Neys 1994). Imprisonment can thus also be best described as 'a total sanction'. A series of 'processes of mortification' attack the identity of the prisoners in a thorough way (Goffman 1961). Their environment is reduced to the immediate prison context. The offence that landed them behind bars degenerates into 'a psychological abscess'. Almost all attention is given to 'survival' in the prison situation.

The introduction of the victim and the community leaves the door open to prisoners for processing what has happened and taking up responsibility. To throw the door to restorative justice wide open, structural aspects of the Belgian prison system need to be readjusted. This was already to some degree grasped in the action research. A number of initiatives already provide prisoners with the possibility to give their punishment a restorative justice touch.

In the first year of the action research, the approach to the prison personnel was at the centre. Only a few sporadic activities took place with the prisoners.

Via the Leuven Auxiliary prison newsletter and in a presentation to the central group of prisoners[24] at the Hoogstraten Penal Educational Centre, restorative justice and the role of the project worker/researcher were introduced. At the same time, education on victimization and the needs of victims was organized. In Leuven Auxiliary, a discussion evening was held on mediation for redress. Using role-playing, the 15 participating prisoners received an experiential interpretation of empathy and victim perception (Brouckmans *et al.* 1998). Other offender-oriented initiatives concerned a discussion evening with volunteers from the Victim Support Service, making juridical office hours available to prisoners and initiating the course 'The Portrayal of the Victim' (Van Camp 2001).

In 1999 and 2000, the level of activity with the prisoners was increased. After a first year of operation, the time was ripe to approach the prisoners in a more focused way. We will briefly run through the action taken and analyse it within three dimensions (accessibility, specificity and intensity).

Thus to provide information to as many prisoners as possible and to increase sensitivity, attention was, in the first instance, firmly focused upon providing both general and specific information. Posters and brochures relating to restorative detention were disseminated in each of the three trial prisons. This gave prisoners immediate access to information concerning the project. Via information evenings, specific information was provided on topics that included the redress fund, civil action and mediation for redress. Furthermore, the action researchers tried to sensitize prisoners by showing and discussing films with themes such as victimization, the needs of the victim, and restorative justice (Van Camp 2001).

Secondly, the practice of juridical office hours were the subject of further follow-up. This met a number of basic rights of the prisoners, more specifically, the right to information regarding their juridical situation, while juridical advice and procedural assistance was also provided for. Lawyers, but also organizations from the field of welfare, handled the juridical office hours. This initiative must be situated against the background of the Act of 23 November 1998 pertaining to the Commissions for Juridical Assistance.[25] Having office hours available in the prisons also complies with the requirement for social assistance and services to prisoners such as introduced in the Strategic Plan of the Flemish Community (Van Camp 2001).

Parallel to the personnel training, prisoners were given the opportunity to become acquainted, in a non-confrontational way, with the experiences of victims. In 1999 the *course* still bore the name 'Victims and Restorative Justice', but the following year this programme received the name 'Offenders and Victims'. This shift in accent was motivated by the fact that it was also desirable to give prisoners the space to be able to reflect on their own life and experiences and on their own victimization.

With respect to content, the course consisted of examining and discussing a film on themes around the issue of victimization. Video testimony and the contribution of a volunteer from the Centre for Victim Support increased the impact of the programme. There was also reflection on and discussion of a number of positions. Finally, a link was made back to oneself as subject of concrete victimization. This programme was open to all prisoners.

The two-day *workshop* 'Victims and Restorative Justice' emphasized the importance of the dialogue between the prisoner and his or her victim, while also underscoring the importance of dialogue between the prisoners and the criminal justice system. This rather short workshop had a higher level of intensity and more selective entrance qualifications.[26]

An increase in knowledge and insight on the one hand, and stimulating the ability to empathize on the other, were the primary objectives. At the same time communication skills were emphasized, and the workshop attempted to stimulate a change in attitude with respect to victims and restorative justice (Van Camp 2001).

The first day of the workshop included an introduction, a proposition game, looking for associations with the word 'victim' and reflection on one's own experience as victim. During the second day, a police officer explained the restorative justice approach at the police department and victims testified regarding their experiences and needs. Evaluations by the participating prisoners and victims indicate that the workshop was always held in high esteem (Christiaensen *et al.* 2000).

Then we focused our attention on the intensive *course* 'The Portrayal of the Victim', a course that asks much of its participants. This was organized for the first time in 1998 at Hoogstraten Penal Educational Centre, but during the following project year the course was also offered at the two other project prisons. 'The Portrayal of the Victim' was not offered in 2000, but was resumed over the course of 2001 in a few Flemish prisons.[27]

Before prisoners may participate in The Portrayal of the Victim, an admission interview takes place. Thus each prisoner is evaluated regarding his or her suitability and motivation regarding the course.[28]

The course The Portrayal of the Victim generally covers seven days. There are phases. First comes the acquisition of knowledge and insight, then the strengthening of the ability to empathize. A third phase is focused upon bringing about a change in attitude among the prisoners. The consciousness-raising of the offender regarding the effects of his or her offence functions as leitmotiv throughout the three phases of The Portrayal of the Victim (Vandeurzen *et al.* 1999). To that end, use is made of newspaper cuttings, video testimonies, group discussions, discussions with guest speakers up to and including the writing of a letter to the victim.[29]

A final action that we wish to briefly discuss deals with the above-mentioned mediation for redress. In an attempt to bridge the wide gap between offender and victim, mediation seems an appropriate method. Yet there was still no structural framework for mediation regarding the punishment. An appeal for mediation was made a number of times to mediators from the non-profit-making organization Suggnomè. The description of these first prison mediations as 'pioneering' within the Belgian prison system is thus by no means an exaggeration.

Only in the autumn of 2000 was a project approved that made possible mediation for redress in punishment at Leuven Central Prison and the Hoogstraten Penal Educational Centre. Mediators from Suggnomè handled the mediation between prisoner and victim. Other initiatives encourage a more indirect and cautious approach by both parties (e.g. the redress fund, see below) (Christiaensen 2000; Van Camp 2001).

Working at the periphery of the prison or 'introducing society'[30]

'Restorative detention' – both as a project and, since the Ministerial Circular of 4 October 2000, as a new objective of prison praxis – will only succeed if supported by 'the outside world'. The project must then also strive to stimulate interaction between the prison milieu and 'the outside world'.

In discussing the broader social context of the prison, two major components are relevant. On the one hand, there are a number of external services for (forensic) social work and work in socio-cultural education, whose contribution within the framework of a more restorative justice oriented detention can be significant. On the other hand, possibly more significantly, 'fellow citizens from free society' can become involved with the project. We will discuss both components.

Even before the pilot project, there was of course collaboration between the internal prison Psychosocial Services and external social services. This collaboration received an enormous boost by adding the victim to the picture at the level of the punishment. Indeed, until then, care for the victim and a client-centric treatment of the offender were 'strangers' to each other. Via this project, the researchers were charged with the task of finding initiatives to bridge the gap. This task is now being further worked on by the restorative justice consultants.

During the first year of the project, the main goals were bringing the social workers 'from within' and 'from without' into contact with each other, informing them as much as possible, allowing them to reflect on the project, its positioning, the methodological and deontological problems and obstacles, as well as to search for feasible forms of collaboration. In 1998 the Psychosocial Service staff members of the Auxiliary Prison of Leuven, together with the members of the 'early assistance' team of

Judicial Social Work Leuven, constituted a 'restorative detention sub-team'. The organization of a prison visit for the staff members of Victim Attention from the public prosecutor's office in Leuven also deserves mention. A meeting with the Psychosocial Service team of the institution was linked to this visit. It represented an initial acquaintance between the two services.

A consultation platform provided the required space to sensitize the relevant actors, to assess their attitude regarding restorative detention, and to achieve feasible forms of collaboration. The partners in communication around this consultation table were the Psychosocial Services of the prisons involved, the directors of the Psychosocial Service at the level of the Directorate-General of Penal Institutions, the services for Victim Attention at the offices of the public prosecutor, and the centres for Victim Assistance.[31]

Social workers dealing with victims and counsellors of prisoners quickly experienced the need for methodological support. In this respect, it has already been indicated that a search was under way in the field of contextual therapy and in systems theory. Both approaches were explained by external organizations. Here again reference can be made to the 'open' character of this educational activity. Thus the three-day training on contextual thinking was followed by two mixed groups, namely the Psychosocial Service workers from the pilot prisons and a group of social workers who work with offenders from the community, and a number of social workers who deal with victims.

The external social work and socio-cultural education also became visible with other information-oriented and sensitizing activities. Even in the first year of the project, an appeal was made to the non-profit-making organization Slachtofferhulp Vlaanderen (Victim Assistance, Flanders), among other things, to organize the course 'The Portrayal of the Victim' in the pilot prisons.[32] Other, more custom-tailored training programmes also came into being at the initiative of an external organization. Thus the Leuven Centre for Victim Support provided the introductory programme 'Victims and Restorative Justice'. In the Hoogstraten Penal Educational Centre there was a deep commitment on the part of an external professional with years of experience as a psychologist–therapist in the care of victims. With this background she supervised, among others, a number of workshops for prisoners.

Since 1988 Judicial Social Work Leuven has been organizing juridical office hours in the Central Prison of Leuven. 'Despite the fact that this form of providing information to prisoners is outside the domain of restorative detention, there are a number of things that can be done to support the project. That is, the project provides an occasion to meet additional and specific juridical informational needs among prisoners' (Christiaensen 2000). Based upon this need for information and also as dictated by the act on juridical assistance of 23 November 1998 and the Strategic Plan of the Flemish Community of July 2000, one can ask whether and how far other prisons might organize juridical office hours (Christiaensen *et al.* 2000).

Several 'external' organizations were mobilized primarily to tackle the issue of debt among prisoners. This is treated in more detail below, but it can already be stated here that the project constitutes a significant bridge between the prison and the Public Social Welfare Centre. Thanks to the Social Stimulus Fund, from September 2000 a social worker has been working on the debt issue half-time at Leuven Auxiliary.

'The reciprocal communicative repositioning of offenders, victims and society is an objective that in the course of the project was realised by concrete initiatives designed to bring "people from outside" in touch with the prison world' (Christiaensen 2001). We will now briefly indicate how this was given content in practice.

At the start of the project, the Hoogstraten Penal Educational Centre was the experimental site *par excellence* to bring 'society' inside. The Penal Educational Centre indeed enjoys a strong reputation so far as its regime is concerned, and it has a tradition of volunteer help. The first initiative brought volunteers from the Herentals Centre for Victim Support to the Hoogstraten Penal Educational Centre and the nearby Turnhout Penal Institution. After this, two discussion evenings between prisoners, prison personnel (the board, Psychosocial Service and prison officials) and visitors followed. Each discussion was a window into the world of the discussion partner. Contrary to the often-heard cry for more severe punishment and the complaint about prisons being three-star hotels, many volunteers were impressed with the prisoners' stories. In the evaluations of these evenings, only positive reactions were heard from all sides (Brouckman *et al.* 1998).

A further step was taken the following year. The group of volunteers from victim support was expanded to include teachers, people from youth protection, punishment mediators, a lawyer, police officers, and some ten direct or indirect victims. Concerning the participants from the prison system, it seemed more interesting (at least based upon the evaluation) to involve a number of prison officials and prisoners. The participating parties were prepared for the discussion evening. The evaluations indicated again that the initiative was well received (Vandeurzen *et al.* 1999).

'Outsiders' were also used with the Offenders and Victims programme already discussed. Thus a police officer explained how restorative justice works with the police department, and several victims testified about their own experience.

A final initiative worthy of mention concerns the layout of an information brochure on various aspects of the prison sentence. The inspiration for this came from Canada, where the pamphlet *Questions and Answers on the Prison System and Parole* has been used since 1993 (Vandeurzen *et al.* 1999).

The pamphlet has a two-fold purpose: 'meeting the need for information on the part of the victims of the crimes for which the offender is behind bars', and 'sensitizing and broadening the outlook of victims' (Vandeurzen *et al.* 1999). A survey informed the researchers about the most important themes of specific interest to the victims in connection with the punishment. The surveys revealed that victims desire more information on the differing conditions relevant to the punishment and especially on the decision concerning the early release from prison.

In a press conference on 20 October 2000, the Minister of Justice presented the brochure 'When the offender disappears behind bars ...What to expect as victim?'[33]

The issue of debt among prisoners

In our modern society the prevailing method to quantify damage is in terms of money (loss of income, work disability, value of stolen articles). While in the personal experience of victims certain losses are irreplaceable (due to the high emotional value attached to them), in official discourse everything receives a monetary value. This is also the case with criminal offences.

When a person who commits an offence is sentenced by the criminal judge to the payment of compensation to one or more civil parties, then the offender is obliged to pay this compensation. Given that it concerns a civil conviction, in the settlement of this payment, the rules of civil law apply. Central here is the principle that 'debt payment is feasible'. If the convicted person does not spontaneously pay, the aggrieved party must then take legal steps to enforce payment (Vandeurzen 2000).

From the beginning of the 'restorative detention' project, a number of important decision makers have emphasized that payment of compensation is a form of restorative justice (Vandeurzen 2000). The researchers themselves underlined the fact that the payment of the civil-action settlement can be only a part of restorative justice activity, and that compensation implies a sign of admission only if it is also the result of commitment on the part of the prisoner. Similar views constitute the foundation for the initiatives concerning civil action.

When the researchers in the three trial prisons also involved civil action in their approach, a number of bottlenecks were quickly identified. These were brought together in a 'civil action bottleneck memorandum'. Payment of the civil action settlement from prison is problematic, if only because prisoners are poorly or not at all informed of their civil sentence. Furthermore, reference can also be made to the insolvency of many prisoners, the high rate of unemployment in the prisons and the low salary levels. Also notable is the fact that convicts must still give priority to payment of the legal costs (pay them before the civil-action settlement). The rule that convicts in sentences involving fines of more than 12,500 Euros must pay taxes or a registration fee of 3 per cent that has priority over the payment of the civil action settlement itself is certainly not friendly to the cause of the victim. In addition, prisoners often have other debts to pay, and in their eyes the support of their own family is often a higher priority.[34]

The attention paid to these problems is thus fully justified. We will successively examine two initiatives that address a number of aspects of the debt issue. First, we will look closely at the redress fund, then we will focus attention on the 'debt settlement' project.

Redress-oriented working within the prison context means, among other things, the creation of possibilities for prisoners to assume their responsibility. The 'restorative detention' project checked whether it might not be possible, following the example of the Settlement Fund for minors,[35] to establish a fund for prisoners. After a preliminary investigation, the non-profit-making organization Welzijnszorg (Care for Welfare) came forward as sponsor for a fund, and a 'redress fund committee' was established that would handle the preparations required to finally start a redress fund (Daeninck 2001).

The committee decided to locate the redress fund with the non-profit-making organization Suggnomè. The reasons behind this are easy to understand. It seemed better that a neutral external organization decided upon the admissibility of an application.[36]

The fund is meant to provide prisoners with the possibility of some degree of rapprochement with their victim. The amount that can be granted remains limited to half of the amount owed, with a ceiling of 1,250 Euros. This limitation is, after all, in line with the principles of restorative justice. The first objective of the redress fund is the promotion of communication between prisoner and victim. The limit emphasizes the symbolic significance of the repayment, not the immediate paying off of the civil action settlement (Daeninck 2001).

If a prisoner wishes to appeal to the fund, he or she can submit an application to that end to the committee. When the committee approves an application, the prisoner must perform a number of hours of community service in exchange for the money. Moreover, the prisoners themselves must first search for an institution that is prepared to have the community service performed. Only when an institution has been found may they formulate a proposal that describes the institution and the community service.

If the committee gives its blessing, a mediator is appointed who will submit the proposal to the victim. The decisive voice lies ultimately with the victim. If a positive answer is forthcoming from this side, the prisoner may begin the community service. The prison must do all that is required to make the community service possible (Daeninck 2001).

If the prisoner completes the community service successfully, the committee will pay the amount agreed to the victim. If both offender and victim desire direct contact, this can be organized by the mediator. Further settlement of the balance of the debt can also be arranged in an indirect way by the mediator.

So far the redress fund remains framed in an experimental setting. An attempt is made to engage as many prisoners as possible in the making and distributing of folders, the organizing of information evenings and the hanging of posters. The initial findings provide a completely positive picture of this initiative (Daeninck 2001).

Another activity strikes at the entire burden of debt borne by prisoners. An initial requirement in tackling one's own debt is to obtain an overview and to come to grips with it. In the Auxiliary Prison of Leuven, a desire was evident to make the burden of debt manageable and to include the civil action settlement in the list of debtors. But managing the debt, negotiating with creditors, and the drawing up of payment plans is an almost impossible task for the staff members of the Psychosocial Service.

This was the occasion for initiating a 'debt settlement' project that was a bridge to the Public Social Welfare Centre of Leuven. The intention was to work out whether it was possible from prison to manage debt, negotiate with creditors and draw up payment plans. A project was submitted to the Social Stimulus Fund. After approval, as already indicated earlier, beginning September 2000, a social worker was employed half-time. The Social Stimulus Fund plans to finance this project until the end of 2002 (Christiaensen et al. 2000).

If upon being received at the Auxiliary Prison a prisoner makes it known that he or she has a debt and wishes assistance or support in managing it, they will be referred by the system. The prisoner may also contact the social worker afterwards.

Within the framework of the debt settlement project, the Public Social Welfare Centre actually takes upon itself the assistance and education at the level of the individual. In addition to individual assistance, there is also an educational package that treats topics connected with budgeting.[37] After all, the intention is to provide prisoners with sufficient means to manage their budget as independently as possible.

There are often consultations with the debt regulator, and initiatives are supported and stimulated. Thus, in October 2001, the project at Leuven Auxiliary organized a number of information sessions (for instance on attachment, civil action, the redress fund) (Daeninck 2001).

A few closing remarks

This wide-ranging yet necessarily selective description of the Restorative Detention project perhaps leaves the impression that the penal context itself does not have many problems.

With a prison system derived largely from the nineteenth century, we encounter enormous structural shortcomings. Most Belgian prisons were built according to the philosophy of confinement in cells. Too many of these old buildings still have to be modified to allow elementary comforts such as running water and a toilet in the cell. Moreover, due to this history, possibilities for organizing communal activities are often lacking. A considerable number of prisoners spend more than 20 hours per day in their cell. (The precise number is difficult to measure due to the lack of clear information about various regimes.)

That the Belgian prison system also continues to suffer from a crisis of legitimacy (Peters and Goethals 1981) can best be understood when one realizes that within the last decade alone, the prison population has increased by almost 50 per cent, while work continues on initial basic legislation regarding the principles of confinement that safeguard the basic rights of prisoners.

The restorative justice consultants have ample knowledge of prison praxis. They are charged with an enormous task in which expectations are high. That is why they are always able to count on support from the universities. But the research teams have few ready-made answers. The actual position of 'restorative justice' in Belgian 'detention' situations must gradually take shape in collaboration with restorative justice consultants and research teams.

In addition we need to point out the problems with *imprisonment*. As the British criminologist David Garland wrote, 'penal practices exist within a specific penal culture which is itself supported and made meaningful by wider cultural forms, these, in turn, being grounded in society's patterns of material life and social action' (Garland 1990).

In a society where individualism is increasingly evident and misuses of victimization also appear on the front page of the newspapers, the concern remains to continue to guarantee adequate means and support in the near future for the integral approach of 'restorative detention'. Hopefully, Belgium can better manage the confinement figures and flatten the growth curve. This has not been the case until now, but a quickening of the pace in this direction throughout Europe can be discerned.[38]

Moreover, we must avoid the danger that imprisonment, with all of its known disadvantages, is 'packaged as restorative justice'. The hijacking of restorative justice initiatives is a real threat, certainly when it concerns a possible new legitimation of imprisonment.[39]

Stanley Cohen once wrote 'good intentions become bad practices'. Let us hope that restorative justice does not follow this path.

Notes

1. For more in-depth information, you are referred to the various research reports.
2. Due to this paradoxical character of the project name, we will use quotation marks when referring to 'restorative detention' throughout this text. The research agreement with the Ministry of Justice mentions 'restorative punishment', but this designation does not do justice to the real research assignment, which on the one hand is limited to the situation of detention and on the other hand is not limited to a given category of prisoner.
3. This part was greatly inspired by the presentation of T. Peters (2001).
4. The penology and victimology research group is part of the Department of Criminal Law, Criminal Procedure and Criminology, Faculty of Law, KU Leuven.
5. In the second part of this paper, action research is given more attention.
6. The *stock* has repercussions for the daily number of prisoners; the intake or flow is generally calculated by counting the number of prisoners from 1 January through 31 December of the same year.
7. A 'total institution' is defined as 'a place of residence and work where a large number of like-situated individuals, cut off from the wider society for an appreciable period of time, together lead an enclosed, formally administered round of life'.
8. But in recent years it could be said that (mass-)confinement, seen purely from an economic perspective, but also from a *law and order*-oriented policy point of view, creates and fills a profitable gap in the market. Until now the tentacles of neo-liberalism have not yet fastened themselves to the Belgian penal establishment. In the *race to incarcerate*, Belgium still remains in the pack. (See for example Christie, N. (2000).)
9. This vision is given extensive treatment in T. Peters (1984).

10. Minister of Justice (1996). For a comprehensive discussion of the pathetic legal status of prisoners under Belgian penal law, see G. Smaers, (1996).
11. L. Dupont (1998). An abstraction is here made from the further developments of this proposal, but we can mention here that it has recently found its way into parliament, where it is now (in 2002) awaiting a vote.
12. The Act of 12 March 1998 for the improvement of the administration of criminal justice at the stage of the investigation and the judicial inquiry is better known as the Franchimont Act.
13. The acts of 5 and 18 March 1998 replace the so-called 'Lejeune Act' of 31 May 1988. It shifts the granting of parole from the penal administration to five so-called Parole Commissions, chaired by a judge.
14. The division of the research is not independent of the federal structure of Belgium. While the prison system is still regulated at the federal level, the authority for assistance is situated at the level of the Communities. Because different services have developed in the field of welfare within the Communities and each university team has a good knowledge of the services within its own language area, the division into two teams is not a big surprise.
15. For an attempt to theorize about the 'restorative detention' project using a number of basic restorative justice models, see P. Daeninck, T. Van Camp and T. Van Win (2001): 35–39.
16. This ran counter to the expectations of the research team that had counted on a gradual introduction of restorative justice consultants. (Christiaensen *et al.* (2001): 127.)
17. Already early in the research, the presence of a 'culture of respect' arose as a *conditio sine qua non* for 'restorative detention'. Everyone must be approached with *dignity* (see among others P. Brouckmans *et al.*, p. 73).
18. Working towards a restorative justice prison culture constitutes an integral part of the job responsibilities of the restorative justice consultants. Indeed, the tasks of the restorative justice consultant are located at the structural level (*Ministerial Circular* no. 1719 of 4 October 2000).
19. This question arose explicitly primarily at the Auxiliary Prison of Leuven. See Vandeurzen *et al.* (1999): 20–1.
20. These three parts are: (1) an overview of the needs, expectations and handling of victims of criminal offences; (2) developing a 'restorative detention' programme and (3) an introductory course 'The Portrayal of the Victim', see among others, in Vandeurzen *et al.* 21–22; Van Win, 2001: 2.
21. The communication skills course focused upon active and passive listening, non-verbal communication, correct timing, and open and closed questions. A motivational discussion techniques programme continued in that direction and, using exercises, introduced a number of general basic skills (Vandeurzen *et al.* 1999: 30; Van Win 2001: 2).
22. It is not the intent of this article to deal in depth with what this contextual approach precisely is. For this see among others Nagy, I. (2000).
23. Thus, for example, questions were addressed regarding which processes make it so difficult for prisoners to empathize with others; soundings were also made regarding the way(s) in which social workers who work with offenders might

be able to expand the tunnel vision of prisoners such that space is created for them to see/recognize the position, the vision, the interests, the emotions and the values of others, ... In other words, a search for ways to impart empathy (Van Win 2001: 3).

24. A group of 20 prisoners voluntarily joined the central group. Among other things, they worked on group projects for the other prisoners. Prisoners are eligible to join the group only after a residency of at least 3 months in the Hoogstraten Penal Educational Centre.

25. The Act of 23 November 1998 proposed accessible first-line assistance and furthermore also gave priority to the goals of consultation and coordination between the differing organizations dealing with legal assistance, all this to provide everyone with the opportunity to defend his or her rights.

26. Participation was on a voluntary basis. On the other hand, preference was given to prisoners (convicts) closest to their parole date. Due to its short character, the workshop is more accessible to the accused, who are usually in custody for an unknown, often rather short length of time. See S. Christiaensen, I. Vandeurzen and H. Verhoeven, o.c., 53; T. Van Camp, o.c., 3.

27. Christiaensen et al. 2000: 60–61; Van Camp 2001: 4. We will examine below the reason for this interruption.

28. The conditions for participation are the following: the presence of a demonstrable victim; a readiness to speak about the offence; no sexual offenders; no serious addiction problem; no serious psychiatric problem; the abilities to speak Dutch sufficiently and to function in a group. At the same, time the prisoner must be able to communicate and must have the capacity for openness and trust. (Vandeurzen et al. 1999: 34, 36).

29. Only if the prisoner explicitly requests to send this letter to the victim are the required steps taken to assess whether the victim is ready for this communication.

30. Based upon Christiaensen, S. (2001). Opzet van het project, unpublished memorandum, pp. 5–9.

31. This consultation platform did not meet again in 2000. With the arrival of the restorative justice consultants and the restorative-justice coordinators, it seemed best to wait for these people to take up their positions before further consultation took place (Christiaensen et al. 2000: 107).

32. 'The Portrayal of the Victim' is intended primarily for education within the framework of alternative (penal) measures outside the prison (Christiaensen 2001: 7). The courses were organized as freelance activities due to the lack of a mandate, which brought with it a high cost. This was the main reason why 'The Portrayal of the Victim' did not take place in 2000 (Christiaensen et al. 2000: 60–61). Beginning in 2001, there were prisons that again organized 'The Portrayal of the Victim' (Van Camp 2001: 4).

33. The King Baudouin Foundation provided the subsidies that made possible the making of the brochure. The Ministry of Justice published the brochure (Christiaensen et al. 2000: 121).

34. Vandeurzen, 2000: 2–3. In the three annual reports contained in the research, close attention is also paid to the problem of debt.

35. Within the framework of mediation for redress with minors, a young person may appeal to the *Settlement Fund*. This fund provides a sum of money to a young person who wishes to compensate the victim. The basic condition for this is agreement by the young person to the performance of a number of hours of volunteer work. If the young person fulfils this condition, his or her good intentions are transferred to the victim in the form of a sum of money (often rather symbolic in amount). The *redress fund* that was established functions according to the same philosophy.

36. In addition, the administration and the financing of the redress fund provides a nice example of how society can provide possibilities for solutions to deal in a constructive way with criminality and the damage brought about by criminality. In this way the redress fund also remains separate from the prison system and does not degenerate into the umpteenth gadget of policy on criminality. Of course, as part of the restorative justice movement, this could be 'hijacked' by the 'establishment'.

37. Individual assistance consists of the following: an inventory of debt; management of debt; providing information and advice regarding debt; negotiating with creditors; drawing up payment plans; referral to other Public Social Welfare Centres or other services where the prisoner can obtain assistance after detention (Christiaensen *et al.* 2000: 63).

38. See Christie (2000) in particular his chapter on *penal geography*: 25–40.

39. With this, prison as locus of the story of correctional improvement would receive new legitimation and thus be reconfirmed in the public discourse on punishment (Daems, T. 2000: 25–45).

References

Aertsen, I. and Peters, T. (1995) 'Actie-Onderzoek, een Hefboom voor Beleidsontwikkeling?' [Action Research, Driving Force for Policy Development?], *Panopticon*, p. 237.

Brenzikofer, P. (1997) 'Een Ervaringsbericht uit de Zwitserse Gevangenis van Saxerriet' [A Message of Experience from the Swiss Prison of Saxerriet], *Metanoia*, pp. 97–107.

Brouckmans, P. *et al.* (1998) p. 11.

Brouckmans, P. *et al.* (1998) pp. 26, 29–30.

Brouckmans, P. *et al.* (1998) pp. 46–49.

Brouckmans, P. *et al.* (1998) p. 73.

Brouckmans, P. *et al.* (1998) p. 38.

Brouckmans, P. *et al.* (1998) p. 42.

Brouckmans, P. *et al.* (1998) pp. 60–63.

Cayley, D. (1998) *The Expanding Prison. The Crisis in Crime and Punishment and the Search for Alternatives*, House of Anansi Press Ltd., pp. 15–88.

Christiaensen, S. (2001) *Opzet van het Pilootproject [Organizingthe Pilot Project]*, unpublished memorandum, p. 1.

Christiaensen, S., Vandeurzen, I. and Verhoeven, H. (2000) *Herstelgerichte detentie. Van Actie-Onderzoek naar Beleidsvorming* [Restorative Detention. From Action Research to Policy Making], Leuven: KU Leuven, Faculty of Law, Department of Criminal Law, Criminal Procedure and Criminology, p. 9.

Christiaensen, S (2001) p. 2.

Christiaensen, S. (2001) p. 3.

Christiaensen, S. (2001) pp. 3–4.

Christiaensen, S. *et al.* (2000) pp. 18–19.

Christiaensen, S. (2000) p. 23.

Christiaensen, S. *et al.* (2000) pp. 26–30.

Christiaensen, S. *et al.* (2000) pp. 58–60.

Christiaensen, S. *et al.* (2000) pp. 102–103; Van Camp, T. (2001) p. 5.

Christiaensen, S. (2000) p. 8.

Christiaensen, S. *et al.* (2000) p. 104.

Christiaensen, S. (2001) p. 8.

Christiaensen, S. *et al.* (2000) p. 63.

Christie, N. (2000) *Crime Control as Industry. Towards Gulags, Western Style*, London: Routledge.

Clemmer, D.R. (1940) *The Prison Community*, N.Y.: Holt, Rinehart and Winston, N.Y., 1958, p. 299.

Daems, T. (2000) 'Op Weg Naar een Nieuwe Etappe in het Verbeteringsverhaal: De Responsabilisering van de Gedetineerde' [Toward a New Stage in the Correctional Story: Making the Detainee Responsible], *Metanoia*, pp. 25–45.

Daeninck, P. (2001) *Het Aanreiken van Middelen tot Materieel en Symbolisch Herstel* [Providing the Means for Material and Symbolic Restorative Justice], unpublished memorandum, p. 4.

Daeninck, P. (2001) pp. 4–5.

Daeninck, P. (2001) p. 6.

Daeninck, P. (2001) pp. 6–7.

Daeninck, P. (2001) p. 9.

Daeninck, P. *et al.* (2001) *Herstelgerichte Detentie: Poging tot Verduidelijking. Een discussienota [Restorative Detention: An Attempt at Clarification. A working paper]*, KU Leuven, Faculty of Law, Department of Criminal Law, Criminal Procedure and Criminology, pp. 35–39.

Dupont, L. (1998) Proeve van een Voorontwerp van Beginselenwet Gevangeniswezen en Tenuitvoerlegging van Vrijheidsstraffen in L. Dupont (ed.) *Op Weg naar een Beginselenwet Gevangeniswezen*, Leuven: Leuven University Press.

Fattah, E. (1991) *Understanding Criminal Victimization. An Introduction to Theoretical Victimology*. Scarborough, Ontario: Prentice-Hall, pp. 149–150.

Garland, D. (1990) *Punishment and Modern Society*, Oxford: Oxford University Press, Oxford, p. 211.

Goffman, E. (1961) *Asylums. Essays on the Social Situation of Mental Patients and Other Inmates*, Garden City, N.Y., Anchor Books.

Goffman, E. (1961) pp. 12–48.

Immarigeon, R. (1996) 'Prison-Based Victim-Offender Reconciliation Programmes', in B. Galaway and J. Hudson (eds), *Restorative Justice: International Perspectives*, Monsey, New York: Criminal Justice Press, pp. 463–476.

Marshall, T. (1998) *Restorative Justice. An Overview*, unpublished.

Minister of Justice (1996) *Oriëntatienota Strafbeleid en Gevangenisbeleid [Orientation Memorandum on Penal and Prison Policy]*, Ministry of Justice, Brussels, especially pages 50–57.

Minister of Justice (2000) *Federaal Veiligheids -en Detentieplan*, Ministry of Justice, Brussels, available at just.fgov.be [2000].

Nagy, I. (2000) *Grondbeginselen van de Contextuele Benadering* [Basic principles of the contextual approach], Haarlem: De Toorts, p. 182.

Neys, A. (1994) 'Gevangenisstraf als Doorleefde Realiteit' [Imprisonment as lived reality] in A. Neys, T. Peters, F. Pieters and J. Vanacker (eds) *Tralies in de Weg. Het Belgische Gevangeniswezen: Historiek, Balans en Perspectieven*, Leuven: Leuven University Press, Leuven.

Peters, T. and Goethals, J. (1981) 'De Legitimiteitscrisis van de Gevangenisstraf' [Imprisonment's Crisis of Legitimacy], *Streven*, pp. 316–327 and 364–365.

Peters, T. and Goethals, J. (eds) (1993) *De Achterkant van de Criminaliteit. Over Victimologie, Slachtofferhulp en Strafrechtsbedeling*, Leuven University Press, Leuven.

Peters, T. (1984) 'Pleidooi voor een Radicaal Reductionistisch Opsluitingsbeleid [Plea for a Radically Reductionist Policy of Confinement]', *Panopticon*.

Peters, T., *et al.* (1999) 'Bouwstenen voor een Coherent Herstel – en Slachtoffergericht Justitiebeleid' in B. Van Doninck, L. Van Daele and A. Naji (eds), *Het Recht op Het Rechte Pad?*, Maklu, Antwerp-Apeldoorn, Maklu, 1999. Also as 'Fondements d'une Politique Judiciaire Cohérente Axée sur la Réparation et sur la victime' in B. Van Doninck, L. Van Daele and A. Naji (eds), *Le droit sur le droit chemin?*, Antwerp-Apeldoorn; Maklu.

Peters, T. (2001) *Restorative Prisons: A Belgian Practice*, a paper presented at the 5th International Conference on Restorative Justice, Leuven, 16–19 September 2001.

Peters, T. (2001) pp. 1–2.

Smaers, G. (1996) *Rechtsbescherming voor Gedetineerden [Protecting the Rights of Prisoners]*, Brussels: Federal Offices for Research, Technical and Cultural Affairs.

Sykes, G. M. (1958) *The Society of Captives*, Princeton, NJ: Princeton University Press.

Vandeurzen, I. *et al.* (1999) *Slachtoffer -en Herstelgerichte Detentie. Visie -en Activiteitenverslag* [Victim and Restorative-Oriented Detention. Vision and Report of Activities], Leuven: KU Leuven, Faculty of Law, Department of Criminal Law, Criminal Procedure and Criminology, p. 11.

Vandeurzen, I. *et al.* (1999) p. 18.

Vandeurzen, I. *et al.* (1999) pp. 18–19.

Vandeurzen, I. *et al.* (1999) p. 19.

Vandeurzen, I. *et al.* (1999) p. 30.

Vandeurzen, I. *et al.* (1999) p. 24.

Vandeurzen, I. *et al.* (1999) p. 26.

Vandeurzen, I. *et al.* (1999) pp. 28–29.

Vandeurzen, I. *et al.* (1999) pp. 32–33.

Vandeurzen, I. (2000) *Knelpuntennota: Burgerlijke Partij en Detentie* [Bottleneck Memorandum: Civil Action and Detention], unpublished memorandum, p. 1.

Vandeurzen, I. (2000) *et al.* p. 44.

Van Camp, T. (2001) *'Activiteiten voor de Gedetineerden'* [Activities for the Detainees], unpublished memorandum, p. 1–2.

Van Camp, T. (2001) p. 2.

Van Camp, T. (2001) pp. 2–3.

Van Camp, T. (2001) pp. 3–4.

Van Win, T. (2001) *Vorming Personeel* [Educating Personnel], unpublished memorandum, p. 1.

Van Win, T. (2001) pp. 1–2.

Van Win, T. (2001) p. 2.

Van Win, T. (2001) p. 2.

Chapter 6

Victims of severe violence in dialogue with the offender: key principles, practices, outcomes and implications

Mark S. Umbreit, William Bradshaw and Robert B. Coates

Restorative justice focuses upon the harm caused to individual victims and the community while emphasizing the importance of engaging key stakeholders (victims, community and offenders) in the process of developing a restorative response to the crime (Bazemore and Umbreit 1994, 1995; Van Ness and Strong 1997; Zehr 1990). Restorative justice theory is having an increasing impact upon communities, and even entire justice systems, throughout North America, Europe and the South Pacific (Alder and Wundeersitz 1994; Bazemore and Walgrave 1999; Galaway and Hudson 1996; Hudson *et al.* 1996; Messmer and Otto 1992; Umbreit 1998; Umbreit and Stacey 1996; Umbreit and Zehr 1996; Wright and Galaway 1989).

The oldest, most widely disseminated and documented practice throughout the world, and empirically grounded expression of restorative justice is victim–offender mediation (VOM). With more than twenty-five years of experience and research, involving many thousands of annual case referrals to programmes in more than 1,200 known communities throughout North America and Europe (Umbreit and Greenwood 1999; Umbreit and Neimeyer 1996; Umbreit 1995b, 1995c, 1993a, 1991b, 1986a, 1985), VOM (often referred to as victim–offender reconciliation or victim–offender conferencing) remains a strong empirically grounded pillar within the growing restorative justice movement.

A growing amount of empirical data has emerged from more than 40 studies of VOM in property crimes and minor assaults, in the US, Canada, and England. High levels of client satisfaction with the mediation process and outcome has been consistently found over the past 20 years in studies throughout Europe and North America (Coates and Gehm 1989; Collins 1984; Dignan 1990; Galaway 1988; Galaway and Hudson 1990; Gehm 1990; Marshall and Merry 1990; Perry *et al*. 1987; Umbreit 1988, 1989a, 1991a, 1993b, 1994a, 1995a, 2001; Umbreit and Bradshaw, 1997, 1999; Umbreit and Coates 1992, 1993, 1995c, 1996, 1998, 1999; Umbreit and Roberts 1996; Wright and Galaway 1989), with some studies finding higher restitution completion rates (Umbreit 1994a), reduced fear among victims (Umbreit and Coates 1993; Umbreit 1993b, 1994a, 1994b), and reduced future criminal behaviour (Nugent and Paddock 1995; Nugent *et al*. 2001; Schneider 1986; Umbreit 1994). It is becoming increasingly clear that the VOM process humanizes the criminal justice experience for both victim and offender; holds offenders directly accountable to the people they victimized, allows for more active involvement of crime victims and community members (as volunteer mediators) in the justice process and suppresses further criminal behaviour in offenders.

During the early 1980s, many questioned whether crime victims would even want to meet face-to-face with their offender. Today it is very clear, from empirical data and practical experience, that the majority of victims of property crimes and minor assaults presented with the opportunity of mediation chose to engage in the process, with victim-participation rates often ranging from about 60 to 70 per cent in many programmes. A state-wide randomized public opinion survey in Minnesota found that 84 per cent of citizens, including many who had been victimized by crime, indicated they would be likely to consider participating in VOM if they were the victim of a property crime (Pranis and Umbreit 1992). A more recent state-wide survey of victim service providers in Minnesota found that 91 per cent felt that VOM was an important service to be made available to victims on a volunteer basis and that it should be offered in each judicial district of the state (Minnesota Department of Public Safety 1996).

Victims of severe violence: a search for meaning

Both restorative justice in general, and VOM specifically, continue to be identified with primarily, if not exclusively, addressing non-violent property crimes, and perhaps even minor assaults. This chapter will challenge such assumptions by providing empirical evidence which suggests that many of the principles of restorative justice can be applied in crimes of severe violence, including murder. Some would even suggest that the deepest healing impact of restorative justice is to be found in addressing and responding to such violent crime.

An increasing number of victims of sexual assault, attempted homicide, and survivors of murder victims are requesting the opportunity to meet the offender to express the full impact of the crime upon their life, to get answers to many questions they have, and to gain a greater sense of closure so that they can move on with their lives. In most cases this occurs many years after the crime occurred and the actual mediation/dialogue session is typically held in a secure institution where the offender is located. In the mid-1980s, only a handful of such cases in scattered locations throughout the United States were provided with the opportunity for a mediated dialogue. As we approach the end of the century, Victim Services Units in six states are at various levels of developing a state-wide protocol for allowing such an encounter between a victim/ survivor of a severely violent crime and the offender. In Texas, there has been a waiting list of more than 300 victims of severe violence, including many parents of murdered children, who have requested a meeting with the offender through the Victim Offender Mediation/Dialog (VOM/D) Program of the Victim Services Unit, Texas Department of Criminal Justice. A growing number of victims of severe violence in Canada and Europe have also expressed interest in a mediated dialogue session with the offender. The Canadian Ministry of Justice has for many years supported the development of these services by the Victim Offender Mediation Program of the Frasier Area Community Justice Initiatives in Langley, British Columbia.

Victim sensitive offender dialogue (VSOD): differing approaches

In response to the growing number of requests over the past decade from victims and survivors of severely violent crime to meet the responsible offender, a small but increasing number of programmes and practitioners are offering this service. Most often, this is made available by highly experienced and trained mediators familiar with the basic VOM process in property crimes and minor assaults and working closely with victim services agencies. The largest programmes to date in the United States have been offered through victim services units of departments of corrections in several states. These developments, however, have not come about without controversy. The concept of restorative justice and VOM remains highly controversial to many in the victim-rights movement, even though far more victim advocates and organizations have become active stakeholders in the restorative justice movement than in earlier years. To date, the use of mediation and dialogue in such cases through state-wide programmes in the United States described below is entirely victim-driven. Crime victims themselves initiate the process.

While the process of VOM in property crimes and minor assaults is well tested and empirically grounded, the basic model is not adequate for working with severely violent crimes. To do so would be to likely re-victimize crime victims and even offenders. Far more advanced training of mediators and preparation of the parties is required in cases of severe violence such as sexual assault, attempted homicide, and murder.

The use of mediation and dialogue in cases of severely violent offences has a number of distinguishing characteristics. These include the following: emotional intensity, extreme need for non-judgmental attitude, longer case preparation by mediator (6 to 18 months), multiple separate meetings prior to joint session, multiple phone conversations, negotiation with correctional officials to secure access to inmate and to conduct mediation in prison, coaching of participants in the communication of intense feelings, and boundary clarification (mediation/dialogue versus therapy). Because of the intense nature of these cases, there are a number of clear implications for advanced training for any person who chooses to work in this area. The field of restorative justice and VOM is only beginning to come to grips with how the basic mediation model must be adapted to serve the more intense needs of parties involved in serious and violent criminal conflict. Far more extensive training of mediators is required, as is an entire new generation of written and audio-visual training resources. For example, mediators will need special knowledge and skills related to working with severely violent crimes, in addition to the normal mediation skills. Advanced training would not focus on the mechanics of negotiation/mediation. Instead, it would emphasize an experiential understanding of the painful journey of the participants. Such advanced training would need to focus on the process of facilitating a direct and frank dialogue between the parties related to the violent crime that occurred, the journey of grief being experienced by the victim and/or surviving family members, and the possibilities for closure and healing through a process of mutual aid.

From the victim perspective, it will be important for the mediator to have the following: understanding of the victimization experience/phases, dealing with grief and loss (our own and others'), understanding post-traumatic stress and its impact, and the ability to collaborate with psychotherapists.

From the offender perspective, mediators will need the following: a thorough understanding of the criminal justice and corrections system, an understanding of the offender and prisoner experience, the ability to relate to offenders convicted of heinous crimes in a non-judgmental manner, and the ability to negotiate with high-level correctional officials to gain access to the offender/inmate.

The earliest known use of mediation and dialogue in severely violent crimes is found during the early 1980s in the pioneering work of the Genessee County Sheriff's Department in Batavia, New York. The work of Dennis Whitman, director of the programme, stands alone as the earliest and most creative, if not courageous, use of mediation and dialogue to serve the needs of highly-traumatized victims and survivors as they chose to meet with the offender(s). The programme in Genessee County serves many crime victims and offenders a year through such restorative justice interventions as community service and a wide range of victim services. While handling only a limited number of mediation/dialogue cases in severe violence each year in this small upstate New York community, the work of Dennis Whitman and his colleagues in Genessee County represents some of the deepest and most well integrated expressions of restorative justice at both an interpersonal and systemic change level known in the United States.

Another early expression of the use of mediation and dialogue in crimes of severe violence is seen in its periodic use with victims of severe violence and incarcerated juvenile offenders in Anchorage, Alaska. The work of Donis Morris at the McLaughlin Youth Center in Anchorage (Flaten 1996) is the only known example of working with juvenile offenders in such severely violent cases.

Communication and dialogue between interested victims of severe violence and the offenders currently occurs in a number of different forms, ranging from highly therapeutic models developed and used by Dave Gustafson in Langley, British Columbia and David Doerfler in Austin, Texas to non-therapeutic dialogue models developed and used by Mark Umbreit in St. Paul, Minnesota and Karen Ho in Columbus, Ohio.

As the practice of VSOD in crimes of severe violence becomes more widespread both through the services provided by individual mediators and state-wide services offered by victim services units within correctional departments, it is becoming evident that there are a number of different approaches. Drawing upon the experience in British Columbia, Texas, Ohio, Pennsylvania, and a number of mediators trained in Minnesota and operating in a number of different states, we have developed the typology described below. Brief descriptions of each programme are also provided.

Victim-sensitive offender dialogue (VSOD) typology

Interviews with staff and volunteers in VSOD programmes and a review of descriptive literature regarding these programmes make clear that while programmes designed under this rubric have much in common, there remain significant differences in intent and scope. Each programme attempts to help victims and offenders deal with the pain of injury and loss and take responsibility for their own actions. While information about the total range of VSOD programmes currently in operation is still incomplete, the outline of a preliminary typology of such programmes is beginning to take shape.

The differences between types of VSOD approaches are a matter of emphasis. At present, three foci are frequently referred to in interviews and in the literature: (1) therapeutic, (2) narrative and (3) empowerment. Existing programmes refer to these three in varying degrees. In other words, while each programme is concerned with all three foci, one focus emerges as dominant or most central to the philosophy and practice of each.

The director of the Texas VSOD project states, 'The purpose of the process is healing. While it is not therapy, it's very therapeutic.' This emphasis upon healing/therapeutic comes to the forefront when staff seeks volunteers for training. 'We are looking for people who think outside the box and who want to help people heal.' (Source: VSOD research project.)

Empowerment is the key word heard when talking with staff and volunteers in the Ohio programme. While healing and being therapeutic are goals, as is getting victims and offenders to tell their stories regarding the crime and its consequences, the director notes that 'whatever victims want to get out of a dialogue is of paramount importance.' Staff and volunteers are not engaged in long term, in-depth therapeutic work. 'The key things that I want to make sure', says the director, 'are that we're having something that's going to be safe for both offender and victim, and in the end it's going to benefit both of them … much of our goal is to help them keep on track.' (Source: VSOD Research Project.)

The central focus within humanistic mediation VSOD programmes is narrative, that is, for each participant to speak to the impact of the crime: 'The telling and hearing of each other's stories about the conflict, the opportunity for maximum direct communication with each other, and the importance of honouring silence and the innate wisdom and strength of participants are all central to humanistic mediation practice.' (Umbreit *et al.* 1999). The humanistic mediation narrative approach to VSOD is practised and taught in Minnesota, as well as numerous other locations.

To summarize, the three goals which are identified by programme staff and literature are: narration, or telling the story; empowering victims and offenders to define their own needs and take responsibility for meeting those needs; and providing a healing/therapeutic experience. All VSOD programmes for which information is available include all three of these goals in their programme objectives. However, in practice, one of these areas emerges as a central focus.

Three preliminary types of VSOD programmes emerge from the interview data and the available programme literature. The resulting typology is outlined in Table 1 below. The three types which are apparent at present tend to place more of an emphasis on therapeutic, narrative or empowerment goals. It must be underscored that this typology is preliminary in nature and that it will inevitably shift and change as more data are gathered on additional programmes.

The three foci discussed in Table 6.1 receive emphasis in the following order: therapeutic, narrative and empowerment. An example of the therapeutic type is the Texas VOM/D programme; an example of the narrative type is Humanistic Mediation, where the focus rank order is: narrative, empowerment and therapeutic; the Ohio Victim Offender Dialogue programme is an example of the empowerment type; where focus rank order in this programme is empowerment, narrative and therapeutic.

Certainly other variations of rank ordering are possible within VSOD types. Based on the review of literature only, the Victim Offender Mediation Project (VOMP) in Langley, British Columbia would fall under the therapeutic type, and its rank-ordered foci would be therapeutic, empowerment and narrative. For example, the director of the programme states that the programme was established 'to meet some of the

Table 6.1. Victim-sensitive offender dialogue typology

	Type I	Type II	Type III
Rank ordered foci	Therapeutic Narrative Empowerment	Narrative Empowerment Therapeutic	Empowerment Narrative Therapeutic
Example	Texas VOM/D Canadian VOMP (Langley, British Columbia)	Minnesota VSOD – humanistic mediation/ dialogue (University of Minnesota)	Ohio VOD Pennsylvania VOD

therapeutic needs unique to survivors of serious criminal trauma as well as to offenders responsible for those harms' (Gustafson 1997). A research report on VOMP describes therapy in that context as 'time spent with individuals working through deep emotions' (Roberts 1995). The director also underscores the importance of empowering individuals as it relates to the dominant therapeutic goal: 'autonomy, and its exercise, is fundamental to trauma recovery.' The narrative is also important in VOMP as programme staff often use letters and taped videos in preparation for a possible meeting between the victim and offender. It may be that more empirical data would lead to categorizing this programme as therapeutic with a rank ordering of therapeutic, narrative and empowerment. In either instance, it would remain a therapeutic type approach to VSOD.

The utility of such a typology is threefold. First, such a typology makes clear that there exist similar but different approaches to VSOD. While there are shared principles across the approaches, there is no single way to do VSOD.

Second, such a typology, when linked with more detailed information regarding actual practice, can illustrate how a dominant focus is related to or determines practice. For example, with its therapeutic emphasis, the Texas VOM/D programme struggles with the concept of closing a case, for in their therapeutic view a case may never be closed. In Ohio, with its empowerment emphasis, a case is typically closed within a month or two after mediation. If the victim and offender feel that their questions have been answered as well as they are likely to be, then the case is closed. This difference regarding closed cases does not make one programme right and the other wrong; each is consistent with its own guiding philosophy and purpose.

Third, such a typology can be helpful to jurisdictions thinking about establishing a VSOD programme. Planners will be better able to determine what they might implement given their own philosophies, desired impact and available resources. A jurisdiction might desire to adapt one of the current approaches, create a variation within a current type, or develop a new type entirely. However it chooses to proceed, an empirically grounded victim-sensitive offender typology will serve to provide a context in which to assess policy and practice.

Project descriptions

Victim Offender Mediation (VOM) project, Langley, British Columbia

A pilot for the VOM Project (VOMP) began in February 1991 under the auspices of the Correctional Services of Canada. The programme works with offenders and victims in cases of serious crime such as sexual assault, serial rape, murder and armed robbery. The primary focus is on healing for both victims and offenders. Professional staff are trained trauma recovery clinicians (Gustafson 1997).

VOMP has its roots in the Victim Offender Reconciliation Programs (VORPs), which the Fraser Region Community Justice Initiatives Association (CJIA) had pioneered in Langley since 1979. Individuals within the justice system as well as offenders and victims acknowledged the value of VORPs as they worked with less serious cases and wondered whether something could not be done in cases where the trauma was far greater. CJIA staff, over a period of years with input from victims and offenders, developed the VOMP that emphasizes healing rather than reconciliation.

Cases may be referred by victims or by criminal justice officials on behalf of offenders. The cases are referred after sentencing and post-incarceration. Face-to-face meeting of victim and offender is not regarded as necessary for healing, but such a meeting occurs in over half the cases. Formal agreements are rare, as they are not a goal of VOMP process and are not regarded as particularly relevant for healing.

Assessment and preparation are often lengthy and are therapeutic in nature. A three-member VOMP staff team works with each of the parties. Individuals participate in shaping their own process, which may include communication between victim and offender through letters, videotaped interviews, and exchange of video statements. Most often one or more face-to-face meetings between victim and offender will result, with a meeting 'convened and chaired' by programme staff. Two mediators are always present in these meetings. One mediates and the other runs the video camera and may also contribute to the substance of the mediation. Meetings average three to five hours and are structured around a two-hour break. Occasionally, a case may involve more than one meeting.

VOMP does not use volunteers in their programme. Staff are trained in offender treatment issues and victim trauma recovery as well as mediation. Follow-up is also likely to be lengthy and intensive and may involve additional family members. Feedback by victims and offenders to an independent research team is very positive regarding the VOMP experience.

Victim–offender dialogue – Ohio

The Ohio Victim–Offender Dialogue Program operates within the Office of Victim Services under the auspices of the Ohio Department of Re-habilitation and Correction. The underlying premise of Victim–Offender Dialogue (VOD) is to help victim and offender define their own needs regarding meeting one another, and that the programme exists to facilitate that meeting in a manner that is safe for all involved. While the process is victim-driven, that is, victim-initiated, offenders are not coerced into participation. Victim and offender are to be viewed as equal partners by the facilitators (Ho 1999, 2000).

The Ohio programme conducted its first victim–offender mediation in May of 1966 after months of programme development within the state as well considering models emerging in other states. In March of 1999, thirty-three volunteers from within and without the Department of Rehabilitation and Correction underwent an intensive five-day training session to prepare them to be facilitators.

In this process, two volunteers act as co-facilitators and share responsibility for preparing and bringing victim and offender together for a joint dialogue. In most instances, one facilitator is employed by the Department (although functioning as a volunteer when working with VOD) and the other is from the community at large.

The focus of VOD is empowering victims and offenders to identify their needs and a process whereby progress can be made in meeting those needs. Whereas it is not expected that a meeting of victim and offender will result in wounds being healed or grief being eliminated, it is hoped that such a dialogue will be a step in that healing journey.

Preparation time will depend largely on the scope of what the victim or offender desire to pursue in face-to-face interaction. The victim may only be interested in pursuing a couple of questions. In that instance, the preparation may be rather short. The offender and victim as well as the facilitator have a fairly clear idea of what will be discussed during the meeting. This is part of providing for a safe place. The actual face-to-face meetings typically take two to four hours with breaks. Seldom is more than one meeting necessary. Follow-up is typically completed within a month after the meeting and may involve direct contact with the volunteer or phone contact.

Feedback from victims and offenders to an independent research team is very positive regarding their experience with VOD.

Victim–offender mediation/dialogue programme – Pennsylvania

The Pennsylvania Victim–Offender Mediation programme operates within the Office of Victim Advocate under the auspices of the Department of Corrections. The programme works with a range of violent crimes including those where an offender has a death sentence. This programme does not handle domestic abuse cases.

The programme has been designed and refined over a five-year period with a restorative justice framework in mind. Its focus is on generating a dialogue whereby the victim may share the impact and trauma of the crime and receive answers and additional information from the offender. It 'provides an opportunity for the victim to be heard' and 'gives the offender an opportunity to accept responsibility for his/her actions … (and) to express his/her feelings about the crime and its consequences.'

Request for mediation is victim-initiated and victim-driven. Victim participants must be 18 years of age or older. Offender participants must be cleared by the institutional psychologist. Mediator/facilitators are community volunteers who have gone through 'intensive training'. Most mediations involve co-mediators. Cases require 'extensive preparation' before the two parties come to a face-to-face mediation. Indirect dialogue is also an option within this programme.

Victim–offender mediation/dialogue programme – Texas

The Texas VOM/D is housed in the Victim Services of the Texas Department of Criminal Justice. Its purpose 'is to provide victims of violent crime the opportunity to have a structured face-to-face meeting with their offender(s) in a secure, safe environment in order to facilitate a healing, recovery process.' The programme was begun in December 1993. Referrals come from victims. A long waiting list exists of victims who have expressed interest in participating in the programme. Offenders are invited to participate and must do so voluntarily (Doerfler 1997).

The process is intense and extensive. The actual face-to-face meeting is regarded as only one important point along a 'continuum of care' from point of referral, through preparation, through meeting, to post-mediation follow-up. Preparation will easily require six months and often longer. Participants are offered a series of protocols designed to facilitate their coming to grips with their fears and their grief and to help them move along in the process of healing and recovery. Mediators work with very detailed protocols, which guide their preparatory work with victims and offenders. Mediators continually assess the victim's readiness to meet with the offender and vice versa.

The actual face-to-face meeting typically lasts from three and a half to eight hours, with eight being normative. Mediators have a detailed checklist to follow for the meeting, but the emphasis is on providing a minimal presence allowing the dialogue between victim and offender to flow without undue guidance or restriction. Most mediated cases are done by paid staff. However, a cadre of volunteer mediators have been trained, some of whom are beginning to work cases. In rare instances, the programme uses co-mediators.

Follow-up post-mediation is extensive and ongoing. Contact has been maintained with some participants for months and years after mediation.

It remains uncertain within the programme when a case is actually closed. Feedback to a team of independent researchers by victims and offenders is very favourable regarding the VOD experience.

Victim sensitive offender dialogue programme (VSOD) – Minnesota

The VSOD programme for crimes of severe violence began as a modest and quite limited initiative in 1991 in direct response to a small but growing number of victims and survivors of severe violence who requested assistance from Dr Mark Umbreit at the University of Minnesota, School of Social Work, in meeting the involved offender. These offenders were typically inmates in a maximum-security prison. The programme initially worked with a limited number of cases in Minnesota and other states.

The VSOD programme is currently in a transition period from its initial effort involving primarily Dr Umbreit and a handful of others as mediators or co-mediators to a fully developed state-wide initiative at the request of the Minnesota Department of Corrections. Approximately 15 to 20 mediators will be trained and supported to work in this broader initiative. The Center for Restorative Justice and Peacemaking will continue to respond to victim-initiated requests from other states. Cases from other states always require an on-site co-mediator to assist extensively with case development. Today the VSOD programme consists of three components: case services, training, and research.

Case services component

With rare exceptions, nearly all cases are victim-initiated and victim-driven. In all cases, involvement of the parties in a mediated dialogue is entirely voluntary and has no direct effect on the legal or institutional status of the offender/inmate. The vast majority of cases (70 per cent) have been homicides, most first or second-degree murder (many involving parents of murdered children). Several cases involved negligent homicide from drunk driving, sexual assaults, one murder resulting from a large terrorist act, and one case involving a serial murderer. The VSOD services are provided by highly trained volunteer mediator(s), with no cost to the participants. About two-thirds of case referrals to the VSOD programme in Minnesota come from within the state, with the remaining cases referred periodically from a variety of other states.

Recognizing and honouring the importance that spirituality and/or religion may play in the lives of those affected by violent crime is central to the healing process offered through VSOD. Of tremendous importance is the recognition that any discussion of or action related to the spiritual needs of the involved parties must be anchored in their expressed needs, their culture, and their mutual agreement. The mediator must never impose issues related to spirituality that are based on the mediator's own needs or assumptions.

The basic elements of the VSOD model, in one form or another, tend to be used by many as a foundation for practice. There is, however, a considerable amount of diversity and creativity used by individual practitioners and programmes. The VSOD model (Umbreit and Bradshaw 1995), should be understood more as a process or an approach, rather than a rigid model. It requires a tremendous amount of compassionate listening, patience, and self-care on the part of the practitioner throughout the entire case, in addition to the specific phases and tasks required.

Training component

Over the past seven years, several hundred people from throughout North America, Canada, Europe, and other parts of the world have attended the advanced training in VSOD in crimes of severe violence offered by the Center for Restorative Justice and Peacemaking at the University of Minnesota. This training has been co-sponsored by the National Organization for Victim Assistance and directors of similar programmes in Texas and Ohio have served as co-trainers, along with several others. This advanced training is now six days (48 hours) long. The use of a humanistic model of mediation and dialogue (described below) is central to the VSOD approach presented in the training.

The VSOD approach (Umbreit and Bradshaw 1995) consists of three essential phases that often occur over a six to twelve month period of time: case development, involving extensive preparation of the parties; the victim–offender dialogue, including pre- and post-dialogue briefing with all parties; and follow-up, which may involve a final dialogue between the parties. Some cases have required up to 18 months of preparation. The actual length of case development time is determined by the specific needs of the involved parties, the legal and correctional context of the case, and the mediator's assessment. The VSOD approach provides a 'road- map' for working with cases of severe violence. In practice it is far less linear than it appears and is continually adapted to the specific needs of the involved parties. It is particularly important to adapt the process to any presenting cultural needs that may be present in the case.

Research component

In 1998, the Center for Restorative Justice and Peacemaking at the University of Minnesota initiated the first and largest multi-site study (Umbreit, Brown, Coates and Vos 2001) to date of the impact of mediation and dialogue in crimes of severe violence, focusing on state-wide programmes in Texas and Ohio. Whereas more than 42 empirical studies of VOM in property crimes and minor assaults have been conducted in North America and Europe, only four such smaller studies that focused on crimes of severe violence have been completed, with the largest in Canada (Roberts 1995). The final report of the Center's study of the programmes in Texas and Ohio will be available on the Center's website by early 2003. Preliminary data is reported below in 'What We Are Learning from Research'.

Humanistic mediation: creating a safe place for dialogue

Humanistic mediation (Umbreit 1997) represents a 'dialogue-driven' rather than 'settlement-driven' approach to confronting conflict. It emphasizes the importance of the following elements: meeting with the parties individually and in person prior to the joint mediation session, in order to listen to their story, build rapport, explain the process and prepare them for engagement in a mediated dialogue; a non-directive style of mediation in which the parties are primarily speaking to each other with minimal intervention by the mediator; and a mediator attitude of unconditional positive regard and connectedness with all parties, while remaining impartial (e.g. not taking sides).

While the focus of the mediator's work is upon the creation of a safe, if not sacred, place to foster direct dialogue among the parties about the emotional and material impact of the conflict, written settlement agreements often occur but are not central to the process. Humanistic mediation is a specific practice application of the broader theory of transformative mediation (Bush and Folger 1994). It is grounded more in a paradigm of healing and peacemaking than problem-solving and resolution. The telling and hearing of each other's stories about the conflict, the opportunity for maximum direct communication with each other, and the importance of honouring silence and the innate wisdom and strength of the participants, are all central to humanistic mediation practice. It is particularly important to use a humanistic style of mediation when working with crimes of severe violence, since the primary issues are typically focused on exchanging information, expressing feelings, reconstructing the event, and for many, a search for meaning following such a devastating event in their lives.

Qualities of the mediator that are central to VSOD through humanistic mediation include: being fully present and centred on the needs of the involved parties; feeling compassion and empathy for all the involved parties; being comfortable with silence, with ambiguity, and with intuition; maintaining a spirit of humility about one's own contribution to the healing process; and bearing witness to the enormous courage, strength and capacity of the parties to help each other, and honouring the meanings they place on the encounter.

What we are learning from research

There exist many anecdotal stories from victims and offenders who often speak of their participation in a mediated dialogue as a powerful and transformative experience that helped them in their healing process. Parents of murdered children have expressed their sense of relief after meeting the offender/inmate and sharing their pain as well as being able to reconstruct what actually happened and why. One such mother whose son was murdered stated, 'I just needed to let him see the pain he has caused in my life and to find out why he pulled the trigger.' A school-teacher who was assaulted and nearly killed commented after meeting the young man in prison, 'It helped me end this ordeal … for me, it has made a difference in my life, though this type of meeting is not for everyone.' An offender/inmate who met with the mother of the man he killed stated, 'It felt good to be able to bring her some relief and to express my remorse to her.' A doctor in California whose sister was killed by a drunk driver and who was initially very sceptical about meeting the offender, following the mediation session stated, 'I couldn't begin to heal until I let go of my hatred … after the mediation I felt a great sense of relief … I was now ready to find enjoyment in life again.'

Only three studies of VOM in crimes of severe violence have been conducted in the US, two were small exploratory initiatives that each examined four case studies; the third study has just recently begun and represents the first major initiative in the US involving multiple sites.

The first study (Umbreit 1989) found that offering a mediated dialogue session in several very violent cases – including a sniper shooting case – was very beneficial to the victims, offenders and community members or family members that were involved in the process. Three of these four cases (all adult offenders) were handled by a police department in upstate New York (Genesee County) that operates a comprehensive restorative justice programme. The second study (Flaten 1996) involving four cases of severely violent crime committed by juvenile offenders found very high levels of satisfaction with the process and outcomes, from both victims and offenders. The offenders were inmates in a juvenile-correctional facility in Alaska.

A third study (Umbreit, Brown, Coates and Vos 2001) is a multi-site, multi-year study (initiated in 1998) that represents the largest initiative in the United States to examine the impact of VOM and dialogue in crimes of severe violence. Programmes in Texas and Ohio were examined, along with a number of cases in other states.

A total of 80 interviews with victims and offenders have been completed. Of the 20 mediated cases in Texas, 70 per cent involved homicide.

Of the 21 cases mediated in Ohio, 57 per cent involved homicide. For the victims interviewed at both sites, post-mediation interviews indicated that 90 per cent were very satisfied and 10 per cent somewhat satisfied with the case preparation; 76 per cent felt the meeting with the offender was very helpful and 24 per cent felt it was somewhat helpful; and 100 per cent were very satisfied with their overall involvement in programme. For the offenders interviewed at both sites, post-mediation interviews indicated 93 per cent were very satisfied and 7 per cent somewhat satisfied with the case preparation; 93 per cent felt the meeting with the victim was very helpful and 7 per cent felt it was somewhat helpful; 81 per cent were very satisfied and 19 per cent somewhat satisfied with their overall involvement in the programme.

A far more descriptive picture of the impact the mediated dialogue session had upon their lives is offered in the participants' actual statements. The following victim comments illustrate common themes:

'I told him, "When you murdered my daughter, you murdered me." My kids, they didn't just lose their sister, they lost their mother because I was not able to function after that, I was brain dead for the longest period of time.'

'It's probably the best thing I've ever done.'

'On a scale of one to ten, it's a hundred.'

'I think in a lot of ways that this is probably the hardest thing that [the offender] ever did, was to sit in front of me and accept responsibility; he didn't have anything besides his own well being to gain from it. And I think that he had to look at some really hard things in himself to do that.'

'My daughter's dead ... but I know I'm better, I can sleep at night, I know it's a good feeling not to hate some monster, and I know my daughter didn't give him any reason to kill her.'

'Before, he was just, you know, a murderer ... after, he was a human being.'

Offender comments included the following themes:

'I think I'm more alive now than I ever have been at any one point in time ... I feel like I'm actually living life now, instead of just existing, you know? Very much at peace ... I told the mediator I felt cleansed. I felt washed, refreshed, ... I felt a great burden had been lifted off my shoulders. I felt joy.'

'Okay, I did this, now I need to move on, I need to work with inside myself, to say … now what else can I do to make this better, is there something that I can do? … That you've done something positive, that at least something positive will come out of this.'

'It felt good to be able to mend that broken spot in her life. Though I can't ever replace what was lost.'

And, in answer to the question, what surprised you most? 'Her compassion, her deep feeling for not only my family and my daughter's and my friends, but her deep feeling for me. I met another face of God that night. And the face God wore that night was hers. The God I know is a God of mercy, a God of love, a God of forgiveness, and that night I met all those things in her.'

The only other known study, completed in Canada (Roberts 1995), examined the Victim Offender Mediation Project in Langley, British Columbia. This community-based Canadian programme, after having pioneered the early development of VOM and reconciliation with property offences and minor assaults many years ago, initiated in 1991 a new project to apply the mediation process with crimes of severe violence involving incarcerated inmates. Prior to initiating this project, a small study (Gustafson and Smidstra 1989) had been conducted by the programme to assess whether victims and offenders involved in severely violent crime would be interested in meeting with each other in a safe and structured manner, after intensive preparation, if such a service were available. A very high level of interest in such meetings was found.

In the study conducted by Roberts (1995), virtually all of the 22 offenders and 24 victims who participated indicated support for the programme. This support was reflected in their belief that they found considerable specific and overall value in the programme, felt it was ethically and professionally run, and would not hesitate to recommend it to others. The overall effects of the mediation session expressed by victims included: they had finally been heard; the offender now no longer exercised control over them; they could see the offender as a person rather than a monster; they felt more trusting in their relationships with others; they felt less fear; they weren't preoccupied with the offender any more; they felt peace; they would not feel suicidal again; they had no more anger.

For offenders, the overall effects of a mediated dialogue with the victim included: discovering emotions; feelings of empathy; increasing awareness of impacts of their acts; increasing self-awareness; opening eyes to the outside world, rather than closed institutional thinking; feeling good about having tried the process; achieving peace of mind in knowing one has helped a former victim.

Implications for policy and practice

As additional states consider developing policies to provide opportunities for interested victims of severe violence to meet with the offender/inmate, we offer the following recommendations for consideration.

Policy

(1) Departments of Corrections should consider developing specific procedures for responding to the requests of those victims who request a mediation/dialogue session with the responsible inmate.

(2) Public funding should be appropriated to support the development and management of victim-sensitive offender dialogue services in crimes of severe violence.

(3) Consideration should be given to amending current state crime-victim compensation laws to allow reimbursement for the cost of victim-initiated mediation/dialogue services with the responsible inmate, when such an encounter is clearly related to their healing process and when such services are provided only by mediators who can document that they have received advanced training in providing victim-sensitive offender dialogue services in crimes of severe violence.

Practice

(1) Only persons who can document that they have received at least 32 hours of advanced training in victim-sensitive offender dialogue in crimes of severe violence and who are under the supervision and support of a mentor should be allowed to provide such services.

(2) When providing victim-sensitive offender dialogue services, a minimum of two in-person preparation meetings with each party should be conducted. In most cases, it is more likely that four to six, or more, preparation meetings will be required.

(3) The process of victim-sensitive offender dialogue in crimes of severe violence should be entirely voluntary for all parties.

(4) Victim-sensitive offender dialogue in crimes of severe violence should be victim-initiated. When inmates initiate the process, their letter should be kept on file in case their victim(s) later request a mediation/dialogue session.

(5) The planning, development and implementation of victim-sensitive

offender dialogue services should be conducted with active
ment of victim services providers along with correctional
other persons familiar with the VSOD process, preferably on
completed the advanced VSOD training.

Conclusion

It is clear that the principles of restorative justice can be applied in selected
cases of severe violence, particularly through the practice of VOM and
dialogue. A far more intense case development process is required and the
'dialogue-driven' humanistic model of mediation offers a more victim-
sensitive process that is also likely to engage the offender in a dialogue
about the full impact of the offence. Preliminary data indicates
exceptionally high levels of client satisfaction with the process and
outcome of VOM and dialogue in crimes of severe violence. This bodes
well for the future development of this emerging restorative justice
intervention. While these studies provide important preliminary data
related to the impact of the mediation and dialogue process in crimes of
severe violence, particularly homicide, they are suggestive at best. Far
more rigorous studies involving larger samples are required before any
conclusions can be drawn. A great deal of caution, however, must be
exercised in applying restorative justice principles in such cases. There
have already been numerous examples of well-intentioned criminal-
justice officials and individual mediators who are too quick to refer or
facilitate the use of mediation and dialogue in crimes of severe violence
without having first secured advanced training and mentoring. Many
unintended negative consequences could result from such initiatives,
including a significant re-victimization of the victim.

There remain many unanswered questions, as well. For whom, under
what circumstances, and when is the use of VOM in crimes of severe
violence most appropriate? How extensive should the case development
process be? Is there significant variance in the degree and length of pre-
mediation case preparation based on characteristics of individual cases?
What type of crime victim and offender respond best to such an
intervention? How can VOM/D services, in crimes of severe violence, be
offered as a voluntary restorative justice intervention on a larger scale and
in a cost effective manner? How extensive should advanced training be?
To what extent should families and other support persons be routinely
involved in the process, at what points, and to what degree? Can state
victim compensation laws cover the cost related to victims of severe
violence who request this intervention? While nearly all cases to date are

victim-initiated, is there a place for offender-initiated cases without triggering the unintended consequence of re-victimizing the victim? Far more rigorous longitudinal, qualitative and quantitative studies are clearly needed in this emerging area that holds the potential for exceptionally high positive impact on participating parties while including significant risks.

At its core, the process of VOM and dialogue in crimes of severe violence is about engaging those most affected by the horror of violent crime in the process of holding the offender truly accountable, helping the victim(s) gain a greater sense of meaning, if not closure, concerning the severe harm resulting from the crime, and helping all parties to have a greater capacity to move on with their lives in a positive fashion. This emerging restorative justice practice certainly warrants further development and analysis, along with an attitude of cautious and informed support.

References

Alder, C. and Wundersitz, J. (1994) *Family Conferencing and Juvenile Justice: The Way Forward or Misplaced Optimism?* Canberra, AUS: Australian Institute of Criminology.

Bazemore, G. and Umbreit, M. S. (1995) 'Rethinking the Sanctioning Function in Juvenile Court: Retributive or Restorative Responses to Youth Crime', *Crime and Delinquency*, 41(3): 296–316.

Bazemore G. and Walgrave L. (1999) *Restorative Juvenile Justice: Repairing the Harm of Youth Crime.* Monsey, NY: Criminal Justice Press.

Bradshaw, W. and Umbreit, M. S. (1998) 'Crime Victims Meet Juvenile Offenders: Contributing Factors to Victim Satisfaction with Mediated Dialogue in Minneapolis', *Juvenile and Family Court Journal*, 49(3): 17–25.

Bush, R. and Folger, J. (1994) *The Promise of Mediation, Responding to Conflict Through Empowerment and Recognition.* San Francisco, CA: Jossey-Bass.

Coates, R. B. and Gehm, J. (1989) 'An Empirical Assessment' in M. Wright and B. Galaway (eds) *Mediation and Criminal Justice.* London: Sage Publications.

Collins, J. (1984) *Final Evaluation Report on the Grande Prairie Community Reconciliation Project For Young Offenders.*

Dignan, (1990) *Repairing the Damage: An Evaluation of an Experimental Adult Reparation Scheme in Kettering, Northamptonshire.* Sheffield: Centre for Criminological Legal Research, Faculty of Law, University of Sheffield.

Doerfler, D. (1997) 'Facing the Pain that Heals', *The Victim's Informer*, 1(3), Texas Department of Criminal Justice Crime Victim Clearinghouse 1 (3).

Flaten, C. (1996) 'Victim Offender Mediation: Application With Serious Offenses Committed by Juvenile' in B. Galaway and J. Hudson (eds) *Restorative Justice: International Perspectives.*

Galaway, B. and Hudson, J. (1996) *Restorative Justice: An International Perspective.* Monsey, NY: Criminal Justice Press.

Gehm, J. (1990) 'Mediated Victim–Offender Restitution Agreements: An Exploratory Analysis of Factors Related to Victim Participation' in B. Galaway and J. Judson (eds) *Criminal Justice, Restitution, and Reconciliation*. Monsey, NY: Criminal Justice Press.

Gustafson, D. L. (1997) 'Facilitating Communication Between Victims and Offenders in Cases of Serious and Violent Crime', *The ICCA Journal on Community Corrections*, 8(1): 44–9.

Gustafson, D. L. and Smidstra, H. (1989) 'Victim Offender Reconciliation in Serious Crime: A Report on the Feasibility Study Undertaken for The Ministry of the Solicitor General (Canada)'. Langley, BC: Fraser Region Community Justice Initiatives Association.

Ho, K. (1999) 'DRC Victim Offender Dialogue Program Launches Training', *Community Justice Beacon* (Ohio Department of Rehabilitation and Correction), 1(1): 12–14.

Ho, K. (2000) 'A Journey Toward Healing', *Community Justice Beacon* (Ohio Department of Rehabilitation and Correction), 2(1): 8–9.

Hudson, J., Morris, A., Maxwell, G. and Galaway, B. (1996) *Family Group Conferences: Perspectives on Policy and Practice*. Monsey, NY: Criminal Justice Press.

Marshall, T. F. and Merry, S. E. (1990) *Crime and Accountability – VOM in Practice*. London: HMSO.

Messmer , H. and Otto, H.-U. (1992) *Restorative Justice on Trial: Pitfalls and Potentials of Victim Offender Mediation – International Research Perspectives*. Dordrecht, NETH: Kluwer Academic Publishers.

Nugent, W. R. and Paddock, J. B. (1995) 'The Effect of Victim–Offender Mediation on Severity of Reoffense', *Mediation Quarterly*, 12(4): 353–67.

Nugent, W. R., Umbreit, M. S., Wiinamaki, L. and Paddock, J. (2000) 'Participation in VOM and Re-Offense: Successful Replications?' *Journal of Research on Social Work Practice*.

Perry, L., Lajeunesse, T. and Woods, A. (1987) *Mediation Services: An Evaluation*. Manitoba Attorney General: Research, Planning and Evaluation.

Pranis, K. and Umbreit, M. S. (1992) *Public Opinion Research Challenges Perception of Widespread Public Demand for Harsher Punishment*. Minneapolis: MN Citizens Council on Crime and Justice.

Roberts, T. (1995) *Evaluation of the VOM Program in Langley, BC*. Victoria, BC: Focus Consultants.

Schneider, A. (1986) 'Restitution and Recidivism Rates of Juvenile Offenders: Results from Four Experimental Studies,' *Criminology* Vol. 24, pp. 533–552.

Umbreit, M. S. and Bradshaw, W. (1995) *Advanced Victim Sensitive Mediation in Crimes of Severe Violence Training Manual*. Center for Restorative Justice and Mediation, University of Minnesota.

Umbreit, M. S. and Bradshaw, W. (1997) 'Crime Victim Experience with Mediation: A Comparison of Mediation with Adult vs. Juvenile Offenders', *Federal Probation*, 61(4): 33–9.

Umbreit, M. S., Bradshaw, W. and Coates, R. B. (1999) 'Victims of Severe Violence Meet the Offender: Restorative Justice Through Dialogue', *International Review of Victimology*, 6(4): 321–44.

Umbreit, M. S. and Brown, K. (1999) 'Victims of Severe Violence Meet Offenders in Ohio', *The Crime Victim Report*, 3(3): 35–6.

Umbreit, M. S. and R. B. Coates (1993) 'Cross-Site Analysis of Victim Offender Mediation in Four States', *Crime and Delinquency*, 39(4): 565-85.

Umbreit, M. S. and Coates, R. (1999) 'Multi-Cultural Implications of Juvenile Restorative Justice', *Federal Probation*, 58(2): 44–51.

Umbreit, M. S., Coates, R. B. and Roberts, A. W. (2000) The Impact of Victim Offender Mediation: A Cross-National Perspective. *Mediation Quarterly*.

Umbreit, M. S. and Greenwood, J. (1999) National Survey of VOM Programmes in the United States. *Mediation Quarterly*.

Umbreit, M. S. and Niemeyer, M. (1996) 'Victim Offender Mediation: From the Margins Toward the Mainstream', *Perspectives*, 20(1): 28–30.

Umbreit, M. S. and Roberts, A. W. (1996) *Mediation of Criminal Conflict in England: An Assessment of Services in Coventry and Leeds.* Center for Restorative Justice and Mediation, University of Minnesota.

Umbreit, M. S. and Stacey, S. L. (1996) 'Family Group Conferencing Comes to the US: A Comparison with Victim Offender Mediation', *Juvenile and Family Court Journal*, 47(2): 29–38.

Umbreit, M. S. and Vos, B. (1997) 'Homicide Survivors Meet the Offender Prior to Execution: Restorative Justice Through Dialogue', *Homicide Studies*, 4(1): 63–87.

Umbreit, M. S. and Zehr, H. (1996) 'Restorative Family Group Conferences: Differing Models and Guidelines for Practice', *Federal Probation*, 60(3): 24–9.

Umbreit, M. S. (1989) 'Violent Offenders and Their Victims' in M. Wright and B. Galaway (eds) *Mediation and Criminal Justice.* London: Sage.

Umbreit, M. S. (1994) *Victim Meets Offender: The Impact of Restorative Justice and Mediation.* Monsey, NY: Criminal Justice Press.

Umbreit, M. S. (1995) The Development and Impact of VOM in the US, *Mediation Quarterly*, 12(3): 263–76.

Umbreit, M. S. (1997) 'Humanistic Mediation: A Transformative Journey of Peace-Making', *Mediation Quarterly*, 14(3): 201–13.

Umbreit, M. S. (2001) *The Handbook on VOM: An Essential Guide for Practice and Research.* San Francisco: Jossey-Bass.

Van Ness, D. and Strong, K. H. (1997) *Restoring Justice.* Cincinnati: Anderson Publishing.

Wright, M. (1996) *Justice for Victims and Offenders.* Philadelphia, PA: Open University Press.

Wright, M. and Galaway, B. (1989) *Mediation and Criminal Justice.* London: Sage.

Zehr, H. (1990) *Changing Lenses, A New Focus for Crime and Justice.* Scottsdale, PA: Herald Press.

Chapter 7

Corporations, crime and restorative justice

Marianne Löschnig-Gspandl

General remarks

One of the very many aspects and facets of restorative justice is the question of how restorative justice deals with corporate crime as well as corporations as crime victims. At first glance, that question seems to be perfectly clear, but when going into details, one finds out rather quickly that it requires exact definitions to deal with at least two terms – 'restorative justice' and 'corporate crime' – that cover very different topics.

Restorative justice

As far as restorative justice is concerned, this chapter follows the approach in which restorative justice measures are linked to the criminal justice system: wrongful acts or omissions performed either by individuals or corporations that are to be considered criminal acts according to our current terminology because of their serious social inadequacy, should also in future be treated within the framework of our traditional criminal justice systems. But our traditional criminal justice systems – keeping the punitive system as a background – should be (and already have been) changed in a fundamental way towards being a much more restorative system. This means as many restorative elements as possible should be included, such as compensation orders, alternative dispute resolution and settlement strategies as well as diversion and restitution in the context of (suspended) sentences etc, considering restitution and reconciliation to be an important, comprehensive purpose of criminal law in its own right (Löschnig-Gspandl 1996: 71ff). Adequate responses to crime, therefore, should use the effectiveness of the criminal justice system rather than seeking to replace it. Thus, the right motto is improvement instead of abolition of the criminal justice system.

Crimes are supposed to be the most serious violations of other people's, corporation's, or the community's interests so that a response by means of civil or administrative law alone would not be sufficient to result in general and individual prevention of these crimes. But thanks to the principle of subsidiarity which is also true within the criminal law – meaning that punishment (fines and imprisonment) has to be the *ultima ratio* even within the criminal sanctioning system – every criminal law should introduce alternative, and therefore also restorative, sanctions, or better: restorative measures. Restorative measures have the ability to serve as additional alternative criminal (not penal) reactions as far as they meet the purpose of prevention. And beyond that: they are the only legal sanctions that meet the purpose of restitution.

The criminal justice system should serve primarily the purposes of prevention and restitution. After a crime has been committed, the balance in society has to be restored by focusing on reparation and restoration as far as possible. The parties involved – from the victim to the offender to the community – should get the opportunity to participate actively in the criminal proceedings or in diversionary proceedings.

From a restorative justice point of view crime is not primarily seen as a violation against the state, but as an act (either arising from a longer lasting conflict or at least causing a conflict) that results in injuries to individual or corporate victims, communities and also the offender him/herself. The debts offenders owe are not to an abstract entity called 'the state' but to their victims and actual communities.

A criminal justice system that provides the possibility of restorative justice measures as additional instruments of the sanctioning system in suitable cases can react in a much more adequate, socially con-structive, and even more efficient way in terms of crime prevention by restoring public peace after the offence and by re-establishing the social link between offender, victim (be they individuals or corporations) and community.

Corporate crime

Corporate crime in this context is understood as being various crimes (acts to be prosecuted by criminal justice authorities) committed by corporations, which actually means committed by their representatives for the benefit of or on behalf of the corporation. The corporations in question usually are enterprises and beyond that also legal entities (juristic persons), including public corporations.[1] Crimes include economic crime (such as offences against property, bribery, money laundering, violations of antitrust law, price fixing, restraint of trade, bankruptcy offences, tax evasion, etc), misrepresentation in advertising, production and sale of unsafe products, deceptive packaging, environmental crime, but also crimes against persons including crimes causing injury or death and many more. These crimes are committed by and within a legitimate organization, in accordance with the organizational goals, and victimize either individuals (including employees and customers), other corporations, or the general public.

Talking about corporations or legal persons, one also must not forget the role of corporations as victims. Obviously there are legal scholars and criminologists who understand the term corporate crime in a comprehensive sense, not only covering crimes of/for corporations, but also crimes against corporations (Ruggiero 1996: 5). I do not think the latter should be incorporated into the definition of corporate crime, at least German-speaking authors usually do not do so. I do intend, however, to include the issue of corporations as victims in my comments on corporate crime and restorative justice to draw a complete picture of corporations, crime and restorative justice.

Consequences

Combining elements of corporate crime with restorative justice means that, at the very least, we must search for the methods, procedures and strategies necessary to react appropriately to offences 'committed' by legally liable corporations. These reactive measures must stress or contain elements of restitution, compensation or mediation, thereby extending and enriching the current sanctioning systems. Moreover, we must create comparable reactive measures in cases in which corporations are victims of crimes.

Coming from Austria (therefore having more or less the same legal, theoretical and especially the same dogmatic background as German criminal lawyers), talking about this topic is particularly precarious: corporations as victims do not constitute a problem, but corporations as offenders do. Up to now, corporate liability has not existed in the Austrian criminal justice system. Thus, for Austria not only is the question of restorative justice and corporate crime a challenge, but so too is the underlying question of criminal corporate liability (Löschnig-Gspandl 2000: 157ff, 2002: 241ff). It is true, however, that Austria – due to obligations laid down in international treaties – is thinking of implementing provisions making corporations liable for crimes; and Austria is considering a criminal (not only administrative) corporate liability (Zeder 2001: 630ff). Whereas the German legislature has so far decided not to invent anything new but stick to the existing sanctions in the *Ordnungswidrigkeitengesetz*, which also fulfil the aforementioned international and European obligations.

The Austrian Ministry of Justice is considering the introduction of a true criminal liability for at least two reasons: firstly because of the principle of equality as well as its necessity for effective crime prevention; secondly, because of the fact that in the long run we certainly will also be obliged to do it by European legal instruments; the tendency clearly goes towards a criminal corporate liability. Many other European countries, e.g. the Netherlands, UK, France, Norway, Denmark, Finland and Belgium, either implemented it many years ago or have at least recently begun introducing criminal corporate liability (Heine 1998: 173ff; 2000 7: 871; Leigh 1982: 1508ff).

The position advanced in this paper is that the idea of introducing criminal liability of corporations into the Austrian criminal justice system as a whole has to be accompanied by restorative measures. A criminal sanctioning system that knows restorative elements with regard to individual offenders and victims certainly has to provide for adequate measures as far as corporations are concerned.

Corporations as offenders

Coming from a country that does not yet even recognize retributive criminal sanctions for corporations, I have to say a few words about the theoretical background.

Corporate liability as a necessity from a criminal policy point of view

There is one thing that seems to be clear: a general criminal liability for corporations (legal persons) should be incorporated in Criminal Codes for several compelling reasons (Dannecker 2001: 101ff). First of all, one has to recognize the increasing importance of legal entities in society, especially in the areas of commerce and trade, quite apart from the issues of internationalism and e-business. As a consequence, corporate crime also came into existence or increased, causing danger and damage in huge dimensions and eventually threatening the whole economic and social order. Approximately two-thirds of all serious economic crimes in Germany are committed by corporations, especially in the fields of building trade, transport, tourism and banking (Kaiser 1996: 863; Schünemann 1979: 60).

It is obvious that the real actors on the stage are usually corporations: buying and selling retail products is physically carried out by employees, but everybody understands that it is the employer who is the real partner in the transactions. If you buy something at a department store, nobody would come away with the idea that they are making a deal with the person operating the cash register. Everybody understands that environmental crimes committed for the benefit of a corporation are crimes committed by the corporation, for it is the actual profiteer.

So if the real actors or offenders are corporations, it is not quite clear why it is always only the individual who is subject to sanctions, *if* this happens at all. Sometimes nobody who can be held responsible is found, because of the structure and internal organization of the enterprise, the division of labour or responsibilities within the corporation; therefore quite often there is a *gap* in accountability for corporate behaviour, because no single individual meets all the conditions for criminal liability. Look at corporate fraud: often no individual completes *all* the required paperwork *and* has the criminal intent.

But even if somebody responsible is found, sanctions – be they punitive or restorative – have to be assessed according to the individual's circumstances. Thus the monetary situation of an individual manager will be calculated instead of the financial state of the corporation. This process does not have any preventive effect on the corporation at all. Moreover, individual employees are easily replaceable. A corporation can only be discouraged from criminal behaviour by hurting its capital or its image – which in the end again means its capital.

The relevance of corporations has been acknowledged by private law as well as by public law (administrative law). Legal persons do possess rights and duties, are civilly liable for damage caused by their organs or representatives, even their reputation/credit is protected by civil law. Internal harmonization of the legal system then requires extension to criminal law. If legal persons are treated by law on an equal basis to natural persons, then they also have to be equally responsible themselves, especially for such serious wrongful acts. Crimes cannot be answered by civil and administrative means only.

Why should an individual who has committed a comparable crime for his own benefit be prosecuted, whereas corporations may escape sanctions? It is a paradox that liability is lacking exactly where the risks are biggest.

Dogmatic background

Being convinced that criminal corporate liability is necessary from a criminal policy point of view, the Austrian legislature is not alone in having to face fundamental dogmatic problems when trying to implement adequate provisions. In this context these problems will merely be mentioned without further elaboration (Heine 1996: 211, 1998: 180; Löschnig-Gspandl 2000: 157ff).

Our traditional systems of criminal liability have been created with exclusive regard to human beings as offenders. Fundamental elements of criminal law like the principle of culpability seem to collide radically with the idea of corporate criminal responsibility. Legal entities are neither able to act themselves, nor to form a guilty state of mind in terms of intent or negligence which, however, are the basic components of crime.

One of the main characteristics of the legal system, however, should be its ability to develop in response to social change. And there actually have been many attempts to create concepts of corporate guilt (Tiedemann 1988: 1169; Fisse and Braithwaite 1988: 483, 1993). As it is clear that it can be only individuals who act on behalf of a corporation, the key dogmatic question should be whose act can be *attributed* to the corporation. What are the criteria that should let a criminal act be viewed as an act committed by the corporation?

According to the Second Protocol to the Convention on the Protection of the European Communities' Financial Interests of 1997 (ABl C 221/11, 19.7.1997), for instance, the member states of the European Union are obliged to take the necessary measures to ensure that legal persons can be held liable for fraud, active corruption and money laundering committed for their benefit by any person, acting either individually or as part of an organ of the legal person, who has a leading position within the legal person, based on

- a power of representation of the legal person,
- an authority to take decisions on behalf of the legal person or
- an authority to exercise control within the legal person,

as well as for involvement as accessories or instigators in such fraud, active corruption or money laundering or the attempted commission of such fraud.

Apart from these cases each member state shall take the necessary measures to ensure that a legal person can be held liable where the lack of supervision or control by a person referred to above has made possible the commission of a fraud, an act of active corruption or money laundering for the benefit of that legal person by a person under its authority. Liability of a legal person shall not exclude criminal proceedings against natural persons who are perpetrators, instigators or accessories in the fraud, active corruption or money laundering.

Although this does not constitute an obligation to introduce a criminal corporate liability, it seems to be clear – for the reasons mentioned above – that this is the only way that makes sense.

So if there is an agreement on the necessity of criminal liability for corporations, one has to look for meaningful, adequate forms of criminal sanctions or responses. These should be responses that fit into a criminal law with the purposes of prevention and restitution.

Possible (restorative) sanctions

The following section does not deal with sanctions for the (individual) representatives of corporations who physically commit the crime. As they are individuals, our traditional sanctioning system is to be applied. The challenge is to find adequate sanctions that can be directly imposed on the corporation. To do this seriously, empirical research on the likely effects of corporate sanctioning should be the basis; especially when it comes to Europe, however, little is known so far about the impact of sanctions imposed on corporations.

The range of options in imposing sanctions upon corporations is a wide one: reactive, preventive and proactive approaches can be found in modern jurisdictions, and even restorative ones. During the last few years, a shift from a purely punitive approach to one of prevention and direct or indirect structural intervention is to be seen in this context (Heine 1999: 238).

Corporations are not only punished by fines (Hawke 2000: 250) or other monetary sanctions such as profit-stripping, which means the imposition of an increased fine based on an amount equal to the financial benefit acquired by the corporation as a result of the commission of an offence (up to total confiscation of property), which brings the problem of quantifying the monetary benefit (Hawke 2000: 254). Other punitive sanctions exist, such as restrictions on business activities (suspension of certain rights, withdrawal of licenses, seizure of certain goods or rights, prohibition of certain activities, regulating organization and production, removal of managers, sequestration, publication of the court decision, appointment of a trustee, closure or winding-up of the enterprise), or exclusion from advantages (withdrawal of tax advantages or subsidies) (deDoelder 1996: 306); but there is also a broad spectrum of other orders and conditions as well as corporate probation (see below).

The Second Protocol of the European Union calls upon the member states to ensure that a legal person is punishable by effective, proportionate and dissuasive sanctions, which shall include criminal or non-criminal *fines* and may include other sanctions such as

- exclusion from entitlement to public benefits or aid,
- temporary or permanent disqualification from the practice of commercial activities,
- placing under judicial supervision or
- a judicial winding-up order.

Of course, this is not a final enumeration, and many other sanctions may be created. But, when looking at the types of sanctions enumerated, it is a pity one cannot find any restorative elements at all. The working group 'Penal law/Community law' of the Council of the European Union did not even think of restorative measures (besides confiscation).

Diversion, conditional discharge, deferred sentence or probation should be applied: thus letting the corporation go free without immediate punishment (such as a fine or maybe the disqualification from the practice of commercial activities, etc) on condition that it compensates the victim for the damage done. Of course, several different conditions or orders, or even punishment and restitution, may also be combined.

Corporate probation (as it is applied in the US) (Bergman 1992: 1312) is an alternative sanction, serving in particular the purpose of prevention by reforming the enterprise. At the same time the extreme consequence of complete financial ruin may be avoided. Corporate probation includes a rich spectrum of orders, such as reorganization: the court may, for instance, compel the senior management to make a series of changes concerning safety procedures, structural reorganization, etc. Compensation or even community service may also be imposed. According to Heine (1999: 249), for example, a large bakery may be ordered to supply bread to slums, or a company may be ordered to assist, through the transfer of know-how, a non-profit organization in developing re-integration programmes for prisoners. Préfontaine (1999: 281) calls 'a community-service order requiring a corporation to undertake some work or activity that is of benefit to the community' an 'interesting and powerful restorative component of a probation order'. Corporate probation may impose greater deterrence than mere economic solutions.

In addition to restitution and compensation, Préfontaine (1999: 283) suggests 'some "redress facilitation" mechanisms which may be set in place by legislation or by the courts. Their aim would be to facilitate the more expeditious compensation of victims for the harm they suffered. For example, redress for victims may be facilitated by requiring a corporation to provide information to litigants, as an enhanced and more intrusive form of discovery.'

When looking for restorative instruments one faces one major problem, however: in the majority of cases, where the greatest damage is done, the victims of corporate crime are either an anonymous group of people one cannot exactly define, or even the general public. Moreover, it will be difficult to quantify (for instance environmental) damage in terms of cost. In these cases symbolic restitution (for instance payments to welfare institutions or community service) seems possible. The question remains, however, whether such measures really are restorative ones in the true sense. Do they not remind us of punishment? (see below). In fact, they seem to be an in-between type of sanction.

An interesting type of sanction in this context also would be the imposition of an 'equity fine', which means that very severe fines should, according to Coffee (1981: 4B), be imposed not in cash, but in the equity securities of the corporation. Such an equity fine could require the convicted corporation to issue such numbers of shares to the state's crime victim compensation fund as would have an expected market value equal to the cash fine necessary to prevent the corporation from re-offending.

Victim–offender mediation (VOM) does not seem to make sense at first glance. VOM concentrates on the relationship between the victim and the offender. These two are the relevant parties having responsibilities associated with participation in the conflict settlement process after a crime has been committed: offenders are responsible for acknowledging the wrong done, reflecting upon the injustice they have done, making apology, expressing remorse and being willing to compensate or to make reparation. The responsibilities of victims are to accept the expressions of remorse made by the offender and to express a willingness to forgive. This personal involvement is the nucleus of VOM.

A legal person as offender is no suitable partner in mediation. Of course, the corporation may send a physical representative to the mediation procedure, but mediation would not have more effects on the corporation itself in terms of prevention than pure compensation for damage. But it seems legitimate to ask if there are not specific cases where this could be in the victim's interest. What about cases where the victim of a corporate crime is an employee (I am thinking of creating health hazards for the workers), or certain individuals, e.g. those living in a polluted area. Maybe in such cases, in which interpersonal contacts are going to continue, an exchange of the different points of view should take place and a settlement beyond material compensation be reached.

What seems to be clear, however, is that restorative measures alone may not always show (sufficient) preventive effects on corporations. The costs of the criminal act for the corporation are far too low; the corporation only risks the *status quo ante*. Not to mention the fact that only a few crimes are detected. Therefore, restitution as a sanction on its own does not seem to make much sense in terms of deterrence unless it is combined with other, non-restorative measures. It should be combined with, or incorporated into, other strategies of responding to the crime, which add the deterrent factor.

Heine's call for corporate sanctions to be increasingly 'grounded in a preventive perspective which leaves room for corporations to amend their ways in the future and bring their practices in full compliance with the law' (Heine 1999: 252) is to be supported. Deterrent effects (Dandurand 1999: 274),[2] however, may sometimes be reached only by imposing (rather drastic) punitive sanctions, thus leading to undesirable consequences for innocent parties, employment opportunities, the economic life of a community, etc. It is clear that the interests of others, e.g. the workforce or creditors, have to be safeguarded adequately. If a sanction leads to bankruptcy or at least forces the company to limit its operations, the corporation's ability to repair the damages it created, to compensate victims, or even to perform a service deemed essential to the community, can also be affected (Préfontaine 1999: 283). This is the main reason for having stressed the importance of sentencing mechanisms such as diversion, suspended or conditional sentences, conditional discharge or probation: they would allow courts or maybe even public prosecutors in the context of diversion to impose very harsh sanctions while at the same time stating that these sanctions would only be executed if the corporation fails to comply with restorative and compliance orders (Préfontaine 1999: 283).

One great value of making restitution a part of the criminal sanctioning system lies in the fact that victims get compensation even in cases where they could not claim for it in civil law or would have to wait for years. Compensation and restitution to the victim, as well as restoration to the former state, should be given a prominent place (EC Rec No R (88)18).

Corporations as victims

'Evaporating' victims?

It is obvious that legal persons or corporations, too, can be and are victims of crime committed either by individuals or other corporations. It is difficult to understand why offences against legal persons, especially if they are enterprises, should be crimes without victims or at least crimes with 'evaporating' victims (Kaiser 1976: 536; but see Schneider 1975: 10ff; 1987: 755).

For the perpetrators, of course, it might be easier to commit an offence against a legal person, because they are not directly confronted with a visible individual who is suffering. As Schneider (1987: 763) puts it: 'Honest' people would never betray or rob their friends or neighbours, but they rather easily commit tax evasion or steal towels in a big hotel. Fattah (1991: 99) talks about 'impersonal' victims,[3] meaning the government, large corporations and organizations. The victim is the concrete (identifiable) legal person itself, represented – as always – by individuals who finally have to share the actual damage.

Empirical data collected in Germany show that corporations have crimes committed against them more often than individuals (Schneider 1987: 756). Economic crime is mainly crime against corporations.[4] Banking establishments, financial institutions and insurance companies as well as other enterprises become victims quite often. Department stores, of course, are permanently victimized by shoplifters.[5] Empirical research also shows that customers commit more thefts than employees do, but employees steal more expensive goods. Corporations, of course, are mainly victims of crimes against property, be it economic crime or classical property offences. Looking at the whole picture of criminality today, property crime is predominant: approximately three-quarters of all reported crimes (excluding traffic offences)[6] in Germany are offences against property. Nearly 48 per cent are thefts. Six per cent of all reported crimes (excluding traffic offences) are shoplifting offences (this is nearly 13 per cent of all thefts). Another 4.8 per cent are burglaries (with the intent to steal something) of business premises, offices, factory buildings, workshops, warehouses, banks, chemist's shops, kiosks and shop-windows.[7]

Restorative sanctions – victim–offender mediation?

If the general public or the state happens to be the victim of a crime, restoration only can be symbolic and at the borderline of punishment. Paying a fixed amount of money to the state as symbolic restitution for a corporate wrongdoing does not seem to be substantively different from paying the same amount of money as a fine. The same is true for community service. Both sanctions contain punitive as well as restorative elements. The voluntariness of both the payment and the community service is not, in itself, a sufficient basis for classifying these two sanctions as restorative.

If a corporation is the victim of a crime, there can be no doubt that this specific corporation may seek, as a legitimate interest, compensation for damage in the same way as any individual victim. And there are several ways to seek redress within criminal proceedings, as existing criminal justice systems provide for various restorative measures in the context of diversion as well as formal sentencing. Regarding these restorative sanctions imposed on individual offenders, criminal law does not differentiate between individual or collective victims.[8] There is only one point at which some authors tend to make a distinction: when it comes to victim–offender mediation (VOM). It is true that the classical VOM procedure takes place between individual offenders and individual victims; this means VOM deals with criminal cases where two people (victim and offender) can sit together after the commission of the offence to discuss and resolve their conflict. This usually does not make sense if the victim is a corporation. Nevertheless there are cases where VOM could be a very useful procedure; think of cases of occupational crimes committed by employees, in which there will be continuing interpersonal contact.

It is obvious that the main reason for applying VOM procedures in these cases is also to be found in the principle of equality, as well as in the idea of individual prevention: offenders who have committed crimes against corporations should not be excluded from mediation procedures which require more personal and socially constructive efforts for reaching an adequate settlement than simply payment of compensation due to the victim. VOM is of special value in these cases, because it is the only way to make the victim more visible to the offenders.

In Austria in 1995, 21 per cent of all victims who participated in a VOM procedure with juvenile offenders were legal persons; with VOM procedures with adult offenders the figure was 4 per cent. The difference might be explained by the types of offences that are assigned to VOM by the public prosecutors and the courts: 62 per cent of all VOM cases with juvenile offenders dealt with property crime, but only 21 per cent of the adult cases. Most of these cases were successfully concluded. Looking at the data of our joint research project on 'VOM with adult offenders in Austria and Germany' (Löschnig-Gspandl and Kilchling 1999: 243), one finds that in Germany legal persons as victims appeared only in 1.5 per cent of all VOM cases, whereas in Austria it was nearly 6 per cent. But what is of more importance is that in both countries, VOM with legal persons were at least as successful as VOM with natural persons.

Victim–offender mediation case

A 36-year-old offender was working at a leather manufacturing and selling firm in a small village in Styria (in the southeast of Austria). From June 1997 until June 1998, he sold several leather goods items to private customers – which he was allowed to do for the firm – but without issuing invoices. The money he charged he spent on himself and his family instead of paying over to his employer. After the discovery that leather goods with an estimated value of €5,000 were missing, the managing director approached the offender, confronting him with the facts. The offender admitted all his criminal acts, insisting, however, that the damage in question would only be €7,000. They reached an agreement that the offender had to pay €21,000 and the management would not report him to the police. Employment was terminated by mutual consent in June 1998. In February 1999, the offender paid the first (and also last) €7,000. In June 2000, the managing director made a report to the police after having tried several times to get the remaining €14,000, ultimately with the assistance of an advocate.

The case was assigned to ATA (*aussergerichtlicher Tatausgleich*, out of court conflict resolution, being the Austrian model of VOM) by the public prosecutor. The offender at that time explained that he had only agreed to pay €21,000 to avoid the report to the police. He had debts of €70,000. The VOM procedure during summer 2000 went very well. First, the offender was contacted by the mediator, asked to give a detailed account of the events from his perspective, whether he was willing to accept responsibility and how he intended to compensate for the damage he had caused. After that, the managing director was invited to explain his/the enterprise's point of view. During the following reconciliation talk, at which all three of them were present, victim and offender agreed on compensation of • 21,000 to be paid in 36 instalments.

Conclusion

A criminal justice system that is to meet contemporary needs has to apply to individual as well as to corporate criminal acts. Thus the spectrum of criminal sanctions has to provide not only sanctions that may be imposed on individual offenders, but also specific corporate sanctions. Although punitive sanctions must come first to make the sanctioning system aiming at prevention work at all, the restorative principle requires the additional implementation of a broad spectrum of restorative measures. The purposes of prevention and restoration should be served equally.

Restorative measures, which may either be imposed in parallel with or in addition to the main penalties, or may even substitute the imposition of regular penalties, and which may either appear in the context of diversion or in the procedural framework of suspended or partly-suspended sentences or fines, or may eventually be imposed as part of the conviction, are perhaps even more important in the field of corporate criminal law than in criminal law for individuals, considering the huge dimensions of damage caused by corporations.

This chapter wanted particularly to draw the attention of European lawyers to the necessity of integrating restorative measures in a corporate criminal law. As in many parts of Europe the idea of corporate criminal liability as such is in its infancy; now seems to be the time when – right from the beginning, so to speak – the importance of restorative justice has to be stressed.

Notes

1. I am *not* including *criminal organizations* deliberately set up for the explicit and sole purpose of the continuous and planned commission of certain serious crimes, aiming at amassing substantial profits and striving to corrupt or intimidate others or to shield from criminal prosecution.
2. The discussion of what really has deterrent effects is deliberately left out in this context.
3. How can a legal *person* be *impersonal*?
4. For Germany: 50 per cent are collective entities (mainly the state and social institutions); 50 per cent of the individual victims are enterprises (Heinz 1993: 591).
5. The real victims are ultimately the (other) customers as well as the economic system.
6. 8.6 per cent of all reported crimes are traffic offences (49.3 per cent of all crimes against persons).
7. Which is a quarter of all burglaries.
8. If the perpetrator is a collective itself see above.

References

Bergman, D. (1992) 'Corporate Sanctions and Corporate Probation', *New Law Journal*, 1312–1313.

Coffee, J. C. (1981) 'No Soul to Damn: no Body to Kick: An Unscandalized Inquiry into the Problem of Corporate Punishment', *Michigan Law Review* Vol 79, 386–459.

Dandurand, Y. (1999) 'Entertaining Realistic Expectations about the Effect of Criminal Sanctions Imposed on Corporate Entities: Canada' in A. Eser, G. Heine, and B. Huber, (eds), *Criminal Responsibility of Legal and Collective Entities*. Beiträge und Materialien aus dem Max-Planck-Institut für ausländisches und internationales Strafrecht Freiburg, vol. S 78, Freiburg im Breisgau, 267–276.

Dannecker, G. (2001) Zur Notwendigkeit der Einführung kriminalrechtlicher Sanktionen gegen Verbände, GA, 101–130.

deDoelder, H. (1996) 'Criminal Liability of Corporations – Netherlands' in H. deDoelder, and K. Tiedemann, (eds), *La Criminalisation du Comportement Collectif*, The Hague, 289–310.

Fattah, E. (1991) *Understanding Criminal Victimization: An Introduction to Theoretical Victimology*, Ontario.

Fisse, B. and Braithwaite, J. (1988) 'The Allocation of Responsibility for Corporate

Crime: Individualism, Collectivism and Accountability,' *Sydney Law Review*, 468–513.

Fisse, B. and Braithwaite, J. (1993) *Corporations, Crime and Accountability*. Cambridge.

Hawke, N., (2000) *Corporate Liability*, London.

Heine, G. (1996) 'Die strafrechtliche Verantwortlichkeit von Unternehmen: internationale Entwicklung – nationale Konsequenzen', *ÖJZ*, 211–219.

Heine, G. (1998) 'New Developments in Corporate Criminal Liability in Europe: Can Europeans learn from the American Experience – or Vice Versa?', *Saint Louis-Warsaw Transatlantic Law Journal*, 173–191.

Heine, G., (1999) 'Sanctions in the Field of Corporate Criminal Liability' in A. Eser, G. Heine and B. Huber, (eds) *Criminal Responsibility of Legal and Collective Entities*, Beiträge und Materialien aus dem Max-Planck-Institut für ausländisches und internationales Strafrecht Freiburg, vol. S 78, Freiburg im Breisgau, 238–254.

Heine, G. (2000) 'Unternehmen, Strafrecht und europäische Entwicklungen', *ÖJZ*, 871–881.

Heinz, W. (1993) 'Wirtschaftskriminalität' in G. Kaiser, H.-J. Kerner, F. Sack, and H. Schellhoss, (eds) *Kleines kriminologisches Wörterbuch*, 3.Aufl, Heidelberg, 589–595.

Kaiser, G. (1976) *Kriminologie*, Eire Einführung in die Grundlagen, 3. Aufl, Heidelberg.

Kaiser, G. (1996) *Kriminologie*, 3. Aufl, Heidelberg.

Leigh, L. H. (1982) 'The Criminal Liability of Corporations and other Groups: A Comparative View,' *Michigan Law Review*, 1508–1528.

Löschnig-Gspandl, M. (1996) *Die Wiedergutmachung im österreichischen Strafrecht*, Wien.

Löschnig-Gspandl, M. and Kilchling, M. (1999) Täter-Opfer-Ausgleich und Wiedergutmachung im allgemeinen Strafrecht von Deutschland und Österreich' in H.-J. Albrecht, (ed.), *Forschungen zu Kriminalität und Kriminalitätskontrolle am Max-Planck-Institut für ausländisches und internationales Strafrecht in Freiburg im Breisgau, Kriminologische Forschungsberichte*, vol 82 243–290. (English summary: Kilchling, M. and Löschnig-Gspandl, M. (1998). 'Evaluating Victim/Offender Mediation Dealing with Adult Offenders in Austria and Germany' in H.-J. Albrecht and H. Kury, (eds) *Research on crime and criminal-justice at the Max-Planck-Institute*, Summaries, Kriminologische Forschungsberichte aus dem Max-Planck-Institut für ausländisches und internationales Strafrecht in Freiburg im Breisgau, Vol 83, 95–97.

Löschnig-Gspandl, M. (2000) 'Die strafrechtliche Verantwortlichkeit juristischer Personen' in Global Business und Justiz, *Richterwoche, Schriftenreihe des BMJ*, Vol. 104, 157.

Löschnig-Gspandl, M. (2002) Zur Beshrafung von juristischen Personen, ögz, 241–252.

Préfontaine, D. (1999). 'Effective Criminal Sanctions against Corporate Entities: Canada' in A. Eser, G. Heine and B. Huber, (eds) *Criminal Responsibility of Legal and Collective Entities*. Beiträge und Materialien aus dem Max-Planck-Institut für ausländisches und internationales Strafrecht Freiburg, vol. S 78, Freiburg im Breisgau, 277–284.

Ruggiero, V. (1996) *Organized and Corporate Crime in Europe*, Aldershot.

Schünemann, B. (1979) Unternehmenskriminalität und Strafrecht, Köln.

Schneider, H.J. (1975) Viktimologie, Tübingen.

Schneider, H. J. (1987) Kriminologie, Berlin.

Tiedemann, K. (1988) Die 'Bebußung' von Unternehmen nach dem 2.Gesetz zur Bekämpfung der Wirtschaftskriminalität, NJW, 1169–1232.

Zeder, F. (2001) 'Ein Strafrecht juristischer Personen: Grundzüge einer Regelung in Österreich', *ÖJZ*; 630–642.

Chapter 8

Restorative justice and corporate regulation

John Braithwaite

Justice that empowers the most powerless

Some of the most moving and effective restorative justice conferences I have seen have been business regulatory conferences, especially following nursing home inspections in the US and Australia. After several days inspecting a nursing home that has had serious complaints about neglect of residents – horrible bed sores, residents left to lie for hours in sheets soaked in their own urine – three government inspectors meet with the six people in the nursing home's management team, a staff representative, a lay member of the Board of Management of this church-run nursing home and a representative of the Relative's Committee. They sit in a circle of chairs in a large meeting room. Then three representatives of the Resident's Committee arrive with assistance from staff. One of them has her bed wheeled into the meeting. It is then tilted forward so the resident can see everyone in the circle. The inspectors discuss their findings. There are still some serious deficiencies in the home. By and large, management accepts their findings. But when they dissent that some of the complaints residents have made are exaggerated, the resident in the bed points out that there are other cases that could have been brought to the attention of the inspectors that are even worse. The Relative's Representative concurs. One story is told to illustrate. The representative from the church says he is distressed that residents could be neglected in this way. Management agrees this is unacceptable and commits to put on some extra staff and introduce a staff training programme to deal with the problem.

Democratic, deliberative empowerment is one of the values of restorative justice. Nowhere is it more profoundly realized than in nursing home regulation at its best, as in the example above. In contemporary societies, no one is more powerless than nursing home residents. As Joel Handler has said, 'even prisoners can riot'. Often residents have no practical capacity to leave a nursing home that is abusing or neglecting them because there is a lot of evidence that such moves can be worse for their health. Often they cannot even speak to complain. Restorative processes like the one described above can compensate by empowering residents and relatives who do have voice to speak up with the stories of those without muscle or voice. This happens during the inspection itself as well. The inspector observes a resident not eating any of her vegetables. They are peas. The resident is no longer able to speak and is very confused. But her roommate speaks up: 'She hates peas but they are always giving her peas.' This view is confirmed with the resident directly. She nods and waves her hand disdainfully across the peas when asked if it is true that she hates them. A citizen who cannot speak has been empowered by this restorative inspection process. In the exit conference it will be agreed that residents must be assured of a capacity to choose an alternative meal. What is restored in this case is a very fundamental right to nourishing food of a kind we choose to eat.

Criminal prosecutions are important in nursing home regulation, but encounters such as that of the conference and the story of the peas are the real stuff of nursing home regulation. Care planning conferences are also important, where best practice is for relatives and residents to meet with the care planning team (nurses, physical therapists, dieticians, etc) to discuss any concerns about neglect and to set new care planning goals. When they are done well, nursing home inspections do a lot to improve nursing home quality of care and compliance with the law. The work of our research group shows that doing nursing home inspection well means the kind of resident empowerment described above, plus giving management a lot of praise when they improve (Makkai and Braithwaite 1993), building the self-efficacy of management – their self-belief in their capacity to improve things for residents (Jenkins 1997), treating management as people who can be trusted (Braithwaite and Makkai 1994), procedural fairness (Makkai and Braithwaite 1996) and practising reintegrative shaming (Makkai and Braithwaite 1994). Figure 8.1 shows the reintegrative shaming result. Inspectors who are stigmatising in their regulatory encounters cause compliance to worsen in the two years following an inspection, as do inspectors who are tolerant and understanding toward

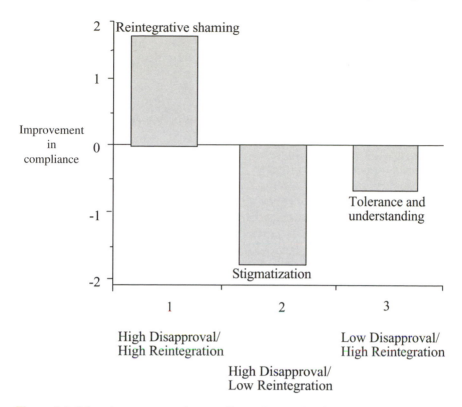

Figure 8.1. Mean improvement in compliance for nursing homes where inspectors used high disapproval and high reintegration styles; high disapproval and low reintegration styles; low disapproval and high reintegration styles ($N = 129$; F-value = 3.58; $p = 0.03$) (from Makkai and Braithwaite 1994)

neglect or abuse of the vulnerable. The inspectors who accomplish improvement have a philosophy of communicating clear disapproval of instances of neglect, while at the same time expressing confidence in the integrity of nursing home staff and management, to improve compliance with the law. Good inspectors treat managers with respect, with a rule of optimism at first, even when their belief is they are greedy, rapacious operators who care about the bottom line to the neglect of their residents' needs. The assumption of the sophisticated inspector is that we all have multiple selves – greedy egoistic selves, incompetent selves and socially responsible, caring selves. A sophisticated regulatory strategy can entice the worst of us to put our best self forward. If it fails to do so, as it often will, then it may be necessary to escalate up an enforcement pyramid (Ayres and Braithwaite 1992) to strategies based on deterrence, and then if deterrence fails, by incapacitation. Just as restorative justice will often fail, so deterrence will often fail, for example because managers are simply incompetent to meet the challenges of running a nursing home. Then it may be necessary to take away their licence.

Reintegrative shaming, empowerment and safety regulation

Rees's (1994) research on nuclear safety regulation was also interpreted by him as supporting the efficacy of reintegrative shaming in business regulation. Rees studied US nuclear regulation after Three Mile Island. The industry realized that it had to transform the nature of its regulation and self-regulation from a rulebook, hardware orientation to one oriented to people, corporate cultures and software. The industry's CEOs set up the Institute of Nuclear Power Operations (INPO) to achieve these ends. Peers from other nuclear power plants would take three weeks off their own jobs to join an INPO review team which engaged the inspected facility in a dialogue about how they could improve. Safety-performance ratings were also issued by the review team; comparative ratings of all the firms in the industry were displayed and discussed at meetings of all the CEOs in the industry and at separate meetings of safety officers. Rees (1994) sees these as reintegrative shaming sessions. Here is an excerpt from a videotape of a meeting of the safety officers:

> It's not particularly easy to come up here and talk about an event at a plant in which you have a lot of pride, a lot of pride in the performance, in the operators … It's also tough going through the agonizing thinking of what it is you want to say. How do you want to confess? How do you want to couch it in a way that, even though you did something wrong, you're still okay? You get a chance to talk to Ken Strahm and Terry Sullivan [INPO Vice Presidents] and you go over what your plans are, and they tell you, 'No, Fred, you've got to really bare your soul.' … It's a painful thing to do. (Rees 1994: 107).

What was the effect of the shift in the centre of gravity of the regulatory regime from a Nuclear Regulatory Commission driven by political sensitivities to be tough and prescriptive to INPO's communitarian regulation (focused on a dialogue about how to achieve outcomes rather than rulebook enforcement)? Rees (1994: 183–6) shows considerable improvement across a range of indicators of the safety performance of the US nuclear power industry since INPO. Improvement has continued since the completion of Rees's study. For example, more recent World Association of Nuclear Operators data show scrams (automatic emergency shut-downs) per unit declined in the US from over seven per unit in 1980 to one by 1990 and 0.1 today.

Earlier Rees (1988) studied the 'Cooperative Compliance Program' of the Occupational Safety and Health Administration between 1979 and 1984. OSHA essentially empowered labour-management safety committees at seven Californian sites to take over the law enforcement role, to solve the underlying problems revealed by breaches of the law. These were similar in the essentials to the restorative nursing home regulatory processes discussed above. Satisfaction of workers, management and government participants was high because they believed it 'worked'. It seemed to. Accident rates ranged from one-third lower to five times as low as the Californian rate for comparable projects of the same companies, as the rate in the same project before the cooperative compliance programme compared with after (Rees 1988: 2–3).

Even less deliberative forms of occupational health and safety inspection seem to have an effect in reducing accidents. Workplace injuries fell after OHSA inspections or when inspection levels increased (Scholz and Gray 1990), even when the penalties imposed were far too small to be a credible deterrent to business, similar results to the coal mine inspection results (Braithwaite 1985). John Scholz and other business-regulatory scholars think this might be because inspectors simply remind employers of their obligations, prick their consciences. Qualitative fieldwork, including my own with both occupational health and safety and nursing homes, suggests that employers have good strategies for protecting themselves from day-to-day knowledge of their organization's failures to meet its legal obligations. The primary function of restorative inspection is therefore simply to squarely draw the attention of chief executives to these failures. In my theoretical terms, this means making it impossible for managers to avoid confronting their shame over failures to keep their organizations safe for people. Deterrence is only needed in cases where this restorative approach repeatedly fails. In another theoretical frame, it is what Black (1997, 1998) has called 'conversational regulation' that does the real work of regulatory inspection.

I found the safety leaders in the coal industry were companies that not only thoroughly involved everyone concerned after a serious accident to reach consensual agreement on what must be done to prevent recurrence, they also did this after 'near accidents' (Braithwaite 1985: 67) and they discussed safety audit results with workers even when there was no near-accident. The same analysis applies to why commercial air travel is so safe today. Airlines and their regulators learnt early that it was a mistake to discourage the reporting and open discussion of near misses by punishing those responsible.

In a remarkable foreshadowing of what we now believe to be reasons for the effectiveness of whole-school approaches to bullying and family group conferences, Davis and Stahl's (1967: 26) study of twelve companies which had been winners of the US coal industry's two safety awards, found one recurring initiative was 'Safety letter to families of workers enlisting family support in promoting safe work habits.' That is, safety leaders engaged a community of care beyond the workplace in building a safety culture. In *To Punish or Persuade* (Braithwaite 1985), I shocked myself by concluding that after mine disasters, so long as there had been an open public dialogue among all those affected, the families of the miners cared for, and a credible plan to prevent recurrence put in place, criminal punishment served little purpose. The process of the public enquiry and helping the families of the miners for whom they were responsible seemed such a potent general deterrent that a criminal trial could be gratuitous and might corrupt the restorative justice process that I found in so many of the 39 disaster investigations I studied.

Just as with the nursing home work, I found that when trade unions were empowered to be involved in the coal-mine inspection process, inspections were more effective in improving safety. DeMichiei *et al.*'s (1982: i) comparison of mines with exceptionally high injury rates with matched mines with exceptionally low injury rates found that at the low injury mines: 'Open lines of communication permit management and labor to jointly reconcile problems affecting safety and health; Representatives of labor become actively involved in issues concerning safety, health and production; and Management and labor identify and accept their joint responsibility for correcting unsafe conditions and practices.'

The ideas of regulation that is conversational and empowering reducing corporate harmdoing are related ideas. The relationship is established by Pranis's (2000) contribution to restorative-justice theory that storytelling is empowering. Let the workers, the consumers, the nursing home residents tell their story and they are empowered. Pranis says you can tell how much power a person has by how many people listen to their stories and how attentively they listen. It follows that an effective path to empowerment is simply to listen. Wheeling the bed of that nursing home resident into a room full of fairly important people who listen attentively to her stories of neglect is extraordinarily empowering.

Building democracy, building community

Giving the least powerful people in our societies voice – like nursing home residents, workers in dangerous industries, children in whole school anti-bullying programmes (see generally Morrison 2002) – is an important restorative justice value. Storytelling is the simple method that can move us from a thin form of representative democracy for people such as these who do not or cannot vote to a thicker form of deliberative democracy. Moreover, people who are unsafe in their nursing home, their workplace or their school tend to want to be heard about safety. Restorative justice circles therefore can deliver a kind of deliberative democracy that matters to some of our least powerful citizens.

At the same time, such regulatory conversations can build micro-communities in contexts where they are sorely needed. Community-building in schools is vital to the development of the young; community-building in workplaces is vital to creating employment; community-building in nursing homes has a special significance for people who have been wrenched late in life from the communities that have given their lives meaning for decades. Representatives of staff, management, the church, the government, the Relatives Committee sharing the stories of residents in a healing circle can have profound effects in building micro-community in nursing homes. The discussion of community in criminology is deeply distorted by its utter preoccupation with the geographical community of neighbourhood. In late modern conditions this is not nearly as important as the local democracy of schools, workplaces or nursing homes that have a much more profound grip on peoples' lives.

Political scientists may say that such local conversations do not go to the heartland of the democratic process. True. But how can citizens hack a path to the heartland of the democracy if the democracy has no strategy for teaching them how to be democratic citizens? Circles and conferences about matters ordinary people care about in their lived experience can teach them. If all students experience and witness serious acts of bullying at school and care about this, then before they reach adulthood, all can have the experience of participation in a circle that solves a difficult problem on which there are multiple perspectives. If they then move into workplaces where they have opportunities to tell their stories of abuse or neglect of their needs, the democratic lessons of their school experience can be reinforced.

And democracy is something that must be taught. We are not born democratic. We are born demanding and inconsiderate, disgruntled whiners, rather than born listeners. We must learn to listen, to be free and caring, through deliberation that sculpts responsible citizenship from common clay (Barber 1992).

Punitive criminal justice, like the accountability mechanisms of the contemporary state more generally, teach us not to be democratic, not to be citizens. This is because of their passive model of responsibility (Bovens 1998). Passive responsibility occurs when we hold someone responsible for what they have done in the past. Circles and conferences, in contrast, teach active responsibility (Braithwaite and Roche 2000). Active responsibility means taking responsibility. In a healing circle, most citizens in the circle are not passively responsible for any wrongdoing; they are certainly not held responsible for criminal wrongdoing. Yet the hope so often realized is that they will take active responsibility for solving the problem. This is part of the ambition of putting the problem rather than the person in the centre of the circle. In the most moving conferences, participants take active responsibility for confronting structural problems like racism in a community (see the Country Womens' Association case study on the Real Justice website: realjustice.org), sexual exploitation and domination of girls by boys in a school (Braithwaite and Daly 1994), even a Prime Minister taking responsibility for restructuring the regulation of the Australian insurance industry (Braithwaite 2002: Chapter 1). But mostly the active responsibility is more banal – the nursing home laundry worker who proposes a new system for turning around soiled sheets to prevent residents from having to put up with lying in their own urine; the environmental manager of a factory who proposes a new system for recycling waste that will both reduce pollution and the risks of chemical exposures for workers. The lesson that democracy requires active responsibility is being learnt in the banal and personal cases just as it is in the less common cases that grapple with structural change. The outputs we hope for are not only solving the problem but also building community and building democracy or at least the competence to be democratic.

To rebuild a rich democracy, we need to do more than motivate people to participate in circles that address problems of living which directly affect their personal relationships. The extra step to democratic citizenship is taken when the citizen moves from participating in a restorative justice conference to being active in some way in the social movement for restorative justice. The extra step is taken when a citizen moves from supporting the residents of mum's nursing home in an exit conference following an inspection, to being an aged-care advocate. It is taken when a young woman who learns in a whole school anti-bullying programme how to confront bullying and then applies those skills to confront corporate bullies who destroy forests on which our wildlife depends.

Of course restorative-justice experiences will never be the principal way that social movement activists acquire the consciences and skills to be actively responsible. On the other hand, when we broaden our conception of restorative justice to include the learning of restorative practices in everyday life (Wachtel 1997), it may be that much of the learning to be actively responsible has always arisen from restorative everyday practices in families, workplaces and peer groups.

A civic republican programme for restorative problem-solving can help teach active responsibility, thereby motivating the making of the personal political, thereby motivating social movement politics and grass-roots engagement with the representative democracy. Elsewhere (Ayres and Braithwaite 1992: Chapter 3; Braithwaite 1998) I have made the case that active social movement politics is the key to controlling corporate abuses of power. Without an environmental movement, environmental crimes would never be shameful and our environmental problems would spiral more deeply into crisis.

Learning from corporate crime

Shearing's (1997: 12) historical analysis of the rise of restorative justice is more about governmentalities of post-Fordist capitalism than the history of pre-capitalist village moots: 'Restorative justice seeks to extend the logic that has informed mediation beyond the settlement of business disputes to the resolution of individual conflicts that have traditionally been addressed within a retributive paradigm ... In both a risk-oriented mentality of security [actuarialism] and a restorative conception of justice, violence loses its privileged status as a strategy to be deployed in the ordering of security'. My own story of the history of coal-mine safety regulation in the British Commonwealth is one of extraordinarily punitive regulation in the late nineteenth and early twentieth century that was not very effective, followed by moves toward more restorative forms of regulation that were more effective in saving lives (see Braithwaite 2002: Chapter 1). In Australia, for example, black lung, which still afflicts generations of former and current miners in the United States and elsewhere, had mostly, though not universally disappeared as a health problem by the 1950s. The empowerment of union-elected safety inspectors whose salaries were paid by the state to coordinate the conversational regulation of coal mines was an important part of this accomplishment (Braithwaite 1985).

Another lesson we have learnt from the conversational regulation of corporate abuses of power is the value of widening the circle. Orchestrated scapegoating is one reason why circle-widening is so important with corporate crime. In my fieldwork 20 years ago, I discovered several pharmaceutical companies who had 'vice presidents responsible for going to jail' (Braithwaite 1984). They were promoted to vice president on the basis that they would take the blame if corporate crime were detected; after a period of faithful service as the vice president responsible for going to jail, they would be promoted sideways to a safe vice presidency. Elsewhere (Braithwaite 2002: Chapter 4) I have discussed my experiences both as a regulator and an observer of regulatory encounters where initially the state meets implacable resistance when it sits down with responsible business executives in the hope of negotiating a restorative resolution. The regulator invites the boss of the responsible executive into the circle and he proves an even tougher nut who even more strongly rejects any corporate responsibility for the harm that has occurred. But the strategy is to keep widening the circle, going right up to inviting the Chairman of the Board into the circle if you have to, until you find a soft target who is moved by a sense of shame, by moral reasoning about ethical corporate conduct. There have been instances where, using this method, Chairmen of Boards who were socially responsible targets fired CEOs who were hard targets (Fisse and Braithwaite 1993). Many kinds of common crime, for example school bullying, are also collective phenomena. Even if they are not, for example a husband acting alone beating his wife, it may still be necessary to keep widening and widening the circle again until responsible members of the extended family are found who will disapprove of the violence and offer to take active responsibility for putting preventive measures in place.

A theoretical conclusion

There has been important evidence under our noses for a long time that restorative practices can help prevent corporate crime. It is rather like the overwhelming evidence from developmental psychology that restorative child-rearing practices prevent violence and other forms of misbehaviour in children, when compared with punitive and laissez-faire child-rearing (Braithwaite 1989). Because they are not 'criminological' forms of evidence, even though they might involve superior measurement than the notoriously unreliable measurement of crime, even though they might be utterly apposite to assessing restorative justice theory, criminologists ignore them.

Underlying the evidentiary claims of this essay, there is a theoretical proposition. This is that regulatory theory needs restorative theory. I have tried to illustrate this, for example, by marrying Black's (1997, 1998) theory of conversational regulation with Pranis's (2000) thinking on restorative storytelling. Second, the subtext has been that restorative justice can learn from regulatory theory, particularly from responsive forms of regulatory theory – widening the circle in response to ears that are deaf to stories of oppression, deploying advocacy NGOs to hold regulatory processes accountable, seizing terrible instances of oppression as an opportunity to build democracy, to strengthen communities and to make the personal political.

References

Ayres, I. and Braithwaite, J. (1992) *Responsive Regulation: Transcending the Deregulation Debate*. New York: Oxford University Press.

Barber, B. R. (1992) *An Aristocracy of Everyone: The Politics of Education and Future of America*. New York: Oxford University Press.

Black, J. (1997) *Rules and Regulators*. Oxford: Oxford University Press.

Black, J. (1998) 'Talking About Regulation', *Public Law* Spring, 77–105.

Bovens, M. (1998) *The Quest for Responsibility*. Cambridge: Cambridge University Press.

Braithwaite, J. (1984) *Corporate Crime in the Pharmaceutical Industry*. London: Routledge.

Braithwaite, J. (1985) *To Punish or Persuade: Enforcement of Coal Mine Safety*. Albany: State University of New York Press.

Braithwaite, J. (1989) *Crime, Shame and Reintegration*. Cambridge: Cambridge University Press.

Braithwaite, J. (1998) 'Institutionalizing Distrust, Enculturating Trust' in *Trust and Democratic Governance* V. Braithwaite and M. Levi (eds). New York: Russell Sage Foundation.

Braithwaite, J. (2002) *Restorative Justice and Responsive Regulation*. New York: Oxford University Press.

Braithwaite, J. and Daly, K. (1994) 'Masculinities, Violence and Communitarian Control' in T. Newburn and E. Stanko (eds) *Just Boys Doing Business*. London and New York: Routledge.

Braithwaite, J. and Makkai, T. (1994) 'Trust and Compliance', *Policing and Society*, 4: 1–12.

Braithwaite, J. and Roche, D. (2000) 'Responsibility and Restorative Justice' in M. Schiff and G. Bazemore (eds) *Restorative Community Justice*. Cincinnati, OH: Anderson.

Davis, R. T. and Stahl, R. W. (1967) 'Safety Organization and Activities of Award-Winning Companies in the Coal Mining Industry', *Bureau of Mines Information Circular 8224*. Washington, DC.

DeMichiei, J. M., Langton, J. F., Bullock, K. A. and Wiles, T. C. (1982) *Factors Associated with Disabling Injuries in Underground Coal Mines*. Washington, DC: Mine Safety and Health Administration.

Fisse, B. and Braithwaite, J. (1993) *Corporations, Crime and Accountability*. Cambridge: Cambridge University Press.

Jenkins, A. L. (1997) 'The Role of Managerial Self-Efficacy in Corporate Compliance with Regulatory Standards'. Unpublished PhD Dissertation, Australian National University.

Makkai, T. and Braithwaite, J. (1993) 'Praise, Pride and Corporate Compliance', *International Journal of the Sociology of Law*, 21: 73–91.

Makkai, T. and Braithwaite, J. (1994) 'Reintegrative Shaming and Regulatory Compliance', *Criminology*, 32(3): 361–85.

Makkai, T. and Braithwaite, J. (1996) 'Procedural Justice and Regulatory Compliance', *Law and Human Behavior*, 20(1): 83–98.

Pranis, K. (2000) 'Democratizing Social Control: Restorative Justice, Social Justice, and the Empowerment of Marginalized Populations' in M. Schiff and G. Bazemore (eds) *Restorative Community Justice*. Cincinnati, OH: Anderson.

Rees, J. V. (1988) *Reforming the Workplace*. Philadelphia: University of Pennsylvania Press.

Rees, J. V. (1994) *Hostages of Each Other: The Transformation of Nuclear Safety Since Three Mile Island*. Chicago: University of Chicago Press.

Scholz, J. T. and Gray, W. B. (1990) 'OSHA Enforcement and Workplace Injuries: A Behavioral Approach to Risk Assessment', *Journal of Risk and Uncertainty*, 3: 283–305.

Shearing, C. (1997) *Violence and the Changing Face of Governance: Privatization and Its Implications*. Cape Town: Community Peace Foundation.

Wachtel, T. (1997) *Real Justice. How we can Revolutionize our Response to Wrongdoing*. Bethlehem, PA: The Piper's Press.

Chapter 9

Confession, apology, repentance and settlement out-of-court in the Japanese criminal justice system – is Japan a model of 'restorative justice'?[1]

Toshio Yoshida

Introduction

Apart from bodily injury or manslaughter caused by negligence in traffic offences, the Japanese police registered 2,033,546 Criminal Code offences in 1998. The ratio of frequency, that is, the number of criminal cases registered by the police per 100,000 residents amounts to 1,608. Japan's crime rate decreased from 1948 to 1978 almost continuously (1948: 2,000; 1973: 1,091), but since then it has gradually increased (1974: 1,095; 1997: 1,506). Still, Japan shows lower figures when compared to Western industrialized states (Research and Training Institute of the Ministry of Justice 1999).[2] Japan's crime rate, being the lowest of all advanced nations, may astonish Western observers. Some criminologists in foreign countries, such as Haley (1989, 1991, 1999) from the United States and Braithwaite (1989) from Australia have looked for the causes of the low Japanese crime rate. They say that it results mainly from the underlying assumption of 'restorative justice' that has traditionally been practised in Japanese criminal justice. Haley states that 'victim–offender mediation' 'is an essential feature of Japan's success and should be expanded in the United States and other criminal justice systems along with other elements of the restorative model, while 'there are no victim–offender mediation programs in Japan. No mediator training agencies exist. There are no statistics or studies. Mediation is a normal aspect of daily life.' So the practice and theory of Japanese criminal justice deserves a closer look.

Internationally there have been developments which have, on the one hand, shown a tendency to help and protect crime victims. On the other hand the tendency has been to seek to introduce and extend forms of conflict resolution, especially 'victim–offender reconciliation', 'victim–offender mediation' or, in the last ten years, 'family conferencing' combined with diversion measures reflecting a new 'restorative justice' philosphy. Is Japanese criminal justice really an exemplary model of 'restorative justice'?

Confession, apology and repentance in practice

Arrest

In the Japanese criminal justice system, the principle of far-reaching discretionary prosecution is very much in evidence. The Code of Criminal Procedure gives the police discretion to close minor offences with the general agreement of the chief public prosecutor of a district (para. 246 CCP). They must report minor offence cases in consolidated form monthly. Criteria for dismissal of proceedings are laid down in advance by the official directions for internal use only. Particular points can vary locally. They are, however, not published. In all likelihood, the losses to the victim caused by an offence on the one hand and the responsibility of the offender on the other hand have to be rated low. It is unclear whether victim compensation or pardon is of importance in the police's decision. According to a textbook of criminal procedure written by an ex-public prosecutor (Nakano 1996), the dismissal of proceedings often has little to do with whether an out-of-court settlement has been reached and, therefore, the victim does not hope for the punishment of the offender. Article 200 of the Criminal Investigation Standards states that police should advise the suspect to provide restitution, to make an apology, or to take other appropriate measures for victims. There are, however, no conditions for dismissal of criminal proceedings.

Detention and its wider effects

The Code of Criminal Procedure gives public prosecutors the exclusive discretion for indictment (para. 247 CCP). The principle of discretionary prosecution is prescribed in this connection. Para. 247 of the Code of Criminal Procedure provides as follows: 'When public prosecution is unnecessary due to considerations of the character, age and circumstances of the offender, the gravity and nature of the offence, and(/or) the circumstances after the offence, prosecution can be suspended.'

Public prosecutors in Japan are allowed to suspend prosecution on their own initiative. They take on as socially formative a function as do judges. In fact, they make very considerable use of these measures. During 1998, 32 persons (2.3 per cent) out of 1,386 persons under suspicion/investigation for homicide were suspended from prosecution, while 497 suspects were not indicted for other reasons (e.g. weak evidence). Seventy-five persons (2.5 per cent) out of 3,041 persons under suspicion/investigation for robbery (including robbery resulting in death, robbery and rape) were suspended from prosecution, while 213 persons were not indicted for other reasons. Concerning persons under suspicion/investigation for bodily injury, blackmail, larceny, fraud, rape, bodily injury and death caused by negligence in traffic, the figures were as follows:

Offence	Persons under suspicion/ investigation	Persons suspended	Per cent	Persons not indicted
Bodily injury	26,733	3,695	13.8	706
Blackmail	10,369	1,120	10.8	425
Larceny	148,231	17,781	12.0	3,274
Fraud	11,524	2,547	22.1	1,146
Rape	1,786	101	5.7	615
Bodily injury & death (traffic)	681,473	545,893	80.1	13,766

Research and Training Institute of the Ministry of Justice 1999: 475.

It is noteworthy that summary proceedings based on documentary evidence, in which fines of less than 500,000 Yen (about $5,000 US at current exchange rates) or those involving a minor fine (less than 10,000 Yen (about $100 US) are paid, play a significant role in Japan (para. 461 CCP). If either side is not satisfied, they can demand a formal trial. In 1998, 68,078 defendants (6.3 per cent) were judged in the First Formal Instance, while 1,018,474 defendants (93.7 per cent) were judged in the summary proceedings (Research and Training Institute of the Ministry of Justice 1999: 44).

Judging from these figures, the Japanese criminal justice system seems to be very lenient. It seems as though circumstances after the offence, such as an out-of-court settlement, compensation for damages or an apology could influence the discretion exercised by the public prosecutors. In fact, the starting point for considerations of diversion was, without doubt, the desire to relieve the workload of public prosecutors and judges, and reducing expenditure. It is evident that settlement out-of-court, compensation for damages, an apology or expression of repentance produce a powerful effect on the degree of discretion of public prosecution in cases relating to bodily injury and deaths by negligence in traffic. In other words, the suspects can expect prosecution to be suspended if they settle a case out-of-court, pay for damages, promise compensation, or make an apology to their victim.

One should not jump to the hasty conclusion, however, that 'restorative justice' is practised in the various phases of investigation. The Japanese Code of Criminal Procedure states that Japanese police can hold an arrested suspect for up to 48 hours before they must bring him before a prosecutor (para. 203 of CCP). The prosecutor then has 24 hours to bring the suspect before a court to ask for a detention order (para. 205 of CCP). If the judge decides that the suspect should be detained pending trial, he can give his approval for a ten-day period of detention. Following this, if the prosecutor so requests, the judge can approve a ten-day extension of the detention period. Also, for certain special crimes (rebellion, preparations and plots for private combat, and riot), an additional five-day extension can be approved (para. 208 of CCP). Thus, investigators can hold suspects for interrogation for 23 days, or, in special cases, 28 days.

In almost all cases, unsentenced detainees are detained in police station cells, that is, a substitute prison (in Japanese, 'daiyo-kangoku') (para. 1 III of the Prison Law states that 'a police cell may substitute for a jail'), although they should in principle be in detention houses under the authority of the Justice Ministry, not the investigators (para. 1 I of the Prison Law). This is a case of putting the exception before the principle. A suspect is usually held in a police cell for 23 days following arrest. The main reason why prosecutors ask for detention in a substitute prison is that it is more convenient for police interrogators. This substitute prison system, which was originally established in 1908 by the 'Prison Law', is still in effect today as a temporary one to supplement a shortage of detention houses and will not be abolished in the near future (Foote 1992).

A suspect's daily life at a substitute prison is continually monitored and restricted by police officers who have total control over the detainees. Communication with visitors is severely restricted. They need legal protection in particular. But Japan's system of state-appointed attorneys is available only to a suspect who has already been indicted (paras 36–38 of CCP). Therefore, during the pre-indictment stage the suspects must find their own attorneys and pay the expenses from their own money (para. 30 of CCP). In fact, very little defence is actively carried out on behalf of unindicted suspects.

The Japanese Constitution guarantees the right to counsel (para. 34) and the Code of Criminal Procedure provides for the right to confer with counsel as well (para. 39). At the same time however, the Code of Criminal Procedure recognizes a principle that severely restricts this right 'when it is necessary for investigation'. The right of 'designation of lawyers visits' given to prosecutors permits them to restrict lawyers' visits. Permission slips are issued, designating the day, hour and number of minutes of duration of visits (para. 39 III of CCP). In serious cases, or in cases in which the suspect denies the charge, this power to restrict the right to counsel is exercised.

It is no exaggeration to say that the key purposes of the investigation are interrogating the suspect, demanding a confession, and pursuing other related crimes. While having the right to remain silent during questioning (para. 198 of CCP), a suspect who is under arrest or detention has no right to leave the investigation room. It is true that the Japanese share a propensity to confess easily, and indeed, most suspects confess to the police. Ninety-two point three per cent of the criminal defendants confessed in 1998 during the first instance of the summary court or district court (General Secretariat of the Supreme Court 1998: 133). This propensity to confess is certainly partly conditioned by child-rearing practices. (Those who are honest are trusted. But there is also a Japanese proverb: 'Honesty does not pay'.) But it can largely be attributed to the influence of the immediate environment by which they are surrounded (in Japanese, 'seken'). Stated another way, it is the influence of the groups to which they belong – family, relationships of blood and marriage, the neighbourhood, their school, college, or company, their leisure groups, and even the state and so on (the concept 'seken' therefore comprises the whole of these groups). People live in groups structured like families, dependant on others, and in close association with the others, in which the *autonomical I* or, in other words, the '*in*dividual' in the western sense, has no place or is devalued. Japanese society consists of, we might say, innumerable groups, not individuals. Each member represents these groups to the outside (Kühne and Miyazawa 1991; Rahn 1990; Wagatsuma and Rosett 1986). Already the fact that a member of a group may have committed a crime and has been apprehended could publicly shame not only themselves, but also other members of the group. The very fact of a suspect being under 'arrest' is widely regarded as an admission of guilt by the neighbours, the media and the public. The suspect loses the respect of others for breaking the social norm that one should have nothing to do with the police. The other members will be ashamed of being in the same group. A strained relationship will arise between the group and the public. Inside the group, the so-called 'forced harmony' which restricts the behaviour of the members will be broken, and therefore unrest will be released.

Indeed, you can shame offenders into apologizing. But it is almost impossible for them to make good their shame, because this does not concern the particular criminal acts but is an act of personality. They feel ashamed, but that cannot be changed from one day to the next. In addition, it is very hard for them to bear shame for a long time because they can have no communication with others about it. On the other hand, they can deal with their own offence more easily, since acknowledging guilt and making an apology can follow. They can receive a victims' forgiveness so communication takes place there. Offenders push their feelings of shame into the background and give their feelings of guilt special emphasis. They make a confession, apologize to the investigators, and apologize at the same time to the members of their groups for breaking the law, and shed tears of remorse for their misbehaviour. Only then can they be released from any psychological burden (Lynd 1958). But this remorse is passive rather than active behaviour.

If the suspect does not make any unexpected confession, and the investigators are convinced that he is guilty, they then make every effort to obtain a confession during the pre-indictment period. Inadmissible measures are used according to circumstances, such as questioning from early morning until late at night, day after day, for over ten hours per day, the beating, poking and kicking of the suspect's body by several policemen at the same time, binding fingers unbearably tight and so on, in order to produce a confession (Japan Federation of Bar Associations 1993). It is most important for police officers and public prosecutors that the suspect makes a confession, accepts moral responsibility and expresses remorse because they think that only then can he be reintegrated into society. Otherwise, he cannot be corrected. In other words, only by expressing great repentance for the alleged offence can we expect the suspect to readjust to the community. We could speculate that he will not commit any further offence. So we take the subject's confession as the first step toward reintegration. That is why confessions play a central role in the Japanese criminal justice system. However, attention should be drawn to the fact that the suspect makes an apology to the investigators as representatives of public interests for having broken a law, but not to the crime victim for the material and immaterial harm caused to them.

The suspect can make an apology at first, feel remorse, and then make a confession, as the case may be. Japanese are inclined to apologize even for matters for which they are not really responsible, simply because they caused trouble to other members of their group. Besides, it is absolutely normal for subordinates and juniors to make apologies to superiors and seniors, respectively, even for trivial things in the vertically and quasi-hierarchically structured society of Japan where each one has a position fixed in the order of precedence (Nishimura and Hosoi 2000). In addition,

Japanese people have always been, and still are today, in awe of ruling authorities. Police officials tend to take advantage of this mode of behaviour, compelling suspects to confess. If the suspect's repentance is taken as sincere, they are accorded preferential treatment in return, as if a dam across a river that had been broken was suddenly restored.

The other members of the group to which the offender belongs can certainly take action on their part. For example, family members or relatives, with the attorney-at-law, can at times visit the victim or his dependants and make apologies to them. On these occasions, presents such as flowers, a cake or a gift of money can be brought. They seek letters from the victim to the effect that no further penalty need be imposed. The offender's neighbours can send petitions on their part to the public prosecutors concerned, hoping for more lenient measures. The offender's co-workers can collect signatures for a petition at their work-place as well, in which they apologize to the offender's victim and the victim's dependants. Of course, they also hope for more lenient measures. But one can assume that their main wish is to avoid further shaming, especially public prosecution. On the one hand, the once-lost social prestige should be restored as far as the outside is concerned. On the other hand, the once-broken harmony should be restored inside as fast as possible.

It should not be overlooked, however, that in Japan a group has some negative aspects. The family cannot assert itself against pressures from outside. Interesting enough, in modern Japan, the old Chinese idea of 'joint guilt/collective responsibility' takes effect. This holds that 'guilt extends even to nine generations: his great-grandparents, his grandparents, his parents, the person himself, his children, his grandchildren, his great-grandchildren and great-great-grandchildren' (Sakuta 1967). They are all partly responsible. Once the offender has been devalued, his relatives cannot look the world in the face, either. Their groups can expel them. Even his father may with much prostration beg an apology from his groups. He can be dismissed from his place of employment or even resign his office from a sense of responsibility. On top of that, he can commit suicide. The offender's mother can make an earnest apology to the public at large for the fact that the whole family, not just the offender, has created a sensation. So the family members can be victims of their own members, as well. The family which became a laughing stock for a less serious crime, or is being shamed for more serious crimes in their neighbourhood, will have to keep away from the community. The family will have to take the public into consideration and agree to accept 'public opinion', including that of the mass media. It will not be able to reintegrate the offender who has damaged its respect. It cannot defend him but has to expel him from itself. The offender's father can or even should demand the death penalty. These deficits of the protective and defensive function of Japanese families were understandably caused and increased by the Empire of Japan, the government before 1945. Japan's government took advantage of the patriarchal family as a foundation for strengthening fanatical ultra-nationalism until the end of World War II. Japanese families were not allowed to protect their members from accusations of being a liberal, democrat or communist. They were able to exert little resistance to pressures from outside. These circumstances have continued to have influence on Japanese families today. Japanese families' bonds or cohesion are still today not as strong as might be thought. To put it briefly, the offender will be pursued, punished and stigmatized, and his relatives will be condemned to the point of his detachment or expulsion (Abe 1999).

This is true for other groups, as well. If they are brought to a crisis and their members are not sure whether the groups will be able to continue, they may quickly expel the offender who caused it. They will save appearances and maintain themselves by taking this action.

If one can assume that the low crime rate of Japan takes root in these social-cultural mechanisms, in the underpinnings peculiar to Japan, in 'soft' mutual restriction, control or interdependence, individuality and freedom will be sacrificed.

Prosecution and sentencing

Japanese judges have broad authority to suspend execution of sentences (para. 25 of the Penal Code). They also carry out their duties as leniently as public prosecutors do. In 1997, of 638 criminal defendants who were sentenced to prison for a limited time due to homicide, 136 persons (17.4 per cent) had the sentence suspended. Of 782 defendants who were sentenced to prison for a limited time due to robbery (resulting in death), 114 persons (14.6 per cent) had their sentence suspended. As far as bodily injury, blackmail, larceny, fraud, rape and death caused by negligence in the conduct of business is concerned, the figures were as follows:

Crime	Sentence	Suspended	Per cent
Bodily injury	3.079	1.792	58.2
Blackmail	1.721	1.062	61.7
Larceny	5.683	2.683	39.9
Fraud	3.453	1.625	47.1
Rape	641	199	31
Death	4.499	3.845	85.5

Research and Training Institute of the Ministry of Justice 1999: 480–481

This makes it seem as if settlements out-of-court, compensation for damages or apologies play a very significant role in sentencing. The influence of this performance on sentencing should nevertheless not be overestimated, it is usually thought.

Last but not least, we cannot shut our eyes to the fact that the attitudes of the population and the criminal justice system toward capital punishment can be characterized as quite punitive. In Japan, the death penalty is not only provided by the law in eight crime-constituting conditions (in German, 'Tatbestände'), but also sentenced and executed. Finally binding death-penalty sentences in 1993, 1994, 1995, 1996, 1997 and 1998 amounted to 7, 3, 3, 3, 4 and 7, respectively. As at 31 December 1998, 52 persons were waiting for the execution of capital punishment (Research and Training Institute of the Ministry of Justice 1999: 43).

Apology and compensation reflected in questionnaire research

The Japan 'Working Group for Investigating the Present Situation of Crime Victims', founded in April 1992, conducted a survey using questionnaires. The crime victims who were surveyed were divided into three crime categories. A questionnaire corresponding to each type was prepared.

Questionnaire A was directed at the victims of crime such as attempted homicide, bodily injury, robbery resulting in bodily injury, bodily injury on the occasion of robbery and bodily injury caused by negligence in the conduct of business (excluding traffic and professional negligence). The concept of 'victims of bodily-injury crimes' are used as a generic term in this chapter.

Questionnaire B was directed at the dependants of those who were killed in crimes such as homicide, murder on the occasion of robbery, robbery resulting in bodily injury, bodily injury resulting in death and so on. This research was restricted to the circle to whom the 'Law concerning compensation for victims of deliberate violent crimes' of 1980 was applied. The concept of 'dependants' is used as a generic term in this chapter.

Questionnaire C was directed at the victims of crimes such as theft and fraud. The concept of 'victims of property crimes' is used as a generic term in this chapter (Miyazawa *et al.* 1996; Takahashi 1997; Yoshida 1997a, 1997b and 1999).[3]

The Research and Training Institute of the Ministry of Justice also conducted a comprehensive survey using questionnaires and published comparable results in the Japanese 'White Book on Crime 1999' (Research and Training Institution of the Ministry of Justice 1999) (abbreviated as 'RTI-questionnaire research'). The persons questioned were (1) dependants of victims of homicide (excluding infanticide) and bodily injury resulting in death (called 'homicide and so on' in the 'White Book'), (2) dependants of those who had suffered bodily injury caused by negligence resulting in death, (3) victims of attempted homicide, bodily injury that takes more than one month to heal (called 'bodily injury and so on' in the 'White Book'), (4) victims of bodily injury caused by negligence in traffic that takes more than one month to heal, (5) victims of larceny, (6) victims of fraud (excluding defrauding a restaurant, defrauding the railway and so on, credit-card fraud), embezzlement (excluding embezzlement of lost articles (called 'fraud and so on' in the 'White Book'), (7) victims of robbery, (8) victims of blackmail, (9) victims of rape and (10) victims of obscenity by compulsion (Research and Training Institute of the Ministry of Justice 1999).[4]

As far as apology in the first place is concerned, according to the questionnaire research of the working group 41.0 per cent of the victims of bodily injuries, 22.6 per cent of the dependants of those killed, and 25.9 per cent of the victims of property crimes answered that 'the offender or his substitutes made an apology'; 6.2 per cent of the victims of bodily injuries, 3.4 per cent of the dependants of those killed, and 1.4 per cent of the victims of property crimes answered that 'the offender or his substitutes offered an apology, but I refused this.' In addition, the victims who answered that 'the offender or his substitutes made an apology', were asked whether they believed 'the offender or his substitutes made an honest apology'; 41.9 per cent of the victims of bodily injuries, 22.0 per cent of the dependants of the killed, and 31 per cent of the victims of property crimes answered this question affirmatively.

According to the RTI-questionnaire research the proportion of the persons asked who answered that 'the offender made an apology on his part' is as follows: among victims of death caused by negligence in traffic 78.6 per cent, among victims of bodily injury caused by negligence in traffic 63.4 per cent, among victims of obscenity by compulsion 55.0 per cent, among victims of blackmail 45.5 per cent, among victims of robbery 43.2 per cent, among victims of fraud 42.6 per cent, among victims of bodily injury 41.4 per cent, among victims of rape 41.0 per cent, among victims of larceny 35.3 per cent, among victims of homicide and so on 24.5 per cent. In about 54 per cent, the offender's substitutes made an apology; in about 39 per cent of apologies, the offender made an apology in person. In cases of death caused by negligence in traffic (about 89 per cent) and bodily injury by negligence in traffic (about 89 per cent), the offender made an apology, in most cases in person.

Concerning settlement out-of-court and compensation for damages for victims of bodily injury and dependants, the questionnaire research of the working group shows that the share of the persons who negotiated a settlement out-of-court or compensation for damages and agreed on it amounts to 34 per cent of the victims of bodily injury and 10 per cent of the dependants. Those who received money paid by way of settlement out-of-court or compensation for damages, regardless of whether they received this in whole or in part, amounted to about one-half (44.1 per cent) of the victims of bodily-injury crimes and about one-fifth (19.9 per cent) of the dependants. Those who were satisfied with compensation or damages, regardless of whether they received this in whole or in part, amounted to 27 per cent of the victims of bodily-injury crimes and 10 per cent of the dependants. Of the victims of bodily-injury crimes who had an opportunity to negotiate with their offender about settlement out-of-court or compensation for damages, it was the offender's side in many cases that initiated settlement out-of-court or compensation for damages (67.4 per cent). With regard to the dependants, in contrast, where the victim's side initiated settlement out-of-court or compensation for damages the figure was 48.9 per cent. These differences were statistically significant (P < 0.01). The fact that the dependants were reduced to poverty must have made them initiate negotiations. About one-half (45.2 per cent) of the dependants indicated that they were unable to make a living after suffering damage, while only one-fifth (18.5 per cent) of the victims of bodily-injury crimes indicated that they were unable to make a living after suffering injury.

As far as the circumstances of the victims of property crimes are concerned, about one-half (43.5 per cent) of the victims of property crimes had an opportunity to negotiate with their offender about a settlement out-of-court. Four-fifths (80 per cent) of those who had such an opportunity agreed on a settlement out-of-court. Therefore, about one-third (35 per cent) of the total cases were settled privately out-of-court. In response to the question: 'What kind of satisfaction does the conclusion of the settlement out-of-court bring you?' (multiple answers allowed), the victims asked answered as follows: 'the offence was cleared up to some extent' (67.1 per cent), 'restoration of financial damage' (30 per cent), 'restoration of psychological equilibrium' (27.1 per cent), and 'I was able to understand the offender'(5.5 per cent). In response to the reverse question: 'What kind of dissatisfaction does the conclusion of settlement out-of-court bring you?' (multiple answers allowed), the interviewees answered as follows: 'the offender is not sincere enough' (24.6 per cent), 'the offender was not punished' (15.9 per cent), 'I am not satisfied with damages' (14.5 per cent), and 'the money was paid too late' (1.4 per cent).

According to the RTI-questionnaire research, 58.1 per cent and 26.4 per cent of the dependants of the persons who suffered death caused by negligence in general or by negligence in traffic respectively concluded a settlement out-of-court or negotiated it. For the other offences the percentages were as follows; blackmail, 43.2 per cent, 1.1 per cent; larceny, 41.2 per cent, 2.6 per cent; obscenity by compulsion, 37.7 per cent, 1.3 per cent; fraud and so on, 36.8 per cent, 4.7 per cent; bodily injury and so on, 34.4 per cent, 8.3 per cent; rape, 32.0 per cent, 4.0 per cent; robbery, 31.7 per cent, 2.0 per cent; bodily injury caused by negligence in traffic, 31.4 per cent, 36.4 per cent; homicide and so on, 10.0 per cent, 10.0 per cent. It was 66.0 per cent of the dependants of the victims of homicide and so on, 58.4 per cent of the victims of robbery, 50.0 per cent of the victims of larceny, 48.1 per cent of the victims of fraud and so on, 38.7 per cent of the victims of rape, 34.4 per cent of the victims of bodily injury and so on, 33.8 per cent of the victims of obscenity by compulsion, and 31.8 per cent of the victims of blackmail that answered that 'the offender did not offer me any conversation'. 22.7 per cent of the victims of rape, 22.1 per cent of the victims of obscenity by compulsion, and 20.5 per cent of the victims of blackmail answered that 'the offender offered me conversation, but I refused it.'

As the results of both questionnaires show, offenders do not make an apology as often as apologies are usual in everyday life in Japan. What stands out is that offenders do not make an apology to the dependants of killed persons or the victims of property crimes so often. This could be put down to the offender and their victims being separated or being distant from one another in severe criminal cases such as homicide. In criminal cases such as property crimes, the restoration of damage could be more important than apology. Therefore, an apology in these cases could not be to the benefit of the offender in the criminal procedure. On top of that, it is remarkable that quite a few victims do not think that their offender made a sincere apology.

Out-of-court settlements, which take place in the shadow of the civil law, does not aim at immaterial restoration but exclusively at paying compensation. Much less mentioned is the empowerment of the participants. Indeed, in about four-fifths of deaths caused by negligence in traffic and about seven-tenths of bodily injuries caused by negligence in traffic, a settlement out-of-court is concluded or negotiated. But in other criminal cases, such as robbery, rape, and especially homicide, the share of the conclusion or negotiation of the settlement out-of-court is rather low. This may have to do with the fact that a (potential) conclusion of settlement out-of-court has little influence on public prosecution or sentencing in the latter cases.

Responsibility and punishment in theory and practice

Punishment and responsibility

According to the currently predominant theory in Japanese criminal law, the basis of punishment as an inflicting of evil against the criminal act is the 'normative particular act responsibility' (in German, 'die normative Einzeltatschuld'). It is the responsibility of the offender to suffer the punishment, resulting from an individual–moralistic and social-ethical culpability of the criminal act. The condition of culpability is the consciousness of freedom, that is, not being predetermined. In fact, on the level of being, namely empirical science, this is neither proved nor disproved. But freedom of will should be postulated, because human beings have the consciousness of self-determination from everyday experiences, except for the cases in which an expert proves that an anti-social urge is determined by a cause such as mental illness. This is the firm belief of law-abiding citizens, based on the experience of their everyday lives. Their recognition of the possibility to self-determinedly act in accordance with the norm is what creates the culpability, and the need for involvement of the criminal law.

The offender is to be blamed for his crime because, although having the choice of acting legally or illegally, he chose to act illegally. When the responsibility for a particular act is investigated, the personality of the offender is considered, so far as it has found expression in the offence. This is because the will is closely linked to the personality at the time of the offence.

From this point of view, according to one theory (Nishihara 1977), the punishment appropriate to the offender's responsibility should be understood as retribution. The essentials of punishment are that the normative retribution demands the infliction of evil. But it is only the response to the culpable criminal act and has nothing to do with retaliation. This theory recognizes, however, that punishment has various functions, namely satisfying retaliatory feelings, rendering harmless, expiation and prevention (deterrence, rehabilitation). The retributive infliction of evil should aim at avoiding too extensive use of punishment for crime prevention (the so-called 'relative theory of retribution'). According to another theory (Ohya 1997), the punishment as duty placed upon the state aims at preventing crimes and maintaining social safety. Therefore, the legal basis of punitive power is the effectiveness of crime prevention. According to this theory, the demand for retribution, the belief that the misdeed must be countered with evil, as it is firmly anchored in 'sound popular feeling', should be still taken into consideration. Only retributive punishment will be perceived as righteous by the offender and the public and will have both general and specific preventive effects.

Aside from fundamental doubts about the normative requirements of the doctrine of 'freedom of will' and the individual–moralistic responsibility in combination with this doctrine as a matter of the state, it is very questionable whether the punishment should take into account and satisfy the retaliatory feelings of crime victims, dependants and the public. In addition, the prevailing theory views, on the one hand, the offender only as the object of criminal sanction and, on the other hand, the victim not as a subject in the criminal justice system. They both stay on the margins. This is a reason why the individual–moralistic culpability which leads to the retaliation demands the infliction of evil as part of punishment, but without apology to victims or active repentance. It does not empower either the victim or the offender to resolve the unexpected problems independently and considerately. This theory leaves no room at all for a social-constructive crime resolution like 'victim–offender reconciliation (mediation)' (Ohya 1999).[5]

The function of the criminal justice system

This is true for the attitudes of criminal justice practitioners toward the aims of criminal justice, as well. According to the results of the 'questionnaire research of the working group', almost all police officers (99.3 per cent), public prosecutors (100 per cent), attorneys-at-law (90.3 per cent), judges (100 per cent) and probation officers (89.7 per cent) answered with 'yes' or a 'definite yes' with regard to the punishment of offenders as an aim of the criminal justice.

With regard to truth-finding as an aim of the criminal justice system, almost all police officers (99.2 per cent), public prosecutors (97.3 per cent), attorneys-at-law (93.1 per cent), judges (96.2 per cent) and probation officers (100 per cent) answered with 'yes' or a 'definite yes', as well.

As far as the conflict resolution between offender and victim as an aim of the criminal justice system is concerned, less than the half of the police officers (46.0 per cent), public prosecutors (30.6 per cent), attorneys-at-law (14.5 per cent), judges (19.6 per cent) and probation officers (48.5 per cent) answered with 'yes' or a 'determined yes' (chi^2 = 28.02; df = 4; p = 0.000).

As for compensation for damage as an aim of the criminal justice system, less than half the police officers (40.9 per cent), public prosecutors (20.0 per cent), attorneys-at-law (17.4 per cent), judges (7.7 per cent) and probation officers (48.6 per cent) answered with 'yes' or a 'determined yes' (chi^2 = 92.72; df = 4; p = 0.000). In response to the question: 'Should settlements out-of-court be an official instrument in which the criminal justice system participates?', most interviewees answered negatively. More than half the probation officers (68.8 per cent) asked, however, answered positively.

Concerning psychological healing as an aim of criminal justice, the people asked answered differently. More than half the police officers (81.9 per cent), public prosecutors (62.9 per cent) and probation officers (71.4 per cent) answered with 'yes' or a 'definite yes'. In contrast, less than half of the attorneys-at-law (35.8 per cent) and judges (38.5 per cent) answered with 'yes' or a 'definite yes' (chi^2 = 53.35; df = 4; p = 0.000).

As far as an assessment of the meaning of settlements out-of-court for the victims is concerned, the following answers were offered: (1) appeasing feelings of the victims, (2) commutation of punishment, (3) conflict resolution, (4) compensation for damages, (5) retribution for the crime, (6) apology and (7) no meaning (multiple answers were not possible to this question).

In response to the question: 'What meaning do settlements out-of court presumably have for victims of bodily-injury crimes, assault–battery, robbery and attempted homicide?', 32.3 per cent of police officers indicated 'appeasing the feelings of the victims'. The same percentage of police officers indicated 'commutation of punishment'. About one-half (48.6 per cent) of public prosecutors indicated 'appeasing the feelings of the victims'. Almost two-thirds (64.6 per cent) of judges indicated 'appeasing the feelings of the victims'. About one-third (36.1 per cent) of attorneys-at-law indicated 'appeasing the feelings of the victims'. The same percentage of attorneys-at-law indicated 'apology'. About two-fifths (43.2 per cent) of probation officers indicated 'appeasing feelings of the victims'. These differences were statistically significant ($p < 0.01$).

Criminal justice practitioners were also asked: 'What meaning does settlement out-of-court presumably have for dependants whose relatives were killed by way of homicide, murder on the occasion of robbery, robbery resulting in death or bodily injury resulting in death?' About one-third (33.3 per cent) of public prosecutors indicated 'appeasing feelings of the victims', and the same percentage of them reported 'apology'. 37.5 per cent and 45.8 per cent of attorneys-at-law indicated respectively 'appeasing feelings of the victims' and 'apology'. About one-third (37 per cent) of judges and about two-fifths (41.9 per cent) of probation officers indicated 'apology'. About one-quarter (25.2 per cent) of police officers indicated 'commutation of punishment', while as many as 31.9 per cent of them recognized 'no meaning'. These differences were statistically significant ($p < 0.01$).

Furthermore, the criminal justice practitioners were given the question: 'What meaning do settlements out-of-court presumably have for victims of property crimes?' 90.8 per cent of attorneys-at-law, 88.2 per cent of judges, 71.8 per cent of probation officers, 67.7 per cent of police officers, and 46.4 per cent of public prosecutors indicated 'compensation for damages'.

In response to the question: 'What meaning does settlement out-of-court presumably have for victims of sexual crimes?', 44 per cent of police officers asked indicated 'commutation of punishment', while 50 per cent of public prosecutors and 56.8 per cent of judges indicated 'appeasing the feelings of the victims'. Fifty-six per cent of attorneys-at-law and 56 per cent of probation officers, however, indicated 'apology'. These differences were statistically significant ($p < 0.01$).

Concerning the influence of settlements out-of-court upon the suspension of prosecution almost all practitioners answered that settlements out-of-court have a great or fairly great influence upon it. As to the influence of settlements out-of-court upon sentencing and suspending sentence, more than the half the public prosecutors (54.1 per cent) and attorneys-at-law (50.7 per cent) answered that it has a great influence, while only 32.7 per cent of the judges asked were of the same opinion. These differences were statistically significant ($p < 0.05$).

On the one hand, the findings presented above show that 'conflict resolution' and 'compensation for damages' as aims of the criminal justice system have far fewer adherents than 'punishment of an offender' and 'truth-finding'. The attitudes of police officers asked about psychological healing as an aim of the criminal justice system contrast remarkably with those of attorneys-at-law. Probably this comes from the fact that, in general, it is thought that satisfying the requirement of retribution gives victims 'psychological healing'. Therefore the new international trend in criminal policy and criminal law seems not to be acceptable to criminal justice practitioners. This could result from the fact that, according to criminal law, they have only the classical forms of responding to crime. Nevertheless it seems strange enough, because on the other hand many practitioners recognize that settlements out-of-court are important for crime victims. What is more, criminal sanctions are possibly influenced by them. These findings might be understood as follows: settlements out-of-court are considered by criminal justice practitioners, above all by public prosecutors, primarily as an indication of the return to law and order, thus achieving reintegration from the offender-oriented perspective. This could be against the background of the so-called 'combining theory' which says that retribution is the substance of punishments; they are resorted to, however, only in accordance with the necessities of general deterrence and rehabilitation (the so-called 'relative theory of retribution').

Practicability of 'victim–offender reconciliation (i.e. mediation)' in Japan

Crime and society

In the liberal–democratic social–constitutional state, the law expresses the notion that right behaviour by individuals or the public at large should be encouraged by both criminal law, and civil law. The law should therefore primarily not be understood as the formal outer norm of order and coercion in which the offender's internal sense of value is of no importance, but rather, as an expression of social–ethical attachment – although the traditional conception that this law represents the 'authorities' against 'subjects' is still held by criminologists and others, influenced by the 'pure law theory' of Hans Kelsen. The formal thinking of law, however, should never be anything more than a supplement to the material thinking of law. The liberal–democratic social–constitutional state's judicial system requires a socially-integrated understanding of law. Crime is not an infringement of the power of the authorities, but a deviation from the value convictions shared by people in the society, which form its social ethics. The conflict of the offender with the criminal law, therefore, should be interpreted rather as social conflict than as 'abstract law infringement'.

Criminal law applies to intolerable forms of behaviour which severely disturb peaceful and orderly human life and offend legally protected collective interests. Criminal law has, in other words, the task of removing the disappointment of expectations of society that the individual abides by legal norms through social control by means of appropriate reactions, and of re-establishing, maintaining and protecting legal peace and order.

Thus, it is also necessary to embrace the change from removing the consequences of crime in the lives of its victims to it being a duty of the criminal law to do this, and to acknowledge the victim's legal status in it. This is because the re-establishment of legal peace as a duty of the criminal law system can be better achieved through restoration of the victim's psychological and physical integrity and reimbursing financial losses caused. This is much better than retributive punishment. In this way, the law as an expression of the general consensus of society will re-establish social stability in the public consciousness. Besides, taking the victim's interests into consideration will meet the demand of the unified community, in other words, the principle of the modern welfare state. The protection of the offender's interests, therefore, should be an independent aim which should be considered on all levels of criminal proceedings.

The above-mentioned concept of law and the experimental, practical impossibility of proof of the offender's freedom of choice compel us to a concept of criminal law responsibility which is not targeted on the inner morality of the person. This means that the offender's responsibility does not lie in individual moralistic culpability, but only in the social–ethical culpability that the deficiency of the offender's attitude expressed in the crime. This is in contradiction to the values acknowledged in the legal conditions of crime. Responsibility expresses the expectation that the law is disappointed because a law-abiding person would not have committed the crime (the concept of the objectivized, social–ethical responsibility) (Moos 1996; Dölling 1992; Yoshida 2001).

Formal blame is an essential feature of normal life. The repressive inflicting of evil should not be, however, an essential element of modern criminal law. The inflicting of evil through imposing a loss of life, freedom or property as a response of the state to crime does not necessarily follow social blame conceptually, because the inflicting of evil is by no means necessary for strengthening common values. The criminal law system should not be equated with a punitively oriented penal law. Other responses which confirm and support the law on the part of the public are legally conceivable and desirable.

Punitive or restorative justice?

Is there in reality a basis for introducing a restorative system like 'victim–offender reconciliation (mediation)' into the Japanese criminal justice system? The 'questionnaire research of the working group' asked the victims of property crimes the following question: 'What kinds of measures would you demand if you suffered from another such loss by another crime?' The order of precedence is as follows (multiple answers allowed): (1) Imposing prison sentence or fine; Yes – 46 per cent, No – 54 per cent. (2) Making the offender write a written explanation and making him swear not to commit any more crime: Yes – 35.8 per cent, No – 64.2 per cent. (3) Making the offender understand that he is guilty of a criminal act, rather than making him give back money or things or apologize: Yes – 31.2 per cent, No – 68.8 per cent. (4) Personal negotiation between victim and offender, followed by making the offender compensate for damages: Yes – 26 per cent, No – 74 per cent. (5) Negotiation between the representative of the victim with the offender, followed by making the offender compensate for damages: Yes – 25.1 per cent, No – 74.9 per cent. (6) Making the offender apologize in an official place for committing the crime: Yes – 13 per cent, No – 87 per cent. (7) Bringing the case before court and making the offender compensate for damages by the force of law: Yes – 12.1 per cent, No – 87.9 per cent. (8) Making the offender apologize for committing the crime after consultation: Yes – 11.6 per cent, No – 88.4 per cent. (9) All is a whim of fate, therefore I will submit to fate: Yes – 5.6 per cent, No – 94.4

per cent. In response to the question of whether settlements out-of-court should be institutionalized publicly (police, public prosecutors, court and so on), about four-fifths (83 per cent) of the victims of property crimes gave answers in favour of its institutionalization (necessary: 60.8 per cent; rather necessary: 22.2 per cent). However, most criminal law practitioners gave negative answers (see above, 'the function of the criminal justice system').

The RTI-questionnaire research also asked crime victims: 'What is the most important thing the offender should do to make up for his crime?' Those who gave the answer that 'the offender should start a new life' amounted to 60.7 per cent of the victims of larceny, 49.5 per cent of the victims of blackmail, 39.3 per cent of the victims of robbery, 39.2 per cent of the victims of obscenity by compulsion, 29.9 per cent of the victims of bodily injury and so on, 23.1 per cent of the victims of rape, 21.9 per cent of the victims of bodily injury caused by negligence in traffic, 20.9 per cent of the dependants of the victims of death caused by negligence in traffic, and 10.4 per cent of the dependants of the victims of homicide and so on. Thirty three point eight per cent of all the victims and dependants asked viewed the rehabilitation of the offender as most important. Those who gave the answer that 'the offender should serve time in prison or pay a fine' amounted to 38.5 per cent of the victims of rape, 35.4 per cent of the dependants of the victims of homicide and so on, 33.6 per cent of the victims of robbery, 24.3 per cent of the dependants of the victims of death caused by negligence in traffic, and 21.5 per cent of the victims of obscenity by compulsion. Twenty-two point two per cent of all the victims and dependants asked saw punishment as most important. Those who gave the answer that 'the offender should conclude a settlement out-of-court and fulfil it' amounted to 33.6 per cent of the victims of fraud and so on, 25.4 per cent of the victims of bodily injury caused by negligence in traffic, 21.6 per cent of the victims of bodily injury and so on, and 14.6 per cent of the dependants of the victims of homicide and so on. Thirteen point seven per cent of all the victims and dependants asked concluded that a settlement out-of-court was most important. Those who gave the answer that 'the offender should make an apology to his victim or his dependants' or 'the offender should get the victim's or dependant's forgiveness' amounted to 33.6 per cent of the dependants of the victims of death caused by negligence in traffic, 31.6 per cent of the victims of bodily injury caused by negligence in traffic, 20.9 per cent of the dependants of the victims of homicide and so on, and 20.6 per cent of the victims of bodily injury and so on. Eighteen point two per cent of all the victims and dependants asked viewed apology or forgiveness as most important.

Overall, it is hardly an exaggeration to say that punitive thinking does not outweigh the orientation towards rehabilitation or compensation, although the former seems still influential today. The way to 'restorative justice' is not totally closed.

Conclusions

The Japanese criminal law system today still knows only the traditional punishment which dissociates the offender and the victim from each other. Modern criminal law, however, can no longer be equated with the infliction of punishment. A varied palette of responses to crimes can and should be offered. The Japanese criminal justice system is in considerable need of reform which will enable the remorseful offender to take on his or her accountability voluntarily. It is above all desirable to lay the legal foundations for victim–offender reconciliation or mediation, including the infrastructure necessary to support this.

Extending the use of punishment is no panacea against criminality, as is widely thought. A stronger orientation of the criminal justice system towards restorative justice not only helps to address the consequences of crime, but will also contribute to a lowering of the crime rates. What the concept of restorative justice means differs depending on its advocates. But there are many points at which they meet common ground, in particular a voluntary and constructive collective response to the offence, including the peaceful settlement of conflict between victim and offender, community service and payment of money to charity or similar under the control of the criminal justice authorities (Meier 1998) (to name but a few, Kerner, H.-J., Schöch, H. and Rössner, D. from Germany; Moos, R. and Jesionek, U. from Austria; Walgrave, L. and Peters, T. from Belgium; Zehr, H., Umbreit, M.S., Van Ness, D.W. and Bazemore, C. from the United States of America; Wright, M. and Marshall, T. from England; Fattah, E.A. from Canada; Braithwaite, J. from Australia). In Japan, supportive and protective measures for victims have been implemented in various legal reforms. But it is clear that they have all been taken in a framework in which they are compatible with the traditional offender-oriented retributive criminal law theory. Therefore, I would not suggest that Japan is a model of the idea of 'restorative justice'. What is necessary is a shift in perspectives or paradigms, that is to say, a change in our thoughts from the concept of an individual–moralistic retributive criminal law to that of the victim–offender community–state interrelated act criminal law (Zehr 1990; Van Ness and Strong 1997; Miklau 1993) (in German, 'Tatstrafrecht') among public prosecutors, judges and people of all social standings in order for the idea of 'restorative justice' to be realised. Without their support, it will never come into being in Japan.

Notes

1. Revised version of a paper presented at the 4th International Conference on Restorative Justice for Juveniles, Tübingen, Germany, October 1–4, 2000.
2. It should be noted, however, that the police criminal statistics only show the first of all those aspects of their activity which they want to record, and therefore, that the statistics should be interpreted rather carefully. (See, Kerner, H.-J. 1993; Kury, H. 2000).
3. Miyazawa, K. *et al.* (eds) (1996). The researched crimes were limited to the crime cases which happened before 31 December 1991. Answers were expected by 15 December 1993. The response rates of the three questionnaires lay between 66 per cent and 70.9 per cent. Regarding questionnaire A, 350 copies were passed on and 231 were responded to (response rate: 66.0 per cent). Regarding questionnaires B, 395 copies were passed on and 273 were responded to (response rate: 69.1 per cent). Regarding questionnaire C, 320 copies were passed on and 227 were responded to (response rate: 70.9 per cent). Altogether

Homicide Rates – USA, UK, Germany, France and Japan 1985–1997

Year/item	USA	UK	FRG	France	Japan
1995					
Homicide cases reported	21,606	1,379	3,960	2,563	1,312
Crime rate	8.2	2.7	4.9	4.4	1.0
Clearance rate	64.8	90.8	88.2	75.1	96.3
1996					
Homicide cases reported	19,645	1,353	3,531	2,385	1,257
Crime rate	7,4	2,6	4,3	4,1	1,0
Clearance rate	66,9	91,1	92,1	74,9	98,5
1997					
Homicide cases reported	18,209	1,391	3,312	2,085	1,323
Crime rate	6.8	2.7	4.0	3.6	1.0
Clearance rate	66.1	91.4	92.8	81.9	95.3

Note. The statistics on reported homicide cases are based on the following criteria in the respective countries:

USA	Murder and manslaughter (negligent manslaughter and attempted cases are not included)
UK	Murder, attempted murder, manslaughter, and infanticide
FRG	Murder (Mord), manslaughter (Totschlag), murder on demand (Tötung auf Verlangen), and infanticide (Kindestötung)
France	Homicides, tentatives d'homicides
Japan	Murder, manslaughter, and robbery causing death

'Crime rate' means the number of reported and recorded offences per 100,000 population
'Clearance rate' means (number of offences cleared/number of offences reported and recorded) × 100
From Research and Training Institute of the Ministry of Justice 1999: 27.

Larceny Rates – USA, UK, Germany, France and Japan 1995–1997

Year/Item	USA	UK	FRG	France	Japan
1995					
Larceny cases reported	12,063,935	3,650,25	3,848,308	2,289,348	1,570,492
Crime rate	4,591	7,044	4,720	3,945	1,251
Clearance rate	17.6	21.5	27.7	12.6	37.4
1996					
Larceny cases reported	11,805,323	3,510,641	3,672,655	2,217,217	1,588,698
Crime rate	4,450	6,750	4,489	3,806	1,262
Clearance rate	18.1	21.8	30.0	12.1	35.6
1997					
Larceny cases reported	11,540,297	3,146,453	3,537,610	2,128,422	1,665,543
Crime rate	4,312	6,026	4,314	3,639	1,320
Clearance rate	17.9	22.9	31.5	11.1	35.2

Note. The statistics on reported larceny cases based on the following criteria in the respective countries:

USA	Larceny-theft, motor-vehicle theft, and burglary
UK	Theft and burglary
FRG	Theft (Diebstahl ohne erschwerende Umstände), and weighted theft (Diebstahl unter erschwerenden Umständen)
France	Theft (vols) (vols avec violences, recels and so on are not included)
Japan	All kinds of theft

From Research and Training Institute of the Ministry of Justice 1999: 27.

a total of 1,065 victims were sent questionnaires, of whom 227 victims (21.3 per cent) responded. In addition, after questionnaires A, B and C, the Japanese 'working group' gathered information from criminal justice practitioners (police officers, public prosecutors, judges, probation officers and attorneys-at-law) in 1994. Of a total number of 150 police officers, 137 police officers responded to the written standardized questionnaire (response rate: 91.3 per cent). Of a total number of 178 public prosecutors, 38 public prosecutors responded (response rate: 21.4 per cent). Of a total number of 147 judges, 53 judges responded (response rate: 36.1 per cent). With regard to probation officers, 74 copies were passed on and 40 probation officers responded (response rate: 54.1 per cent). Of a total number of 197 attorneys-at-law, 72 attorneys-at-law responded (response rate: 35.3 per cent). Altogether a total number of 746 criminal justice practitioners were sent questionnaires, of whom 340 practitioners (45.6 per cent) responded. See also, Takahashi, N. 1997; Yoshida, T. 1997a and 1997b.

4. The researched crimes were limited to the crime cases in which defendants were found guilty between January 1st 1997 and March 31st 1999. Altogether a total of 1,132 victims or dependants responded. Regarding Nos. (1)–(10) in the text, respectively 111; 131; 104; 124; 142; 127; 123; 104; 81; 85.

5. According to Ohya, M. (1999), crime victim aids should not be combined with offenders' aids, but should be fulfilled separately. This is a logical consequence of his theory on crime responsibility.

References

Abe, K. (1999) *Nihonshakai de Ikirutoiukoto* (*Living a Life in Japanese Society*). Tokyo, Japan.

Bärmann, J. (1990) 'Alternativen zum Strafverfahren vor Gericht: Ein japanisches Modell' in G. Ballod and K. Kremb (eds) *Beiträge zur Landeskunde Japans*, Vol. 2. 38–50. Germany: Schriften des Gymnasiums Weierhof.

Braithwate, J. (1989) *Crime, Shame and Reintegration*. Cambridge, UK: University Press.

Dölling, D. (1992) 'Der Täter-Opfer-Ausgleich.' *Juristenzeitung*, 47: 493–9.

Eser, A. and Walther, S. (eds) (1997) *Wiedergutmachung im Kriminalrecht. Internationale Perspektiven, Vol. 2*. Freiburg: Max-Planck-Institut für ausländisches und internationales Strafrecht.

Eser, A. and Yamanaka, K. (2001) *Einflüsse deutschen Strafrechts auf Polen und Japan*. Baden-Baden: Nomos.

Foote, D. H. (1992) 'The Benevolent Paternalism of Japanese Criminal Justice', *California Law Review*, 80: 316–90.

General Secretariat of the Supreme Court (1998) *Shiho Tokei Nenpo, Keijihen* 1998 (*The Year Book for Court Statistics – Criminal Cases – 1998*). Tokyo: General Secretariat of the Supreme Court.

Haley, J. O. (1989) 'Confession, Repentance and Absolution' in M. Wright and B. Galaway (eds) *Mediation and Criminal Justice*. London, Newbury Park and New Delhi: Sage Publications.

Haley, J. O. (1991) 'Victim–Offender Mediation: Japanese and American Comparisons' in H. Messner and H.-U. Otto (eds) *Restorative Justice on Trial*. Dordrecht, NETH and Boston, MA: Kluwer.

Haley, J. O. (1999) 'Apology and Pardon: Learning from Japan' in A. Etzioni (ed.) *Civic Repentance*. Lanham MD: Rowman and Littlefield.

Japan Federation of Bar Associations (1993) *What's Daiyo-Kangoku? Abolish 'Daiyo-Kangoku – Japan Police Custody System' Now*. Tokyo: JFBA.

Kerner, H.-J. (1993) 'Kriminalstatistik' in G. Kaiser, H.-J. Kerner and H. Schellhoss (eds) *Kleines kriminologisches Wörterbuch* (3rd edn). Heidelberg: C. F. Müller Juristischer Verlag.

Kühne, H.-H. and Miyazawa, K. (1991) *Kriminalität und Kriminalitätsbekämpfung in Japan* (2nd edn). Weisbaden: Bundeskriminalamt Wiesbaden.

Kury, H. (2000) 'Das Dunkelfeld der Kriminalität – Höher als vermutet?', *Hokkaigakuen Hogaku Kenkyu* (*The Hokkaigakuen Law Journal*), 36(1): 165–208.

Lynd, H. M. (1958) *On Shame and the Search for Identity*. London: Routledge and Kegan Paul.

Meier, B. D. (1998) 'Restorative Justice – A New Paradigm in Criminal Law?' *European Journal of Crime, Criminal Law and Criminal Justice*, 6(2): 125–39.

Miklau, R. (1993) 'Der Modellversuch "außergerichtlicher Tatausgleich" ist nicht verfassungswidrig', *Österreichische Juristenzeitung*: 697–9.

Miyazawa, K., Taguchi, M. and Takahashi, N. (eds) (1996) *Hanzaihigaisha no Kenkyu (Empirical Researches on Crime Victims in Japan)*. Tokyo: Seibundo.

Moos, R. (1996) 'Der Schuldbegriff im österreichsischen StGB' in K. Schmoller (ed.) *Festschrift für O. Triffterer zum 65. Geburtstag*. Wien and New York: Springer.

Nakano, Y. (1996) *Keijisoshoho (Criminal Procedure)*. Tokyo: Kyoiku System.

Nishihara, H. (1977) *Keiho Soron (Criminal Law. General Principles)*. Tokyo: Seibundo.

Nishimura, H. and Hosoi, Y. (2000) 'Shazai; (Yurushi to Nihon no Keijishiho – Kankeishufukuseigi o Kangaeru' (Apology, Forgiveness and the Japanese Criminal Justice: Considerations on Restorative Justice.) in T. Atsumi *et al.* (eds) *Miyazawa Koichi Sensei Koki Shukuga Ronbunshu (Festschrift for Miyazawa) Vol. 1*. Tokyo: Seibundo.

Ohya, M. (1997) *Keiho Kogi Soron (Lectures on Criminal Law. General Principles)*. Tokyo.

Ohya, M. (1999) 'Hanzaihigaisha Taisaku no Rinen' (Ideas of the Policy for Crime Victims), *Jurist*, 1163: 7–12.

Rahn, G. (1990) *Rechtsdenken und Rechtsauffassung in Japan*. Munich: C. H. Beck.

Research and Training Institute of the Ministry of Justice (1999) *Hanzai Hakusho 1999*. (*The White Book on Japanese Criminality* 1999). Tokyo: Research and Training Institute of the Ministry of Justice.

Sakuta, K. (1967) Haji no Bunka Saiko (*Reconsiderations on the Culture of Shame*).

Takahashi, N. (1997) 'Wiedergutmachung als Aufgabe der Strafjustiz' in A. Eser and S. Walther (eds) *Wiedergutmachung im Kriminalrecht, Vol. 1*: 355–371.

Van Ness, D. and Strong, K. H. (1997) *Restoring Justice*. Cincinnati, OH: Anderson Publishing.

Wagatsuma, H. and Rosett, A. (1986) 'The Implications of Apology: Law and Culture in Japan and the United States' *Law and Society Review*, 20(4): 461–98.

Yoshida, T. (1997a) 'Außergerichtlicher Vergleich und Schadenswiedergutmachung in der japanischen Strafrechtspflege' in A. Eser and S. Walther (eds) *Wiedergutmachung im Kriminalrecht, Vol. 1*: 373–463.

Yoshida, T. (1997b) 'The Present Situation of "Settlement Out-Of-Court" and its Significance in Japanese Criminal Justice', *Indian Journal of Criminology*, 25(1): 35–42.

Yoshida, T. (1999) 'Opferhilfe und Wiedergutmachung in Japan' in Weisser Ring (ed.) *Wiedergutmachung für Kriminalitätsopfer – Erfahrungen und Perspektiven*. Mainz: Weißer Ring.

Yoshida, T. (2001) 'Der japanische strafrechtliche Schuldbegriff von gestern, heute und morgen – Recht, Schuld, Strafe, Strafzumessung und Wiedergutmachung in A. Eser and K. Yamanaka (eds) *Einflüsse deutschen Strafrechts auf Polen und Japan*.

Zehr, H. (1990) *Changing Lenses*. Scottdale, PA: Herald Press.

Chapter 10

Legal rules and safeguards within Belgian mediation practices for juveniles

Els Dumortier

Introduction

Since the beginning of the Belgian experiments with victim–offender mediation for juveniles, a lack of legal rules and standards obliged and still obliges Belgian Mediation Centres to establish their own procedures, rules and standards. In this chapter I would like to analyse the ways in which basic procedural safeguards are organized (or not) within mediation practices for juveniles in Brussels and, more specifically, in the Mediation Centre BAS! and its linked Restitution Fund. BAS! means *Begeleidingsdienst Alternatieve Sancties* or 'Counselling Service for Community Service'. Originally they only counselled juveniles who had to serve a court-imposed community service. But in 1996 they started an experiment with victim–offender mediation at the level of the Public Prosecutor. The argument for co-operating with the Public Prosecutor is that in this way the young offender is able to avoid a procedure before the Juvenile Judge (diversion). Moreover, both victim and offender have to accept mediation on a voluntary basis. Hence, it is said, a lack of procedural safeguards on this level would be defensible. The question arises however if, *in practice,* both voluntary acceptance and the avoidance of a Juvenile Judge actually counterbalance the need for legal rules and procedural safeguards for the minors involved.

Voluntary co-operation and diversion *vs.* legal rules and safeguards?

As mentioned above, within the discourse on mediation, the voluntary acceptance and commitment on the part of the offender and the victim are often stressed. Within the mediation practices of BAS!, however, it seems that certain minors in particular participate because they want to avoid a prosecution. Even certain minors who see themselves as being innocent are prepared to accept mediation in order to avoid any further legal procedure. Other minors seem to accept unreasonable damage claims in order to avoid such a prosecution. Recent Belgian research on mediation practices confirms that young offenders are, of course, also motivated to participate in a mediation process in order to avoid further judicial consequences (Stassart 1999: 105). This instrumental motivation on the part of young offenders (to avoid further negative consequences) raises serious questions concerning the concept of 'voluntary commitment' to victim–offender mediation. After all, it is hard to pretend that, in practice, a minor has a free choice and is in no way obliged to participate, when his unwillingness to co-operate can be sanctioned by prosecution before the juvenile court (Trépanier 1993). Following this discourse in which mediation is described as 'extra-judicial, not obligatory, free to accept, voluntary commitment, etc.', no legal rights (like the right to legal assistance, proportionality, the right to appeal, etc.) are, in practice, organized either. This situation seems to resemble the heavily-criticized treatment model (criticised also by restorative justice advocates: Walgrave 1980), where youngsters were not punished either, at least not following the treatment discourse, and therefore did not need proper procedural guarantees (Dumortier 2000). Because the pressure on minors to participate in victim–offender mediation and/or accept repair agreements can be quite high in practice, the need for rules and procedural guarantees as a defence against this pressure also grows.

Besides, avoiding an appearance before a judge does not seem to be realised in practice either. In Belgium there are no legal rules, nor guidelines, that state what kind of juvenile cases are appropriate for mediation on the level of the Public Prosecutor. The issue tends to be settled in local co-operation agreements between the Mediation Centre and the Public Prosecutor's Office. Initially, BAS! asked the Public Prosecutor's Office to select and divert only serious cases that normally would have been prosecuted. Nevertheless, five years later, the BAS! mediators unfortunately have had to come to the conclusion that minor cases in particular, which normally would not have been prosecuted at all, are sent to BAS! Hence, instead of avoiding a judge, a widening of the net has taken place: juveniles who are normally left alone by the judicial system now face mediation. This net-widening effect need not be seen as a negative outcome in all respects, if only because more victims can be taken care of and can have their damage repaired. From a pedagogic point of view, moreover, it may be better to respond in a restorative way to a minor's first offence. Nevertheless, net-widening does pose a problem when too great a burden is placed on a young offender who has only committed a minor, often a first, offence. After all, in the name of restoration, youngsters can also be obliged to carry out a considerable amount of work (see further). Therefore, procedural safeguards as a defence against illegal or disproportionate responses from or on behalf of the state or (other citizens of) the community remain a necessity even within voluntary and diversionary experiments (Dünkel 1996). In the rest of this chapter, I would like to discuss three bottlenecks – related to the lack of legal rules and safeguards – that have regularly surfaced as being problematic within the five years of BAS! mediation practice: (1) proportionality, (2) legal assistance and (3) the influence of mediation on subsequent judicial proceedings.

Restorative proportionality in practice

Taking into account the low severity of the cases BAS! handles, victim–offender mediation often seems to amount to, within BAS! practices, making a financial arrangement. This often implies that the insurance company or the parents of the youngster intervene in order to restore financially the material damage claimed by the victim. Within this scheme, victim–offender mediation (or should we call it 'financial arrangements'?) and net-widening only seem to lead to more restored victims without imposing sanctions on the youngster. Hence it does not seem that problematic. Sometimes, however, it is not that easy to financially repair the damage claimed by the victim: if parents have not taken out insurance for instance, if the insurance company refuses to intervene, if parents are poor, if parents are unwilling to pay anything, if the juvenile has no pocket money, if the victim insists on being restored financially by the minor himself, etc. In all these cases, if the minor does not want to drop out of mediation and risk a prosecution, he is obliged to take a job. In certain Belgian districts, such as the district of Brussels, the mediator can also make an appeal to a Restitution Fund. These funds are composed of donations from private persons as well as public authorities and make a certain amount of money (approximately 5 Euros) available for each hour that the minor labours for the community (Dumortier and Eliaerts 1998). An example: if a young offender has to repair a damage of 100 Euros, by earning 5 Euros an hour, he will have to work for 20 hours for the community. At the end of this paid community service, it is the victim who receives the money earned and not the young offender. Although, some young offenders are able to repair the damage and avoid a possible prosecution, as a result of these Restitution Funds some problems do also occur.

First of all, Restitution Funds handle, in principle, only cases that have been sent by the Public Prosecutor to a Mediation Centre and afterwards by the Mediation Centre to the Restitution Fund. Hence, Restitution Funds also deal with less serious net-widening cases. But certain minor offences (such as spraying graffiti) cause huge material damage. So by using a form of restorative proportionality instead of a penal one, certain young minor offenders are obliged to do a considerable amount of work, sometimes even more than youngsters punished by the Juvenile Judge for the same kind of offences.[1] Using restorative proportionality also implies, in practice, that minors who commit rather minor offences with a high degree of material damage sometimes have to work more than young offenders who commit more serious offences with a lower degree of material damage (such as intentionally breaking someone else's nose).

Another problem concerning this restorative proportionality is the fact that some victims demand unreasonable damage claims. As a consequence, young offenders sometimes have to work more than they actually deserve (even on the basis of a restorative proportionality). The BAS! mediators often feel uncomfortable in these situations, because if the mediator says the claim is unreasonable, the mediator might lose the victim's confidence. As a consequence, mediation might totally fail, and an unsuccessful mediation might trigger a prosecution on the part of the Public Prosecutor. Moreover, the conflict should belong to both offender and victim. Hence, if both reach an agreement, even when it is an unreasonable one, it still is their choice. At the same time, nevertheless, the BAS! mediators often have the impression that minors accept these unreasonable damage claims specifically out of ignorance or for fear of subsequent prosecutions.

The (low) earnings a minor receives by working for the Restitution Fund can also lead to severe and/or unfair repair efforts. Within the Restitution Fund covering the district of Brussels, for example, the young offenders receive the equivalent of the minimum wages minors earn in the free-market system. But the less a minor earns an hour, the more hours he or she will have to work to repair a certain amount of damage. Taking into account the less serious character of the (net-widening) cases, disproportionate repair actions can easily be created. The free-market wages also imply that older minors earn more money an hour than younger minors.[2] After all, younger minors are capable of doing less than older minors. Hence, following the free-market philosophy, they should earn less than the older ones. However, the question arises whether this argument deserves more weight than the argument that this same system also implies that fifteen-year olds have to fulfil more hours of Community Service than eighteen-year olds, when they have caused the same amount of damage. From a pedagogical point of view, this situation is quite difficult to defend, because the older you are, the more responsibility you can and should bear.[3]

Another argument, defending the (low) free-market wages, is said to be victim related. If young offenders could earn more, this would not be acceptable in the eyes of the victim. It would look as if we were giving the youngster too much in compensating the victim. Some victims might feel victimized again by it being made too easy for young delinquents. But, is this kind of thinking not akin to the retributive philosophy (*'they have to feel it!'*)? Would not those victims be better off in a real trial instead of going through a restorative procedure in which punishing youngsters (and making it not too easy on youngsters) is not at stake (at least not following the discourse on mediation)?

Finally, it is also said that the minor is not forced to work for the Restitution Fund, because the mediation procedure is a voluntary process, and so is the choice to work at a minimum rate for the Restitution Fund. But, as said before, we believe that, in practice, very little freedom is involved, because if the damage is not repaired, the minor risks being prosecuted by the Public Prosecutor. Moreover, in the mediation practice of BAS! it seems that certain parents put a lot of pressure on minors to make them accept the execution of voluntary paid community service. This way parents, who are normally civilly liable for their children, do not have to make a financial contribution. But is it fair that juveniles have to pay the price for this kind of parental attitude? Such an attitude on the part of the parents causes problems especially when several minors have committed an offence together. In such cases, some parents are prepared to repair everything, others want their son or daughter to take part in the repair actions and some parents refuse to pay a penny. Hence the young offenders involved, who know one another, all have to fulfil different repair actions. These situations definitely undermine the principle of equality.

Implications for policy

(Restorative) proportionality remains a difficult problem within mediation practices. Ignorance, poverty, unwilling parents, coercion and fear of being pursued might encourage young offenders to restore and to work to a greater extent than they think is just. Therefore, we must then ask whether there should not be guidance available that would leave freedom to negotiate, but that would also avoid unwarranted disparity (Van Ness 1999: 274–5). This need for proportionality does not imply the use of strict retributive proportionality. Instead, the creation of a retributive minimum and a retributive maximum related to the seriousness of the offence and the age of the minor could offer the retributive limits within which victims and offenders can agree on forms of reparation. Moreover, these retributive limits could also act as a 'default setting' in cases where no informal resolution proved possible (Cavadino and Dignan 1997: 248) and the case is passed on to the criminal justice system.

Besides, to prevent minors from fulfilling excessive reparations on the level of the Public Prosecutor, the question arises as whether it would not be advisable to put a clear (legal) limitation on the hours a minor should (or feels obliged to) work for the community. After all, within Belgian juvenile justice, procedural safeguards (such as the presumption of innocence, the right to legal assistance, appeal, etc.) are only organized on the level of the Juvenile Judge and not on the level of the Public Prosecutor. Following the Dutch juvenile justice act (which is a penal one), a clear limitation of 40 hours of community service appears reasonable at the level of the Public Prosecutor. If we want minors to work and repair more, then maybe the mediation procedure should be continued at the level of the Juvenile Judge. At this level, the minor's legal rights are, normally, better guaranteed. Hence, the hours a minor wants (or feels obliged) to work for the damage repair can be higher (Dumortier 2000).

The need for legal assistance in practice

Taking into account the minor's age and sensitivity to persuasion and pressure (from parents, the victim, the mediator and/or the Public Prosecutor), BAS! recently signed a local co-operation agreement with the Brussels Bar Association. For each juvenile involved in a victim–offender mediation (offender as well as victim), a lawyer will be appointed. This lawyer will write a letter to the client stating that the youngster can always contact him in order to receive free (legal) advice. However, usually this lawyer may not attend the real mediation process, where the offender meets the victim. With this scenario, BAS! hopes, on the one hand, that minors can and will more easily, and for free, contact a (specialized) lawyer. On the other hand, by not accepting the presence of the lawyer during the real meeting, they want to prevent a 'rejuridication' (Groenhuijsen 2000: 446) of the conflict, with lawyers taking over.

Although this recent co-operation with the Bar is definitely a positive initiative, the question arises whether this *right* to legal assistance should not be an *obligation*. After all, within the traditional juvenile justice system, we notice that whenever the right to legal assistance is not obligatory, many minors are simply not represented because, it is said, they have waived their right to legal assistance. These waivers are probably due to the fact that minors, on the one hand, are not well informed on what exactly the benefits of legal assistance are and that this is, at least in Belgium, free of charge for minors. On the other hand, the perceived low quality of legal assistance might also play an important role.

Implications for policy

In order to enable a practice where legal assistance is always foreseen, the quality of legal assistance should be guaranteed. On the one hand, lawyers should therefore specialize in juvenile law and the problems closely linked to it. On the other hand they should also receive special instruction in restorative justice and its underlying principles. Well-informed lawyers could give relevant advice to the young offenders concerning their decision on whether or not to participate in the mediation procedure. At the end of the negotiation, but before signing the final agreement, the lawyer could also prevent the young offender from accepting unreasonable damage claims and/or unreasonable repair actions. Besides, it must be mentioned that arranging damage repair is a difficult problem, which triggers a number of questions in which legal advice also might be very relevant (Dumortier *et al.* 1998: 362).

Finally, a fundamental question still remains. Should there not also be a lawyer during the real victim–offender meeting? After all, minors can be put under enormous pressure by their parents and extended family, by the victim, by the mediator, etc. In contrast to adults, minors might be more in need of (legal) assistance during the process than we assume.

The influence of the mediation outcome on the traditional justice system in practice

In Belgium, there is no legal instrument that determines whether and to what extent the prosecutor has to take into account the outcome of mediation in cases in which minors are involved. In practice, the issue tends to be settled in referring to local co-operation agreements between the Mediation Centre and the Public Prosecutor. This lack of legal rules definitely creates an inequality between minors, depending on the district they live in. Moreover, following international regulation on mediation in penal matters (UN Draft Declaration 2000: no. 11 and European

Recommendation 1999: p. 5) guidelines and standards should address 'the handling of cases following a restorative process'.

In the local co-operation agreement between BAS! and the Brussels Public Prosecutor's Office, it is stipulated that the prosecutor dismisses the case when the outcome of the mediation procedure proves successful. This demand is made in the interests of the young offender's rights and to prevent the minor being (or feeling) punished twice, once during the mediation and once by the judge (Dumortier *et al.* 1998). Nevertheless, the demand for a dismissal probably reinforces the net-widening effect. After all, Public Prosecutors will hesitate (in the interests of society) to send serious cases to a mediation centre, if afterwards they lose all rights to prosecute.

Being aware of this, BAS! decided to extend its activities. In the future, BAS! also intends to set up victim–offender mediation in cases that have already been prosecuted by the Public Prosecutor. In this scenario, the Juvenile Judge, the social services or the lawyer involved can suggest to a minor that he contacts BAS! If afterwards the young offender and the victim are prepared to mediate, a victim–offender mediation can then start. Such a way of working has nothing to do with diversion, because both the young offender and the victim know they will face a judge at the end of the road. Nevertheless, this scenario still incorporates certain advantages. First of all, net-widening will probably occur less, because the Public Prosecutor normally only prosecutes the more serious cases. Secondly, the legal rights and procedural safeguards are better guaranteed on the level of the Juvenile Judge (as contrasted with the level of the Public Prosecutor). Thirdly, victim and offender are offered the possibility of influencing the judge's decision. Finally, the evaluation of the mediation outcome by an independent and impartial judge can be seen as a procedural guarantee for the offender and the victim, as well as for society. After all, a judge must take the interests of all parties involved into consideration. Besides, if one of the parties does not agree with the evaluation of the judge, appeal is always possible. Therefore, judges should always give reasons for why they accept or refuse to take a mediation outcome into consideration (Eliaerts and Dumortier 2000). Moreover, proportionality limits (as mentioned above) can help the Juvenile Judge to consider whether the mediation outcome can be considered proportionate, fair and sufficient (for offender, victim and society).

Implications for policy

If Belgian authorities claim victim–offender mediation is a defensible alternative for the traditional juvenile justice system, they should at least create 'guidelines, with legislative authority when necessary, defining and governing the use of mediation in penal matters. Such guidelines should in particular address the conditions for the referral of cases to restorative justice programmes and the handling of cases following a restorative process' (European Recommendation 1999: no. 7; UN Draft Declaration 2000: no. 11). These guidelines are indispensable for avoiding the exercise of discretion on the part of the judicial actors and to bring clarity to the young offenders, as well as to the victim(s) (Dünkel 1996).

Moreover, within Belgium legal traditions, the presumption of innocence and the right to defend oneself require a fair trial before any punishment or educational measure can be imposed. Hence, it might be advisable to organize victim–offender mediation on the level of the Juvenile Judge instead of the level of the Public Prosecutor. The legal safeguards for the youngsters and children involved (such as the right to legal assistance, the right to appeal, the right to be heard by the judge, etc) are only organized on the level of the Juvenile Judge. Besides, the Juvenile Judge is a specialized judge, with special knowledge of children's affairs. As a consequence, he might be the ideal figure to evaluate whether mediation is a feasible and constructive option in certain cases. Taking into account his specialization and the informal procedures that characterize Juvenile Courts, the Juvenile Judge might even be an ideal mediator.

Conclusion: clarity on rules and rights

To conclude, it seems that victim–offender mediation and Restitution Funds have become well-established experiments in Belgian juvenile justice practice. Nevertheless, many questions still arise about the organization of victim–offender mediation and Restitution Funds, their relation with and their influence on the traditional juvenile justice system. Moreover, the basic legal safeguards for the minor as well as the victim remain obscure. Hence, establishing a legal framework and guidelines becomes an increasingly urgent need. We must not forget that as long as legal rules and rights are not established, restorative experiments will remain vague techniques for responding to criminal behaviour committed by youngsters. Vagueness in procedures and definitions has proved in the past to lead to arbitrariness within the practice of the juvenile justice system. Already we notice that within different Belgian districts, different solutions are invented for the bottlenecks and different policies are implemented. Although this situation might be acceptable during an experimental phase, it becomes quite difficult to defend on a permanent basis. Unless, of course, uniformity and clarity on procedures, practices and rights becomes totally neglected as a goal of a (restorative) justice system. But is a (restorative) justice system based on diversity, discretion and obscurity actually in the best interest of the child, the victim and society at large?

Notes

1. Within this scheme the material damage is of course not restored, but the parents, as civilly liable persons, will be ordered by the Juvenile Judge to financially compensate the victim.
2. But, since working under the age of sixteen is forbidden by Belgian laws and hence no minimum wages are available for these minors, the Restitution Fund covering the district of Brussels itself established a wage rate for minors below sixteen. The Steering Group governing this Restitution Fund decided that minors under sixteen would earn the same amount of money as the sixteen-year-olds (see Dumortier and Eliaerts 1998).
3. From 1 January 2002 all youngsters will earn the same amount of money for each hour they labour (Henckens 2002, 175). Hence, it seems that this assessment has been partially met.

References

Cavadino, M. and Dignan, J. (1997) 'Reparation, Retribution and Rights', *International Review of Victimology*, 4, 233–53.

Dumortier, E. (2000) 'Neglecting Due Process for Minors: A Possible Dark Side of the Restorative Justice Implementation?', paper presented to the 10th UN Congress on the Prevention of Crime and the Treatment of Offenders, 13th April 2000, Vienna, Austria, available at www.restorativejustice.org

Dumortier, E. and Eliaerts, C. (1998) 'Does Restorative Justice in Action Always Equal Restorative Justice in Books?', paper presented to the 2nd International Conference on Restorative Justice for Juveniles, Fort Lauderdale, November 1998.

Dumortier, E., Eliaerts, C. and Vanderhaegen, R. (1998) 'Critical Assessment of Community Service and Mediation for Juvenile Offenders in Brussels. A discussion of the Project BAS!' in L. Walgrave (ed.), *Restorative Justice for Juveniles. Potentialities, Risks and Problems*, Leuven; Leuven University Press.

Dünkel, F. (1996) 'Täter-Opfer-Ausgleich. German Experiences with Mediation in a European Perspective', *European Journal on Criminal Policy and Research*, 44–66.

Eliaerts, C. and Dumortier, E. (2000) 'Restorative Justice for Juveniles and its Need for Procedural Safeguards and Standards', paper presented to the 4th International Conference on Restorative Justice for Juveniles, Tübingen, 1–4 Oktober 2000.

European Recommendation on Mediation in Penal Matters (N° R (99) 19) (1999) adopted by the Committee of Ministers of the Council of Europe, 15 September 1999.

Groenhuijsen, M.S. (2000) 'Mediation in het Strafrecht (Mediation in penal law)', *Delikt en Delinkwent*, (5), 441–8.

Henckens, F. (2002) 'BAS! en de praktijk inzake herstelbemiddeling (BAS! and the mediation practice)' in C. Eliaerts (ed.), *Constructief sanctioneren van jeugddelinquenten (Punishing youth delinquents in a constructive way)*, Brussel, VUB Press.

Stassart, E. (1999) *Wetenschappelijke Ondersteuning bij de Implementatie en Ontwikkeling van het Provinciaal Vereffeningsfonds (Scientific Support for the Implementation and Development of the Provincial Restitution Fund)*, Leuven; Katholieke Universiteit Leuven.

Trepanier, J. (1993) 'La Justice Réparatrice et les Philosophies de l'Intervention Pénale sur les Jeunes', paper presented at the 9th Journées Internationales de Criminologie Juvénile, Vaucresson, June 1993.

UN Draft Declaration (2000) UN Preliminary Draft Elements of a Declaration of Basic Principles on the Use of Restorative Justice Programmes in Criminal Matters, annexed to the ECOSOC Resolution 2000/14, 27 July 2000).

Van Ness, D. (1999) 'Legal Issues of Restorative Justice' in G. Bazemore, and L. Walgrave, *Restorative Juvenile Justice: Repairing the Harm of Youth Crime*, Monsey/New York: Criminal Justice Press.

Walgrave, L. (1980) *De Bescherming Voorbij*, Antwerpen/Arnhem: Kluwer/Gouda Quint.

Chapter 11

Re-offending after victim–offender mediation in juvenile court proceedings

Dieter Dölling and Arthur Hartmann

Introduction

Subject of the research project

The Institute of Criminology of the University of Heidelberg has been engaged in a research project on behalf of the Bavarian Ministry of Justice on re-offending rates among defendants who had taken part in model tests on victim–offender mediation (VOM) in the juvenile criminal justice system in Munich and Landshut, as well as in model tests in the adult criminal justice system in Nuremberg and Aschaffenburg. The re-offending profile of these groups will not only be described but also compared with re-offending (further official diversions and convictions) of a control group of defendants who had not taken part in VOM.

The data collection for the model projects in Munich and Landshut is complete, and the progress of the evaluation permits a first interim report on the research outcomes. Concerning the model test on VOM in the adult criminal justice system in Nuremberg and Aschaffenburg, data on re-offending are presently being collected, so we can only report on the results for Munich and Landshut.

Problems of comparative research in re-offending

Some basic problems of this kind of research should be mentioned – in order to facilitate the evaluation of the results. One difficulty is that of developing a research instrument which permits the interpretation of differences in re-offending as a result of a different form of treatment – in this case VOM *versus* normal procedure. This is possible if the two groups only differ in type of treatment but are identical in every other respect. Since, however, there are never two identical defendants and no identical cases, science must get by using sophisticated research techniques. A generally-accepted procedure consists of distributing a larger number of persons randomly to the test and control group; thus, the laws of statistics permit us to assume that only the different treatment is reflected in the result since all other factors are distributed equally in the two groups. However, such a procedure is not possible with this research project on re-offending since the random use of criminal procedures is not permitted for legal and ethical reasons. It is, therefore, necessary to make use of an alternative which is to construct a control group which is as close as possible in profile to the VOM group after the criminal procedure. This is, of course, not as valid as a random experiment.

Concerning re-offending research, it is pointed out from a criminological point of view that the aim of VOM is, in the first place, not to avoid re-offending but to find an agreement between victims and offenders and to reduce harm. Support for VOM has even been generated by crisis of confidence in penological theories of crime prevention (Hartmann 1995: 99). However, VOM cannot be conceptualized outside the present structure of criminal law (Dölling 1992) – especially when it is connected to a criminal procedure. From this perspective, it is legitimate and necessary to examine the influence of VOM on re-offending even if the prevention of offences might not be the sole or decisive aim of VOM.

Research conception

In Munich as well as in Landshut, the data on the VOM cases had already been collected for the project description. First it had to be decided whether the control samples had to be taken from the same courts as for the VOM group or from other courts. It had to be taken into consideration that the VOM cases had been selected very carefully and individually by the prosecutors. Thus the assumption could be made that during the same period of time no control cases can be found at the same place. On the other hand, empirical studies show that a significantly higher number of cases could have been treated by VOM – this under consideration of the basic criteria for a VOM, i.e. injury to a personal victim, clear evidence or confession of the defendant, and offences that are usually treated in VOM (see Kuhn *et al.* 1989: 92, 193; esp. for Munich, Hartmann 1995: 193). In addition, an investigation of the selection of cases for the model project in Munich also showed that there was great variation in the numbers of cases referred to VOM by individual prosecutors which strongly suggested that the upper limit of potential referrals had not been reached (Hartmann 1995: 193). These considerations led to the assumption that the cases for the control group can be collected from the caseload of the same jurisdiction as the VOM cases. To use cases of a different jurisdiction as a control group would lead to potentially false comparisons between the VOM and control groups arising from different geographical profiles of criminal behaviour and defendant characteristics. This is especially true of Munich, for which a comparable city may hardly be found within Bavaria. Thus, the control samples have been taken in the same cities where the VOM projects also took place.

Establishing comparability

The VOM cases were analysed as a complete census, i.e. every mediation case falling into the period of time being investigated was analysed. However, the control group had to be limited to a sample by a method of random selection such that basic statistical procedures, e.g. the calculation of significance values, could be used. Only such cases were selected for the sample which corresponded to the basic selection criteria: a personal victim and a confession of the offender, no dismissal due to lack of evidence and no expulsion to another country of the defendant during the time of the research project, since otherwise re-offending cannot be registered reliably. The data for the selected cases were collected by analysing court files. After this, all cases comprising offence categories which were not found in the VOM group were excluded. Furthermore, comparability was established by means of statistical procedures. As a first step, the variables correlated with re-offending were analysed. When calculating the influence of VOM on re-offending, these variables have been used as controlling variables, i.e. the influence of these variables on re-offending has been eliminated by calculation. This procedure is explained in detail in the following section presenting the multivariate empirical findings.

Extent of data collection

The extent of data collection for the sample is determined by statistical considerations. The question of whether re-offending is higher in the VOM or in the control group should be answered without exceeding the error probability of 5 per cent (significance level $p = 0.05$) usually tolerated in social sciences.

In order to ensure validity, the calculated number of cases for the control group has been duplicated. For Munich, inquiries to the Federal Penal Registration Office have been made for 209 VOM and for 575 control cases; for Landshut, for 145 VOM and for 89 control cases. It was not possible to find more than 89 control cases in Landshut.

Sample

Numerous cases could not be included in the sample, due to a variety of difficulties. Some reasons for this were, in particular:

- No inquiries to the Federal Penal Registration Office could be made due to missing data;

- the defendant had completed his 24th year when making the inquiry to the Registration Office (with the consequence that certain registrations are deleted at this time);

- cases have been excluded from the control group which comprised offence categories which were not part of the VOM group.

Finally, a total of 130 cases in the VOM group, with 85 cases showing a successful VOM, and 140 control cases in Munich and Landshut together were available for analysis. The VOM group comprised far fewer cases than expected. A separate analysis of re-offending for Munich and Landshut was thus no longer possible.

Description of cases

In this section, we will provide an overview of the characteristics of the samples and a comparison between them. Since this research project is about re-offending in cases in which VOM has been successful, only the 85 successful cases in the VOM group are of interest. Those cases are regarded as successful in this study where a mediation has led to an agreement between offenders and victims. There is no further differentiation as to whether this agreement has been made in a joint mediation session, by 'shuttle diplomacy' on part of the mediators without a mediation session, or on a private basis without direct involvement of the mediator; all these cases are 'successful' mediation cases if an agreement has been carried out. Thus, cases in which agreements have been reached but not carried out are counted as part of the successful VOM group. However, cases in which the offenders and victims had first agreed to a mediation but then withdrawn their agreement, or where they had not reached any agreement and thus withdrawn from mediation, are not part of the VOM group. This is because criminal proceedings against the defendants were continued in the normal manner and concluded with a usual sanction, whereas the successful mediations had in most instances led to dismissal of cases without further sanctions. Thus, in the case of a failed mediation the influence of the VOM on re-offending cannot be separated from the influence of the normal criminal procedure on re-offending. It is, however, the aim of this research project to analyse the influence of VOM and of the normal procedure on re-offending separately in order to make a comparison. However, re-offending with failed mediations and with the different kinds of successful cases is shown separately in the following section to make possible an overview.

Offence characteristics

Two major characteristics of an offence are the type of offence and the numbers of participants in the event. As shown in the following tables, there are hardly any differences between the VOM cases and those of the control group. In so far as the control group comprised cases with offences which were not represented in the VOM group, these were excluded. The share of damage-to-property cases is significantly higher in the control group (12.9 per cent) than in the VOM group (5.9 per cent). Violent crimes and felonies, which are especially important for this research, are, however, more strongly represented in the VOM group (see Table 11.1), so that there is no need to be concerned about a bias resulting from a weighing of minor cases in the VOM group. An index of the seriousness of the offences using the range of punishment for this offence was also calculated. This index showed no massive differences between the two groups, nor did the number of offenders (see Tables 11.2 and 11.3).

Tables 11.4–9 give further details of victims, Tables 11.10–14 of defendants.

Table 11.1. Types of offences

Type of offence	VOM cases		Control group	
	Frequency	Per cent	Frequency	Per cent
Bodily injury	29	34.1	44	31.4
Theft	41	48.2	77	55.0
Damage to property	5	5.9	18	12.9
Robbery/extortion	3	3.5	6	4.3
Felonies	3	3.5	3	2.1
Violent crimes	32	37.6	47	33.6

Table 11.2. Index of offence gravity

Gravity of offence	VOM cases		Control group	
	Frequency	Per cent	Frequency	Per cent
1.00	20	23.5	25	17.9
2.00	30	35.3	63	45.0
3.00	13	15.3	21	15.0
4.00	17	20.0	13	9.3
5.00	1	1.2	4	2.9
6.00	4	4.7	5	3.6
7.00	—	—	8	5.7
11.00	—	—	1	0.7
Total	85	100.0	140	100.0
Average	2.5		2.7	

Table 11.3. Number of offenders

Number of offenders	VOM cases		Control group	
	Frequency	Per cent	Frequency	Per cent
1	35	41.2	50	37.8
2	23	27.1	40	28.0
3	15	17.6	18	14.7
4	5	5.9	7	5.3
5	—	—	17	7.6
6	3	3.5	8	4.9
7	2	2.4	—	—
8	2	2.4	—	—
Total	85	100.0	140	100.0
Average	2.3		2.5	

Table 11.4. Sex of victims

Sex	VOM cases		Control group	
	Frequency	Per cent	Frequency	Per cent
Female	39	45.9	44	33.8
Male	40	47.1	79	60.8
Juristic person	6	7.1	7	5.4
Total	85	100.0	130 (n.i. = 10)	100.0

n.i. – no indications.

Table 11.5. Nationality of victims

Nationality	VOM cases		Control group	
	Frequency	Per cent	Frequency	Per cent
German	70	88.6	104	89.7
Not German	9	11.4	12	10.3
Total	79	100.0	116	100.0
	(n.i. = 6)		(n.i. = 24)	

n.i. – no indications.

Table 11.6. Age of victims

Age	VOM cases		Control group	
	Frequency	Per cent	Frequency	Per cent
0–13	9	12.0	13	11.2
14–17	17	22.7	34	29.3
18–21	7	9.3	14	12.1
22–29	12	16.0	15	12.9
30–39	6	8.0	6	5.2
40–49	12	16.0	13	11.2
50–59	3	4.0	12	10.3
60–69	2	2.7	5	4.3
70–79	5	6.7	3	2.6
80 and older	2	2.7	1	0.9
Average	31.2		29. 0	
Total	75	100.0	116	100.0
	(n.i. = 10)		(n.i. = 16)	

n.i. – no indications.

Table 11.7. Physical injury of victims

Degree of injury	VOM cases		Control group	
	Frequency	Per cent	Frequency	Per cent
No injury	55	67.1	77	65.3
Slight injury	7	8.5	18	15.3
Medical treatment	14	17.1	17	14.4
Hospital (in-patient)	6	7.3	6	5.1
Total	82	100.0	118	100.0
	(n.i. = 3)		(n.i. = 22)	

n.i. – no indications.

Table 11.8. Material damage of victims

Material damage	VOM group		Control group	
	Frequency	Per cent	Frequency	Per cent
No material damage	32	39.0	43	35.8
Material damage	50	61.0	77	64.2
Total	82	100.0	120	100.0
	(n.i. = 3)		(n.i. = 20)	

n.i. – no indications.

Table 11.9. Demand for prosecution by the victims

Demand for prosecution	VOM group		Control group	
	Frequency	Per cent	Frequency	Per cent
No demand	35	43.2	55	43.7
Demand	46	56.8	71	56.3
Total	81	100.0	126	100.0
	(n.i. = 4)		(n.i. = 14)	

n.i. – no indications.

Characteristics of defendants

Since the greatest influence on re-offending can be expected from the characteristics of the defendants, much information has been collected on the defendants, a selection of which is presented in the following tables. In contrast to the characteristics of offences and victims, there are, concerning the defendants, many significant differences between VOM and control group. It must be pointed out that the VOM group does not comprise adolescent defendants, and that the findings of this research project thus only refer to young defendants. In German law, adolescents are young people at the age of 18 to 21 years.

There are further significant differences between VOM and control group as to the family circumstances of the defendants and the number of times there has been an official diversion or conviction. In the VOM group, 67 per cent of the defendants were brought up by both parents; in the control group, only 50 per cent (see Table 11.15). Table 11.16 indicates the extent of acquaintance of defendant and victim prior to the offence. There are significantly more first offenders (81 per cent) in the VOM group than in the control group (68 per cent). Finally, from information provided by the Federal Penal Registration Office, the highest number of official diversions and convictions is up to three in the VOM group and up to five in the control group (see Table 11.17).

Table 11.10. Age of defendants

Age	VOM group		Control group	
	Frequency	Per cent	Frequency	Per cent
Juveniles	84	100.0	134	95.7
Adolescents	0	0	6	4.3
Total	84 (n.i. = 1)	100.0	140	100.0

n.i. – no indications.

Table 11.11. Sex of defendants

Sex	VOM group		Control group	
	Frequency	Per cent	Frequency	Per cent
Female	11	13.1	17	12.2
Male	73	86.9	122	87.8
Total	84	100.0	139	100.0
	(n.i. = 1)		(n.i. = 1)	

n.i. – no indications.

Table 11.12. Formal education of defendants

School qualifications	VOM group		Control group	
	Frequency	Per cent	Frequency	Per cent
None	1	1.2	5	3.9
Special school for people with learning disabilities	2	2.5	5	3.9
Elementary school	58	71.6	96	75.6
Middle school	16	19.8	10	7.9
Grammar school	1	1.2	11	8.7
University – Technical University	3	3.7	0	0.0
Total	81	100.0	127	100.0
	(n.i. = 4)		(n.i. = 13)	

n.i. – no indications.

Table 11.13. Income of defendants

Income	VOM group		Control group	
	Frequency	Per cent	Frequency	Per cent
Regular	62	88.6	96	89.7
Not regular	8	11.4	11	10.3
Total	70	100.0	107	100.0
	(n.i. = 15)		(n.i. = 33)	

n.i. – no indications.

Table 11.14. Living situation of defendants

Defendent lives with	VOM group		Control group	
	Frequency	Per cent	Frequency	Per cent
Own family/alone	0	0	1	0.8
Parents	53	63.9	70	55.6
One parent	26	31.3	44	34.9
Grandparents or other relatives	4	4.8	11	8.7
Total	83	100.0	126	100.0
	(n.i. = 1)		(n.i. = 14)	

n.i. – no indications.

Table 11.15. Bringing up of defendant by mother/father

	VOM group		Control group	
	Frequency	Per cent	Frequency	Per cent
Upbringing by mother				
Mother only	12	14.6	32	26.4
With biological father	55	67.1	60	49.6
With other partner	6	7.3	15	12.4
Mother does not bring up	9	11.0	14	11.6
Total	82	100.0	121	100.0
	(n.i. = 3)		(n.i. = 19)	
Upbringing by father				
Father only	6	7.4	4	4.5
Father with other partner	1	1.2	2	2.3
Father does not bring up	19	23.5	47	53.4
Total	26	100.0	53	100.0
	(n.i. = 1)		(n.i. = 87)	

n.i. – no indications.

Table 11.16. Acquaintance of defendant and victim before offence

	VOM cases		Control group	
Degree of acquaintance	Frequency	Per cent	Frequency	Per cent
No acquaintance	50	60.2	88	65.2
Seen before offence	9	10.8	22	16.3
Known	24	28.9	25	18.5
Total	83	100.0	135	100.0
	(n.i. = 2)		(n.i. = 5)	

n.i. – no indications.

Table 11.17. Number of previous official diversions and convictions

Number of further official diversions and convictions (re-offending)	VOM cases		Control group	
	Frequency	Per cent	Frequency	Per cent
0	69	81.2	95	67.9
1	12	14.1	29	20.7
2	3	3.5	12	8.6
3	1	1.2	2	1.4
4	–	–	1	.7
5	–	–	1	.7
Total	85	100.0	140	100.0
Average	0.3		0.5	

Table 11.18. Re-offending according to Federal Penal Registration Office

Number of further official diversions and convictions (re-offending)	VOM cases		Control group	
	Frequency	Per cent	Frequency	Per cent
0	32	37.6	49	35.0
1	28	32.9	21	15.0
2	8	9.4	15	10.7
3	7	8.2	24	17.1
4	5	5.9	12	8.6
5	1	1.2	9	6.4
6	2	2.4	3	2.1
7	2	2.4	4	2.9
8	—	—	1	0.7
9	—	—	1	0.7
10	—	—	1	0.7
Total	85	100.0	140	100.0
Average	1.4		2.1	

The simple comparison of re-offending shown in Table 11.18 leads to a rather favourable result in the VOM group. In this group, 38 per cent of the defendants did not acquire any further registration at the Federal Penal Registration Office, compared to 35 per cent in the control group. There were up to 10 further registrations in the control group, compared to seven in the VOM group. On average, an offender who had taken part in VOM had 1.4 further registrations in the Federal Central Register, compared to 2.1 of a defendant of the control group. That is to say, the amount of re-offending is reduced by 33 per cent by using VOM instead of the conventional procedure and sanctions.

However, a simple comparison between the VOM and the control group does not permit a statement on the significance of the influence of the VOM on re-offending. Since other characteristics such as the type of procedure could also have influenced re-offending, these must be checked before drawing any conclusions.

Bi-variate investigations on re-offending

Table 11.19 shows the relation between re-offending and either conventional legal processing, or successful VOM. It indicates the average number of further official diversions and convictions (re-offending).

Table 11.19. Re-offending in control groups

Group	n	Average number of re-offending	Standard deviation
Successful VOM	85	1.4	1.69
Control sample	140	2.1	2.19

Following Table 11.19, on a bi-variate level there is, on average, less re-offending in the VOM group than in the control group. The measure of association eta reaches a value of 0.17. The association cannot be regarded as being very strong (eta can have values between 0 and 1), but it is nevertheless considerable for social science investigations. With a probability of error of 1.2 per cent, the association is significant despite the low number of cases. To give a summary, Table 11.20 shows the average re-offending for the different types of mediations separately.

Obviously, the number of cases in the single sub-groups is too low to interpret the single results soundly.

Table 11.20. Re-offending, separated according to course of VOM

Course of VOM	n	Average number of re-offending	Standard deviation
VOM with mediation session	52	1.19	1.33
VOM without mediation session	16	1.06	1.81
Settlement without mediator	17	2.18	2.32
Defendant refused VOM	2	0.50	0.71
Defendant could not be contacted	5	1.20	0.84
Defendant did not appear	2	3.00	4.24
VOM stopped due to further proceedings against defendant	1	1.00	—
Victim refused VOM	28	2.36	2.13
No agreement between defendant and victim in VOM	6	1.50	1.76
Total	123	(n.i. = 1)	

n.i. – no indications.

Selection of control variables for multi-variate analysis

As already shown, there are several distinguishing characteristics between VOM and the control group. These differences might be the reason for the lower re-offending rates in the VOM group. The possibility of a given variable producing a bias effect depends on whether it occurs with different frequency in the VOM and the control group and, in addition, on whether this variable influences re-offending.

Taking these into consideration, nearly all the variables that had been collected by the documentary analysis of court and prosecutor files have been examined to discover whether there could be a bias effect. One objection to this method could be that numerous characteristics which might influence re-offending cannot be identified by analysing court files. This is certainly correct; however, the prosecutors who selected the VOM cases did not have more information than that found in the files. Thus, it might rightly be assumed that information that is not found in the files does not influence the selection of cases. Characteristics that do not influence the selection should occur in equal proportions in the VOM and in the control group and can therefore cause no bias in the relation of re-offending between the VOM and the control group.

In individual cases, however, a prosecutor might already have more information about an offender from an earlier case or, after having read the file, might come to a general impression which cannot be identified sufficiently in the variables of a file analysis. This potential bias cannot be excluded, but, as shown below, it can be estimated by using quasi-experimental research methods.

For reasons of clarity, the complete process of selection of variables cannot be explained here.[1] Only the following variables were selected:

- variables which are significantly correlated with the number of further official diversions and convictions (level of significance $p < 0.05$);

- variables which occur with different frequency in the VOM and in the control group, if this difference is significant (level of significance $p < 0.05$).

In relation to the second criterion, it must be pointed out that there are several options for setting up the control group:

first, the successful mediation cases can be compared with the cases of the control group (subgroup A in Table 11.21);

second, re-offending can be examined with the successful and the failed mediation cases (subgroup B in Table 11.21).

third, a control group can be set up composed of cases from the control sample and the failed mediation cases (subgroup C in Table 11.21).

If the distribution of a variable differed significantly between the successful VOM cases compared to one of the three kinds of control groups, it was selected for further analysis. In addition, a variable was selected for further analysis if it occurred with significant different frequency in the VOM cases (successful and failed cases) compared to the cases of the original control group (subgroup D in Table 11.21). Thus, tendencies in the selection of cases by the prosecutors were taken into consideration, even if they do not have a significant effect on the successful VOM cases.

Only two variables corresponded to the criteria indicated above: a variable to which belong all offences without material damage – especially violent crimes – and a variable including the number of pre-punishments. Either cases arising from non-material damage or cases with higher previous official diversion and conviction numbers are associated with higher re-offending levels. There is a very strong and highly significant relationship between the number of previous official diversions and convictions and the number of re-offending, with $R = 0.36$.

Table 11.21. Selected control variables

Variable	Re-offending	A	B	C	D
	Correlation (Pearson's R) (significance p–two-sided)				
No material damage	0.15	0.07	−0.02	−0.31	−0.18
(0 = no, 1 = yes)	(0.01)	(0.29)	(0.69)	(0.00)	(0.00)
Number of previous official	0.36	−0.15	−0.16	−0.23	0.08
Diversions and convinctions	(0.00)	(0.02)	(0.01)	(0.01)	(0.19)

Table 11.22. Further variables correlated with the number of re-offending

Variable	Correlation (Pearson's R)	Significance (p)
Offence theft (0 = no, 1 = yes)	−0.12	0.03
Demand for prosecution by victim (0 = no, 1 = yes)	0.16	0.01
Sex of defendant (1 = f, 2 = m)	0.17	0.00
Formal education (0 = no qualifications – 5 = University/Technical University)	−0.19	0.00

Table 11.22 shows the variables which are correlated with re-offending but show no significantly different distribution in the VOM and the control groups.

Taking the control variables from Table 11.21 and all further variables from Table 11.22 to predict re-offending, there is a correlation of $R = 0.45$. Since R can take values between 0 (no correlation) up to 1 (total dependence), this is a considerable and significant value. This means that in the documentary analyses variables have been found which have a considerable influence on re-offending. However, re-offending cannot be predicted completely from the presence of these characteristics. Therefore, there must be other characteristics influencing re-offending which could not be identified by the documentary analysis. This fact can be quantified by the calculation of R. This is necessary to get an idea of the extent to which differences between the VOM group and the sample can be controlled by the variables that turned out to be relevant for re-offending.

For quantification of prediction, it can be added that the percentage reduction of the prediction error can be obtained when squaring value R. In this case it means that value $R = 0.45$ results in an R^2 of 0.18. This means, compared to a prediction of the number of further official diversions and convictions merely based on accident, the number of wrong predictions is reduced by 18 per cent upon knowledge of the correlations analysed here. The research project further revealed that for this prediction, the number of former official diversions and convictions is the most meaningful variable. This variable solely reached a value of $R = 0.36$, respectively $R^2 = 0.13$. If the variable 'no material damage' is included in the calculation, this results in an R of 0.39 and in an R^2 of 0.15. This shows that predictability cannot be improved significantly by including further variables which are significantly correlated to re-offending, because all variables together result in $R = 0.45$ as shown above. In addition, these variables do not show a significantly different distribution in the VOM and the control group. For this reason, a bias effect on the correlation between VOM and re-offending might not be expected from these variables.

Re-offending under control of the number of pre-punishments and the variable 'no material damage'

It is now time to return to the calculation of how strong the influence of VOM on re-offending is when eliminating the influence of the control variables selected above. Technically, this can be done by a partial correlation (Bortz 1985: 550, 552). The above-mentioned effect of VOM on re-offending will be confirmed if it can be preserved to a significant extent after having eliminated the influence of the two selected control variables.

The effect of VOM first of all results from a comparison of successful VOM cases with the control group (subgroup A). It should, however, also result from a comparison between the successful VOM cases with the cases in the control group plus the failed VOM cases (subgroup B). Finally, this effect should also be proven by a comparison of the successful VOM cases with the failed VOM cases (subgroup C). However, there should be no significant difference in re-offending between the failed VOM cases and the cases of the control group. If there is a difference here, it can only arise from the selection of VOM cases. If there is then less re-offending among the offenders of the failed VOM cases compared to the control group, this result can be taken as evidence that the prosecutors have selected less serious offenders for VOM using information that could not be controlled by the variables obtained from the document analyses. This holds good provided one does not assume that the offer of VOM alone could have produced a positive effect.

Table 11.23 presents partial correlations with respect to the influence of the type of procedure (VOM/conventional) upon re-offending.

Table 11.23. Partial correlations concerning influence of type of procedure (VOM/conventional procedure) on re-offending

Groups compared	Control variables	Partial correlation with number of re-offending	Significance (p)
Successful VOM cases (code 1), control sample (code 0)	No material damage	–0.14	0.04
Successful VOM cases (code 1), control sample and failed VOM cases (code 0)	and no. of pre-punishments	–0.11	0.08
Successful VOM cases (code 1), failed VOM cases (code 0)		–0.05	0.54
Failed VOM cases (code 1), control sample (code 0)		–0.09	0.21

There is a correlation of –0.14 between the type of procedure – successful VOM cases versus control sample, i.e. normal juvenile criminal procedure – and the number of re-offendings; this correlation is significant with $p = 0.04$. The negative correlation of –0.14 means that if the value of the type of procedure increases (code: 1 = VOM cases versus 0 = control group), the number of re-offendings declines. In other words, the average number of re-offendings is lower in the VOM group than in the control group, although the influence of the number of former formal diversions and convictions and of the kind of offence has been eliminated.

Comparing the successful VOM cases with the cases of the control group enlarged by the failed VOM cases, there is again less re-offending in the VOM group; however, the relation is weaker with –0.11 and no longer significant with $p = 0.08$.

Comparing the successful VOM cases with the failed VOM cases, the successful ones only show a slightly better result, the effect not being significant with $p = 0.54$. This may lead to the assumption that the influence of VOM when compared with the control group is over-estimated. This can be assumed because only the offenders of the successful VOM cases have had the experience of a mediation process. If this experience reduces re-offending, then the level of re-offending should be lower among the successful VOM cases compared to the failed cases. Since a favourable effect can, however, hardly be found here, this shows that the favourable re-offending finding of the VOM cases compared to the control group must at least partly be put down to the selection of VOM cases. Since the influence of the two control variables which have been identified by the document analysis has been eliminated, there seem to be latent characteristics which could not be obtained by the document analysis. It must, however, be stated that this result is based on very small groups: 85 successful and 44 failed VOM cases. For this reason alone, a significant difference could not be expected. In addition, the number of failed VOM cases falls below the minimum of 55 cases which justifies the assumption of normal distribution.

The last result of Table 11.23 also tells against the findings just mentioned. The failed VOM cases only show a slightly lower re-offending than the cases of the control group, the relation is not significant. If in fact only defendants with a favourable legal prognosis had been selected for VOM – as can be assumed from the above findings – this should also have a much stronger effect on the comparison between the failed VOM cases and the control group.

Course and result of criminal proceedings

Up to now, it has only been found that VOM, compared with the normal juvenile criminal procedure, has a favourable effect on re-offending. However, especially in the field of sanctions, the juvenile criminal procedure has many different possibilities, so that a more specific explanation must be given on the kinds of procedures and the sanctions in the control groups.

In the group of successful VOM cases, all but three of the criminal proceedings have been dropped by the prosecutor without further sanctions. The three cases mentioned have been brought before the juvenile court judge. These three cases were dismissed according to para. 47 JGG (Juvenile Court Act) by the judge. As far as is known, no further sanctions were imposed. The number of further official diversions and convictions (re-offending) for these three cases is 2 on average, with the other cases it was 1.34.

According to the Federal Penal Registration Office, the cases of the control sample have been treated as indicated in Table 11.24.

It is remarkable that the average number of those re-offending is higher for the cases of the control group which have been dropped or dismissed according to paras 45, 47 JGG than for the VOM cases. The same holds true when comparing the VOM cases and the cases of the control group which have resulted in the imposition of a sentence. In the 27 cases of the control group with a sentence, the defendants have been sentenced to the

Table 11.24. Results of procedures in the control sample

Results of procedure	Control sample		
	n	%	Re-offending[a]
Dropped by prosecutor according to para. 45 JGG without sanction	43	38.4	2.09
Dismissal by judge according to para. 47 JGG after educational measure	42	37.5	1.93
Sentence	27	24.1	3.15
No indications	28	—	—

[a]Average number of re-offending in the respective group.

Table 11.25. Results of procedures with failed mediation cases

Results of procedure	Failed mediation cases		
	n	%	Re-offending[a]
Dropping acc. to para. 45 JGG without sanction	12	33.3	1.42
Dropping acc. to para. 45 JGG with judicial measure	1	2.8	0
Dismissal acc. to para. 47 JGG after educational measure	15	41.7	2.47
Sentence	8	22.2	1.63
No indications/unknown	9	—	—

[a]Average number of recividisms in the respective group.

following sanctions: 5 × prison sentence for juveniles between 8 and 10 months, all on probation, but in one case the probation was withdrawn and the offender taken into the prison; 1 × short arrest of five days, 5 × weekend arrest, 1 × payment of a fine, 3 × warning, 16 × instructions, 2 × official educational care and supervision.

According to the Federal Penal Registration Office, the failed VOM cases have been treated as indicated in Table 11.25.

When comparing the successful and the failed VOM cases, there are different results; however, the results are based on a very small number of cases. With cases ending with a dropping, a dismissal or the imposition of a sentence, the average number of recidivisms with the successful VOM cases is more favourable, except category para. 45 III JGG which, however, comprises only one case. The sanctions for the eight cases ending with the imposition of a sentence were as follows: 1 × weekend arrest, 1 × excuse, 2 × fine, 2 × warning, 6 × instructions and 2 × official educational care and supervision.

Evaluation of results

The research project revealed a favourable influence of VOM on re-offending. With the successful mediation cases, the average number of re-offendings was 1.36, as opposed to 2.06 with the control sample. This relation was also confirmed by a partial correlation where the influence of control variables was eliminated. With a partial correlation coefficient of 0.14, this correlation is not very strong; however, it is significant. Checks have been made on whether the result is influenced by latent bias effects which cannot be controlled by the available variables. However, the indicators for such an influence are contradictory. Only a small number (85 successful mediation cases, 44 failed mediation cases and 140 cases of the control group) could be analysed, mostly due to the fact that the names of defendants are removed from the Education Register for defendants upon having completed their 24th year (according to 63 I BZRG – Federal Penal Registration Office Act). Therefore, the extent of the favourable effect of VOM on re-offending is not fully quantifiable in this study. Fears that the preventive effect of criminal law could be weakened by VOM are, however, not supported by these results.

Notes

1. The control variables were mainly selected by using the β-values in multiple regression calculations.

References

Bortz, J. (1985) *Lehrbuch der Statistik,* (2nd edn), Springer-Verlag: Berlin.
Dölling, D. (1992) Der Täter-Opfer-Ausgleich, *Juristenzeitung,* pp. 493–9. Mohr Siebeck.
Hartmann, A. (1995) *Schlichten oder Richten*, Wilhelm Fink Verlag: Munich.
Kuhn, A. *et al.*, (1989) *'Tat-Sachen'* als Konflikt Forum Verlag Godesberg: Bonn.

Chapter 12

Captains of restorative justice: experience, legitimacy and recidivism by type of offence

Lawrence W. Sherman, Heather Strang
together with Daniel J. Woods

Introduction

Restorative justice is a ripe subject for the science of sanction effects (Sherman 1993, 2000). While both theory and practice have grown at a rapid rate in recent years, the science of restorative justice (RJ) has lagged far behind. That is only natural, since science takes time, especially time to follow up on the long term effects of different kinds of justice. But it may also take time for science to discover the important questions about any subject, as well as some answers.

One of the most important emerging questions about RJ concerns its consistency and variability. While philosophers and practitioners of RJ can readily distinguish their work from the retributive or legalistic modes of justice, such distinctions merely describe central tendencies, or average differences. Varieties of RJ programmes, as well as the overlapping boundaries of their territory with that of other innovations in justice, have recently been made clearer as a matter of theory and philosophy (McCold 2000). Yet even within the various categories of RJ programmes, it is increasingly clear that actual practices vary widely.

The state of RJ practice today is not unlike the state of sailing ships in the eighteenth century. As Benjamin Franklin described it after three round trips across the Atlantic, debates about the practice of sailing were focused on the best design and construction of a ship. His contribution to that debate was to observe that even when ship design is held constant, the performance of a ship varies widely depending on the details of how a ship captain sails it.

> It has been remarked, as an imperfection of shipbuilding, that it can never be known, till she is tried, whether a new ship will or will not be a good sailor; for that the model of a good-sailing ship has been exactly follow'd in a new one, which has been prov'd, on the contrary, remarkably dull. I apprehend that this may partly be occasion'd by the different opinions of seamen respecting the modes of lading, rigging and sailing of a ship; each has his system, and the same vessel, laden by the judgment and orders of one captain shall sail better or worse than when by the orders of another…
>
> Even in the simple operation of sailing when at sea, I have often observ'd different judgments in the officers who commanded the successive watches, the wind being the same. One would have the sails trimm'd sharper or flatter than another, so that they seem'd to have no certain rule to govern by. *Yet I think a set of experiments might be instituted*, first, to determine the most proper form of the hull for swift sailing; next the best dimensions and properest places for the masts; then the form and quantity of sails, and their position, as the wind may be; and, lastly , the disposition of the lading. *This is an age of experiments*, and I think a set accurately made and combin'd would be of great use. I am persuaded, therefore, that ere long some ingenious philosopher [scientist] will undertake it, to whom I wish success.
>
> (Franklin (1788) 1996: 129–30 emphasis added.)

Similarly, the design of different RJ programmes may turn out to be less important than how they are implemented. Like the captains of sailing ships, the leaders of RJ processes may have enormous influence on the success or failure of those processes.

Benjamin Franklin's observation about the variable speed of ships built with a uniform design is a powerful metaphor for any social policy. The complex details of implementing a policy can produce wide variations in practices, with wide variations in results. This fact is often used to attack the value of conducting experiments in social policies to determine their average effects compared to the average effects of other policies. Yet as Franklin suggests, the variability of implementation creates opportunities for even greater benefits of experimentation to produce useable knowledge. Had the invention of the steamboat not put an end to the age of commercial and naval sailing ships, it seems likely that the experiments Franklin proposed would have been conducted, and that captains could have used that knowledge to sail ships much faster – on average.

In this chapter we suggest that RJ could benefit from a similar set of experiments, designed to reveal how differences in implementation may cause differences in outcomes. The primary focus of our analysis is repeat offending. While reducing repeat offending is by no means the only goal we envision for RJ (Braithwaite 1998; Strang 2002), it is a major issue for the adoption of RJ policies in the United States, the United Kingdom and elsewhere, just as it is in Australia, where our research was conducted. Our central question is *whether qualitative differences from case to case in the conduct of a standardized RJ process can produce different effects on repeat offending.*

We take the metaphor of 'captains' of RJ from Franklin's discussion of sailing ships. This metaphor aptly suggests the kind of role that Australian Federal Police officers play while serving as 'facilitators' of the diversionary conferences in Canberra that are described in the RJ literature as 'family group conferences' (Strang *et al.* 1999). In this metaphor, a RJ conference is a vessel that is loaded by the police facilitator and others who determine how many people of various dispositions are in attendance at the conference. That vessel travels on a journey that may take more or less time to complete. During that time the vessel may encounter 'winds' of variable direction and intensity in the attitudes and conduct of the offenders and others participating in the conference. As captains of these vessels, the police officers serving as conference facilitators bring a wide range of personality traits to the conferences that affects their judgements about how to respond to highly variable combinations of mood and statements. They also bring varying amounts of experience in the job as measured by the numbers of prior conferences they have led. Like sea captains of Franklin's era, Canberra police facilitators had relatively few prior 'voyages' as experience with different combinations of factors present in each case. Just as ten trans-oceanic voyages represented a relatively high level of experience for an eighteenth-century sea captain, it was in the upper range of experience for a Canberra police facilitator in RISE, the Reintegrative Shaming Experiments that we conducted from 1 July 1995 through 30 June 2000.

We examine some, but not all, of these variable aspects of the delivery of a RJ conference with a focus on the police facilitator. The RISE data include observational measures taken during the conferences as well as interview measures taken several weeks after the conferences. This chapter relies on interview measures to examine varying perceptions of offenders on the way in which the conference was delivered and how it affected offender attitudes. We then link those data to the prior experience of the police facilitators at the time of the conference and the criminal behaviour of the offenders subsequent to the conference.

Our theoretical perspective emphasizes the procedural justice framework articulated by Tyler (1990, 1998) and others. That framework gives broader implications to the analysis beyond its significance for the Canberra or 'Wagga Wagga' model of family group conferences. For no matter how a RJ process is conducted, the experience and personality of the 'captain' may produce highly variable results for all outcomes. The procedural justice framework suggests that outcomes for repeat offending may be particularly sensitive to the qualitative variations in delivery of RJ. Whether the 'captain' in a RJ process is a judge, a mediator, a probation officer, a social worker or a community leader, the same issues of procedural justice will arise. Any person invested with the authority of the state to reach an agreement with an offender for repairing the harm a crime has caused has the same theoretical power as the Canberra police facilitators to use that authority effectively or ineffectively. Our analysis tests the hypothesis that systematic differences in offender perceptions of such authority figures shapes the future offending rates of offenders placed into RJ processes.

Our practical perspective emphasizes the role of experience as one of the variable that may be most easily manipulated. The quantitative dynamic of experience is that the more cases a decision-maker confronts, the more variability in conditions the decision-maker encounters. Each novel combination of factors creates new opportunities to exercise judgement and to observe the immediate feedback from that judgement. The more experience decision-makers have with the same kind of case, the fewer 'surprises' they may encounter in the future. For a heart surgeon, experience with this variability can help reduce death rates in coronary bypass operations from 12 per cent to 3 per cent (Millenson 1998: 202); the more experience the surgeons have, the lower the death rate. For sea captains, the more experience with winds and storms and defiant crew members they have, the more likely they may be to survive a voyage. And for the captains of RJ, the more prior cases they have had, the more emotional control and respect they may be able to muster in the face of challenges that might shock and distress them the first time they occur. That, at least, is the hypothesis we begin to test.

This chapter does *not* report on the kind of experiments in implementation that Franklin suggested for sailing the same ship in the same winds with different kinds of practices. It provides an analysis that is logically prior to such experiments: an identification of some (though not all) of the factors that such experiments can address in the conduct of RJ.

This analysis works within the framework of four larger randomized experiments comparing the effects of Common Law court and diversionary RJ conferences on victim and offender outcomes. But the analysis itself is non-experimental, using correlations within those larger experiments to suggest hypotheses for future controlled experiments. It is by such a plodding, incremental sequence that we are most likely to build the science of RJ (Zimring 1976).

Legitimacy and offending: the procedural justice hypothesis

This analysis builds on increasing evidence that compliance with law in modern democracies depends highly on a belief by citizens that the law is morally correct, as defined by citizens' personal morality (Tyler 1998). The theological tradition underlying this empirical pattern is described by Baltzell (1979) as originating in Germany during the Antinomian aftershocks of the Lutheran Reformation, and later emerging during the English Civil War in the form of Quakerism, Diggers and Levellers, as well continuing in such Germanic sects as Mennonites, Amish, Hutterites and Moravians. The idea that each individual's own 'inner light' and biblical interpretation was the ultimate theistic source of morality arguably expanded the idea of the 'priesthood of all believers' into the 'lawgiving of all believers' (Sherman 2001). Ghandi's civil disobedience and the rising egalitarianism of the modern world (Friedman 1999) have arguably strengthened the role of personal morality in deciding whether each law is just, one law at a time. The continuing force of evangelical movements attacking intellectual and statist sources of moral interpretation (Hofstadter 1963: 47) continues to undermine such principles as a 'government of laws, not of men'. For modern democracies to create legitimacy, it seems the government must persuade each citizen that each law is moral, one citizen at a time.

  The challenge of creating legitimacy for a legal system has been increased by the breakdown or decline of social capital in the US (LaFree 1998; Putnam 2000) and arguably elsewhere. The less time people spend in face-to-face relationships with other citizens on activities of common community purpose, such as schools, youth organizations and religious institutions, the less interdependence and social trust they create. Declining participation in community life reduces both trust in other citizens and trust in government. It may also make citizens more sensitive to perceived insults by other citizens, including citizens working for the government. As Fukuyama (1992) has suggested, it is the 'in-dignation' people feel when they think government fails to accord them sufficient dignity and recognition that fuels resentment against government and law. And as Tyler (1998) has shown in surveys of citizens about their experiences with the criminal justice system, their personal judgement that the law is moral may depend upon their judgement that the human agents of the legal system have treated them with respect.

There is increasing quasi-experimental evidence that the quality of sanctioning decisions can affect offending and repeat offending rates, as distinct from the effects of the severity of sanctions *per se*. The evidence from the Milwaukee domestic violence experiment, for example, shows that the qualitative dimensions of the arrest process can substantially affect the rate of repeat offending (Paternoster *et al*. 1997). The analysis controlled for prior rates of offending and attitudes toward the law, examining offender statements made during independent interviews in jail immediately after arrest. Offenders who said that police had treated them with respect during the arrest process subsequently had a 25 per cent repeat offending rate over the next six months, compared to a 40 per cent rate among offenders who said in jail that police had not treated them with respect. Since this difference held constant the amount of time the offenders were in custody, the difference in repeat offending rates is plausibly connected to the legitimacy of the law against partner abuse-legitimacy created by the personal qualities of the police officers' interactions with the people they were arresting.

A similar finding comes from nursing homes, where more polite (but firm) treatment of nursing home administrators by regulatory agents was associated with higher levels of future compliance with regulatory standards than was harsh and disrespectful treatment by regulators (Makkai and Braithwaite 1994).

Another similar finding comes from the industrial setting, where the way in which factory workers were told of a pay cut predicted the level of employee theft over the duration of the pay cut. In a quasi-experimental design, factory management announced pay cuts in two factories in two different ways. A third factory, which had sufficient orders to avoid a pay cut, was used as a control site. In the first factory, top management conducted a very long and apologetic meeting with workers, explaining why the pay cut was necessary to avoid layoffs and telling the workers that managers would take an identical rate of reduction in pay. In the second factory, a brief announcement was made with minimal explanation and no apology. Over the duration of the pay cut, employee theft rose in both factories suffering pay cuts. But while the rate of theft rose only slightly in the first factory, it rose substantially in the second factory. By building more legitimacy among the workers at the first factory, top management obtained more compliance with rules and laws against stealing company tools and materials than in the second factory. In Fukuyama's (1992) terms, the first factory received more dignity and recognition, while the second factory was deprived of that recognition and its incentive to believe the law to be fair and just.

Similarly, Kinsey (1992) found that among people who had direct or indirect experiences with US tax collectors, survey research showed higher levels of compliance with tax laws when those experiences were favourable. Among respondents who had heard or experienced tax agents being harsh or abrasive in their manner, the respondents admitted to less compliance with tax laws.

Given both research and theory about legitimacy and compliance, there are at least two very plausible hypotheses about RJ. One hypothesis is that by giving offenders more opportunity to talk about the offence they committed and to participate in a decision about how they should be sanctioned for that offences, *RJ processes, on average, should create more legitimacy and more compliance than conventional forms of justice that allow less offender participation.* That hypothesis is tested elsewhere (Strang *et al.* 1999), and is not directly addressed in this chapter; the results of the test vary across offence types.

The second hypothesis is our central concern in this chapter: *the amount of future compliance with law resulting from an RJ process should vary with the degree to which the RJ process 'captains' are able to create legitimacy in the eyes of the offenders being sanctioned.* The more legitimacy each captain can create, the higher the level of future compliance should be. Whether the creation of legitimacy is solely caused by the conduct of the 'captain', of course, may affect the success of this hypothesis. Other factors may be found to have more effect on legitimacy than the personality and behaviour of the RJ leader. Just as a ship may sink for reasons more due to the severity of a storm than to the competence of a ship captain, RJ conferences may be driven off course by factors beyond a facilitator's control. But across numerous conferences, the contribution of an individual leader to both legitimacy and recidivism may become more statistically discernible. While the data we use to explore this question are not ideal for separating individual leadership from situational effects, they at least provide enough data to illustrate the questions and refine the hypotheses for further experimentation.

RJ experience and leadership effects on legitimacy

One of the key questions about any complex and highly variable process is whether experience makes a difference. From sea captaincy to surgery, the common sense hypothesis is that practice makes better (if not perfect), other things being equal. The research on medicine also suggests that frequent practice at a complex technique may be the more relevant variable, as distinct from experience that is not constantly renewed (Millenson 1998). Much may depend, of course, on how experience is processed. 'If experience were the best teacher', as Dr. Johnson observed, 'the streets of London would be the wisest of all.' Learning from experience through the eyes of an experienced supervisor is one method. Learning from systematic rules of observation is another – and a basic definition of science. Yet even when observations of complex processes are insightful or systematic, different people may draw different conclusions from the same experience. Because natural experience lacks the counter-factual design of the controlled experiment (Boruch 1997), different people may employ different biases in imagining 'what if' their conduct had been different. 'Next time', says person A, 'I won't be so easy to give in.' Yet confronted with an identical experience to person A, 'next time', says person B, 'I won't come on so strong.'

The question of experience is especially important at this point in the development of RJ because so many programmes are implemented by people with so little experience in RJ. In many cases, the captains of RJ have had little experience with anything even remotely like RJ. Police officers in particular may have had little experience in running meetings, listening to extended venting of emotional energy, insuring fairness of time allocations across participants, and in restraining their own desire to talk and debate the matters at hand. For the 137 Canberra police officers (out of a total of approximately 550, or almost one out of four officers) who conducted at least one RJ conference in Canberra, most found the experience unlike anything they had previously done in police work. But for the 26 officers who conducted over 15 conferences in five years, RJ became a more familiar and probably less stressful experience.

The comfort level of the person leading the RJ conference may well affect the legitimacy of the process in the eyes of offenders (as well as victims and others). The elements of procedural justice that lead to increased respect for legal agents include an opportunity to correct factual error, as well as the lack of any bias against the suspect or offender based upon personal characteristics. Each of these elements may be delivered more effectively by a facilitator who has more experience at steering an RJ process. Whether experience had that effect in Canberra, however, was not a matter of formal training; these theoretical elements were never included in the formal training they received, at least not in those terms. What experience provided was an opportunity for employing emotional intelligence in learning how to create a group consensus across people with arguably conflicting interests. Success in that endeavour was arguably measured by offender indications of whether they came away from the process with increased respect for the police.

Measuring legitimacy with the concept of 'increased respect for police' is justifiable on the basis of Tyler's (1998) data and theory on the personal relationship citizens have with agents of the law. Tyler shows that citizens seem to generalize from their experience with one or so legal agents to the entire legal system. Thus the answers to our questions about offender attitudes to both police and the legal system were highly correlated, although the effects of RJ were stronger on increased respect for police than for other indicators of legal legitimacy (Strang *et al.* 1999). The fact that RJ was generally far more effective than court in producing increased legitimacy is a major empirical success for RJ, one that makes the challenge of reducing recidivism all the greater.

The connection between that success and legitimacy was only found after the fact, however. Unlike surgical training or sea captaincy, where apprenticeships are supervised by experienced master craftsmen, there were no master craftsmen to supervise new captains of RJ in Canberra. After six years of conducting conferences, the Australian Federal Police still had only one officer who had led more than 50 conferences. This was an intentional strategy pursued by the first police chief in Canberra to adopt diversionary conferences. His view was that RJ should become a standard method of police work that all police officers would learn how to do. Yet as it turned out, some officers enjoyed being captains of RJ far more than others, and sought out more opportunities to lead conferences. Most officers who ever conducted a conference stopped after only doing several. As Table 12.1 shows, most 'captains' steered less than three conferences within the RISE data collection (834 other conferences were conducted over five years without being referred to RISE for random assignment). Yet most RISE conferences were led by facilitators with at least seven prior conferences. Like many other aspects of police work, RJ became something of a speciality, rather than the work of generalists.

The tendency towards specialization increased substantially over time. In the first half of the five-year RISE project (1 July, 1995–31 December, 2000), the average experience level of the facilitators leading each juvenile case was five prior cases. But as Figure 12.1 shows, the average experience level rose dramatically in the second half of the RISE period (January 1, 1998 through July 1, 2000) to 23 prior cases, or about five times higher.

As Figure 12.2 shows, that change was a result less of individual RJ leaders gaining more experience than of the departure of the less experienced RJ leaders from RJ work. The number of different RJ leaders in each quarter of the first half of RISE averaged about eight for juvenile cases

Table 12.1. Analysis of the number of RJ conferences held by police officers in Canberra July 1995 – December 2000.

Maximum no of cases	No of police	No of cases	Cumulative cases	
			No	Per cent
1	23	23	23	4
2	4	48	71	13
3	14	42	113	21
4	9	36	149	27
5	6	30	179	33
6	4	24	203	37
7	6	42	245	45
8	5	40	28	53
9–10	21	47	332	61
11–20	7	89	421	78
21–23	2	45	466	86
25	1	25	491	91
51	1	51	542	100
Total	107	542		

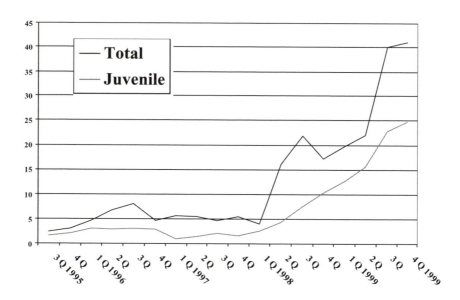

Figure 12.1. Average number of prior total and juvenile conferences by quarter (July '95 to Dec '99)

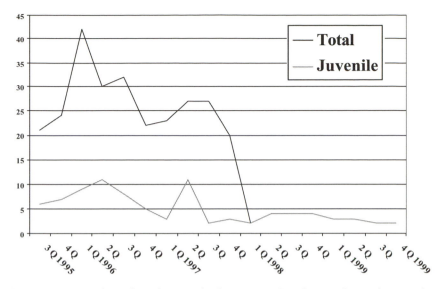

Figure 12.2. Number of conference facilitators total and juvenile conferences by quarter (July '95 to Dec '99)

and 25 for all cases. That dropped in the second half, which was juvenile cases only, to about three facilitators per quarter.

These data raise many questions. What these specialists made out of their growing experience is one question. What they could have made out of their experience had they been trained by a system of supervised apprenticeships is another question. Whether a partnership between an evaluation team and an RJ programme could serve to use interview data to enrich an apprenticeship programme is yet another question. None of those questions can be answered with the available Canberra data.[1]

The question we *can* answer is how effectively officers performed at varying levels of experience, controlling for the expected future offending rate of the offenders in their caseloads. The control for expected offending, based on prior rates of offending, is crucial. Without such controls we may be misled by re-offending rates that simply reflect the kinds of offenders an RJ captain had to steer. Sailing in sunshine produces different results from sailing in storms. First offenders with two loving parents and good educational history provide a very different challenge from repeat offenders from broken homes who have dropped out of school. The differences between such varying types of offenders are largely captured by the prior rate of offending. There is no point in comparing repeat offending rate across officers without adjusting for those rates, and that is relatively easily done (Sherman 1998).

What is less easily done is controlling for risk in the measurement of legitimacy. If we take as a short-term measure of success in steering a conference the offender's statement that their respect for police went up, that statement may also be a reflection of the kind of offender being interviewed. Some kinds of offenders may be far more readily disposed to report increased respect than others would be. Yet without a baseline measure of respect for police before the RJ process, there is no direct way to measure actual change in legitimacy. While the controlled experimental design in RISE allowed us to compare two similar groups, that design is not available at the level of individual RJ facilitators.

This problem is especially important in the Canberra RISE data, given an apparent increase in the prior offending rates of juvenile offenders over time. This change may have reflected the increased pressure on officers to refer cases to RISE after the completion of the drinking-and-driving experiment. The more experience the specialist facilitators got, the higher the prior offending rates were. That increase was about 25 per cent on average for juveniles, a change that could have been a chance difference. But comparisons of legitimacy at different levels of experience may be biased by the changing mix of offenders for the officers leading cases. While it may be possible to distinguish legitimacy effects for first offenders versus repeat offenders, such disaggregation of the data requires a sample size large enough to retain sufficient numbers of cases in each category to produce reliable estimates.

These problems cannot be easily resolved with the current data, given the small numbers of conferences led by officers at each level of experience. Controlling for prior offending in estimates of legitimacy reduces each cell size by about half. Even though we present data here on 542 conferences, 402 of those are for drinking and driving offences. The rest are derived from three separate experiments that should be examined separately, given the fact that the effects of RJ compared to court were quite different for each of the four experiments.

One purpose of raising these problems is to demonstrate a template that could be developed for evidence-based RJ systems in which conference leaders are trained by experienced supervisors, evaluated with survey data, and not penalized for taking on more difficult, defiant offenders. A second purpose is to sensitize the reader to these issues while interpreting the exploratory data analysis this chapter attempts, despite the limitations of the data.

Data and methods

The RISE project compared the effects of standard court processing with the effect of RJ conferencing for four kinds of cases: drink-driving (over 0.08 blood alcohol content) at any age, juvenile property offending with personal victims, juvenile shoplifting cases detected by shop security officers and youth violent crime (under age 30). Cases could be included in the experiments only if they would normally be dealt with in court and were randomly assigned either to formal court processing or to a conference. They were observed both in court and in conference and offenders and victims were interviewed after their case had been dealt with. Outcome measures were primarily re-offending rates, victim satisfaction and perceptions of procedural justice (see generally www.aic.gov.au/rjustice/rise/index.html).

With these observation and interview data we are able to explore the following questions, and lay the foundation for future experiments that might randomly assign the different aspects of leading RJ:

(1) Does offender-respect for police (legitimacy) predict repeat offending rates?

(2) Do offender-recidivism rates vary by individual facilitators, controlling for prior offending rates?

(3) Does offender-respect for police vary by individual facilitator?

(4) Does offender-respect for police vary by facilitator experience?

(5) Does facilitator-experience affect repeat offending rates, controlling for prior offending rates?

Effects of legitimacy on re-offending

The first question for our analysis is whether offender-respect for police after RJ conferences predicts repeat offending risk. This question may reflect the offender's baseline predisposition as much as any aspect of the conference leadership. Nonetheless, it is important to know whether the interviews of offenders shortly after the conferences were completed are useful data for facilitators to examine in learning from their own experience. The policy value of these data is complemented by their theoretical value in identifying all the factors affecting both legitimacy and compliance with law.

Figure 12.3 shows the effect on repeat-offending risk of increased

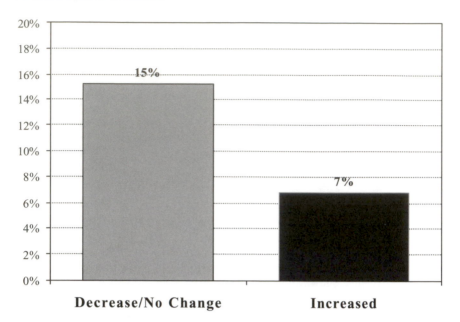

Figure 12.3. Per cent drink-driving recidivism by respect for the police (drink driving cases, $n = 736$). $\chi^2 = 12.831$, $p \leq 0.0004$, $\gamma = -0.425$, $p \leq 0.00009$

respect for police among RISE drinking and driving offenders. These data combine cases randomly assigned to both court and RJ conferences. The follow-up period for measuring repeat offending ranged from two to four years. The average risk of repeat offending for offenders reporting increased respect for police was less than half that for offenders who came away from the legal process reporting no change or a decrease in their respect for police. To the extent that legal agents can manage to alter offender respect, then, there may be substantial opportunity to reduce repeat drinking and driving offences.

Figure 12.4, in contrast, shows that offender respect for police does not have much predictive power for repeat offending across all three juvenile/young offender experiments within RISE. While repeat offending risk is 10 per cent lower for offenders reporting increased respect for police after court or conference, the difference is not statistically significant. Yet Figure 12.4 masks important differences on these data among the three youth offender experiments.

Figure 12.5 shows that offenders committing juvenile property crimes with a personal victim are significantly and substantially less likely to re-offend if they report increase respect for police after their completion of court or conference. Compared to offenders who reported no change in or

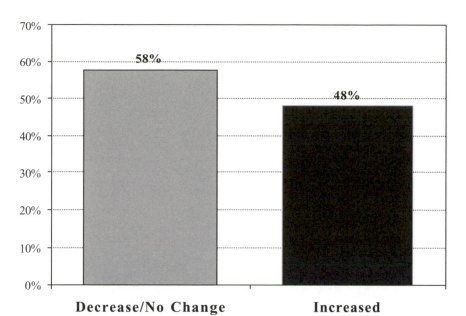

Figure 12.4. Per cent recidivism by respect for the police (all juvenile young offender cases, n = 234). χ^2 = 2.000, $p \leq 0.157$, (*ns*), y = −0.196, $p \leq 0.158$, (*ns*).

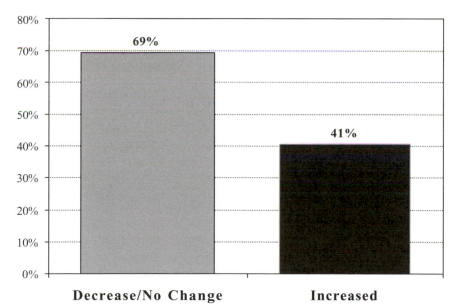

Figure 12.5. Per cent recidivism by respect for the police (juvenile personal property cases, n = 99). χ^2 = 7.929, $p \leq 0.005$, γ = −0.537, $p \leq 0.004$

a decrease in respect for the police, the offenders who report increased respect for police are 59 per cent less likely to be arrested again for crime in the follow-up periods ranging from one month to four years.

Figure 12.6, in contrast, shows that increased respect for police does not predict re-offending after court or RJ conference for juvenile shoplifting offenders. While the re-offending rate is slightly lower among offenders reporting increase respect, the difference from offenders reporting no increase in respect for police is not statistically significant.

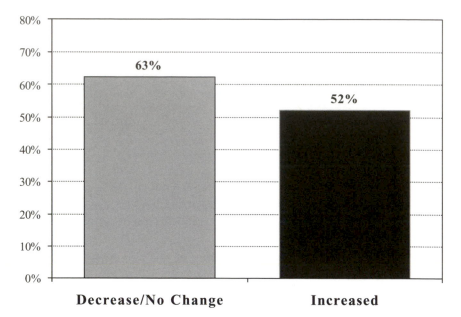

Figure 12.6. Per cent recidivism by respect for the police (juvenile shoplifting cases, $n = 73$). $\chi^2 = 0.749$, $p \leq 0.387$ (ns), $\gamma = -0.212$, $p \leq 0.39$ (ns)

Figure 12.7 shows the same lack of statistically discernible difference for youth violence cases, even though the risk of re-offending actually appears higher among the 13 offenders reporting increased respect for police than among the 49 others in that experiment.

These differences are all the more striking because of the consistent experimental differences between court and RJ conference cases. In the main experimental effects for all four RISE experiments, RJ conferences produce substantially higher levels of offenders reporting increased respect for police. The level of increased respect among RJ conference offenders relative to court case offenders is about:

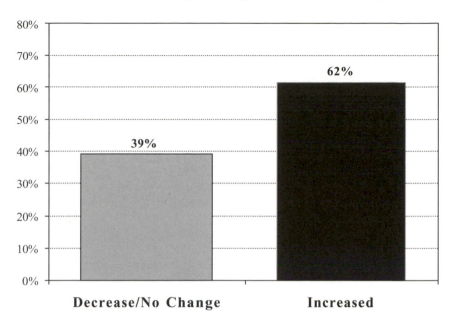

Figure 12.7. Per cent recidivism by respect for the police (juvenile violence cases, $n = 62$). $\chi^2 = 2.162$, $p \leq 0.141$ (ns), $\gamma = 0.433$, $p \leq 0.148$ (ns)

- three times higher in the drinking-drivers experiment;
- twice as high among all three juvenile–youth experiments combined;
- 24 per cent higher in the juvenile property crime experiment;
- three times higher in the juvenile shoplifting experiment; and
- over twice as high in the juvenile violence experiment.

(The data are not displayed, but are based on an updated analysis of data presented in Strang *et al.* 1999).

The answer to the question of legitimacy effects on *repeat* offending (as distinct from *any* offending), based on these data, is that it depends on the offence type. While previous research by Tyler (1990, 1998) and others aggregate all offending, the procedural justice hypothesis may require specification for different kinds of offenders and crimes. While RISE did not concentrate on serious offences, it did concentrate on high volume offences. A high proportion of all offences committed and of all persons who ever offend are captured in the kinds of offences RISE included. In the 1998 FBI Uniform Crime Reports (1999: 210) in the US, for example, over three-quarters of all Crime Index arrests are for offence types that would have been eligible for RISE. Over half of these offences were the larceny–theft offences included in the RISE shoplifting and personal victims of property crimes experiments. Thus it seems well worth exploring the differences in legitimacy that are found by offence type. Police respect seems to matter much more for personal property crime and drink-driving than for shoplifting or violence.

One unexplored factor here is social class. It may be that contrary to Tyler's (1998) observations, legitimacy matters more for middle class compliance than for working class compliance. If the drinking-drivers have different social class characteristics from the juvenile offenders, then the effects of respect would be correlated with a class difference. This question should be addressed in not just the RISE data, but all studies of legitimacy and compliance.

Effects of facilitators on re-offending

The second question is whether different RJ 'captains' produce different repeat-offending rates, controlling for the prior rates of offending of their caseloads. One theoretical basis of that difference could be that there are differences in respect for police produced by the different personalities and RJ leadership skills of the different facilitators. But as the last section demonstrated, respect for police may not be the only link between the nature of a sanctioning experience and the level of repeat offending. If there are differences across RJ facilitators in recidivism outcomes, this may be due to a number of factors.

Figure 12.8 demonstrates that there are substantial differences across RJ leaders in their before-and-after differences in the offending rates of the offenders in the cases they process. These differences are portrayed by individual facilitator, who constitute all eight of the facilitators with at least a total of ten drinking-driver conferences in RISE, out of 29 facilitators who ever conducted a drinking-driver conference; that threshold is set here for reliability of the comparisons. These differences must therefore include all cases handled by each of these eight facilitators, including the early cases they handled without much experience. The range in total experience is from 10 to 51 cases, creating a substantial mix in the average level of experience across these facilitators. Figure 12.8 arrays these differences in by before-and-after differences in offending rate by facilitator. The baseline comparison to the rate of change in offending for all novice facilitators show that even among experienced facilitators, most do better but some do worse than novices.

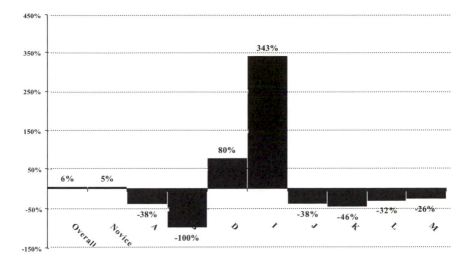

Figure 12.8. Relative change in monthly drink-driving offending rate (pre- and post RISE) by facilitator. Novice category represents facilitators with less than ten completed conferences

Note that the data in all graphics on facilitator effects is presented in terms of cases, with average effects across all offenders in each case. Thus the data represent mean offending rates per offender per month at risk per case. When a case has only one offender, as all drinking-driver cases did, this definition does not matter. But in cases with more than one offender, as many juvenile conferences had, the rates are calculated by taking the average of the individual offending rates within a case. Such procedures are necessary in theoretical terms to reflect the unit of analysis in the experiment, which was the case rather than the offender. It also reflects a reality of juvenile offences, which is that they are predominantly events involving more than one offender (Reiss 1988).

The data in Figure 12.8 suggest that some facilitators do better than others. The range change in before-and-after offending per month varied from a 343 per cent increase to a 100 per cent decrease (no repeat offending). While there is some possibility that these differences reflect selection bias in the kinds of offences or offenders in facilitators' caseloads, the statistical controls for prior offending rates should eliminate that rival hypothesis. Leadership quality seems to affect repeat-offending rates. But how and why that happens remains unanswered as yet.

Effects of facilitators on legitimacy

The answer to the third question may help to explain these differences. That question is whether individual facilitators produce different levels of respect for police. The main limitation in answering that question, as noted above, is the lack of any baseline measure of respect for police. Unlike before-and-after differences in offending, we cannot construct before-and-after differences in legitimacy. But we can at least note that there are post-RJ-conference differences in offender levels of respect for police.

Figure 12.9 arrays the results for different facilitators in rank order of mean levels of respect for police after RJ conferences. While the maximum number of cases each facilitator led may reflect both experience and a preference for RJ kinds of work, the differences in mean results per leader in legitimacy suggest that they may be relevant to accounting for differences across facilitators in their offending rates.

As Figure 12.9 shows, among the 13 facilitators with ten or more RJ conferences in RISE, the mean percentage of post-conference respect for

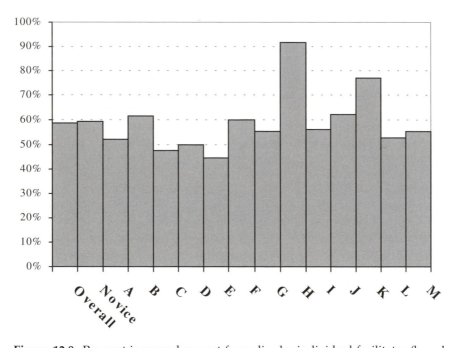

Figure 12.9. Per cent increased respect for police by individual facilitator (based on total conference experience of 10+). Novice category represents facilitators with less than 10 total conferences

police varies widely. The range in average per cent of offenders saying that they had increased respect for police had a minimum of 45 per cent and a maximum of 90 per cent. Yet these differences appear unrelated to experience.

Effects of facilitator experience on legitimacy

The fourth question of whether the level of facilitator experience *per se* shapes respect for police after RJ conferences appears to take 'no' for an answer. At least within the low number of cases we are able to examine, the difference in experience does not cause a difference in respect. Figure 12.10 shows that those who eventually led over ten cases did only a little better than those who did a total of less than ten cases. Since that difference reflects *maximum* cases ever completed, it is a measure of self-selection by facilitators into RJ. Figure 12.10 controls for that self-selection by showing the average effects on respect at each level of experience across all facilitators at that level of experience. Looking just at experience rather

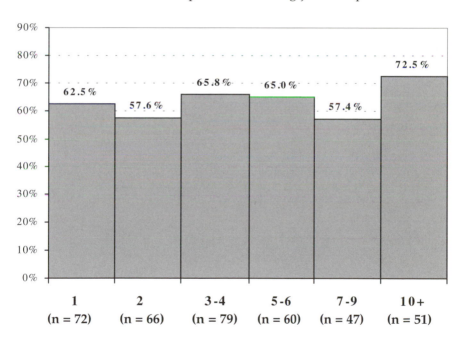

Figure 12.10. Per cent increased respect for police conference facilitator cumulative experience (drink-driving, $n = 375$). $\chi^2 = 3.816$, $p \leq 0.576$ (ns), $\gamma = 0.066$, $p \leq 0.365$ (ns)

than 'commitment' and 'persistence' in leadership, the results show no relationship between prior experience and respect (legitimacy) outcomes. Those with more than ten prior cases do best leading drinking-driver conferences, but not very much better than those who had only led one prior case. At lower levels of prior conference experience there was no consistent improvement as the number of prior cases increased.

Figure 12.11 shows even less evidence that facilitator experience *per se* increases respect for police among juvenile and youthful offenders. The highest levels of respect were found after officers conducted their first conferences. Lower levels of respect were found among facilitators with more experience. That finding was derived from many of the same officers whose success is reflected in the results from their first conference. Whether there was a 'Hawthorne effect' improving the first result that later disappeared is unclear. But it is equally plausible that a change in the case mix over time affected the baseline levels of respect for police. Thus we must repeat the *caveat* that all the legitimacy data lack a baseline comparison. Yet there is still a difference evident between drinking-drivers and juvenile recidivism.

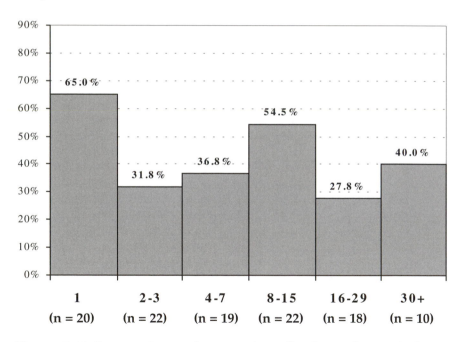

Figure 12.11. Per cent increased respect for police by conference facilitator cumulative experience (juveniles, $n = 111$). $\chi^2 = 8.287$, $p \leq 0.141$ (ns), $\gamma = -0.164$, $p \leq 0.206$ (ns)

Effects of facilitator experience on re-offending

The final and most crucial question is whether facilitator experience makes a difference in re-offending rates. If it does, it would have major policy implications for the organization and management of RJ processes, including selection, training and apprenticeships. Even if there is no clear relationship of experience to legitimacy, the unclear relationship of legitimacy to repeat offending across all cases may allow experience to have a direct link to improved recidivism results.

Figure 12.12 shows that among drink-driving cases, the highest levels of cumulative experience of the officers leading RJ conferences produces the best effects on before-and-after changes in offending rates. This is consistent with the finding that at that level of experience officers produced the highest levels of offender respect for police. This may mean that varying levels of prior experience do not make much difference until an RJ leader has conducted at least ten cases. It also implies that there should be even clearer differences in juvenile cases, which employ far higher levels of prior experience to test the hypothesis than were ever available in the drink-driving experiment.

Yet that implication is false. We cannot test the juvenile effects in the same way as we did for drinking-drivers, because the number of cases at each level of experience was smaller – and because the system for leading conferences changed so dramatically for the juvenile cases. Thus system effects are confounded with experience effects. But we can compare the

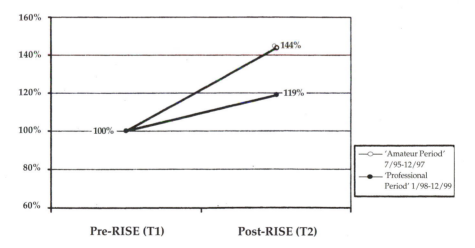

Figure 12.12 Relative monthly drink-driving offending rates before and after RISE during 'amateur' and 'professional' periods

combined effects of the two variables of system (including practice frequency or rate of conference leading) and prior experience.

Figure 12.13 shows a comparison between the experience of RJ leadership in the first and second half of RISE. During the first half of RISE, as noted above, many facilitators conducted conferences, but few of them did so on a regular basis. They also conducted a mix of juvenile and drink-driving cases. During the second half of RISE, only seven facilitators led all of the conferences, with two facilitators leading 80 per cent of the cases. By this time they were highly experienced, with an average of 23 prior total conferences and 13 prior juvenile conferences; the two primary leaders had a mean of 28 total and 15 juvenile priors. The entire system of diversionary conferencing in the second half of RISE was organized around this small number of 'professional' RJ leaders, in contrast to the large number of 'amateur' RJ leaders who had led juvenile conferences in the fist half of RISE.

In Figure 12.14, the substantial difference in the mean cumulative experience of the RJ leaders during the first and second half of RISE is clearly shown to have had no effect on recidivism rates. Among the juvenile cases led by 'amateur' RJ captains in the first half of RISE, the

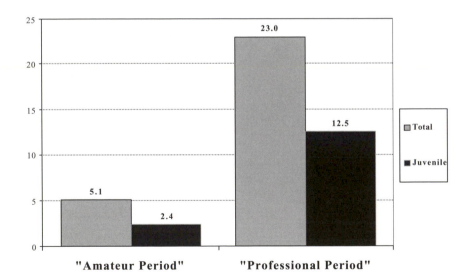

Figure 12.13. Average facilitator prior cumulative experience by RISE time period (total and juvenile only). Total – all conference experience (PCA and juvenile). Subsequent to any conference (PCA or juvenile) juvenile – juvenile conference experience prior to a juvenile conference

mean reduction in the rate of case-based offending from one year before to one year after the conference was 28 per cent. In the second half of RISE, when the caseload became slightly tougher but the leaders were far more experienced, there was a 29 per cent reduction. Figure 12.14 displays the differences in pre-post conference offending rates, using 100 per cent as the baseline rate for both periods, and the relative change from baseline as the post-conference offending rate in each period.

An important caution in interpreting the lack of difference in the two periods is that it confounds experience *per se* and a system of managing service delivery. The first period was short on both, while the second period was strong on both. The effect of *experience* cannot be separated in this analysis from the effect of *practice*, since individual facilitators conducted far fewer cases per year in the first half of RISE (a mean of one juvenile case per facilitator per quarter during the 'amateur' period) than in the second half (a mean of four per quarter per facilitator in the 'professional' period). If the two variables for some reason have opposite effects, they may cancel each other out. We simply do not have enough data to eliminate any of these possibilities on merely theoretical grounds. The fact that none of these analyses are randomized experiments is a powerful caution for all findings, and a reminder of how valuable such research designs are for any research question.

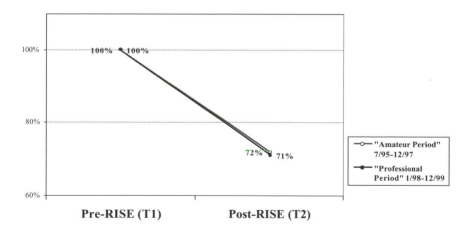

Figure 12.14. Relative monthly offending rates before and after RISE during 'amateur' and 'professional' periods (juveniles). All time differences are not significant

Conclusions and policy implications

This analysis answers some questions and raises others. It shows that respect for police predicts repeat offending for some types of offences but not others. It shows that repeat offending after an RJ process varies widely across different RJ facilitators. It suggests that experience of RJ leaders has little direct relationship with respect for police after RJ conferences. But it also shows that the level of RJ leadership experience may be inversely related to repeat offending rates, controlling for prior offending rates, for drink-driving cases. It also suggests that experience and practice do not affect the impact of RJ on juvenile cases, at least within a two-year time frame with an RJ conference in the middle. It suggests that there may be little difference between a system of experienced 'professional' or 'specialist' RJ leaders running all conferences, at least for juvenile recidivism.

The questions this analysis raises are the same as Benjamin Franklin's questions about practices of sailing ships. If it is true that some leaders get better results than others regardless of levels of experience, there must be specific ways of leading a conference that are produced by the better leaders. This suggests that conferences have dimensions that can be observed and measured in relation to recidivism. The RISE data have substantial observational measures that have not yet been analysed between the two time periods. But now that these findings suggest that there are major difference in recidivism effects by individual leader, future RISE analyses can turn to a wide variety of hypotheses about what differences matter most.

Some possible differences might include the following:

(1) conference preparation – how many offender and victim supporters attend?

(2) leadership air time – what percentage of the conference does the leader talk?

(3) blaming the offender – how much negative commentary about the offender does the leader make or allow others to make?

(4) condemning the offence – how much moral indignation is expressed by the leader, offender supporters, victims and victim supporters, and offenders themselves over the crime in question?

(5) repairing the harm – how substantial was the reparation agreement?

(6) apologizing to victims – how frequently did that happen?

(7) forgiving the offender – how frequently did that happen?

Differences between more and less effective conference leaders on these and other dimensions would be suggestive. While the analysis would not be experimental, it could provide a basis for future experiments. Franklin said his was the age of great experiments. Perhaps we are still in that age, and just beginning to see what we can discover from experiments in human relations.

Notes

1. However, we hope that they will all be answered in the course of the research the authors are undertaking in the United Kingdom, where, building on the experience with RISE, a series of Home Office-funded studies will examine programme research and development at various points in the criminal-justice system and in a variety of locations.

References

Baltzell, E. D. (1979) *Puritan Boston and Quaker Philadelphia*. New York: Free Press.
Boruch, R. (1997) *Randomized Experiments for Planning and Evaluation*. Thousand Oaks: Sage Publications.
Braithwaite, J. (1998) 'Restorative Justice' in M. Tonry (ed.) *The Handbook of Crime and Punishment*. New York: Oxford University Press.
Franklin, B. (1996) *The Autobiography of Benjamin Franklin*. Mineola, NY: Dover.
Federal Bureau of Investigation (1999) Uniform Crime Reports, Washington, DC: USGPO.
Friedman, L. M. (1999) *The Horizontal Society*. New Haven: Yale University Press.
Fukuyama, F. (1992) *The End of History and the Last Man*. New York: Free Press.
Hofstadter, R. (1963) *Anti-Intellectualism in American Life*. New York: Alfred A. Knopf.
Kinsey, K. (1992) 'Deterrence and Alienation Effects of IRS Enforcement: An Analysis of Survey Data' in J. Slemrod, (ed.) *Why People Pay Taxes*. Ann Arbor, MI: University of Michigan Press.
LaFree, G. (1998) *Losing Legitimacy: Street Crime and the Decline of Social Institutions in America*. Boulder, CO: Westview Press.
McCold, P. (2000) 'Types and Degrees of Restorative Justice Practice', *Real Justice Forum*, February, Issue 8: 3.
Makkai, T. and Braithwaite, J. (1994). 'Reintegrative Shaming and Compliance with Regulatory Standards', *Criminology*, 32: 361–85.
Millenson, M. (1998) *Demanding Medical Excellence*. Chicago: University of Chicago Press.
Paternoster, R., Brame, R., Bachman, R. and Sherman, L. W. (1997) 'Do Fair Procedures Matter? The Effect of Procedural Justice on Spouse Assault', *Law and Society Review*, 31: 163–204.

Putnam, R. (2000) *Bowling Alone: The Collapse and Revival of American Community.* NY: Simon and Schuster.

Reiss, A. J., Jr. (1988) 'Co-Offending and Criminal Careers' in M. Tonry and N. Morris, (eds) *Crime and Justice: A Review of Research.* Chicago: University of Chicago Press.

Sherman, L. W. (1993) 'Defiance, Deterrence and Irrelevance: A Theory of the Criminal Sanction', *Journal of Research in Crime and Delinquency*, 30: 445–73.

Sherman, L. W. (1998) *Evidence-Based Policing.* Washington, DC: Police Foundation.

Sherman, L. W. (2000) 'The Defiant Imagination: Consilience and the Science of Sanctions'. Albert M. Greenfield Chair Inaugural Lecture, University of Pennsylvania, Philadelphia; February 24.

Sherman, L. W. (2001) 'Two Protestant Ethics and the Spirit of Restoration' in H. Strang and J. Braithwaite (eds) *Restorative Justice and Civil Society.* Cambridge: Cambridge University Press.

Strang, H. (2002) *Repair or Revenge: Victims and Restorative Justice.* Oxford: Oxford University Press.

Strang, H., Barnes, G., Braithwaite, J. and Sherman, L. W. (1999) 'Experiments in Restorative Policing: A Progress Report on the Canberra Reintegrative Shaming Experiments (RISE).' Canberra: Australian National University, available at www.aic.gov.au/rjustice/rise/index.html

Tyler, T. (1990) *Why People Obey the Law.* New Haven: Yale University Press.

Tyler, T. (1998) 'Trust and Democratic Governance' in V. Braithwaite and M. Levi (eds) *Trust and Governance.* New York: Russell Sage Foundation.

Zimring, F. E. (1976) 'Field Experiments in General Deterrence: Preferring the Tortoise to the Hare', *Evaluation*, 3: 132–5.

Chapter 13

Ways of knowing for a restorative worldview

Barb Toews and Howard Zehr

Over the past 25 years, restorative justice has emerged as a challenge to the assumptions of the dominant criminal justice system. In contrast to a justice model which focuses primarily on laws, blame and punishment, restorative justice emphasizes harms, needs and obligations. Instead of lawyers and judges assuming responsibility for the telling of crime stories and deciding the fate of the offending individual – often at the exclusion of the victim – restorative justice emphasizes the active participation of victims, offenders and community members in recounting their experiences and determining justice.

What we are learning from restorative justice is that a fundamental element of justice has to do with the creation of meaning. Justice is served when the meaning of the crime has been constructed from the perspectives and experiences of those most affected: victim, offender and perhaps community members. Meaning cannot be imposed by outside experts and proxi-professionals; it requires that victims as well as offenders be given a voice. This implies a fundamental reordering of roles and values. Justice professionals and community members often assume roles as facilitators while victims and offenders take centre stage. Dialogue and negotiated outcomes take precedence over imposed solutions. A fundamental respect for all players is essential.

Unfortunately, in our research practices we often fail to operate under principles that are consistent with our beliefs in restorative justice and instead mirror the values of the dominant justice system. Like justice professionals, as researchers we view ourselves as objective experts in the field, assuming responsibility for the stories of the people we study. We collect data and stories, interpreting the meaning without consulting or giving benefit to our subjects. Like the practice of criminal justice, this approach to research disempowers and leads to 'othering' (Fine 1994). To avoid these pitfalls, we are challenged to find ways of knowing and doing research that reflect the values we espouse in restorative justice.

This paper explores some of the similarities in the values and practices of the dominant approaches to research and to justice, and contrasts them with those of restorative justice. It then suggests a set of 'transformative guidelines' for research that are more consistent with the values of restorative justice.

Traditional research and ways of knowing

Kvale (1996) uses the metaphor of a miner to characterize the positivist view of research which until recently has tended to dominate in both quantitative and qualitative approaches to research. In this metaphor, the miner digs up nuggets of buried knowledge that are waiting to be discovered. The pieces of knowledge are then refined and purified through a process that extracts from them the essential elements and shapes them so that they are useable for the researcher's purposes. The miner is expert and arbiter of the outcome; the subject is a passive and unaffected resource in the process.

The traditional view of researcher as objective expert carries with it the power of definition and determination. As the expert, the researcher decides who is worthy of study. They determine how the problem under study is to be defined and what hypothesis is to be tested. Upon completion of the study, the researcher sorts through the gathered information in a process designed to determine what is useful and what is not useful based on their hypothesis, goals and expertise in the problem. Information they deem useless is discarded. They take the relevant information, interpret it and share it with their colleagues. There is little or no collaboration with or accountability to the subjects (Kvale 1996; Fine 1994).

The researcher is bound by a methodology that promotes a strict adherence to rules that are believed to uncover the 'truth' of a problem. If procedures are followed properly, a researcher can find the answer to any social problem. This answer, or truth, is an objective reality that is considered value free (Kvale 1996; Weiss 1994). Being objective knowledge stemming from a patterned world, the answer that is uncovered in research is generalized across situations, people and time. The illusion of objectivity is possible because the researcher does not enter into close relationships with the people under study and their presence does not materially affect the material being collected (Kvale 1996; Fine 1994).

Work in a number of fields – feminist critical theory, studies of racism and oppression, postmodernism – has led to a sharp critique of this approach, arguing in part that it leads to disempowerment and alienation for important elements of society and serves as a tool for domination. Michelle Fine (1994) has called it '… a colonizing discourse of the "Other".'

An important element of this critique focuses on the power that derives from speaking on behalf of the group of people under study. Talking is power. It is through talking that we understand our world. As a result, those who talk control reality and the interpretation of the world around us (Slim and Thompson 1995). By speaking on behalf of research subjects – and by choosing whose talk is worthy of attention – the researcher takes or keeps power from the people under research. Since the subjects are often marginalized populations who have little voice in society, the research process keeps them in their voiceless social positions (Slim and Thompson 1995; Fine 1994).

Despite their appearance as neutral experts – Haraway (1988) has termed this the 'god trick' – a researcher's study and the subsequent interpretation of the information gathered is informed by his or her internal values (Fine 1994). Considering that researchers are educated academics, their values are often based in mainstream biases that in turn affect the interpretation of research results. The story they tell on behalf of the subjects is limited to the information that supports the societal biases and values. Further, the subjects' voice, and the knowledge they have given to the researcher, is often unrecognizable from its original form (Slim and Thompson 1995).

By operating under a pretence of neutrality, the critics argue, this traditional approach to research has important implications for subjects and for society as a whole. It has tended to silence dissonant voices; disempower and disrespect subjects; maintain power in the hands of elites; uphold patterns of oppression; and contribute to a sense of otherness and social distance – the sense that certain groups are different from us, thus deserving of treatment that we would not impose on ourselves (Fine 1994; Slim and Thompson 1995; Kvale 1996). Above all, perhaps, this approach lacks humility about the limits to what we know and a respect for those involved.

This critique may sound strikingly familiar to those who are critical of the Western legal approach to justice.

Traditional criminal justice system

The criminal justice system is another arena in which the acquisition of knowledge and the interpretation of meaning are used to determine the realities of our social world, impacting how we as individuals understand and act within that world. In this arena, the justice process serves as a methodology to uncover the knowledge hidden inside a variety of individuals who are connected in some manner to the criminal offence. This information is used to determine the meaning of the criminal action, and thus the criminal charge, and the nature and degree of punishment that an individual deserves following a criminal offence. This justice system operates with values and practices similar to those of the dominant approach to research, with similar consequences.

From the moment a criminal offence occurs, experts shape the description and meaning of the event. After discovery of the crime, police are often the first individuals on the scene. The officer is likely to write a report describing the criminal event based on the stories of the victim and witnesses. In the course of this documentation, the officer determines what information should be documented and creates a translation of events that becomes the initial 'truth' of the event. The event then falls under the scrutiny and control of another set of 'neutral' experts: attorneys, judges and forensic experts. Attorneys listen to and sort through stories provided by the offender, victim and witnesses to determine what information is the most truthful, relevant and useful for the purposes of prosecuting or defending the offender. They determine the charge that will be filed against the offending individual. They select the most effective course of action to successfully prosecute or defend the case, accepting and rejecting plea bargains on behalf of their clients. The judge and perhaps jury listen to the presentation of the information, determine what is relevant, and make a determination on the outcome of the case.

The traditional criminal justice process relies on the strict adherence to a set of rules and procedures that, if followed correctly, will uncover the real truth of the event and allow for the proper sentencing of the offender. In the television show 'Dragnet,' the detective is known for his often-repeated admonition, 'Just the facts, ma'am.' This slogan provides the framework for the criminal justice process. The prosecution and defence attorneys search for, catalogue and present the factual and permissible truths for the crime to reach the goal of acquittal or conviction and sentencing.

Just as the researcher brings to the research project biases and values that influence the interpretation and outcome of the study, so does the criminal justice system itself and the individuals, the paid experts, who operate within it. What is to be considered a crime punishable by a certain sentence is determined by legislators, who typically come from wealthy, influential and educated backgrounds. These backgrounds constitute a particular perspective and interpretation of the social world with laws being created to preserve that world. For instance, the laws they create determine whether possession of crack cocaine, predominantly used by African–Americans, will carry a heavier sentence than powder cocaine, used more often by European–Americans. Police are permitted a degree of discretion in stopping people for suspected crimes and this too is influenced by their personal values and biases – as is illustrated by the current controversy about racial 'profiling'. Offenders are considered lucky if their case is assigned to a particular attorney or judge because of the use of the personal values in discretionary decisions (Fuller 1998).

Like traditional research, this reliance on presumed 'objectivity' and 'pure' facts results in the exclusion of the voices of those people most affected by the crime, the victim and offender. Little, if any, relationship or connection is made with them as individuals. The key criminal justice players – police, attorneys and judges – speak for the victims and offenders, keeping them essentially voiceless throughout the process. While many people take the stand on behalf of the prosecution or defence, their participation is limited and shaped by those on whose behalf they speak. By removing the victim and offender from the primary role of telling their story of the crime, its impact and their needs for justice, the justice process loses the personal, contextual and subjective meaning that the experience held for the victim and offender. Because the truth of the crime has been constructed by others since the initial police report, their reality and interpretation of the event is often considered unnecessary. The result is 'lawyer stories' which may have little apparent relationship to the existential reality of what the experience meant to the participants. Victims and offenders can feel alienated from their case and disrespected by the lack opportunity to explore the meaning of the crime in ways that might contribute to growth and healing.

The justice process assumes that justice is a generalizable experience – that experiences and outcomes can be fit into pre-established categories, including the nature and degree of punishment. Justice implies that, for instance, murder is murder, regardless of who you are or what your situation may be. One, two or three options for sentencing those who have committed murder are all that is required. Personal knowledge of the meaning and impact of crime and the needs of the victim and offender are not necessary pieces of information required to establish an outcome. This is a narrow and often unfulfilling approach for victims and offenders. Every victim experiences crime differently. Their needs for justice are different based on these experiences. Similarly, every offender experiences the crime he or she committed differently. Their needs for justice and personal transformation will vary from person to person.

Maintaining the crime experience in the hand of experts contributes to othering and the creation of social distance between offenders, victims and the rest of society. The public is never permitted to encounter offenders and victims as multi-dimensional individuals with personal stories and unique experiences. Instead, offenders as well as victims become stereotypes of the 'other.' These others are often associated with ethnic groups and social classes different than the majority of society. Once we create this sense of otherness and social distance, we are able to do things to them that we would not otherwise be able to do if we saw their uniqueness as individuals. As Christie (1982) has pointed out, it is this sense of social distance that allows us to deliver pain to offenders and to ignore and/or blame victims.

In short, the dominant paradigm of justice shares some key elements and outcomes with the dominant paradigm of research. Both have tended to disempower and disrespect primary stakeholders, putting the construction of meaning in the hands of experts presumed to be objective. All too often, both have contributed to othering and the maintenance of dominant patterns of power.

Restorative justice has provided a challenge to the current justice system, calling for a different value set to guide the practice of criminal justice. The values and principles of restorative justice also offer a challenge to traditional research and ways of acquiring knowledge.

Assumptions of restorative justice and transformative research

Restorative justice is based on values that respect and encourage the active participation of both offenders and victims in the justice process. Instead of relegating the primary roles to attorneys and judges, these roles are reserved for those who are affected by the criminal event. Their participation is guided by the exploration of harms experienced by the victim and the resulting obligations that fall on the offender to repair those damages. Their participation is not confined to the question of guilt, blame and punishment. Because the nature and degree of harms differ with each criminal event and with each person involved, the participation of the victim and offender is encompassed in a process based in listening and dialogue. The goal of this process is to elicit each individual's personal experience with the event. The restorative justice process aims to promote restoration and healing for all individuals involved based on these unique perspectives and experiences.

Restorative justice suggests some key elements for a more trans-formative approach to research – ones that seek to respect and empower stakeholders while reducing othering. Highlighted below are several of these values and assumptions that have implications for our ways of knowing.

A respect for the people affected by the criminal event

Listening is one of the foremost acts of respect. As discussed earlier, the ability to talk for oneself or on behalf of others is a source of power. Victims and offenders are often marginalized people who are excluded from active participation in the justice process. By being invited into a process of dialogue and listening, they are empowered to take control of the crime problem that they face and respected for the knowledge they have regarding the event and a justice response.

For a victim who is searching for personal control following the crime, telling their story and articulating their needs can provide an impressive source of empowerment. For offenders who traditionally are passive participants in the justice process, telling their story can be the first step to taking responsibility for their actions and identifying needs for personal transformation. The act of being listened to sends the message to both victims and offenders that their experience is important and meaningful.

A recognition that the meaning of the crime event is subjective, constructed and inter-relational and, as a result, is complex and limits the nature of the justice response

Objectively looking at a crime event without understanding the personal experience is inadequate. Through indirect and direct communication between the victim and offender, the unique perspectives about the crime event emerge. A more holistic understanding of the crime and its im-plications surfaces. The meaning of the event is not something that is out there to be discovered; it is something to be constructed through the interaction and participation of the victim and offender. It is from the mutually constructed meaning of the crime that meaningful justice response will emerge, co-authored by the victim and offender.

The introduction of multiple perspectives on a crime event does not necessarily make for the emergence of an objective singular 'truth' to the crime event. As a result, it is not a simple road on which to travel. The justice response for seemingly similar crime events is not generalizable across all people and experiences. For example, the meaning of an auto theft may vary depending on whether the victim had just bought the car or whether they had owned it for many years. Further, the perspectives of the victim and offender may not seem to be in collusion but rather may actually contradict each other or appear paradoxical. Multiple perspectives may mean multiple interpretations of the same event. These are not troublesome outcomes that need to be eliminated, however. It is through the active participation of the victim and offender as they discover and understand the crime event from each of their perspectives that they, as the authors of the crime event, determine how to proceed.

While we are only beginning to explore the importance of the construction of meaning with offenders, it may have particular importance in a victim's journey. It may be argued that a major dimension of trauma is the destruction of meaning: assumptions that an individual has made about the orderliness of the world, about their own personal autonomy, about where they fit in the web of social relationships – all these are disrupted by crime and provide an important dimension to the trauma that they experience. Recovery from, and transcendence of, the trauma requires them to reconstruct meaning, to reorder their lives. The opportunity to tell and explore their own story, on their own terms, and possibly to hear other participants' stories, is an essential element in this journey.

A process in which the victim and offender are assisted by a person who serves as facilitator who is open to and encourages the emergence of each person's perspective

In the traditional criminal justice system, attorneys and judges assume ownership of the meaning of the event and the subsequent justice response. A restorative justice process, in contrast, is guided by a facilitator whose role is to create an environment in which the offender and victim can dialogue about their perspectives and co-create the meaning of the crime and the justice response to it. Instead of acting as a neutral expert, the facilitator is the caretaker of a dialogue. What is particularly important with this approach is that the facilitator creates a process that meets the needs of the victim and offender. The participants are not expected to adapt to the requirements of the court.

By serving in this process, the facilitator becomes both a collaborator and a 'learner' as well. He or she is impacted by the story of the crime event, and thus is impacted by the feelings and experiences of the victim and offender. By becoming familiar with the victim and offender while they are becoming familiar with each other, the facilitator develops a new awareness of the meaning of crime, the individualism of offenders and victims and the possibilities for justice.

An acknowledgement of the harms, unintended consequences and power dynamics for people who participate in restorative processes

A restorative justice process is a risky venture for both victims and offenders. Victims may relive the original trauma of the crime or discover troublesome information about the crime that they did not know. They may not be able to achieve all that they need for justice to be done. The process itself may re-victimize them. The offender risks facing a victim who is vengeful or who is asking for justice that is beyond their means. The task of meeting the victim face-to-face can be a frightening venture in and of itself. The role of the facilitator is to be aware of these harms and possible consequences and to inform the victim and offender of them. Should they decide to proceed with a restorative justice process, the facilitator assists the victim and offender in responding to the risks that they might encounter before, during or after the process.

Power dynamics can take on several manifestations. First, there is the dynamic between the participants themselves. Victims can feel that offenders are in the power position because they committed the crime and thus have some degree of control over them. Offenders can feel that victims are in the power position because they are seen as holding the key to the criminal justice response. By showing respect for all and validating the harm, the facilitator can act in a way that aims to balance the power between the participants.

Power dynamics can also exist between the facilitator and the participants. By placing the victim's and offender's voices and experiences at the centre of the justice process, the facilitator is turning power over to them. This can be a humbling experience. Through a restorative justice process, the facilitator is invited to listen more and talk less, to learn from others and allow him or herself to be impacted by the stories of others. It encourages them to be aware of their own biographies and biases that influence them and those around them, including the victim and offender. It further challenges the facilitator to limit the influences of their experiences and values so that the stories of the victim and offender may emerge.

An experience of justice that values the process as well as the outcome

The desired goal for a restorative process is an outcome that satisfies the victim, offender and others affected by the crime. It is not simply an ends-oriented process, however. The restorative process itself embodies other benefits that carry a powerful message and challenge our understanding of the social world. The process empowers those who are typically silenced in the justice process. It indicates that people can solve their own problems if given the means to do so. It promotes the importance of dialogue. It builds community and relationships among people who are typically seen as enemies.

Perhaps most importantly, in light of the analysis of the colonizing effect of the criminal justice system, restorative justice processes contribute to the breakdown of othering and social distance. Victims, offenders and those involved in facilitating these processes begin to see beyond stereotypes and generalizations that they have about the people involved in the crime event. They see victims as people deeply wounded by an event and hear the personal impact of the crime on their lives. They hear the individually unique perspective of offenders and their ideas for justice. Through their dialogue, they are no longer in categories of 'us' and 'them' but rather in the category of 'we', shaped by their mutually created meaning of the crime event.

Toward a restorative or transformative approach to justice

As the above indicates, restorative justice is based in the creation of meaning that is constructed by the victim and offender in a process of dialogue and listening. Research and the collection of knowledge are also about the creation of meaning for the world in which we live. From the restorative assumptions we can create a form of research that similarly seeks to decolonize and decrease the degree of othering and social distance inherent to traditional research.

Drawing from these restorative values, as well as the emerging 'new' qualitative research, we suggest the following 'transformative guidelines' as a way of knowing that is appropriate to this work.

Transformative inquiry aims at social action more than 'pure' knowledge

The inquiry process serves a purpose greater than the quest for knowledge. It values the transformative benefits of the process itself to the individuals involved in it. These benefits include building community, promoting dialogue, reducing social distance, challenging 'comforting myths' of who people are, empowering individuals and communities to solve their problems, giving voice to marginalized people, and promoting justice.

Transformative inquiry acknowledges that much knowledge is subjective, constructed, and inter-relational

The inquiry process recognizes that the meaning of the event under study is constructed by those who experience it. In order to construct this meaning, the study participants are invited into relationship and dialogue with each other and with the researcher. The process is one by which the participants and researcher are influenced by each other based on their own biographies.

Transformative inquiry recognizes the complex and limited nature of our findings

The inquiry process recognizes that our 'truths' are often ambiguous, paradoxical, partial and contextual in nature. As a result, the knowledge gained is often not easily generalizable across people, time and space. It recognizes that the 'truth' is susceptible to multiple interpretations.

Transformative inquiry takes seriously the power dynamics inherent in all inquiries

The inquiry process acknowledges and works to limit the influence of power as it is used by the researcher and the research process. This power can be derived from speaking on behalf of others, interpreting another person's experience, and contributing to the existence of othering and social distance.

Transformative inquiry respects subjects as participants in the study

The inquiry process respects individuals by adhering to values such as the collaboration, participation and empowerment of the study participant. The researcher facilitates a process in which the participants can present themselves in their own voice. The researcher views themself as accountable to the participants and acts accordingly. This accountability can be expressed through confidentiality, an acknowledgement of the researchers obligations to the participants, and a transparency of goals, methods and motives. Instead of only sharing the study with those outside the group of study, the researcher prepares a study that benefits the participants and 'returns' the knowledge to them.

Transformative inquiry defines the researcher's role as facilitator, collaborator and learner, rather than neutral expert

The inquiry process is led by a researcher who sees their role as the facilitator of a process to learn from the participants in the study and to create with them the meaning of the event under study. They view themself and act in way that promotes the belief that the researcher is a 'learner' in this experience as opposed to a neutral and detached expert.

Transformative inquiry values process as much as product

The inquiry process values both the end product of the creation of knowledge and the process used to gather that knowledge. The value placed in the process stems from respect for the participants involved in the study and the accountability of the researcher to those participants. The process itself strives to be beneficial for the participant, regardless of the knowledge gained.

Transformative inquiry acknowledges others' realities and the researcher is open to being affected personally by this interaction

The inquiry process, in which the researcher is a facilitator/learner, engages the researcher in a way that invites them to acknowledge and respect the realities of the study participants. In addition, the researcher is open to being personally affected by this participation.

Transformative inquiry is attuned to the potential harms and unintended consequences for subjects and others

The inquiry process is designed to expose potential harms and consequences of the process and the final product as they may be experienced by the participants and others related in some way to the study. These harms and consequences are recognized and responded to in a manner that limits or eliminates their influence.

Transformative inquiry aims at an appropriate balance of subjectivity and objectivity, avoiding co-optation by funders, clients, colleagues or subjects

The inquiry process, while recognizing the subjectivity of knowledge, provides a balance between subjectivity and objectivity. This balance means walking the line between learning from and engaging with the study participants and collaborating with professional colleagues.

This transformative perspective on research offers a challenge to the traditional miner/researcher metaphor presented by Kvale. Instead of a neutral expert digging for knowledge and making it useful, the role of the researcher is that of a traveller, a metaphor Kvale suggests as a contrast to the miner metaphor (1996). The researcher sets out on a journey in which they have conversations with the people they encounter. From these encounters, they hear the many and varied stories of the land through which they are travelling. They meet and become friends with the unique individuals that live in the land. Upon their return, the researcher retells the stories they have heard to colleagues. Using their own voices and words, they reflect on the individualism of the people they have met and communicate the knowledge that has been learned. When returning home they find they are influenced and changed by their travels, just as the participants have been changed (hopefully for the good) by their encounter with them. It is through a transformative inquiry process that researchers 'wander' with the participants of the problem under study. The researcher invites the participants' personal stories and creates space for their voices to prevail. Through their 'storytelling', we learn not only of the similarities and uniquenesses among people but also of our connectedness to those around us. This is fundamental for the reduction of the colonizing effect of othering and social distance.

Conclusion

Over the past few decades we have seen the transformation that is possible for victims, offenders and communities when restorative justice processes are used. By rejecting the dominant form of justice and its colonizing effects, people who were once marginalized and silenced are now experiencing voice and participation. They are given the key position in the creation of meaning regarding the event that they have experienced. They are given the power of definition and the determination of justice. Ultimately, their experiences challenge the way with which we 'know' about crime and justice.

With this restorative approach, a consistency between our practice of research and the goals and values we promote with restorative justice is necessary. Our work and research will benefit if we remember that seemingly objective ways of knowing in fact often reflect and reinforce dominant ideologies and hegemonic constructions or narratives (Lofquist 1997). Just as restorative justice challenges the traditional ways of knowing about crime and justice, our research practices have the potential to challenge the dominant ways of knowing of our social world. If as a society we are to move from a criminology that is violent and a justice that is essentially retributive, we will need to advance ways of knowing which emphasize connectedness above separation and healing rather than suffering. Above all, we are called to embody respect and a deep-rooted sense of humility about the limits to what we can know.

Principles for transformative inquiry (Zehr 1998: 377–85)

(1) Aims at social action more than 'pure' knowledge: building community, promoting dialogue, reducing social distance, challenging 'comforting myths', empowering individuals and communities to

solve problems, giving voice to marginalized people, promoting justice.

(2) Acknowledges that much knowledge is subjective, constructed, and inter-relational:

- our results are inevitably influenced by our biographies;
- meaning is constructed, in part, through the interaction of subject and researcher;
- both subject and researcher influence and are influenced by this process.

(3) Recognizes the complex and limited nature of our findings: our 'truths' are often ambiguous, paradoxical, partial, contextual (not easily generalizable) and susceptible to multiple interpretations.

(4) Takes seriously the power dynamics inherent in all such inquiries.

(5) Respects subjects by promoting values such as:

- collaboration, participation, empowerment;
- accountability;
- confidentiality;
- acknowledgement of obligations to subjects;
- transparency of goals, methods, motives;
- benefits to subjects, including return of knowledge gained;
- opportunities for subjects to present themselves, in their own voice.

(6) Defines the researcher's role as facilitator, collaborator, learner more than neutral expert.

(7) Values process as much as product.

(8) Acknowledges others' realities and is open to being affected personally by this interaction.

(9) Is attuned to the potential harms and unintended consequences for subjects and others.

(10) Aims at an appropriate balance of subjectivity and objectivity, avoiding co-optation by funders, clients, colleagues or subjects.

(11) Utilizes visual as well as verbal, non-linear as well as linear, artistic as well as scientific, methods of elicitation and presentation.

References

Christie, N. (1982) *Limits to Pain*. Oslo, Norway: Universitetsforglaget.

Fine, M. (1994) 'Working the Hyphens' in N. Denzin and Y. Lincoln (eds) *Handbook of Qualitative Research*. Thousand Oaks, CA: Sage.

Fuller, J. (1998) *Criminal Justice: A Peacemaking Perspective*. Needham Heights, MA, Allyn and Bacon.

Haraway, D. (1988) 'Situated Knowledge', *Feminist Studies*, 14: 575–99.

Kvale, S. (1996) *Interviews: An Introduction to Qualitative Research Interviewing*. Thousand Oaks, CA: Sage.

Lofquist, W. S. (1997) 'Constructing "Crime": Media Coverage of Individual and Organizational Wrongdoing', *Justice Quarterly*, 14: 243–63.

Slim, H. and Thompson, P. (1995) *Listening for a Change: Oral Testimony and Community Development*. London: Panos Publications.

Weiss, R. (1994) *Learning From Strangers: The Art and Method of Qualitative Interview Studies*. New York: The Free Press.

Zehr, H. (1998) 'Us and Them: A Photographer Looks at Police Pictures: The Photograph as Evidence', *Contemporary Justice Review*, 1: 377–85.

Chapter 14

Within or outside the system? Restorative justice attempts and the penal system[1]

Thomas Trenczek

Introduction

In this chapter I deal with some problematical aspects and consequences of the implementation of TOA (the German version of victim–offender reconciliation). But, to make it very clear from the beginning, criticism for its own sake is not my intention. None of the thoughts expressed here amount to what the German language calls a 'killer argument' (*Totschlagsargument*) against the implementation of restorative justice elements within the criminal justice system, but they might be a reason to think about the current use and status of victim–offender reconciliation and its further development.

First of all, I need to explain the German term TOA. TOA is the acronym of '*Täter-Opfer-Ausgleich*', literally translated 'Offender–Victim Balancing', which means both settlement and reconciliation (Arbeitsgemeinschaft TAO-Standards: 1989; Kubach *et al*. 1995; Trenczek 1992). The TOA-programmes are quite similar in approach and procedure to the American victim–offender reconciliation programs (VORPs) which aim to emphasize the process of reconciliation and see restitution for the victim as a (symbolic) end of a conflict-resolving process to demonstrate that the harm done is restored. Beyond restitution, 'balance', 'making good' as well as reconciliation, implies a dynamic dimension and an interactive process between at least two parties. Therefore, TOA is and can only be an offer to victims and offenders/the accused to find, with the help of a neutral mediator, a consensual solution of the conflict which led to or came out of the criminal act.

Why do I complain about a TOA practice that seems to be opportunistic? I take the view that in the very beginning, some important directions were set in an incorrect manner and have not been changed since. I do not intend any self-righteous reproach here, because as a founder and supporter of VORP in Germany, I myself have often compromised my beliefs in a similar manner to what I am criticizing. Maybe in the former situation, these directions could not have been taken any differently, given the experience with a model that was totally different compared to traditional thinking. But now the model phase of trial-and-error is over, and we need to start thinking about the structural future of victim–offender reconciliation and restorative justice.

In Germany, we tried from the very beginning to establish victim–offender reconciliation through diversion models or as so-called alternative educational measures for juveniles, because of the understandable search for acceptance and especially funding. This, precisely, is also the problem. In connection with the reformatory efforts in the criminal law system, Feeley (1979) and Zehr (1985) draw attention to the problem that good innovative ideas are not immune to being co-opted by powers within the system. The criminal justice system seems to be 'so impregnated with self-interests, so adaptive that it takes in any new idea, moulds it, changes it until is suits the system's own purposes'. (Zehr 1985: 3) From an organization-related sociological perspective, such a self-referencing co-optation seems to be necessary, because the alternatives are perceived to be threatening to the system. This, according to Feeley and Zehr, is the reason why simple reformatory solutions have to fail. Victim–offender reconciliation in Germany has not failed yet, but if we do not take care, it will be co-opted, it will be changed and adapted to the purposes of the penal system.

A critical review in a criminal law perspective

Provisions in German criminal law which refer to victim–offender reconciliation

One can find several provisions in the German juvenile and criminal code which make it possible to consider victim–offender reconciliation within judicial decision-making. Since 1991, besides the order of restitution (para. 15 sec. 1 No. 1 JGG), victim–offender reconciliation has been explicitly mentioned in the juvenile criminal code as a judicial measure (para. 10 sec. 1

No. 7 JGG). But the prosecutor can also refrain from a formal procedure if the juvenile has made a serious attempt at victim–offender reconciliation (para. 45 sec. 2, 2 Alt. JGG). Even if the so-called legality principle in German law (para. 152 StPO/German Criminal Procedure Code) does not allow for as extensive a use of discretion within law enforcement as in the Anglo-American law systems, there are some unique exceptions to the requirement of mandatory prosecution which refer explicitly to victim–offender reconciliation. Under para. 153a sec. 1, No. 5 StPO, the prosecutor can defer and ultimately refrain from formally charging an accused person in a misdemeanour case if serious attempts at reconciliation with the victim are undertaken. In 1994, the new para. 46a StGB (German Penal Code) was introduced, which explicitly refers to victim–offender reconciliation as a means to mitigate a sentence. Further, the judge is allowed to refrain from imposing the sentence in all cases in which the maximum imprisonment would be one year. In these cases, the prosecutors can also drop the charge (para. 153b StPO). Finally, in 1999, several regulations within the Criminal Procedure Code were established which refer explicitly to victim–offender reconciliation. According to para. 155a StPO, both prosecutor and judge not only have to prove, in every phase of a proceeding, that a reconciliation between victim and offender seems to be attainable, but are also called upon to initiate and foster all attempts of the parties to do so. Therefore, according to para. 155b StPO, they are allowed to refer the case to a victim–offender reconciliation programme, which may be a criminal justice agency such as a probation service, or a so called TOA-programme, a dispute resolution programme run by an association outside the criminal justice system.

Empirical observations and comments

The number and content of the provisions in Germany seem to provide an ideal basis for a substantial use of victim–offender reconciliation within the criminal justice system. However, the inherent nature of criminal law gives victim–offender reconciliation almost no chance of becoming the 'most hopeful alternative' (Schreckling and Pieplow 1989) to the punishment-oriented catalogue of criminal law enactments from the late 1980s. And it gives TOA almost no chance of achieving significant effect. As an instrument of the criminal justice agencies TOA still remains largely in the shadows, and its quantitative and qualitative meaning is inversely proportional to the public and political interest. Five empirical observations are the basis of my assessment.

(a) Because of the peculiarities of the German law statistics, we can only estimate the actual use of victim–offender reconciliation. Overall, the number of decisions to discontinue proceedings (due to restitutive endeavours of offenders) by public prosecutors and courts has increased in recent years, from 6,798 in 1993 to 10,865 in 1997. (Kilchling 1999). Compared to the 530,000 charges and the 250,000 decisions according to para. 153a StPO, this is not a truly impressive number. The fine remains dominant (85 to 90 per cent of the dismissals), and fits better into the experiences and the repertoire of sanctions of the criminal justice system. The practical use of restorative justice elements in the German criminal procedure is described correctly as a 'stagnation on a low level.' (Böttcher 1994; Weitekamp and Tränkle 1998: 9–11).

(b) The same can be noted from the view of the TOA programmes. Most institutions that foster victim–offender reconciliation deal with less than 50 proceedings per year. Altogether, the 368 TOA programmes that were registered at the TOA service bureau, Cologne, until 1995 dealt with about 9,000 cases per year. Even though the number might have reached more than 10,000–15,000 cases a year, it is not an impressive number compared to the one million criminal trials that were taken care of by the courts. Furthermore, the caseload of the VORP concentrates on juvenile cases, victim–offender reconciliation in adult system occuring in less than one-third of the cases.

(c) Not only with regard to the numbers, however, but also with regard to the quality of cases, we have to note that victim–offender reconciliation is being used for the treatment of minor offences and other criminal justice marginalia. Such an assessment by criminal law standards, of course, does not say anything about the meaning for the participants of the conflict. However, I am concerned with the criminal law point of view here. In this view the TOA is supposed to be – I quote from one of the most well known commentaries – only suitable for '*small and minor crimes*' and 'it is hardly imaginable that para. 46a StGB finds any use for crimes where violence against the victim was used or where the victims life and limb was in danger.' (Dreher and Tröndle 1999). Although there are no restrictions referring to the offences in juvenile criminal law and the criminal law in general, the cases that are referred to the VORPs are usually limited to trifles, simple misdemeanours and other minor offences. Because of the previous connection of TOA with the idea of diversion, especially para. 153a StPO, its elements – minor offences, exclusions of felonies – became connected with the character of victim–offender reconciliation. In the practical field, one has to argue with the public prosecutors' office about the appropriateness of a case for mediation without distinguishing between the two points of 'appropriateness', the adequacy of conflict mediation, and the judicial criteria of the dismissal of the criminal procedure. And to keep friends,

TOA programmes and their representatives hurry on ahead to announce at every (in)appropriate opportunity that victim–offender reconciliation 'obviously' is not suitable for serious crimes: 'In the case of aggravated assault with considerable physical and psychological damage, it is quite clear that measures like mediation or restitution would not work. Therefore, it would be most sensible to concentrate on offences of minor and medium severity, because here we have the highest amount of cases' (Hartmann 1994). Why is it *quite clear* that mediation does not work? And what is the standard of success or failure?

(d) A questionable development has occurred when TOA/VORP is used as an educational measure in juvenile proceedings. This very often leads to a misuse of VORP as a rounding of all possible sanctions (so called 'sanction-cocktails') under the slogan 'education can never be bad'. In almost all concepts of the deployment of VORP with young people, the educational effect of VORP is pointed out – with the no doubt justified hope of making TOA popular with the ambitious decision-makers in justice, youth services, and household committees. The reason is quite clear. The juvenile welfare provisions in Germany only allow the financing of remedies if the juvenile is in educational need (cf. paras. 13, 27 ff. SGB VIII/Juvenile Welfare Code). And because nearly every single programme in Germany is financed by the juvenile welfare departments, with the magic of definition victim–offender reconciliation becomes an educational tool, despite the fact that the established VORP standards rightly distinguish victim–offender reconciliation in content and methods from educational measures of the juvenile law and the juvenile welfare system (Trenczek 1996). There are many other reasons relating to the peculiarity of German welfare provisions for avoiding the concepts of TOA as an educating aid, but I will spare you the details. So much for today: besides the increasing budgetary problems of the communities, characterization as an educational remedy (for juveniles) hinders the development of mediation outside the juvenile sector. Furthermore, although victim–offender reconciliation clearly has an intrinsic educational value, the juvenile welfare construction strengthens the danger of misjudging the character of mediation and of abusing it as an instrument for education. A little while ago, a committed TOA mediator did not realize this problem when he confessed: 'If a young person doesn't want to apologize, then I will make him do so.' It is not an isolated case that educative solutions are forced upon a youth to 'successfully' close down the case – of course always in their 'best interest'.

(e) A further questionable development takes place in adult proceedings if the public prosecutor or the court states some preconditions that are conceived of as the result of the mediation process. The same occurs if the amount of a fine or the level of any other sanction that is reserved by the prosecutor is made dependent on the amount of the restitution that the participants will agree on. If the victim renounces a part of the compensation, no matter what the reasons are – it could be that, for example, both participants agreed on another (symbolic) form of compensation – then it is usually the prosecutor's office that demands the compensation, otherwise it would be 'too easy to get away with it' for the offender.

Critical assessment

Since the first introduction of victim–offender reconciliation (TOA) into the (juvenile) criminal code as a judicial 'educational' measure (10 para. 1, No. 7 JGG), attempts have been made to improve its legal position and meaning by other legal enactments. But the introduction of the TOA as a judicial instruction to juveniles ('*jugendrichterliche Weisung*') was criticized from the beginning. It is not only contradictory, but absurd, to sentence a young person to a solution which needs to be balanced out with another party, but it also makes it possible to connect this instruction with other educating and disciplining measures (comparison para. 8 JGG), which hinders a true reconciliation. However, despite these unanimously critical comments, the law was never changed. In December of 1994, the legislature took a decisive step in the criminal law by creating the para. 46a StGB, which asks for an explicit consideration of the TOA within the estimation of criminal responsibility. However, the German criminal justice officials acted with conspicuous caution towards victim–offender reconciliation. One reacted to this in December of 1999, anchoring the TOA in the criminal procedure Code by establishing a duty for prosecutors as well as the courts to recognize as well as to initiate a reconciliation process at every stage of the criminal procedure (para. 155a StGB). This was expressly done 'to give the TOA a wider area of application'.[3] Nevertheless, it is doubtful if criminal justice officials will significantly change their decision-making conduct, because this duty already existed on the basis of general law principles; furthermore, several states had underpinned this duty by internal instructions of their own. In an overall assessment from an European perspective, Löschnig (2000) criticizes the (new) German provisions as not very binding (in regard to para. 155a StPO), without a content or definite line (in regard to para. 153a, 153b, 155a StPO), and as contradictory and therefore not only foreign to the nature of victim–offender reconciliation but also detrimental to it (in regard to para. 153a StPO) (Löschnig-Gspandl 1999). It is not surprising that, according to the new instructions, the TOA and mediation came out as an tool for the criminal justice officials themselves. Criminal justice officials may, but do not have to, refer a case to a specialized institution for mediation; they also have the right 'to reconcile the parties' themselves: the public prosecutor as a mediator. Mediation and reconciliation are perceived as something criminal justice officials have always done. Why do we need professional mediators and expensive victim–offender reconciliation programmes anyway?

As you see, my criticism does not concentrate on that fact that victim–offender reconciliation is integrated in criminal justice decision-making; my point applies to how victim–offender reconciliation is perceived and misused by the criminal justice system. According to the law (para. 46a StGB, para. 153a StPO), based on the present practice of sanctioning in Germany it would be possible to renounce a condemnation to a criminal sanction in 97 per cent of all criminal cases in case a victim–offender reconciliation attempt was carried out (Dölling *et al* 1998: p. 15; Kilchling 1996; Konig and Seitz 1995). As far as that is possible, the TOA/VORP is already a partially abolitionist concept! Actually, one really did not need a law to give TOA a 'wider area of application'. If the criminal justice officials wanted to, they could already use victim–offender reconciliation as an alternative to common sanctions in the criminal law. But apparently, whatever reasons they might have, they do not want that.

Primarily, they give economic reasons for this. Initiating a victim–offender reconciliation has always been refused by the individual prosecutor as time-consuming, because the time advantages (especially the release and exoneration effects with regard especially to appeal or civil law trials) are not credited to the persons who have initiated the mediation. However, the argument that a victim–offender reconciliation procedure might be too time-costly is mostly put forward by such officials who refused a mediation of conflicts because of other reasons. It might be that they do not feel well-informed, it might be because they have no experience of their own with mediation, or because the idea of mediation is just too strange (Meyer 1999). In reality the reason for the low use of victim–offender reconciliation cannot be explained on grounds of cost alone. Rather, it seems partly to be rooted in the way of thinking in the criminal law, thought patterns that have strong meaning within the everyday actions of justice, especially with the interpretation of indefinite law terms and the exercise of legal discretion. For example, what are the 'suitable' cases where, according to the law (para. 155a StPO), victim–offender reconciliation should be used by the public prosecutors? What measures are 'suitable' to remove for the public interest of the criminal prosecution (para. 153a, paragraph 1, sentence 1 StPO), and which standards will be relevant if a trial 'can' (not must) be abandoned? If one opens up to such interpretation, assessment and discretion margins within non-obligatory decision structures, then, those basic standards become relevant. Therefore, my criticism is directed against those values one can find not only in the instruments of law but also in explanations of the so-called 'alternative draft reparation' (Baumann *et al.* 1992) or even in some VORP concepts.

Although the justice system is seen as necessary to guarantee a fair, legal trial, it seems that in practice the prosecutors see themselves more as the guardian of the – however justified – 'governmental claim of punishment'. Therefore, victim–offender reconciliation is seen as a subversive tool, because it does not focus on punishment but on a mutually acceptable solution of a conflict. Mediation and reconciliation, of course, are only an offer to the victim as well as to the offender, they are a new way to solve a conflict (independent of the relevance of the criminal law in the case) through professionally guided negotiations. Both victim and offender should actively and autonomously find a common, forward-looking settlement or solution to the conflict, but mediation does not become preoccupied with a past-orientated, necessarily repressive response to the crime. In the eyes of many criminal justice representatives, victim–offender reconciliation must look like a measure that withdraws the offenders from their just punishment. Ed Watzke, an Austrian colleague, described it humorously but also impressively:

> In one way or the other, they [the mediators] are all accomplices of the offenders because they try to find hundreds of excuses to absolve the offender from responsibility. Therefore it is the fault of traumatic events in the early childhood, the parents, if there are any, the absence of the parents, if they are no longer living, the absence or existence of all possible social relationships, schools, homes, homelessness, unemployment, the society and so on. All of these excuses that are impossible to prove are helpful to show the offender as a victim himself and to withdraw him from the just punishment (Watzke 1997: 77)

The fundamental mistrust of prosecutors and criminal justice officials of social work chimes in with mistrust of mediation, which with a suspect is then associated with counterculture rather than being with a basic request of the law.

This tendency is often strengthened by the way TOA is sold to criminal justice officials and even by the justifications put forward for it on the part of the reform movements (Baumann *et al.* 1992). With the aim of securing 'the highest amount of cases' (cf. above), many programme officials are in danger of corrupting themselves. The assessment that 'it is quite clear that measures like mediation or restitution won't work' might only be understandable from the traditional, punishment-orientated point of view, but VORP should not get mixed up with diversion programmes or traditional sanctions. While asking for more acceptance, TOA/VORP and their officials deny their own basis and potential and anticipate the criteria of the criminal law as a measurement for the evaluation of mediation and conflict resolution.

With the understandable desire to achieve great legal and political acceptance, one can observe the effort to give reasons for the typical criminal law relevance of victim–offender reconciliation and its compatibility with the system of criminal law sanctions and the goals of punishment. Victim–offender reconciliation is presented as a 'third way' (besides punishment and incapacitation) in criminal justice which meets 'the punishment purposes and the need of the victim well or even better than a traditional sanction alone' (Baumann et al. 1992; Roxin 1987; 37–55). This perspective, however, is the dilemma of an 'alternative' measure. On this yardstick, such measures could only replace traditional punishments and be accepted by the criminal justice system if they do justice 'to the punishment purposes ... well or even better than a traditional sanction alone'. From there follows the decisive question: how much reparation is necessary, how punitive must victim–offender reconciliation be that it serves 'as well or even better for punishment than the punishment itself'? In this equation, the chronic overestimation of the importance of the punishment function is already disturbing, as is the premise that the traditional sanctions of the criminal law would do justice or meet the needs of the victim. But it is disastrous for the acceptance of VORP and other restorative devices that this dimension diminishes the essential character of mediation, reparation and reconciliation. Victim-offender mediation and reconciliation (differently from the restitution order, the diversion measures, or incarceration alternatives) are not compatible with the traditional punishment purposes and the vertical system of traditional criminal sanctions. Although restorative remedies may have relevant, inherent effects, they go beyond the restitution and the punishment purposes by including the victim and leaving space for an autonomous and active regulation of the conflict by the parties concerned.

One cannot think about conflict mediation and punishment at the same time. Mediation and reconciliation are not more or less a punishment, but qualitatively an 'aliud,' a different material legal principle that has it own character in the reparation of the peace under the law. As good as it is to rescue the perspective of the damaged victim, it does not make a lot of sense to designate victim–offender mediation and reconciliation as peace-making solutions for the conflict and at the same time subordinate them to the punitive function of the punishment. With such a benchmark, the process and the result of victim–offender mediation cannot be appropriate because of the demands, the overburdening, and the restriction of the traditional view of the judicial system which is constantly reproduced in law schools. This is to view victim–offender reconciliation as just another instrument 'to fight the crime' (BT-Dirs), not as a remedy for conflict resolution.

In contrast to this, the degree of acceptance of a restorative and mediative conflict resolution on the part of the public is a lot greater than many criminal justice officials imagine. In particular the victims of crime do not come over as strong advocates of a repressive criminal justice policy. The punishment needs of the population are – here I can quote Hans-Jürgen Kerner – 'if not only a psycho-hygienically useful fiction of criminal law practitioners, first of all a need for justice and an acknowledgement of the victim as a victim' (Kenner 1991: 206). The simplistic upholding of punishment needs and claims has its source in a judicial authoritarianism that gives special emphasis to a formal order but not to the social peace.

Conclusion: within or outside or transformation of the system – where do we go from here?

Despite our initial enthusiasm, it seems to be a hopeless attempt to establish acceptance for victim–offender reconciliation within the criminal justice system without adaptation and co-optation. Therefore, the path that has been taken hitherto needs to be reconsidered. In view of the persisting powers of the practice of penal law, victim-offender reconciliation stands little chance of making progress. The new restorative paradigm and VORPs seem challenging to the criminal justice system, since they question the traditional point of view of the penal law, focusing on the behaviour-controlling power of the law rather than on the aspect of punishing. But the retraction of the supposed 'claim to punish' by the state is not identical with the removal of the social control of behaviour. Fears of the uncontrolled exercise of power at the expense of the weak and victims are used to discredit mediation, because it is an informal procedure undertaken not priamrily by lawyers but by social workers or psychologists. But even mediation as an informal, extra judicial settlement of the conflict is only possible under the 'rule of law' (Silving 1961: 77). Through the law, it is defined in advance what a legally protected right is, and with that – in case of a violation of the norm – one can determine who is the victim and who the offender. Even if we are in favour of mediation, we should not forget that force and compulsion belong to the law as an instrument of public social control like brakes in a car or reins on a horse. The 'autonomous regulation of the conflict after a crime derives from the fact that there are coercive measures ready in the background' (Rössner 1992: 269–79) and that these can be activated for the defence of the law and the protection of the weak. Nothing should be changed on this. But what is decisive – as *Detlef Frehsee* has put it – is that 'the law is more effective through its shadow than through the actual execution of force' (Frehsee 1991: 51–60). Therein lies, beyond the short-term, functional usage, the wide-ranging potential of reparation of victim–offender reconciliation.

The change of view from a penal, punishment-oriented model of justice to one that is predominantly designed to influence behaviour in the future, the change of paradigms from repression to prevention, opens up the vision of a community-related culture of conflict which is close to the people's orientation. In the practice of German VORPs, it becomes more and more evident that the citizens do not wait until a case is referred by the state attorney's office or other criminal justice agencies, but take up the offer of mediation by themselves right away. This access shows that the mediation of conflicts and victim–offender reconciliation are more connected with daily life than is the judicial system. These close community connections should be extended and – outside of the penal system – should lower the threshold of access to mediation and reconciliation. The practical experience with the TOA in Germany shows that victim–offender reconciliation is not the only or ideal way, but that on a continuum of possible steps in the treatments of conflicts, it is one possible area of use. A community justice centre in criminally relevant disputes as well as civil law disputes (for example, neighbourhood, consumer and family disputes) can be mediated meets the needs of citizens for participation, justice and security. Such a dispute-resolution culture cannot, and will not, replace the judicial system totally, but the parallel system of mediation and ADR can fill a gap that exists between the self-organized regulating mechanism in the population, which is often left to chance, and the judicial system, which is quantitatively and qualitatively overburdened with the resolution of conflicts. If victim–offender reconciliation as part of the ADR movement is established everywhere and cannot be removed from people's everyday experience, those in the criminal justice system might learn that even criminal law cases cannot be solved through punishment alone.

Notes

1. Paper presented at the 4th International Conference on Restorative Justice, Tübingen, 1–4th October, 2000.
2. In 1997, the restitution conditions played a role in only 2.3 per cent of the public prosecutors' dismissals according to para. 153a I No. 1 StPO (without important changes to the previous years). It was a little bit more with the judicial dismissal of the proceeding according to para. 153a II (7.8 per cent) and with the decisions

according to para. 15 I JGG (3.4 per cent of the imposed conditions).
3. Explanation of the Federal government for the law proposal from 29.10.1999, BT-Drs. (German Federal Congressional Publication) 14/1928, p. 1.

References

Arbeitsgemeinschaft TOA-Standards (1989) *Täter, Opfer und Vermittler. Beiheft 10 zum Rundbrief Soziale Arbeit und Strafrecht.* Bonn, DBH.

Baumann, J. *et al.* (1992) *Alternativentwurf Wiedergutmachung* München: AE-WGM. 37; Roxin, C. (1987) 'Die Wiedergutmachung im System der Strafzwecke' in H. Schöch, (ed.) *Wiedergutmachung und Strafrecht.* München.

Böttcher, R. (1994) 'Täter-Opfer-Ausgleich. Eine kritische Zwischenbilanz bisheriger Praxiserfahrungen und Forschungsergebnisse, *Bewährungshilfe*, 41; 45–8.

BT-Drs. (German Federal Congressional Publication) 12/6853, p. 1.

Dölling, D. *et al.* (eds) (1998) p. 15. *Täter-Opfer-Ausgleich. Eine Chance für Opfer und Täter durch einen neuen Weg im Umgang mit Kriminalität*, Bon, Forum Verlag Godesberg.

Dreher, E. and Tröndle, H. (1990) Strafgesetzbuch. Kommentar. 47. ed. München 1995, para. 46a Rn. 3; cf. just renewed in Tröndle and Fischer 49. Auflage (1999).

Feeley, M. (1979) *Court Reform on Trial. Why Simple Solutions Fail,* New York 1979.

Frehsee, D. (1991) 'Täter-Opfer-Ausgleich aus rechtstheoretischer Perspektive' in Bundesministerium der Justiz (ed.).

Hartmann, U. (1994) 'Victim–Offender Reconciliation with Adult Offenders in Germany', paper presented at the 8th International Symposium on Victimology, Adelaide, 1994, *KFN-Forschungsberichte* (27, 6).

Kerner, H.-J. (1991) 'Täter-Opfer-Ausgleich: Modererscheinung auf ihrem Höhepunkt oder realistische Sanktionsalternative' in Bundesministerium der Justiz (ed.): *Bonner Symposium*. Bonn.

Kilchling, M. (1996) 'Aktuelle Perspektiven für Täter-Opfer-Ausgleich und Wiedergutmachung im Erwachsenenstrafrecht. Eine kritische Würdigung der bisherigen höchstrichterlichen Rechtsprechung zu para. 46a StGB aus viktimologischer Sicht.' *NStZ* 16; 309–11.

Kilchling, M. (1999) 'TOA-E versus ATA-E – empirische Befunde zur Praxis des Täter-Opfer-Ausgleichs mit Erwachsenen im deutsch-österreichischen Vergleich' paper presented to the Conference of the New Criminological Society (NKG),Herausforderungen der Kriminologie im Europa des 21. Jah. 30 Sept. – 2 Oct 1999, Göttingen.

König, P. and Seitz, H. (1995) 'Die straf- und verfahrensrechtlichen Regelungen des Verbrechensbekämpfungsgesetzes' *Neue Zeitschrift für Strafrecht*, 15: 1–6.

Kubach, T., Netzig, L., Petzold, F., Schadt, M. and Wandrey, M.: (1995) *TOA-Standards – Ein Handbuch für die Praxis des Täter-Opfer-Ausgleichs.* Bonn/Hannover: DBH/WAAGE.

Löschnig-Gspandl, M. (1999) TOA-E versus ATA-E – Ausgewählte Fragen zu den normativen Grundlagen: Gesetz zur strafverfahrensrechtlichen Verankerung des Täter-Opfer-Ausgleichs – Strafprozeßnovelle.' Paper presented at the

Conference of the New Criminological Society 'Herausforderungen der Kriminologie im Europa des 21. Jah.' , 30 Sept – 2 Oct 1999, in Göttingen.

Meier, B. (1999) 'Wiedergutmachung im Strafrecht? Empirische Befunde und kriminalpolitische Perspektiven,' paper presented at the Conference of the New Criminological Society (NKG) 'Herausforderungen der Kriminologie im Europa des 21. Jah.' 30 Sept – 2 Oct 1999, Göttingen.

Rössner, D. (1992) 'Autonomie und Zwang im System der Strafrechtsfolgen' in Arzt, G. (ed.) *Festschrift für Jürgen Baumann*. Bielefeld.

Schreckling, J. and Pieplow, L. (1989) Täter-Opfer-Ausgleich: Eine Zwischenbilanz nach zwei Jahren Fallpraxis beim Modellprojekt 'Die Waage'. *Zeitschrift für Rechtspolitik*, 22; 10–15.

Silving, H. (1961) ' "Rule of Law" in Criminal Justice,' in G.O.W. Mueller, (ed.) *Essays in Criminal Justice*, South Hackensack, NJ/London.

Trenczek, T. (1996) *Strafe, Erziehung oder Hilfe? Neue ambulante Maßnahmen und Hilfen zur Erziehung – Sozialpädagogische Hilfeangebote für straffällige junge Menschen im Spannungsfeld von Jugendhilferecht und Strafrecht*, Bonn; Forum.

Watzke, E. (1997) 'Von Strafjuristen und Sozialarbeitern' in *Äquibrilistischer Tanz zwischen Welten*, Bonn.

Weitekamp, E. and Tränkle, S. (1998). 'Die Entwicklung des Täter-Opfer-Ausgleich in der Bundesrepublik Deutschland: Neueste Ergebnisse und Befunde' Friedrich-Ebert-Stiftung (ed.) *Der Täter-Opfer-Ausgleich (TOA): Moderner Beitrag zur Konfliktregulierung und zur Sicherung des sozialen Friedens*. Potsdam.

Zehr, H. (1985) *Restributive Justice, Restorative Justice*, USA: USA: Elkhart.

Chapter 15

Zero tolerance criminal policy and restorative justice: a hidden link?

Peter Lindström

Introduction

The Swedish criminal justice system can be seen as an entity made up of a number of different parts – police, prosecution service, courts and prison service[1] – each with different functions but which share a common responsibility for the overall political goals of crime policy: to reduce crime and increase levels of public security.

In order to achieve the goals of reduced crime and improved public security, it is often claimed – not least by politicians – that what is needed are reduced levels of tolerance for crime and clearer signals from the justice system in relation to those committing offences. One doctrine that has been much discussed over recent years is that of zero tolerance in relation to crime and offenders. This requires among other things that the police should respond to any and all offences, including minor public-order offences and other less serious crimes, and that offending should result in the punishment of the offender. A recurring demand in the crime policy debate is that the justice system reacts particularly clearly with respect to young offenders.

In most countries, including Sweden, there are several ways for the justice system to wind up a case against an offender without it coming to court. In practice, therefore, court proceedings constitute only a small part of society's responses to offending. This is true for both young offenders and adults. Ten years ago, a leading professor in criminal law pointed out that 'the sentences produced by Swedish courts in criminal cases today do not reflect even in general the actual administration of justice in the area of criminal law. An extremely intensive weeding-out process takes place among the offences against the criminal law that are reported and discovered. This weeding-out process has now assumed such proportions that one can with good reason ask the question: Are we still working on the principle of an obligation always to prosecute offences?' (Löfmarck *et al.* 1986: 3).

The question of an absolute *contra* as a relative form of the compulsory prosecution of criminal offences has been taken up by different inquiries on a number of occasions (see for example SOU 1976: 47; SOU 1992: 61). In countries where the justice system is based on an absolute duty to prosecute, the fundamental principle is that the bodies within the justice system treat all offences against the criminal law in a formal and similar manner. The police, for example, have a duty to investigate offences that are reported, and prosecutors have a duty to prosecute where there is enough evidence against a person. In states whose justice system rests on the relative form, both the police and the prosecution service have considerable discretion to decide how to react when an offence is committed.

In an inquiry report entitled 'A Reformed Prosecution Service' (SOU 1992: 61), it is suggested that the absolute duty to prosecute be retained, but that the content of the concept be toned down. The inquiry argued that in the international arena, Sweden has obligated herself to introduce a greater degree of discretion when it comes to deciding whether or not to prosecute and that, in spite of the absolute duty principle, there are opportunities for the use of discretion at the level of the individual case. The discretionary alternatives provided by Swedish legislation involve, on the one hand, the police's ability to decide not to report a case to the prosecutor ('*rapporteftergift*'), and on the other the prosecutor's ability not to prosecute a case through the courts even though there is sufficient evidence to do so ('*åtalsunderlåtelse*').

Over the course of recent years, discussions in the area of crime policy have on the one hand focused on a reduced level of tolerance in relation to offenders (expressed in its most simplified form with the term zero tolerance) and on the other hand on increased possibilities of winding up a case at an earlier stage of its path through the justice system. But is it really possible to integrate the concept of zero tolerance with increases in the degree of discretion exercised by police and prosecutors? Is it not rather the case, as Harding and Dingwall (1998) pointed out, that the less tolerant a society becomes, the less often discretionary methods are employed in the criminal justice process?

One interesting question to be answered is whether the goal of reducing crime and increasing levels of security can be reached by means of a reduction in the use of discretionary powers by the police and the prosecution service. In order to illuminate this issue further, this chapter first examines trends in the number of decisions by the police not to report offences to the prosecutor, primarily in relation to the offence of shoplifting. Besides being an offence where this particular discretionary power is used, shoplifting is interesting from the perspective of crime policy for several reasons. For one thing, it is a so-called 'everyday crime' and should thus, in accordance with directives from the government, be given priority by the police. It is also an offence that according to official crime statistics is committed by both younger and older people. Furthermore, perceptions of this form of offending have changed over time. In order to illustrate society's reactions to less serious offending in more detail, the chapter goes on to examine trends in the way the system reacts to the crimes of young offenders.

The obligation of the police to report offences

The tasks of the police include preventing crime and conducting surveillance and investigations in connection with offences that fall under the remit of the public prosecutor. How well the police succeed in these tasks has been a recurring theme in the public debate over the years. Knut Sveri, formerly Professor of Criminology at Stockholm University, asks whether it is not in fact the case that 'the job of the modern police force involves so many and such disparate tasks that it fails to carry out any of them completely satisfactorily' (Sveri 1992: 38).

Finding suitable measures of how 'well' the police do their job is undoubtedly a complicated issue. In contrast to what many people believe, for example, a reduction in the number of reported offences in many cases constitutes a very unsuitable measure of police effectiveness. For certain types of offences, primarily those discovered by the police, higher levels of reports may indicate that the police are doing the work required of them by the government. Although in certain cases the work of the police may have a direct effect on crime, research findings indicate that the possibilities for affecting crime trends in any substantial way by means of police work are rather limited (Bayley 1998). The general conclusion is that it is primarily factors other than the work of the police that affect more general crime trends.

As in any other operation, the police decide priorities and weigh alternatives when it comes to which tasks will be carried out. Decisions must be taken, for example, as to whether a traffic check is to be implemented and if so, when and on which roads; as to whether to cooperate in a school-based drug prevention programme, and how many police are to be assigned to the task of preventing violence against women.

The tasks involved in police work are obviously affected by political decisions as manifested in legislation. Increases in the level of penalties for drug use introduced in 1993, for example, provided police with the opportunity to use a number of more invasive surveillance techniques. Each year now, 10,000 blood or urine samples are taken from people suspected of having used narcotics – a task which the police had not previously undertaken. The criminalization of the purchase of sexual services constitutes a more recent example of legislation involving new tasks for the police.

In addition to direct legislative changes, the work of the police is also affected by the demands placed on them by the social context. The local police reforms implemented in recent years, for example, have meant that the police have increasingly come to work in cooperation with the public in a more preventive and problem-orientated way than was previously the case. Because of the variety of tasks included in the work of the police, discussions over recent years have focused, among other things, on attempts to identify what the essential core of police work actually comprises. One goal has been to try and sift out those activities that are not counted among the principle tasks of the police.

With respect to crime, the opportunities for reductions in the number of tasks assigned to the police are inevitably limited. According to the Police Act (SFS 1984: 387), 'when an offence under the remit of the public prosecutor comes to the attention of a police officer, he is to report this to his superior at the earliest possible opportunity.' In the case of certain offences, however, the police are able to decide not to report the offence to the public prosecutor. The Police Act states that 'an officer may choose not to report an offence to the public prosecutor if the circumstances of the specific case are such that the offence is insignificant and it is clear that the offence would not lead to a sentence other than a fine.' This option is not unique to Sweden, but rather exists in most comparable countries.

A decision not to report an offence to the prosecutor may be made directly in connection with the commission of the offence. The offences involved in such cases are primarily minor forms of public order and traffic offences. In these instances, as a rule, no police report is filed, but the suspect, or the person previously referred to as 'the offender', is verbally cautioned by a police officer that he or she has committed an offence. There is no other form of reaction than this verbal notification and the person in question is not recorded in the police register. There are no statistics relating to the annual number of such immediate decisions not to report offences to the prosecutor; the number is likely to be very high, however.[2] The decision not to report an offence to the prosecutor may also be taken once an offence report has been filed. The circumstances in which this type of decision may be taken have been regulated since 1961 (for a historical overview of the decision not to report to the prosecutor, see Rikspolisstyrelsen (1988)). The National Police Board issues directives on the implementation of decisions not to report offences to the prosecutor.

National Police Board directives on the non-reporting of offences to the prosecutor

Directives of a more detailed nature with respect to the non-reporting of offences to the prosecutor were issued for the first time in connection with the passing of the Police Act in 1984. These directives have since been revised on two occasions. In 1990, altered directives were issued in connection with, among other things, a governmentally commissioned evaluation by the National Police Board of the way the police implemented their discretion not to report offences to the prosecutor. New directives were again issued in 1998 as a result of the transference of the regulations concerning non-reporting from the Police Ordinance into the Police Act.

A content analysis of the three versions of these directives turned up both similarities and a number of significant differences. The National Police Board directives from 1984 state that 'decisions not to report to the prosecutor can be taken in connection both with offences where a fine is the only penalty and offences where a prison sentence is included in the penalty scale. In those cases where the offence may lead to a prison sentence, a decision not to report the offence to the prosecutor may only be taken if it is clear that were the case to lead to a conviction, the sentence passed would not exceed a fine' (RPS FS 1984: 6). In the directives from 1990, crimes for which the penalty scale includes a prison term are not mentioned explicitly. Instead, a section of the directives entitled 'General conditions for non-reporting of offences to the prosecutor' states that 'it should be clear that in the case of a conviction, the sentence passed would not exceed a fine' (RPS FS 1990: 3). In theory, then, it is still the case that a decision not to report an offence to the prosecutor could be taken for such offences as shoplifting, vandalism and minor drug offences. In practice, however, it is primarily in connection with shoplifting offences that such decisions have been implemented.

The possibility of deciding not to report an incident to the prosecutor in connection with shoplifting offences has been regulated in law since 1972

(SFS 1972: 24). The directives from 1990 contain a special section on non-reporting in connection with shoplifting. This states, among other things, that decisions of this kind should not be taken if 'in a particular case, it is adjudged that a decision not to report the offence to the prosecutor and the caution that is issued in connection with this decision, will not have a sufficiently restraining effect.' This formulation is also included in the 1998 directives. In the directives from 1984, the use of this discretionary power in connection with shoplifting is mentioned only under the heading 'Offences against the Penal Code and other criminal offences for which a prison sentence is included in the penalty scale', and even here the only directive is that a complete assessment should be made of the circumstances of the offence.

The 1984 directives state that the suspect should be informed verbally of the decision not to pass the case on to the prosecutor. The directives from 1990 clarify this point such that a verbal notification should in particular be given when a decision applies to youths aged 15 to 17. The 1998 directives indicate that guardians should also be informed of the decision.

While the different sets of directives indicate that implementation of the decision not to report offences to the prosecutor has become somewhat more restrictive, demands for restrictions on the use of this discretionary power have come primarily from the political arena. A number of motions placed before Parliament by parties from the centre and centre right have made the point that the number of such decisions should be reduced (e.g. Motion 1979/80: Ju612; Motion 1986/87: Ju621; Motion 1990/91: Ju615; Motion 1990/91: Ju821). The Justice Committee has up to now rejected all motions suggesting the imposition of restrictions on the use of decisions not to report offences to the prosecutor.

Trends in the number of decisions not to report offences to the prosecutor

In the preamble to the Police Act, which was enacted in 1984, the head of the Ministry stressed that the discretionary power not to report an offence to the prosecutor should be expanded to apply even to offences for which the penalty could include a prison term not exceeding six months. The object of widening the police's discretionary power in this way was to limit the time the justice system spent dealing with very minor offences and, in so doing, to concentrate these resources on more serious crime.

Decisions not to report offences to the prosecutor are included in the official crime statistics under the heading 'Cleared Offences'. In 1980, 4,200 such decisions were taken once an offence had already been registered.

The vast majority (around 95 per cent) of the offences not reported to the prosecutor related to incidents of shoplifting. In 1998, 1,950 decisions not to report an offence to the prosecutor were taken (90 per cent relating to shoplifting). Figure 15.1 presents the annual numbers of decisions not to report an offence to the prosecutor taken between 1979 and 1998.

Between 1979 and 1984, the number of such decisions increased from 4,000 to 6,000. With the introduction of the Police Act and the new directives issued by the National Police Board, the number rose dramatically and during the period between 1985–91, between 8,000 and 9,000 such decisions were taken annually. As Figure 15.1 indicates, the number dropped substantially after 1991. The greatest decrease occurred between 1992 and 1993, when the number of such decisions taken was reduced by half.

It has not been possible to find a single – or a simple – explanation for the substantial decrease in the number of decisions not to report an offence to the prosecutor since the beginning of the 1990s. There is nothing to indicate that crime has become so much more serious that the police are no longer able to exercise this discretionary power, for example. As was mentioned earlier, the directives from the National Police Board were changed in 1990, and certain parties to the political discussion expressed the opinion that the police should be more restrictive in their use of this power. No legislative changes were made, however.

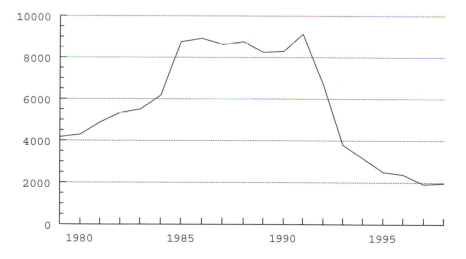

Figure 15.1. Number of decisions taken annually by the police not to report an offence to the prosecutor, 1979–98

The non-reporting of shoplifting offences to the prosecutor

As has been mentioned, decisions not to report an offence to the prosecutor are most commonly taken in association with minor shoplifting incidents. During the 1980s a little over 15 per cent of all cleared shoplifting offences resulted in such a decision. The corresponding proportion in recent years has been under five per cent. Figure 15.2 presents the number of shoplifting offences reported to the police and the number of decisions taken not to report offences to the prosecutor during the period 1975–98.

As can be seen from Figure 15.2, the two series relating to numbers of reported shoplifting offences and numbers of decisions taken not to report offences to the prosecutor follow one another very closely between 1975 and 1991. Thereafter, the number of decisions not to report to the prosecutor drops sharply while the number of reported shoplifting offences falls until 1994, only to increase again in the following period (preliminary statistics for 1999 indicate, however, that the number of shoplifting offences reported to the police has fallen by 10 per cent compared to 1998).

Since the beginning of the 1980s, shoplifting offences reported to the police have comprised approximately six per cent of the total number of penal code offences reported annually. With the exception of recent years, the proportion of offences cleared by the police has been high, since as a rule the offender is caught at the scene of the offence. In the evaluation of

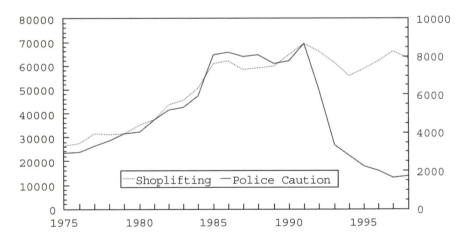

Figure 15.2. Number of shoplifting offences reported to the police (left-hand scale) and number of decisions taken not to report a shoplifting offence to the prosecutor between 1975 and 1998

the application of decisions not to report offences to the prosecutor published by the National Police Board in 1988, it was found that 43 per cent of the suspects were aged 60 or over while 17 per cent were youths aged between 15 and 19. Of all those suspected of shoplifting during the year in question (1986), 24 per cent were between the ages of 15 and 19, and 10 per cent were 60 years of age or older. In 1997, the relation between the number of young and old suspects was much the same (26 per cent of the suspects were aged between 15 and 19, and nine per cent were 60 or over).

One consequence of the reduction in the number of decisions not to report shoplifting offences to the prosecutor, at least to begin with, was that an increased number of elderly persons had their cases examined by the prosecutor. Between the years 1992 and 1993, when the number of decisions not to report shoplifting offences to the prosecutor dropped by almost 40 per cent, the number of persons aged 60 or over convicted of shoplifting increased by 30 per cent. Among youths aged 15 to 17, the increase between these two years was six per cent, and other age groups experienced an increase of 13 per cent. Thereafter, the number of older persons convicted of shoplifting has fallen but the number of youths has increased substantially. The extent to which this reflects actual changes in the age structure of individuals committing shoplifting offences, or rather the way such offenders are dealt with by the justice system, is impossible to determine with any degree of certainty. One possible explanation is that shoplifting offences committed by youths are being given a higher priority by the police. Results from a study into the response system for young offenders show that the time taken to deal with cases of shoplifting committed by youths has been reduced by just over a third between the years 1993 and 1998. In addition, an increasingly large proportion of the youth offences dealt with by the police in 1998 involved shoplifting.

A further possible consequence of the fall in the number of decisions taken not to report offences to the prosecutor may be that more cases of shoplifting are remaining in the hands of the police without being cleared. The proportion of cleared shoplifting offences has fallen from around 75 per cent during the 1980s to approximately 65 per cent in recent years. In 1997, 75 per cent of cleared shoplifting offences were passed on to the prosecutor, while the corresponding proportion for 1987 was 65 per cent. The drop in the clear-up rate for shoplifting offences may be a result of the fact that the time taken to deal with shoplifting offences committed by individuals from other age groups has increased.[3]

The most common penalty for shoplifting offences is a fine issued by the prosecutor. One suggestion that has been tabled by, among others, the Inquiry into the Prosecution Service (SOU 1992: 61) is that the police should be given the power to issue on-the-spot fines in connection with shoplifting offences (see also SOU 1982: 39). This suggestion has not been recognized in any legislation however.

To summarize, then, during the 1990s the police have made less and less use of their discretionary power not to report offences to the prosecutor. The principal explanation for this is probably that such a decision not to report an offence to the prosecutor is viewed as too weak a response to crime, something that has been emphasized in parliamentary bills. Unfortunately, it is impossible to see whether the reduced level of tolerance in relation to shoplifting, as expressed in the fall in the number of decisions not to report such offences to the prosecutor, has led to a reduction in offending and an increase in levels of security. What we can say, on the other hand, is that between the mid 1980s and the beginning of the 1990s, the police use of this particular discretionary power increased substantially with no corresponding increase in the number of shoplifting offences being reported. During the 1990s, the use of this discretionary power decreased, which does not seem to have led to a corresponding drop in the number of reported shoplifting offences.

In other countries, decisions not to report an offence to the prosecutor, or their equivalent, are considerably more common in connection with both shoplifting offences and other minor crimes. In England and Wales, for example, 'police cautions', which involve issuing a warning to an offender which is then registered, were issued in 40 per cent of shoplifting cases. Among youths aged 14–17, this proportion was nearer 70 per cent (Farrington 1999). In most Western countries, efforts are made to take as few young people as possible to court. This is of course also true in Sweden, but developments in recent years have tended towards the prosecution of increasing numbers of young offenders. One question that might be considered is whether this trend is the result of a crime policy based on the doctrine of zero tolerance.

The obligation for prosecutors to bring charges

The guiding principle of an absolute duty to prosecute offenders – and the duty of the police to report offences to the prosecution service – nonetheless allows for the possibility of deviation in certain circumstances. As has been described above, the police may decide not to report an offence to the prosecutor, and a prosecutor, besides being able to decide to wind up the police investigation of an offence even when there is sufficient evidence, may also in certain cases rule not to prosecute an offender but to instead issue what I refer to here as a 'decision not to prosecute'. The possibilities open to a prosecutor to issue such a ruling are regulated in the Law (1964: 167) of Special Regulations relating to Young Offenders (LUL). Regulations relating to decisions not to prosecute are also contained in the Swedish Penal Code (Chapter 20). Over the last two decades, an average of 10 per cent of all convictions have taken the form of rulings not to prosecute.

Decisions not to prosecute and age

Between 1983 and 1998, the median age for all those convicted of offences (i.e. persons who have been issued with a decision not to prosecute, or who have accepted a summary fine or who have been adjudicated guilty in court) rose from 28 to 32 years. Over the course of the last 15 years, the age structure of persons receiving decisions not to prosecute has also changed; the median age has increased from 21 to 27 years. This trend is a result both of the fact that such decisions have been issued to more offenders in young middle age (i.e. 30 to 49 years) and of the fact that fewer of the youths receiving convictions receive them in this form. Of all those issued with decisions not to prosecute, approximately one-third are aged 15 to 17, while less than ten per cent are what the criminal justice system regards as 'older youths' (i.e. aged 18 to 20).

When different offence categories are examined separately, we find that the proportion of decisions not to prosecute issued for certain offences has fallen substantially. In the case of vehicle theft, for example, 18 per cent of those convicted in 1998 with this as the principle offence in the charge received this conviction in the form of a decision not to prosecute. The corresponding proportion in 1988 was 32 per cent. For shoplifting offences, the proportion has fallen by just over one third (from 33 per cent in 1988 to 22 per cent in 1998). For narcotics offences, however, there has been a slight increase in the proportion being issued with decisions not to prosecute. Of all those convicted for narcotics offences in 1998, 21 per cent were issued with such a decision as compared with 17 per cent in 1988. The principal explanation for this lies in the fact that more people are being convicted of minor narcotics offences.

On the whole it appears that decisions not to prosecute are being issued increasingly less often for offences against the Penal Code, and that it is primarily older offenders who are issued with such decisions. This means that the character of the sanction system for young offenders has changed to some extent since the beginning of the 1980s.

Youths and the sanction system

The question of the sanctions that should be applied to youths who commit criminal offences is a recurring theme in the crime-policy debate. A long line of inquiries and reports has emphasized that society's reaction to the crimes of young offenders should be swift and unequivocal. Decisions as to whether a young offender should be prosecuted or if the sanction should be no more than a summary fine or a ruling not to prosecute are taken by the public prosecutor. Such decisions are affected by both the nature and seriousness of the offence, and also by the prior criminal record of the youth concerned. It is difficult to judge the extent to which these decisions are also affected by other factors, such as expressions of political opinion in relation to crime policy.

Each year, approximately 15,500 youths aged between 15 and 17 are convicted by means of a decision by the prosecutor or a judgement by the courts. This constitutes around five per cent of persons in this age group. The most common principle offence, i.e. the most serious of the offences included in a specific conviction, comprises theft offences, followed by crimes against the person and traffic offences. Today approximately one-third (30 per cent) of all youths convicted of offences are charged and receive a court adjudication. The corresponding proportion during the period of 1975–86 was 15 per cent. Thus more youths are prosecuted through the courts today than was previously the case, as can be seen from Figure 15.3.

In connection with an analysis of the Swedish sanction system for young offenders, the American law professor Barry Feld (1994) states that by comparison with the justice system in America, the Swedish system constitutes a commendable model. Feld emphasizes, for example, the relative constancy of the proportion of young offenders that are prosecuted. Figure 15.3 indicates, however, that this assertion of constancy only holds for the period from 1975 to 1986. From the middle of the 1980s, the proportion of young offenders being prosecuted undergoes a successive increases. In recent years, an average of 4,700 youths in this age group have been prosecuted each year. The corresponding figure ten years previously was 2,600 youths.

One consequence of this trend is that criminal justice sanctions have also changed. Table 15.1 presents the sanctions issued to young offenders during the period under study.

At the beginning of the 1980s, 84 per cent of young offenders were convicted by means of a prosecutorial decision. A decision not to prosecute was issued in almost 40 per cent of all cases of conviction, while just under

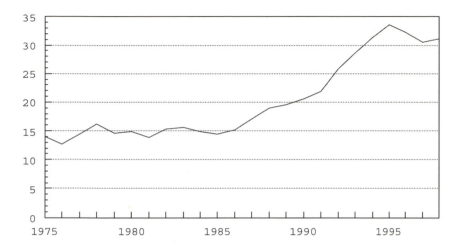

Figure 15.3. Young offenders (aged 15 to 17) prosecuted through the courts as a proportion of all convicted youths in this age group, 1975–98

Table 15.1. Convicted youths (aged 15–17) by principal sanction, for the years, 1988, 1993 & 1998 (per cent)

	1988	1993	1998
Prosecutorial disposition			
Waiver of prosecution	41	26	28
Fine imposed by prosecutor	40	45	41
Judicial disposition			
Fine by judicial sentence	11	17	15
Care under Social Service Act	5	8	13
Other sanctions	3	3	3

half of the convictions took the form of summary fines. Of those prosecuted, the majority were sentenced to fines while around a quarter were placed in the care of the social services. Ten per cent (or 1.5 per cent of all those convicted) were sentenced either to probation, or received a conditional sentence or a prison term. Fifteen years later the picture is different.

In summary, the proportion of young offenders being issued with a decision not to prosecute has fallen, while the proportion being placed in the care of the social services has increased. In 1998, a little under 30 per cent of convictions took the form of decisions not to prosecute issued by the prosecutor. Fines, issued either by the prosecutor or by a court, account for more than half (56 per cent) of the convictions. Almost 13 per cent of young offenders were placed in the care of the social services. And finally, two per cent received one of the other forms of sanction.

This trend is particularly interesting against the background of the fact that the final report of the Youth Committee emphasized that: 'When deciding whether or not to prosecute a case, the question of whether the court's choice of sanction is limited by the various restrictions relating to the application of criminal sanctions to youths should generally be considered. In practice, this relates to the sanction of placement into the care of the social services. In such cases it may appear unnecessary to prosecute a case, particularly considering the risk that a court appearance may have a damaging affect on the youth.' It is remarkable in itself that more young offenders are being taken to court. What is even more remarkable is the fact that this increase is particularly marked among the youngest group of offenders.

Has youth crime become more serious?

One possible explanation for the change in sanctions issued to youths over the last 15 to 20 years might be that the character of police reported youth offending has changed. If more youths had been suspected of serious offences during the 1990s, this would mean that the opportunities for prosecutors to issue decisions not to prosecute will have been fewer.

Of the youths aged 15 to 17 who were sentenced by a court during 1998, just over one fifth were 15 years of age (approximately 1,000 individuals). By comparison with earlier years, this represents a considerably higher proportion of 15-year-olds being convicted by the courts. In 1983, 15-year-olds comprised just over ten per cent of the individuals in this age group who were sentenced by the courts (in absolute figures, approximately 300 fifteen-year-olds were adjudicated in 1983). In 1983, 15 per cent of the 15-year-olds sentenced by the courts had been charged with assault, while the corresponding proportion in 1998 was 30 per cent.

In a study of cases of assault, Andersson (1996) has examined trends in the sanctions issued to young offenders. Between the years 1973 and 1975, 67 per cent of youths who had committed an assault but were without prior convictions were prosecuted. The corresponding proportion for the period 1991 to 1993 was 74 per cent. Of youths with previous convictions, 65 per cent were prosecuted during the first of these two periods, while over 80 per cent were prosecuted during the second period.

The majority of youths suspected of offences have committed a theft offence of some kind. In 1997 just over half (55 per cent) of youths between 15 and 17 years of age suspected of offences were suspected of various kinds of theft (Chapter 8 of the Swedish Penal Code), while just under one fifth (19 per cent) were suspected of crimes against the person (Chapters 3 to 7 of the Penal Code). By comparison with the situation in the 1980s, the change is most marked with regard to youths suspected of violent offences.

Youth offences reported to the police in the 1990s are comprised to a larger extent of assault, shoplifting and vandalism, while other offence types such as car or motorcycle thefts, burglary or unauthorized driving comprise a smaller proportion. Among the more serious offences, also, there is a shift away from theft offences and towards violence. More youths were convicted of serious violent offences, including muggings, during the 1990s than during the 1980s. At the same time it is important to point out that in terms of the actual numbers involved, very few youths were convicted of these types of serious offences during either the 1980s or the 1990s.

Zero tolerance with respect to young offenders

Youth offending and the measures taken to control it have been the subject of a great many reports over the past 15 years. The most comprehensive of these was the report of the Youth Crime Committee (SOU 1993: 35). The departmental memorandum 'Changed regulations regarding decisions not to prosecute young offenders' (Ds Ju 1987: 11) was of significance for trends in the use of decisions not to prosecute, as were the legislative changes that followed in 1988. Few in Sweden will have missed the hot debate surrounding the 'luxury trips' organized for seriously delinquent youths since the mid 1980s. At the same time, opinion survey results have indicated that 'more or less the whole of the population of Sweden ... is in favour of tougher measures against young offenders' (Research Group for Social and Information Studies 1997).

The departmental memorandum 'Changed regulations regarding decisions not to prosecute young offenders' (Ds Ju 1987: 11) points out that 'in the context of the general debate, we hear now and then that the rules relating to decisions not to prosecute young offenders are formulated in a rather unsuitable way. Among other things, it has been contended that the system is constructed so that the young person can easily get the impression that a decision not to prosecute means that society does not repudiate criminal activities' (p. 12). Against this background, it is therefore suggested that 'There is reason to consider whether the existing regulations on the decision not to prosecute might be tightened or complemented in different ways in order to create a system which is a little more nuanced and functional from the point of view of crime policy' (p. 12). At the same time, the memorandum lays down that 'a modified system of regulations should not aim to reduce the number of decisions not to prosecute young offenders. To the extent that regulations relating to the issuing of such decisions are tightened, the result should not be that in general young offenders are prosecuted to a greater extent than is now the case' (p. 13).

In summary, the increase in the number of young offenders being prosecuted through the courts is the result of changes in the regulations relating to the issuing of decisions not to prosecute, particularly in the case of re-offending. Another contributory factor is that more youths have committed assaults, which often leads to a court prosecution. This is not the whole explanation, however. Even young offenders with no previous convictions who have not committed violent offences were prosecuted through the courts more often during the 1990s than was the case earlier. One consequence of the reduced levels of tolerance in relation to youth crime, and of the legislative changes associated with this reduced tolerance, is that even less serious offending is being covered by this more restrictive tendency.

Conclusion

Swedish crime statistics show that during the 1990s, the police decided not to report crimes to the prosecutor in fewer cases, and more young offenders were prosecuted through the courts. These changes can in part be explained by political decisions taken in a 'spirit' of zero tolerance. One example of this crime policy ideology is provided by a former Under-secretary of State at the Department of Justice, who stressed that: 'immediately being placed before the court, once the case has been sufficiently well investigated, is better – even if it may seem organizationally more costly – than a letter from the prosecutor or the social services six months later' (Thelin 1997).

The expression 'is better' is central in the above citation. The question is, however, for whom is it better? For the offender, for the victim, or for the tax-payer? To what extent are levels of crime and security, respectively, affected by prosecuting more youths through the courts? It is self-evident that society has to react to breaches of the law. History and a brief examination of the situation in other countries indicate, however, that this can be achieved in a great many different ways. Using the resources of both the police and the prosecution service to deal with simple cases of shoplifting, for example, as is the case today, seems slightly inefficient. The time has perhaps come to try using summary police fines for shoplifting offences as a means of prioritizing the use of justice system resources in a more efficient way. The real penalty paid by many of those caught shoplifting is probably not the amount they are fined, but rather the fact that they were caught in itself, as Knut Sveri pointed out 30 years ago. Sveri (1968) also pointed out that a decision not to report the offence to the prosecutor, coupled with an opportunity for the police to register the individual, would provide a means of simplifying the justice system's handling of this type of offence.

As regards young offenders, the non-reporting of offences to the prosecutor, possibly in combination with alternative measures such as mediation, could be used to a much greater extent than it is today. The alternative measures employed could be organized by the social services, for example, in cooperation with agents at the local level. Around the country there are a number of pilot mediation projects in progress, where young offenders are given the opportunity to settle with the injured party directly. These mediation programmes run in parallel with judicial process and without actually affecting the judicial sanction. Many important questions remain to be answered, however, before this project can be employed more comprehensively in Sweden.

It is of course unfortunate for the public courts to be transformed into 'youth centres'. This seems, however, to be the trend, since increasing numbers of those being prosecuted are aged between 15 and 17. It is of course clear that certain offences committed by youths must be tried before a court of law. But we should ask ourselves if it is reasonable that one in three young offenders today is dealt with in this way as compared with one in six 15 years ago, and whether this really produces results in relation to the behaviour of young people. The most common sanction issued to these youths is a fine. At the same time, increasing numbers of young offenders are being 'sentenced' to the care of the social services. The resources of the social services are also limited and should be used to give help and support to those most in need.

Finally, the discretionary powers referred to above have an important role to play, since they can sort out those actions that are so culpable that the justice system ought to react with the most forcible means possible. The principle argument in favour of the police being obliged to report offences to the prosecutor, and the prosecutor being obliged to prosecute them through the courts, is that such a system maintains the principle of equality before the law. By expressing the exceptions to this guiding principle in legislation, it becomes possible to have what amounts in practice to a more or less relative system. At the same time, there is a risk that the use of the 'sorting' mechanisms will be affected by prevailing opinion. As one prosecutor expressed it, it is never legally wrong to prosecute where there is sufficient evidence. The relationship between zero tolerance and discretionary powers is complicated, however. Among other things, economic considerations affect the discretionary possibilities open to the police and prosecutors. If all offences where a suspect were found were to result in a trial, the system would simply become totally 'blocked up'. The majority of the cases dealt with by the courts in such a situation would be related to less serious offences. The discretionary powers are thus necessary in order for the justice system to function reasonably well at a reasonable cost to the taxpayer.

It is without doubt a huge task for citizens, police and decision makers at different levels to decide what the justice system should be used for. The goals of reducing crime and increasing security are so general that most people can probably agree on them. One objective of societal reactions to crime should be to redress the injury that has been done. Abandoning the justice system's ability to use discretionary powers in relation to minor offences and to yield to populist slogans promoting zero tolerance runs the risk of generating unreasonable costs for crime policy on both the economic and the social levels.

Notes

1. In the case of young offenders, the social services can also be included in this system.
2. In an evaluation of the employment of the decision not to report offences to the prosecutor carried out by the National Police Board in 1988, it was found that 70 per cent of the police questioned had made at least one such decision over the course of the previous month (RPS Report 1988: 2).
3. The increase in the time taken to deal with shoplifting offences has meant that among other things, the number of offences falling foul of the statute of limitations (which in this case occurs after two years) has increased. Some increase is also visible in the number of shoplifting offences cleared with the motivation 'suspect deceased'.

References

Andersson, J. (1996) 'Påföljder för Våldsbrott åren 1973–1993' in J. Ahlberg (ed.) *Brottsutvecklingen 1994*, BRÅ-rapport 1996:4. Stockholm: Brottsförebyggande rådet.
Bayley, D. (1998) *What Works in Policing?* Oxford: Oxford University Press.

Ds Ju (1987) 11 Ändrade Regler om Åtalsunderlåtelse för unga Lagöverträdare. Stockholm: Justitiedepartementet.

Farrington, D. P. (1999) 'Measuring, Explaining and Preventing Shoplifting: A Review of British Research', *Security Journal*, 2(1): 9–27.

Feld, B. C. (1994) 'Juvenile Justice Swedish Style: A Rose by Another Name', *Justice Quarterly*, 11(4): 625–50.

Harding, C. and Dingwall, D. (1998) *Diversion in the Criminal Process*. London: Sweet and Maxwell.

Löfmarck, M. *et al.* (1986) *Åtalsunderlåtelse: Processekonomi och Absolut Åtalsplikt.* Stockholm: Juristförlaget.

Research Group for Social and Information Studies. Forskningsgruppen för Samhälls- och Informationsstudier (1997) 'Attityder till Rättsväsendet och egen Trygghet mot Brott'. Release ur Kajsa v34, Stockholm.

Rikspolisstyrelsen (1988) 'Rapporteftergift i Praktisk Tillämpning'. RPS Report 1988: 2.

RPS FS (1984; 1990) National Police Board Directives. Stockholm.

SFS (1972; 1984) Police Act Sweden. Stockholm.

SOU (1976) 47 Färre Brottmål. Betänkande av Åtalsrättskommittén. Stockholm.

SOU (1982) 39 Stöld i Butik. Betänkande av Stöldutredningen. Stockholm.

SOU (1992) 61 Ett Reformerat Åklagarväsende. Betänkande av Åklagarutredningen -90. Stockholm.

SOU (1993) 35 Reaktioner mot Ungdomsbrott. Betänkande av Ungdomsbrotts-kommittén. Stockholm.

Sveri, K. (1968) *Butikssnatterier och Andra Smärre Förmögenhetsbrott ur Kriminalpolitsk Synvinkel*. Stockholm: NTfK.

Sveri, K. (1992) 'Professur i Kriminalpolitik', pp. 331–348, i SOU 1992:80. Stockholm.

Thelin, K. (1997) *Noll-Tolerans eller Inget Dalt*. Stockholm: Smedjan.

Chapter 16

Community and problem-oriented policing in the context of restorative justice

Elmar G. M. Weitekamp, Hans-Jürgen Kerner and Ulrike Meier

Introduction

The traditional style of policing was to keep public peace and order, to enforce laws, make arrests, and to provide short-term solutions to problems which occurred. This concept stood in contrast to the policing style proposed by Sir Robert Peel for a professional police force in Great Britain which was passed by the British Parliament in 1829 and which stressed the preventive nature of the new law: 'The principal object to be attained is the prevention of crime. The security of persons and property will thus be better effected, than by the detection and punishment of the offender after he has succeeded in committing the crime' (Radzinowicz 1968: 163). The principles of Peel's policing can again be found since the early 1980s, when community policing emerged as the dominant direction for new ways in thinking about policing. Parallel to the reintroduction of the concept of community policing, Goldstein (1977 and 1979) and later Eck and Spelman (1987) developed the concept of problem-oriented policing. Even though these two concepts, community policing and problem-oriented policing, are analytically separate and distinct, Peak and Glensor (1996: 69) convincingly argue that they are complementary in substance and can be operated together. Peak and Glensor (1996: 68) coined the term 'community oriented policing and problem solving' (COPPS) in which they tried to integrate the two concepts. One important aspect so far is the community and the citizens' welfare and their working together with the police. This is in line with an argument already put forward by Sir Robert Peel: 'The police are only members of the public who are paid to give full time attention to duties which are incumbent on every citizen in the interest of the community welfare' (cited in Melville Lee 1901: ch 12). One may ask, however, how well, even whether at all, this cooperation between communities and the police works in modern, industrialized and socially more or less fragmented societies. In this chapter, we therefore take a rather broad view. We will consider what the core concepts of community and problem-oriented policing are, how the public views and perceives the police and their work in general, and how restorative justice models can incorporate community and problem-oriented concepts, thus leading to better communities and more satisfied citizens.

Community policing

Based on the assumption that in today's world the working together between the police and the citizens is almost non-existent, the concept of community policing was developed in the early 1980s. Among the reasons for the rather loose, sometimes tense or even bad relationship between the police and the community were a lack of trust in and scepticism about the police. This was partly due to the fact that in the past in many regions, cities, and elsewhere, close personal contacts between the police authorities or individual police officers and the citizens, apart from the handling of concrete 'events', were generally rather scarce. However, in order to secure background knowledge about the typical characteristics of the population and their living environment, which was seen as essential in order to achieve an improved crime clearance rate and to better prevent future crimes, a close relationship and good everyday cooperation between the police and the community members seemed absolutely necessary. Therefore the concept of community policing aims to reunite the police with, or to immerse them in, the community. It is a holistic concept, definitely surpassing technocratic solutions favoured by bureaucratic apparatuses. It is also critical about marketing considerations as they were proposed earlier, e.g. the notion of 'Police–Community Relations'. Trojanowicz and Carter (1988: 17) describe the basic philosophy of community policing as follows: 'It is a philosophy and not a specific tactic; a proactive, decentralized approach, designed to reduce crime, disorder, and fear of crime, by involving the same officer in the same community on a long-term basis.'

For the purpose of our analysis we summarize the principles of community policing as follows:

- Community policing is based on the assumption that there is no real distinction between the substantive function of 'policing' between members of the general public and particular office-holders. To put it in a slogan: 'Police are the public and the public are the police'. That means that the police officers are just those who are paid to give full-time attention to the duties of every citizen (Peak and Glensor 1996: 73).

- Community policing is based upon commitment for a far-reaching, broadly problem-oriented service. It is much more than just an addition to the traditional event-oriented policing style.

- Community policing is based upon an organizational decentralization and on the reconstruction of police work in favour of a two-way communication between the police and the citizens (Sparrow 1988: 8–9).

- Community policing requests that the police, representing but one department among many others responsible for improving the quality of life, respond towards the wishes of the citizens and, even in the absence of crime and disorder, to whatever problems disturb the community most.

- The police and their work serve as a catalyst to organize the community and to enhance public co-operation amongst the citizens.

- Community policing concentrates its attention on signs of disorder or incivility such as vandalism, graffiti, abandoned housing, trash, etc. (Wilson and Kelling 1982; Moore and Kelling 1983; Lee-Sammons and Stock 1993).

- Community policing favours foot patrols by the police, which allows the police officer to experientially 'learn his beat' (Alpert and Dunham 1993: 432).

- Community policing supports the idea that local police officers function as 'problem brokers' and coordinate the communication with (other) public institutions and the members and associations of the community.

- Community policing implies a special cooperation between the police and the citizens for crime prevention. Recurring problems are supposed to be solved by going back over and over to the same places in order to evaluate the efforts of both sides (Rosenbaum 1986: 5).

- Community policing tries to involve every citizen of a whole community in activities to reduce and control acute crime problems, drug markets, fear of crime, the decline of the neighbourhood in order to improve the quality of life in the community (Trojanowicz 1994: 6).

- Community policing is based upon the idea that the activities of the police have to be extended in the communities to become an institution that cares and coordinates efforts to improve social cohesion, if and at times when a fragmentation of the community takes place and ties among organizations and citizens of a community become weaker. Crime control in general and combating acute particular crimes still remain important aspects of policing in everyday practice. But community policing has its main focus on keeping the public peaceful, on mediating conflicts, and on coordinating efforts to improve the whole quality of life in the community (Feltes and Gramckow 1994).

Problem-oriented policing

The police authorities have always tried, in addition to clearing up reported criminal incidents and to pursuing suspected offenders, to solve problems occurring within their area of jurisdiction. Individual police officers always took care of problems they were faced with on their beat while on duty. But the concept of what a police 'problem' is all about was rather limited and, in a certain way, typologically 'concretistic'. Keeping public peace and order, clearing a difficult or even dangerous traffic situation, providing first service in cases of personal emergency, effecting first measures and alerting other authorities such as the fire brigade, helping people and animals out of acute trouble, providing guidance for persons in need of care, offering advice for precautionary measures with regard to crime prevention (e.g. installing alarm systems) – this is but a selection of what a responsive and responseful police authority or representative may have done and will still do in their regular work. This is not to be contested. However, problems of that type are probably mere 'surface phenomena'. Seen from the point of view of community policing they may 'emerge' out of deeper seated, more far-reaching if not structural problems affecting the whole 'social space' and the 'social–psychological web' of a neighbourhood, a village, a town or a certain region of a city or metropolitan area. In the past, there existed no guidance or concept on how to detect and tackle such problems in a community.

The philosophy of problem-solving policing aims to improve exactly that situation. It was developed by Goldstein in 1979 out of frustration with the dominant, i.e. more technological if not technocratic model for improving police operations. At the time the police in the US and in many other Western industrialized countries were much more concerned about, for example, how quick they were in responding to a call than about asking what may have caused the fact that that particular call was the 55th arriving from that locality within the last three months. Accordingly, it was important for them to look for the necessary evidence for immediate law enforcement and eventual criminal justice procedures, but it did not matter that much what they did otherwise with persons or situations affected by the event once they arrived at the scene of a crime. The police administrations lacked a concept which offered the police officers ways and means to detect signs of 'problems behind the manifested problem', and particular techniques to address such problems if detected on the occasion or in the aftermath of the event. Problem-oriented policing tries to develop such concepts. It has so far a strong community inclination. In accordance with Peak and Glensor (1996: 79), one can, therefore, conclude that problem-oriented policing relates to different principles than community-oriented policing, but that both are complementary. Problem-oriented policing may thus be perceived as a strategy that puts the community-oriented policing philosophy into practice. The police as organization is supposed to look for and to examine the underlying causes of emerging crimes and disorders, and to find long-term solutions. When grasping the essence of the concept of problem-solving policing every individual police officer should feel enabled to contribute to the continuous task of identifying problems, analysing them rigorously, developing strategies to moderate or even eliminate them, and later to evaluate the outcome. Spelman and Eck (1987: 2–3) call this four-stage problem-solving process S.A.R.A, meaning that the process involves scanning, analysis, response, and assessment.

According to Goldstein (1990: 32), problem-oriented policing means an encompassing plan to improve the work of the police by focusing their attention on the most serious background factors which have far-reaching consequences for all levels of the structure and the organization of their duties. Goldstein argues further that the usual police approaches (strategies, tactics, etc.) are oriented towards the wrong categories. For example, it is not a crime category such as murder which should define the way the police operate and what methods should be applied. Instead, the police have to evaluate and search for the objective causes and subjective reasons (motives, etc.) behind the tangible crime scene, and to develop proactive and long-term problem-solving concepts for an area of social conflict. This does not imply, of course, that a local police authority with a high incidence of homicide cases could or should dismantle an existing and suitably equipped homicide squad or department. Crimes that happen always have to be dealt with in terms of clearance and appropriate law enforcement. The guiding idea is rather pointing at a meta-level of everyday work. According to that idea, the police work may just 'start' on the surface of an event, since that is often the way the responsible persons gain knowledge of what 'happens out there'. Sometimes even a single event can be significant for what 'basically determines the trouble' people and/or localities are suffering from. At least repeated events or continuous nuisances should at least alert the police to look for other than the evident contingencies of the situation. They are supposed to pursue the 'contextual elements' of crime in the community, beyond the concrete cases and independently of the traditional detective tasks and endeavours. To put it in more classical criminological terms, they are expected to tackle the root causes of crime in a given environment, and not just to deal with the surface of individual crimes or series of offences. Consequently, individual police officers should not restrict themselves to thinking about single case solutions but rather strive to contribute to the development of complete societal problem-solving strategies. This should then trickle down in the organization, structure, and the training of the whole police corps, particularly with regard to sensitizing new recruits and experienced officers.

Goldstein argued that several steps must be taken in order to improve the quality of police responses. Eck and Spelman (1987: 3) seem to offer a suitable concept. They developed a twelve-step model of what a problem-oriented policing agency should do:

(1) Focus on problems of concern to the public.

(2) Zero in on effectiveness as the primary concern.

(3) Be proactive.

(4) Be committed to systematic inquiry as a first step in solving substantive problems.

(5) Encourage the use of rigorous methods in making inquiries.

(6) Make full use of the data in police files and the experience of police personnel.

(7) Group like incidents together so that they can be addressed as a common problem.

(8) Avoid using overly broad labels in grouping incidents so separate problems can be identified.

(9) Encourage a broad and uninhibited search for solutions.

(10) Acknowledge the limits of the criminal justice system as a response to problems.

(11) Identify multiple interests in any one problem and weigh them when analysing the value of different responses.

(12) Be committed to taking some risks in responding to problems.

The relationship between problem-oriented policing and community policing

Police experts in the USA sought for two decades alternative ways to reduce the steadily increasing crime rates and to combat crime through preventive measures (Lee-Sammons and Stock 1993: 157). Problem-oriented policing and community policing both have the same philosophical roots and, according to Moore and Trojanowicz (1988: 11), share some important characteristics:

(1) decentralization in order to encourage officer initiative and the effective use of local knowledge;

(2) geographical rather than functionally defined subordinate units in order to develop local knowledge;

(3) close interactions with local communities in order to facilitate responsiveness to, and cooperation with, the community.

Problem-oriented policing mainly tries to solve regional crime problems, however; the main focus is the solving of crimes and the underlying causes of the crime through restructuring of the police force and changes in the police organization. The main focus of community-oriented policing, on the other hand, is the improvement of the relationship between the police and the citizens. Both concepts overlap in those areas where problem-oriented policing depends on information from the public and on having a good relationship with the community. Furthermore, in areas where potential conflict in the population leads to conflicts which problem-oriented policing wants to solve, such conflicts may not have occurred had community-oriented policing been properly implemented. All community-oriented police work includes problem-solving strategies, but not all problem-oriented police work is necessarily community oriented. Problem-oriented policing does not necessarily include long-term evaluations in order to guarantee that the solutions to the problems will be long lasting (Trojanowicz and Bucqueroux 1994: 17). Interventions through problem-oriented policing can change the structure of the community; they are, however, limited since the police come into the community, make changes and disappear. This does not apply to community-oriented policing since in this case the police come into the neighbourhood/community, stay there and take on the responsibility to improve the quality of communal life (Hoover 1992: 10).

Peak and Glensor (1996: 95) engage, as already mentioned above, in formulating an integrated model called 'community-oriented policing and problem solving' (COPPS). They describe the essence of their concept as follows:

> Community-oriented policing and problem solving is a proactive philosophy that promotes solving problems that are criminal, affect our quality of life, or increase our fear of crime, as well as relate to other community issues. COPPS encourages using various resources and police-community partnerships for developing strategies to identify, analyse, and address community problems at their source.

In surveys on citizens' attitudes towards the police, one can find support for the notion that the public view the concepts of problem- and community-oriented policing in a favourable way. We further detected that the expectations of the public to a certain degree reflect what problem- and community-oriented policing postulate. However, since the concepts are at this moment not sufficiently operationalized, one could argue that we can find under the umbrella of problem- and community-oriented policing everything that is new in police work. Therefore, we agree partly with Bayley (1994: 278), who concludes that one will never know whether community policing (as well as problem-oriented policing) will be successful since problem- and community-oriented policing means too many things to different people. The practice varies so much that any evaluation will be completely challengeable, at least in part, on grounds of not representing what problem- and community-oriented policing postulate. A central question in the case of problem- and community-oriented policing seems to be that we no longer have a clear role for the police. Are the duties of the police to combat crime or are they supposed to work like a social worker? If anything in between seems suitable, then what is the appropriate mixture and how could individual police officers combine the very divergent competences needed to fulfil the different tasks? In the case of problem-oriented policing, the police are supposed to identify the main problems of certain groups in the population and to help solve them. However, population groups are not homogenous units, and different groups identify problems differently and also suggest different ways to solve them. Even if the police were able to acknowledge the various sources of trouble, it would often be impossible to reach agreement on how to solve them when the police are forced to work together with different subgroups and organizations in a given community. On the one hand, this would improve the feeling of security to a certain degree, but it would also lead to resignation and frustrations on the other hand for some of the residents who do not approve of the suggested strategies in order to solve the problems.

The concepts and the combination of problem- and community-oriented policing sound very good in theory and might work quite well in countries which adhere to the opportunity principle (e.g. USA, Canada, the Netherlands). They still sound good in theory for countries with the legality principle (e.g. Germany, Austria); however, in countries with the legality principle, the police are obliged by procedural law to embark upon prosecution in every case in which there is a preliminary suspicion that a crime was committed and to report it to the prosecutor's office. Therefore, the concepts are doomed and would fail even before one could start to implement them into practice.

The central principle of problem- and community-oriented policing is that the relationship between the police officers and the public should be improved. This implies that when a police officer wants to build a relationship of trust with the public in order to reach a better understanding of the problems of the community, he/she will hear about situations and events which are in a strict sense illegal according to the law. In countries with the legality principle, this would have the consequence that the police officer would have to report this 'confidential knowledge' of a crime to the prosecutor's office, since the police in general have no discretion whatsoever and have to leave the final decision about whether to prosecute or to drop the charge to the prosecutor's office. In order to build up trust, which is essential to problem- and community-oriented policing, the police officer has to have at least some discretion on how to react when they are informed about acts which according to the law constitute a crime or are on the borderline. If the officer is forced to report the pettiest offences to the prosecutor's office, one cannot expect that they will build up a meaningful relationship with any given community. Discretion and flexibility for police officers in how to interpret certain situations seem to be essential if one wants to implement problem- and community-oriented policing in a community. If one takes these postulates seriously, the concepts cannot function in countries with the legality principle unless they fundamentally change their penal procedural law.

Despite this specific problem for countries with the legality principle, Lustig (1996: 35) rightly concludes that the philosophy of community policing (as well as problem-oriented policing) will in any system be defined by the fact that through the implementation of community and problem-orientated policing, neither the strategy of the police work, nor the logic of guaranteeing security, nor the power of the state will be changed. These three positions will be strengthened through the concepts of community and problem-oriented policing, thus leading to a net-widening effect. While this is basically true, the results of surveys of the public's views and expectations indicate that they are in favour of core elements of community and problem-oriented policing and that through the implementation of these concepts, their feelings of security and thus their quality of life can be improved (Hermannstädter 1986; Hermanutz 1995: 141). Therefore, net-widening effects are not necessarily negative unless they are used to control the public in an intrusive way (Weitekamp 1989). Some projects in the United States of America also support this conclusion, since they were able reduce the number of crimes committed but, even more importantly, reduce people's fear of becoming a victim of a crime. In addition, it was found in these projects that the level of satisfaction with the police was increased among members of the public (Lee-Sammons and Stock 1993: 160). However, despite the reported success of these projects on local levels, one has to be sceptical that the degree of satisfaction with police work in a given population at large would improve overall. In order to improve the general level of satisfaction with the police, one would have to be able to show on a large scale that through measures of problem- and community-oriented policing the quality of life improves. The public will hardly recognize a restructuring of the police force and the implementation of problem- and community-oriented policing unless it happens on a large scale, is continuously reported and favourably backed up by the media, or directly involves them. Scepticism is also justified by the fact that especially problem-oriented policing calls for solving the underlying problems of crime. The experiences in the United States of America, where problem- and community-oriented policing were practised and the relationship between the police, the public and community organizations was excellent and they all worked together, show that this did not necessarily lead to the solving of problems of security and order in those communities. The reason for this is that the police cannot create jobs, improve the schools or get better teachers and often fail even to get the garbage collectors or street services better organized in order to improve the situation of a given community (Feltes and Gramckow 1994: 20).

If one examines the views of citizens who were asked about the perceived causes of the increasing crime rate and their suggestions with regard to measures for crime prevention, one can clearly detect the dilemma which communities are in. The factors which citizens define as causing the increase in crime are mostly structural or economic ones, but when asked what preventive measures should be taken to reduce the crime rates, they primarily suggest increasing the presence of the police in their neighbourhood. This short-term measure cannot solve the underlying economic and structural problems in a city or community, and the increasing rates of youth unemployment are also not affected by more police officers in the streets (Heinz and Spieß 1995: 117). In general, we find a tendency in almost all countries around the world that the public reacts to increasing crime rates with a call for more police and stiffer laws. This reflects the widespread tendency on the one hand to hold the state responsible for the shaping of one's own, personal conditions of life, and on the other hand to believe in the behaviour-controlling power of the penal laws.

Towards a restorative problem-solving police prevention programme (RPSPPP)

In examining the concepts of problem- and community-oriented policing, one finds that the key players in these concepts are the police, represented through its police officers, and members of the public. Members of the public have various levels of fear of crime and feelings of insecurity, and of becoming victims of a crime, which may further affect their level of fear of crime and feelings of insecurity. These citizens and various community organizations, which are usually not described in more depth in the literature, then form the community. One absolutely essential group in the community is completely left out of the concept of problem- and community-oriented policing and serves on a theoretical level as the bogeymen for both the police and the citizens in a given community – the offenders who commit crimes. It seems to be futile to develop a concept of policing which aims to reshape and improve communities, reduce fear of crime, increase feelings of security for its citizens and to leave out the most disturbing group which is usually responsible for a great deal of the problems in the community – the offenders. Offenders are not an inconsiderable group: criminological research has shown that up to one-third of the males in a typical population has been convicted of a crime before the age of thirty.

Of the problem- and community-oriented police concepts proposed so far, one can only expect that the relationship between citizens and the police will improve and lead to lower levels of fear of crime and a higher level of satisfaction with the police, and that nuisances such as garbage in the streets, broken windows and other signs of incivility will be handled more efficiently. However, whether this then leads naturally to fewer crimes or a higher clearance rate for crimes committed seems to be questionable. In addition, leaving out the offenders in the process of rebuilding communities and treating them as the 'common and outside enemy of the police as well as the citizens' is overlooking the fact that these so-called criminals are usually members of the community and are not considered as outsiders by most of the residents of such communities, since they live a very 'normal' life. In order to improve the quality of a community in a meaningful way and not just superficially, one has to develop a concept which includes the offenders in the rebuilding and improving of communities as well.

We propose that a balanced and restorative police–community prevention programme could be the answer and addresses the shortcomings of existing problem- and community-oriented police concepts. We are not arguing that existing concepts are wrong, since they give us essential elements for our model, but we think they leave out very important elements which are of utmost importance for improving the quality of life in communities and societies. We think it is futile to focus on the call for a stronger police force, tougher laws, bringing back law and order, or – as introduced in the United States of America – laws like 'three strikes and you are out' or concepts like 'truth in sentencing', which seems to be the standard reaction of politicians to increasing crime rates and concerns about crime among citizens. On the contrary, one needs to develop concepts which restore peace in communities in a balanced way, develop prevention strategies, improve the relationship between citizens and the police, and mediate between victims and offenders in order to achieve reconciliation between them. While the existing concepts of problem- and community-oriented policing focus their work on improving the relationship between citizens and the police officers, develop prevention strategies, and to a certain degree improve the communities, they fail to realize that one can only restore peace in communities through a restorative approach. One also has to keep this in mind when one develops prevention strategies: it is essential to mediate between victims and offenders in order to achieve reconciliation among them. Victims in this context can be the community as a whole as well as individual members of the community.

Bazemore and Umbreit (1994) developed a model (Figure 16.1) which they called the 'balanced and restorative justice model'. The idea behind this model was to develop a programme for community supervision for juveniles. Frustrated by the criminal justice policy in the United States of America, which is essentially retributive, they wanted to develop a model which protected the community and made sure that the offender was held accountable in a meaningful way. Restorative justice became the guiding philosophical framework of their model. Restorative justice heavily

Figure 16.1. The balanced and restorative justice model of Bazemore and Umbreit

emphasizes maximum involvement of the victim, the offender and the community in the process of restoring peace.

As Figure 16.1 shows, Bazemore and Umbreit's balanced and restorative justice model includes four key elements: accountability, community protection, competency development and balance.

Accountability means that when a crime is committed, an obligation to the victim is incurred. Victims and communities should have their losses restored by the actions of the offenders making reparation, and victims should be empowered as active participants in the juvenile justice process.

Community protection means that the public has a right to a safe and secure community and must be protected during the time the offender is under juvenile justice supervision. The juvenile justice system must provide a variety of interventions which take the risks of the juvenile offenders into account.

Competency development means that the juvenile offenders should leave the justice system as productive and competent members of the community. Rather than just receiving treatment and services aimed at suppressing problem behaviour, offenders should make measurable improvements in their ability to function as productive, responsible citizens.

Balance in the model by Bazemore and Umbreit means that the community, the victim and the offender should receive balanced attention. All three parties should gain tangible benefits from their interaction with the juvenile justice system.

While Bazemore's and Umbreit's model was only developed for the juvenile justice system, it can be easily extended to the justice system in general or employed for a restorative/enhancement approach to community crime prevention, as was done by Brown and Polk (1996: 398–420). Brown and Polk were asked by the state of Tasmania for help in creating a new criminal justice strategy. In evaluating the crime situation in Tasmania, Brown and Polk found that there was a very low crime rate with regard to violent crime, but they also found that the level of fear of crime among Tasmanian citizens was very high. They further detected that fear of crime was as much an issue as crime itself. Knowing that fear of crime often becomes the basis for political campaigns that emphasize the slogan 'getting tough on crime' and usually turn into strategies that require increased use of prisons and longer sentences, Brown and Polk (1996: 400) rightly point out that if fear of crime is as much a problem as crime itself, these hard-line strategies provide no solution to the underlying problem. Tasmania public-policy makers were confronted with two clearly distinct but interlocked problems: the crime problem and the fear-of-crime problem. This led them to the conclusion that they would have to develop a criminal justice strategy which should stress prevention strategies that would help to reduce crime and fear of crime at the same time.

Brown and Polk discovered that the Tasmanian agencies dealing with the crime problem had already been committed to keep the number of incarcerated people extraordinarily small, while at the same time looking for crime prevention and control strategies. In addition, they detected that in Tasmania there existed a widespread interest in and adaptation of aspects of the restorative justice approach known as family conferencing. According to Brown and Polk (1996: 406) 'the family group conference model emphasizes the need to bring together the offender, the victim, and their respective support groups to achieve a mutual understanding of the reasons and circumstances of the crime from both perspectives, and to resolve the matter in such a way that it reinforces the position of the young person as a member of the community rather than an outsider against whom the community has aligned itself.'

Brown and Polk combined these findings and, based upon Bazemore and Umbreit's model, developed what they called a restorative/enhancement approach to community crime prevention (Figure 16.2). Essentially, the model shifts the attention from the state-level criminal justice agencies to local community initiatives and links ongoing restorative justice approaches to a broader community enhancement perspective. Brown and Polk called for more general community enhancement activities to involve citizens from divergent sectors of the community as well as the offenders and victims. This strategy should lead to stronger and more

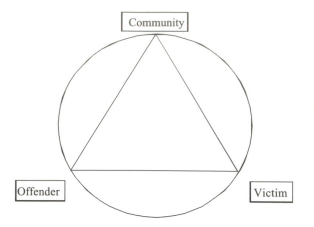

Figure 16.2. The restorative/enhancement prevention model of Brown and Polk (1996: 410)

effective neighbourhoods, which would be able to prevent and cope with the consequences of crime in a better way.

The model of Brown and Polk (1996: 410) is a decentralized strategic model which emphasizes the role of the local communities rather than, as in the past, state-level approaches to crime control and prevention. It further calls for a constant process of evaluation and assessment and is dynamic rather than static in character. The second feature of the model focuses on the restorative and enhancement strategies. Historically, restorative justice paid attention to the relationship between the offender and the victim, but Brown and Polk include the community as a specific element in the criminal justice strategy. In both models, the balanced and restorative justice project for juveniles of Bazemore and Umbreit and the restorative/enhancement approach to community crime prevention model by Brown and Polk, we find three distinctive groups of participants: victims, offenders and representatives of the community.

The traditional criminal justice programmes concentrated essentially on the offender, and the victim was completely ignored or at most used as a witness in trials. The rediscovered restorative justice approach in the 1970s again gave a place to victims. Bazemore and Umbreit, as well as Brown and Polk (1996: 408–9), provide a role for each of the three distinct groups of participants in their models:

Victims in terms of obligations for restorative work assumed by both the individual offender and the community; offenders where accountability is the desired outcome, which can be provided through such restorative processes as restitution, community service, and victim-offender mediation; and communities, where it is argued that communities can play a role in restorative work both at the community level and for individual victims, while it is also important that the community engage in such activities such as competency development with offenders by providing opportunities for learning and service activities.

For the latter, we already have rather good structures and conditions in many states and countries. There exist many volunteer and semi-public organizations for the care and the resettlement of offenders which could be mobilized in the model created above and lead to a further improvement of peace and domestic security (Kerner 1995).

We think that the model of Bazemore and Umbreit, as well as the one introduced by Brown and Polk, is missing one major component and therefore propose a restorative problem-solving police prevention programme in which we want to add an additional distinctive group of participants: the police represented through their police officers (Figure 16.3).

We think it is absolutely necessary to include the police in a model which is supposed to make a community safer, reduce fear of crime levels, create and implement successful prevention strategies, improve the quality of life in a given community, restore peace within the community through a restorative justice approach, and improve the relationship

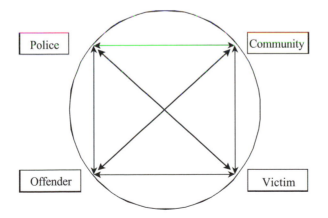

Figure 16.3. The restorative problem-solving police prevention model of Weitekamp, Kerner and Meier.

between the police and citizens in order to achieve higher levels of satisfaction with the police work. As one can see from this list, the police and their officers are necessary for almost every point; or to put it differently, it would be foolish to try to implement anything to improve the situation in a community without the police and their officers. It is short-sighted if one wants to improve a community, but ignores any link to the state and in this case, where we deal with crime and fear of crime, the criminal justice system. Citizens perceive and are in contact with their criminal justice system mostly through contact observing with, or by observing, the police in their neighbourhoods and communities. If the model were right, the police would become even more a part of daily life and, as we have shown, there exists a good chance that they would then be perceived by the public as their friends and helpers. Therefore, we think it is of utmost importance that the police and their officers are incorporated in any model that seeks to improve life in a community.

If one examines the model adapted by us from Brown and Polk, which we simply extended by introducing the police as one more major player in the field, one finds a lot of the key elements which problem- and community-oriented policing concepts are proposing. These concepts advocate decentralization and a local community approach in order to handle crime control and prevention. Furthermore, they propose dynamic objectives which should be evaluated and assessed constantly. These are two of the most essential objectives of problem- and community-oriented policing. Moreover, Brown and Polk ask for more community enhancement activities which should involve residents from divergent sectors of the community, which is again what problem- and community-oriented policing postulate. However, without the restorative justice com-ponent, and that is what problem- and community-oriented policing do not have and postulate, the implementation of such strategies looks rather artificial. The concepts as they are proposed today look like approaches which are structured and imposed on the communities by the police and are thus unnatural. On the other hand, if one adds the restorative justice component, the approach changes so that it becomes structured and implemented by the community, victims, offenders and the police together, and thus becomes balanced. Also one could expect from a policing concept which is built into a community restorative prevention programme that it works more successfully than a programme which is more or less imposed.

How do the views and expectations of the citizens about the police in general, and problem- and community-oriented policing especially, fit into these models? We think they fit rather well. The scattered and meagre results we obtained about citizens' views and expectations of the police point in a direction which clearly favours problem- and community-oriented policing. If one then adds the restorative justice approach and includes the major four players who can improve the quality of life in a community, we think this approach would find even more support among citizens.

We think that both outcomes can be accomplished through our proposed model. By adding to the existing concepts of problem- and community-oriented policing the offenders as an important party, and more clearly stressing the victims' importance, and by introducing a balanced restorative justice model, a positive, developmental approach is possible. This approach includes all aspects in an integrated manner such as crime, fear of crime, crime prevention, and the improvement of the quality of life for all people who are involved. If one examines the wishes of the citizens on how police work could and should be improved, we found above that all suggestions went in the same direction: the community as a whole would be improved along with communication between the police and the residents of communities. In a community where people are content, life is balanced, and the police are visible on the local level, we think that the call for a strong police force fades away naturally, since the underlying causes of the problems which generate fear and annoyance are addressed. Approaching policing and communities the way we suggest in our model constitutes in our opinion a positive, dynamic concept to integrate all people involved in a community. If one implemented this model, it would make obsolete the negative, punishment-orientated policies currently popular in many countries and found in extreme form in the United States of America.

References

Alex, M. (1989) 'Konflikte zwischen Polizei und Bevölkerung im Rollenverständnis von angehenden Polizeibeamten', *Kriminologisches Journal.*

Alpert, G. P. and Dunham, R. G. (1986) 'Community Policing', *Journal of Police Science and Administration*, 14: 212–22.

Alpert, G. P. and Dunham, R. G. (1992) *Policing Urban America*. 2nd ed. Illinois: Waveland Press.

Bazemore, G. and Umbreit, M. S. (1994) *Balanced and Restorative Justice*. Washington, DC: Office of Juvenile Justice and Delinquency Prevention.

Bayley, D. H. (1994) 'International Differences in Community Policing' in D. P. Rosenbaum (ed.) *The Challenge of Community Policing*. London: Sage.

Bennett, S. F. and Lavrakas, P. J. (1989) 'Community-Based Crime Prevention: An Assessment of the Eisenhower Foundation's Neighbourhood Program', *Crime and Delinquency*, 35(3): 345–64.

Beyer, L. R. (1993) *Community Policing: Lessons from Victoria*. Canberra: Australian Institute of Criminology.

Boggs, S. L. (1971) 'Formal and Informal Crime Control: An Exploratory Study of Urban, Suburban and Rural Orientations', *Sociological Quarterly*, 12: 319–27.

Braithwaite, J. (1989) *Crime, Shame and Reintegration*. Cambridge: Cambridge University Press.

Brand, S. G., Frank, J., Worden, R. E. and Bonum, T. S. (1994) 'Global and Specific Attitudes towards the Police: Disentangeling the Relationship', *Justice Quarterly*, 11(1): 119–34.

Brown, L. P. and Wycoff, M. A. (1987) 'Policing Houston: Reducing Fear and Improving Service', *Crime and Delinquency*, 33(1): 71–89.

Brown, M. and Polk, K. (1996) 'Taking Fear of Crime Seriously: The Tasmanian Approach to Community Crime Prevention', *Crime and Delinquency*, 398–420.

Byrne, J. M. (1989) 'Reintegrating the Concept of Community into Community – Based Corrections', *Crime and Delinquency*, 35(3): 471–99.

Cao, L., Frank, J. and Cullen, F. T. (1996) 'Race, Community Context and Confidence in the Police', *American Journal of Police*, 15(1): 3–17.

Chacko, J. (ed.) (1993) *Community Policing in Canada*. 1st edn. Toronto: Canadian Scholar's Press.

Chicago Community Policing Evaluation Consortium (1995) *Community Policing in Chicago, Year Two: An interim Report*. Illinois.

Christie, N. (1978) 'Conflicts as Property', *British Journal of Criminology*, 17: 1–15.

Covington, J. and Taylor, R. B. (1991) 'Fear of Crime in Urban Residential Neighbourhoods: Implications of Between- and Within-Neighbourhood Sources for Current Models', *The Sociological Quarterly*, 32(2): 231–49.

Cox, S. M. and Fitzgerald, J. D. (1996) *Police in Community Relations*. 3rd edn. Chicago: Brown and Benchmark.

Dölling, D. and Feltes, T. (ed.) (1993) *Community Policing – Comparative Aspects of Community Oriented Police Work*. Holzkirchen: Felix-Verlag.

Dunham, R. G. and Alpert, G. P. (1993) *Critical Issues in Policing. Contemporary Readings*. 2nd edn. Illinois: Waveland Press.

Eck, J. E. and Spelman, W. (1987) *Problem-Solving: Problem-Oriented Policing in Newport news*. Washington, DC: Police Executive Research Forum. Reprinted in: *Critical Issues in Policing* R. G. Dunham and G. P. Alpert, (eds). Illinois: Waveland Press.

Eck, J. E. and Spelman, W. (1993) 'Problem-Solving: Problem-Oriented Policing in Newport News' in R. G. Dunham and G. P. Alpert (eds) *Critical Issues in Policing*. Dunham, IL: Waveland Press.

Feltes, T. (1990) Polizei, Bürger und Gemeinwesen, *Neue Kriminalpolitik*, 4.

Feltes, T. (ed.) (1995) *Kommunale Kriminalprävention in Baden-Württemberg*. Holzkirchen: Felix-Verlag.

Feltes, T. and Gramckow, H. (1994) 'Bürgernahe Polizei und kommunale Kriminalprävention', *Neue Kriminalpolitik*, 3: 16.

Fleissner, D. (1992) *Community Policing in Seattle: A Model Partnership between Citizens and Police*. Washington, DC: US Department of Justice, Office of Justice Programs.

Friedmann, R. R. (1992) *Community Policing: Comparative Perspectives and Prospects.* 1. publ. New York: Harvester Wheatsheaf.

Glensor, R. W. (1993) *Community Policing: An Empirical Assessment of the Influence of Contact on Citizen's Perceptions of Police Performance.* Ann Arbor, MI: UMI Dissertation Services International.

Goldstein, H. (1977) *Policing a Free Society* (Cambridge, MA.: Ballinger, 1977).

Goldstein, H. (1979) 'Improving Policing: A Problem-Oriented Approach', *Crime and Delinquency*, 25: 236–58.

Goldstein, H. (1987) 'Towards Community – Oriented Policing: Potential, Basic Requirements, and Threshold Questions', *Crime and Delinquency*, 33(1): 6–30.

Goldstein, H. (1990) *Problem-Oriented Policing.* Philadelphia: Temple University Press.

Greene, J. R. (1993) 'Civic Accountability and the Police. Lessons Learned from Police and Community Relations' in R. G. Dunham and G. P. Alpert (eds) *Critical Issues in Policing.* Illinois: Waveland Press.

Heinz, W. and Spieß, G. (1995) *Opfererfahrungen, Kriminalitätsfurcht und Vorstellungen zur Prävention von Kriminalität. Ergebnisse der Bevölkerungsbefragung in den Gemeinden Ravensburg/Weingarten im Rahmen des Begleitforschungsprojekts 'Kommunale Kriminalprävention' in Baden-Württemberg.* Konstanz.

Hermannstädter, P. (1986) 'Konzeption zur Erreichung von Bürgernähe', *Schriftenreihe der PFA*: 102–26.

Hermanutz, M. (1995) 'Die Zufriedenheit von Bürgern mit den Umgangsformen der Polizei nach einem mündlichen Polizeikontakt – eine empirische Untersuchung' in T. Feltes (ed.) *Kommunale Kriminalprävention in Baden-Württemberg.* Holzkirchen: Felix Verlag.

Hess, K. M. and Miller, L. S. (1994) *Community Policing: Theory and Practice.* Minneapolis: West.

Hoover, L. T. (ed.) (1992) *Police Management: Perspectives and Issues.* Washington, DC, Police Executive Research Forum.

Ipos (Institut für praxisorientierte Sozialforschung) (ed.) *Einstellungen zu Aktuellen Fragen der Innenpolitik 1991 in Deutschland.*

Kelling, G. L. (1987) 'Acquiring a Taste for Order: The Community and Police', *Crime and Delinquency*, 33(1): 90–102.

Kerner, H.-J. (1980) *Kriminalitätseinschätzung und Innere Sicherheit.* Wiesbaden: BKA Forschungsreihe 11.

Kerner, H.-J. (1995) 'Kriminalpolitik und Innere Sicherheit. Anforderungen an Verbrechensverhütung, Verbrechenskontrolle und Straffälligenhilfe' in *Innere Sicherheit und Soziale Strafrechtspflege* (Hrsg). Evangelische Akademie Bad Boll. Bad Boll: Protokolldienst 23/95, 95–123.

Kratcoski, P. C. and Dukes, D. (1995) *Issues in Community Policing.* Highland Heights, KY.: Acad. of Criminal Justice Sciences, Northern Kentucky.

Lanier, M. M. (1993) *Explication and Measurement of the Theoretical Constructs Underlying Community Policing.* Ann Arbor, MI: UMI Dissertation Services International.

Lee-Sammons, L. and Stock, J. (1993) 'Kriminalprävention. Das Konzept des "Community Policing" in den USA', *Kriminalistik*, 3: 157–62.

Lewis, D. A. and Salem, G. (1981) 'Community Crime Prevention: An Analysis of a Developing Strategy', *Crime and Delinquency*: 405–21.

Lustig, S. (1996) *Die Sicherheitswacht im Rahmen des Bayrischen Polizeikonzepts*, unveröffentlichte Diplomarbeit. Ludwig-Maximilian-Universität München.

Manning, P. K. (1993) 'Community-Based Policing' in R. G. Dunham and G. P. Alpert (eds) *Critical Issues in Policing*. Prospects Heights IL: Waveland Press.

McIntyre, J. (1967) 'Public Attitudes Toward Crime and Law Enforcement', *The Annals of the American Academy*, 374: 34–6.

Melville Lee, W. L. (1901) *A History of Police in England*. London: Methuen.

Moore, M. H. and Kelling, G. L. (1983) '"To Serve and Protect": Learning from Police History', *The Public Interest*, 70: 49–65.

Moore, M. H. and Trojanowicz R. C. (1988) *Corporate Strategies for Policing*, Washington DC: U.S. Department of Justice, National Institute of Justice.

Moose, C. (1993) *The Theory and Practice of Community Policing: An Evaluation of the Iris Court Demonstration Project*. Ann Arbor, MI: UMI Dissertation Services International.

Murck, M. (1992) Zwischen Schutzbedürfnis und Mißtrauen – Einstellungen zur Polizei bei den Bürgern in den neuen Bundesländer, *Die Polizei*: 16.

Peak, K. J. and Glensor, R. W. (1996) *Community Policing and Problem Solving. Strategies and Practices*. Englewood Cliffs, NJ: Prentice Hall.

Pepinsky, H. E. (1989) 'Issues of Citizen Involvement in Policing', *Crime and Delinquency*, 35(3): 458–70.

Radzinowicz, L. (1968) *A History of English Criminal Law and 1st Administration from 1750, Vol. IV: Grappling for Control*. London: Stevens and Son.

Riechers, L. M. and Roberg, R. R. (1990) 'Community Policing: A Critical Review of Underlying Assumptions', *Journal of Police Science and Administration*, 17(2): 105–14.

Rosenbaum, D. P. (1986) *Community Crime Prevention: Does it Work?* Sage Criminal Justice System Annuals, 22. Beverly Hills, CA: Sage.

Rosenbaum, D. P. (1987) 'The Theory and Research Behind Neighborhood Watch: Is It a Sound Fear and Crime Reduction Strategy?', *Crime and Delinquency*, 33(1): 103–34.

Rosenbaum, D. P. (ed.) (1994) *The Challenge of Community Policing: Testing the Promises*. Thousand Oaks, CA: Sage.

Sadd, S., McElroy, J. E. and Cosgrove, C. A. (1993) *Community Policing: The CPOP in NEW York*. Newbury Park: Sage.

Shaw, J. W. (1994) *Community Policing Against Crime: Violence and Firearms*. Ann Arbor, MI: UMI Dissertation Services International.

Skogan, W. G. (1989) 'Communities, Crime, and Neighbourhood Organization', *Crime and Delinquency*, 35(3): 437–57.

Skogan, W. G. (1994) *Contacts between Police and Public: Findings from the 1992 British Crime Survey*. London: A Home Office Research and Planning Unit Report.

Skogan, W. G. (1996) 'The Police and Public Opinion in Britain', *American Behavioral Scientist*, 39(4): 421–32.

Skogan, W. G. and Maxfield, M. G. (1981) *Coping with Crime. Individual and Neighborhood Reactions*. London: Sage.

Sparrow, M. K. (1988) *Implementing Community Policing, Perspectives on Policing*, November 1988, No. 9. Washington, DC: U.S. Department of Justice.

Spelman, W. and Eck J. E. (1987) 'Problem-Oriented Policing'. Washington, DC: U.S. Department of Justice, National Institute of Justice.

Stone, S. S. (1993) *Problem-Oriented Policing Approach to Drug Enforcement: Atlanta as a Case Study*. Ann Arbor, MI: UMI Dissertation Services International.

Taylor, R. and Shumaker, S. A. (1990) 'Local Crime as a Natural Hazard: Implications for Understanding the Relationship Between Disorder and Fear of Crime', *Journal of Community Psychology*, 18(5): 619–40.

Trojanowicz, R. C. (1994) 'The future of Community Policing' in D. P. Rosenberg (ed.) *The Challenge of Community Policing: Testing the Promises*. Thousand Oaks, CA: Sage Publications.

Trojanowicz, R. C. (1998) *Community Policing: A Contemporary Perspective*, 2nd edn. Cincinnati, Ohio: Anderson.

Trojanowicz, R. C. and Bucqueroux, B. (1994) *Community Policing: How to Get Started*. Cincinnati, OH: Anderson.

Trojanowicz, R. C. and Bucqueroux, B. (1991) *Community Policing and the Challenge of Diversity*. East Lansing, MI: National Center for Community Policing.

Trojanowicz, R. C. and Carter, D. (1988) *The Philosophy and Role of Community Policing*. East Lansing, MI: National Neighbourhood Foot Pat.

Trojanowicz, R. C. and Moore, M. H. (1988) *The Meaning of Community Policing*, East Lansing, MI: National Neighbourhood Foot Pat.

Wadman, R. C. and Bailey, S. E. (1993) *Community Policing and Crime Prevention in America and England*. Chicago: Office of International Criminal Justice.

Wagner, A. E. and Decker, S. H. (1993) 'Evaluating Citizen Complaints Against the Police' in R. G. Dunham and G. P. Alpert (eds) *Critical Issues in Policing*. Illinois: Waveland Press.

Weitekamp, E. G. M. (1989) *Restitution: A New Paradigm of Criminal Justice or a New Way to Widen the System of Social Control*. Ann Arbor: University Microfilms.

Wilson, J. Q. and Kelling, G. L. (1982) 'Broken Windows' in *Atlantic Monthly*, reprinted in R. G. Dunham and G. P. Alpert (eds) *Critical Issues in Policing*. IL: Waveland Press.

Worrall, J. L. (1996) 'Book review of : *The Challenge of Community Policing: Testing the Promises by Dennis P. Rosenbaum*', *Justice Quarterly*, 13(1): 181–87.

Wycoff, M. A. and Skogan, W. K. (1993) *Community Policing in Madison: Quality From the Inside Out; An Evaluation of Implementation and Impact; A final summary report presented to the National Institute of Justice*. Rockville, MD: U.S. Department of Justice.

Yeh, Y.-L.S. (1994) *Innovation of Police Policy: A Study on Community Policing*. Ann Arbor, MI: UMI Dissertation Services International.

Index

abuse
  in partnerships, 61
  see also physical abuse; sexual abuse; substance abuse
accountability
  corporate behaviour, 150
  RJ model, 316
acquaintance with victim, re-offending, 219t
action research, 96, 100–2
active responsibility, 168
age
  decisions not to prosecute, Sweden, 295
  of defendants, re-offending, 216t
  of victims, re-offending, 214t
aggression, against police, family violence, 64
airlines, safety regulation, 165
alcohol abuse, VYOS
  by close family members, 11
  by young offenders, 14, 15t
anti-aggression training, 72
anti-social behaviour, youthful offending, 7, 12–13

apologies, Japan
  inclination to offer, 178
  questionnaire research, 180–4
appeasement, out-of-court settlements, Japan, 186–7
arrests, Japan, 174, 177
attention-deficit hyperactivity disorder, 15
attitudes, SAJJ project
  towards law, 40–1t, 43
  towards victims, 39t, 42
  towards young offenders, 44, 45t, 47t
Austria
  corporate crime and restorative justice, 148–9
  police operation law, family violence, 67
  VOM, 157
Auxiliary Prison of Leuven, 101, 104, 106, 109, 112, 115

balanced and restorative justice model, 315–17
BAS!, 197, 198, 202, 204

VORPs *see* Victim Offender
  Reconciliation Programs
VSOD *see* victim-sensitive offender
  dialogue
VYOS *see* Vancouver Young Offenders
  Study

ways of knowing
  criminal justice system, 260–2
  restorative approach to justice, 270
  traditional research, 258–9
  transformative approach to justice,
    266–70
  values and assumptions implicated
    in, 263–6
Welsijnszorg, 113
White Book on Crime, 181
Whitman, Dennis, 127
women
  numbers in battered wives' refuges,
    57–8
  perpetrators of family violence, 56
  social class of battered, 58
  violent offending, lack of research,
    9
working class status, battered women,
  58

young offenders
  Belgian mediation practices,
    197–205
    influence on criminal justice
      system, 203–5
    restorative proportionality,
      199–205
    rules and rights, clarity on, 205
    voluntary co-operation and
      diversion, 198–9
  mediation and dialogue, 128
  respect for police, re-offending,
    242–4
  SAJJ project

attendance at conferences, 33t
attitude towards legal system, 43
attitude towards victims, 39t, 42
demographics, 33t
emotion at conferences, 33t
indicators of restorativeness,
  34–5t
level of restorativeness, 26, 27t
limits of restorative ideal, 28, 29,
  30t, 31t
victims' attitudes towards, 44,
  45t, 47t
Sweden
  non-reporting of offences, 301
  sanctions, 296–8
  zero tolerance, 299–300
TOA as an educational measure,
  276–7
see also school violence; violent
  youth
youth centres, public courts as, 301
youth crime, seriousness, Sweden,
  298–9

zero tolerance, Sweden, 285–302
  conclusions, 300–2
  decisions not to prosecute, 295
  decisions not to report offences,
    290–1
  non-reporting
    National Police Board directives,
      289–90
    shoplifting offences, 292–4
  obligations
    of police to report offences,
      287–9
    for prosecutors to bring charges,
      294–5
  young offenders, 299–300
    sanction system, 296–8
  youth crime, increasing seriousness,
    298–9